ROBERT PRESTON

Forever The Music Man

DEBRA WARREN

PHOTO ACKNOWLEDGMENTS

Photos courtesy of The Pasadena Playhouse archives–page 213
Photos Courtesy of Getty Images–page 213
Photos Courtesy of the New York Public Library for The Performing Arts–pages 213, 214
Photos Courtesy of AP Images–pages 214, 215
Photo Courtesy of Neva Small–page 214
Photo Courtesy of David Krane–page 215
Photos Courtesy of Tracy Palmgren Monroe–page 215

COVER PHOTO

Robert Preston in the stage production of *I Do! I Do!* (1966)
Photo by Friedman-Ables © The New York Public Library for The Performing Arts

Design by Tami Boyce
www.tamiboyce.com

Library of Congress Control Number: 2022912036

Warren, Debra, 1960–
Robert Preston - Forever The Music Man
Includes endnotes, filmography, and index.

1. Preston, Robert, 1918-1987   2. Actors—United States—Biography

ISBN 979-8-9863110-2-9 (hardback)
ISBN 979-8-9863110-0-5 (paperback)
ISBN 979-8-9863110-1-2 (E-Book)

TABLE OF CONTENTS

ACKNOWLEDGMENTS

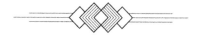

Since I did not have the opportunity to meet or interview Robert Preston during his lifetime, all of the quotes attributed to him were obtained from published interviews or sound recordings as well as from information from family, friends, and co-stars who are directly quoted in this book. I was overwhelmed by the number of individuals who were willing to share their precious memories of Robert Preston for inclusion in his biography. The outpouring of support from people who knew, admired, and loved Preston during his lifetime, and readily shared their anecdotes and remembrances, recordings, and photos with me, stands as the ultimate tribute to his legacy.

Preston's extended family and friends contributed significantly to bringing his story to life. I am indebted to them for the information they provided in interviews and emails and for their willingness to share their precious memories.

This book would also not have been possible without the personal and professional recollections of those who were kind enough to share their memories of Robert Preston for this biography:

There are no words to adequately thank Jennifer Ehle for making the interview with her mother, actress Rosemary Harris, a reality. I am indebted to Rosemary, who starred with Preston both in *The Lion in Winter* on Broadway and *The Chisholms* television miniseries, for graciously sharing memories of her co-star and dear friend for inclusion in his biography.

Christopher Walken, who portrayed King Philip II of France in *The Lion in Winter*, for candidly sharing his conversations and interactions with Preston.

Lesley Ann Warren, who co-starred with Robert Preston in *Victor/Victoria*, for providing invaluable observations about the actor and bringing his natural improvisational talent to light. Thanks also to Kevin Carroll, with Management Production Entertainment in Los Angeles, for coordinating this interview.

Neva Small, who co-starred opposite Preston in the ill-fated musical *The Prince of Grand Street*, which closed in Boston before reaching Broadway; her stories were priceless.

Loretta Swit, Preston's co-star in *S.O.B.*, for sharing her memories of Preston as a gifted actor and raconteur. A special thank you is extended to Los Angeles publicist Harlan Böll for facilitating this interview.

Ruta Lee, who provided information about Preston's 1984 Thalians award ceremony and lent her star power to secure a video of the event from the Academy of Motion Picture Arts and Sciences.

Bob Gunton, who appeared with Preston in the television movie *Finnegan Begin Again*, for his memories of the actor prior to and during the shooting of the HBO film.

Barbara Leigh, who starred in *Junior Bonner* alongside Preston, for her memories of cast interactions on and off the set.

Bethe Austin, who starred with Preston in *Sly Fox* on Broadway, for the enlightening interview about her interactions with the actor.

Leslye Hunter, who played the role of Preston's pre-teen daughter in *Nobody Loves an Albatross,* for sharing her memories of the play and her avuncular bond with Preston.

Brandon Maggart, who recounted his interactions with Preston on and off the set of *The Man That Corrupted Hadleyburg.*

David Krane, the assistant musical director of *The Prince of Grand Street,* for sharing his observations of and interactions with Preston during the musical's previews in Philadelphia and Boston.

Ada Lynn Shrewsbury, a film extra in *The Chisholms* miniseries who shared lines of dialogue with Preston, for her description of Preston on set.

Paul F. Brown, author of *Rufus: James Agee in Tennessee,* for graciously sharing a *Knoxville Journal* article in his collection and information about the Tennessee Archive of Moving Image and Sound (TAMIS).

David Spence, the hybridizer who developed the Robert Preston Iris in honor of the actor, for sharing the backstory of the flower's origin and Preston's reaction to his name-sake bloom.

Ron Spivak, actor, director, and musical theatre historian, for making it possible to hear some rare recordings of Robert Preston in performance.

A special thank you to Preston fan extraordinaire, Ron Fassler, for providing a copy of his 1987 Playbill article, his suggestions, and sharing priceless audio of a Preston performance.

Librarians and archivists were particularly helpful in locating interviews, articles, sound recordings, and video archives.

Special thanks are extended to Tom Lisanti in the Permissions and Reproduction Services department at the New York Public Library as well as the staff in The Billy Rose Theatre Division. Elizabeth Youle at the Margaret Herrick Library at the Academy of Motion Picture Arts and Sciences was equally helpful, as was Edda Manriquez and Taylor Morales in the Academy's film archive. I am also grateful to Mr. Terry Hodge Taylor from the Theater Hall of Fame for providing information about Mr. Preston's induction ceremony.

I extend my heartfelt thanks to the libraries and librarians who went above and beyond the call of duty to provide critical research materials for this biography: Miki Goral, Reference Librarian at the UCLA Library; Eric Dawson, McClurg Historical Collection Audiovisual Archivist in Knoxville, TN; Nancy Spiegel, Bibliographer for Art and Cinema at the University of Chicago Library; Associate Professor Stephen Lawrence Hanson, Director of the Arts and Humanities Division at the USC Libraries; The Boston Public Library; The A.C. Buehler Library at Elmhurst University; Lake Forest Library; The Tennessee State Library and Archives; the periodical collection of Steven Lomazow. M.D.; Becky Biegelsen, Director of Public Relations at The La Jolla Playhouse, and Ross Clark, Archivist at The Pasadena Playhouse.

In addition, the book draws upon fifty years of press interviews and magazine articles that closely chronicled Mr. Preston's life and career in publications throughout the United States. Thanks are extended to Richie Rathsack, Assistant Managing Editor, Digital Content & Analytics, with the *Record-Journal* in Meriden, CT for his helpfulness.

Thanks also to attorney Beverly Berneman for addressing all of the headaches involved with the publication of a biography. You are the best.

A shout-out is in order for Elise Womack for contributing her expertise with the printed word to an analysis of the manuscript.

I am indebted to my son, Gerard Warren, for his filmography research and for diligently applying his red pen to each incarnation of the manuscript and making corrections to the final draft. Each passage of this biography is better because he edited it.

I additionally offer my sincere thanks to any person who provided research material and assistance whose names I may have inadvertently omitted in this acknowledgment.

And last, but not least, to each member of my family—thank you for your patience while this biography was being written and, moreover, for believing in me.

—Debra Warren, 2022

INTRODUCTION

W/hen people hear the name Robert Preston, what typically comes to mind is the iconic role of Harold Hill that he so famously brought to life on the stage and screen versions of *The Music Man*. Yet most are unaware that Preston had an extensive film and stage career both before and after portraying the quintessential Harold Hill. Preston's film career, which began in 1938, is not well known to movie fans of the modern era, and his career as an actor has been overlooked more than many of his prominent contemporaries. As a member of Paramount Studio's stable of stars, Robert Preston appeared in twenty-seven movies between 1938 and 1949. Among the most notable were roles in *Beau Geste, Union Pacific, North West Mounted Police, This Gun for Hire, Reap the Wild Wind, Tulsa,* and *The Macomber Affair*. With his shock of wavy hair and rugged good looks, Paramount chose to overlook Preston's versatile talent. He was instead typecast as a suave villain, detective, soldier, cowboy, and attorney in both lead and supporting roles in a variety of film genres including film noir, westerns, action movies, and crime dramas.

Prior to 1950, the film roles offered to Preston were typically limited by studio typecasting, a short-sighted policy the actor unsuccessfully objected to until winning his release from his Paramount contract in the late 1940s. It was Preston's charisma and natural ability to bring humanity and depth to his roles, even when portraying a scoundrel, that underscored his strength and skill as an actor. These qualities were reflected in the reviews of Preston's films, both the box office hits and those that fell short of the mark, in which critics consistently lavished praise on his performances.

A look at Preston's career reveals the problems endured by many serious actors in Hollywood who decline to "play the game" or hobnob with the regulars on the Tinseltown party circuit. Preston, unmistakably private and the antithesis of everything Hollywood, grappled with the fickleness of the film industry while remaining committed to a life as a working actor. He believed it was possible for an actor to sustain steady employment in the entertainment industry. And his extensive professional résumé proved him right.

Even though a few of his films and plays were considered flops, Preston was not one to regret any of his roles, instead choosing to use each performance as an opportunity to further hone his craft in his tireless pursuit of perfection. To this end, he made important contributions to movies from the late 1930s to the mid-1980s, as well as on the Broadway stage. Over the course of his fifty-year career, the actor appeared in forty-two Pasadena Playhouse productions, forty-five motion pictures, sixteen Broadway plays and musicals (plus two that closed on the road), regional and radio plays, countless television movies and teleplays, and regularly performed with other Pasadena Playhouse alumni in the Eighteen Actors troupe in California.

Robert Preston's work in films and on Broadway garnered him an Academy Award nomination for his role in *Victor/ Victoria* (1982), and Tony Awards for his performances on Broadway in *The Music Man* (1958) and *I Do! I Do!* (1967). Along the way, he received the Golden Laurel Award for Top Male Musical Performance in *The Music Man* (1962), The Los Angeles Film Critics Association Career Achievement Award (1982), The National Board of Review award for Best Supporting Actor in *Victor/Victoria* (1982), and a Western Heritage Award for his role in the television drama *September Gun* (1984). Preston also received several cinema and theater awards and tributes in the years immediately prior to his death. Each event was a celebration of his talent and long career, as well as a testament to his decency and likeability as a human being.

Born Robert Preston Meservey in the suburbs of Boston in 1918, Preston moved with his family to Los Angeles as a toddler. He caught the acting bug in high school and continued as an actor with a Shakespearean acting troupe and at the Pasadena Playhouse before being discovered by Paramount Studios in May 1938 at the age of nineteen. After signing a contract with Paramount, the studio dropped his last name and billed their newly acquired heartthrob by his first and middle name—Robert Preston. Answering the call to military service in 1942, the actor served his country as an S-2 intelligence officer in Combat Intelligence for the Ninth Air Force during World War II and received a citation for distinguished service. Preston met the former Catherine Feltus, known professionally as Catherine Craig, while the two were actors at the Pasadena Playhouse. The couple married in 1940 and remained together until Preston's death, though the marriage endured a few imbroglios resulting from Preston's relationships with songstress

Peggy Lee, and two of his foreign-born, Broadway leading ladies, Glynis Johns and Ulla Sallert.

With his wide grin and disarming manner, Preston possessed the uncanny ability to laser-focus his gaze, appearing to look straight through a person to connect with their soul and read their innermost thoughts. He was known by his peers in Hollywood and on Broadway as a consummate professional, a human dynamo, and a dream to work with—no one who worked with Robert Preston in films or on the stage ever had a bad word to say about him. Preston consistently brought equilibrium, cohesiveness, and camaraderie to stage and screen sets. It is only in his personal life where undercurrents of angst were visible as his private life vacillated between long stretches of calm and happiness and brief periods of complication, uncertainty, and upheaval.

Morton DaCosta, who directed Preston in *The Music Man* and *Island of Love*, aptly described the actor as a perfect gentleman who possessed a sense of proportion about himself—never exhibiting any signs of self-importance or an awareness of being an important star.

DaCosta witnessed Preston's sensitivity and lauded him as a man who would listen with full attention to anyone's problems. Preston did not hesitate to offer support and guidance to fledgling co-stars and treated others in a way that made them feel valued and important. The following pages are punctuated with stories from co-stars and friends who praise him as a wonderful human being. He was a notoriously big-hearted, friendly, and unpretentious chap who treated everyone from luminaries to the wait staff at Sardi's restaurant with equal dignity and respect. Preston was one of the few celebrities who was known to acknowledge restaurant employees on the street and inquire about their families. Actor Christopher Plummer described the talented, magical Preston as just about the best friend anyone could ever have.

Robert Preston was a distinguished actor and gifted artist on the public stage, yet remained a reclusive, enigmatic man in his private life. On a personal and professional level, Preston was unpretentious and wholly unimpressed with the trappings of fame and wealth.

Having achieved star status after appearing in *The Music Man*, he opted to forgo the stress of living in Hollywood or Manhattan and instead sought quiet refuge in rural areas of New York and Connecticut. Although he amassed considerable wealth over the course of his career, money only served to provide Preston with the luxury of being selective with his acting roles.

The actor's relentless drive and professional resiliency were legendary, yet he maintained strong self-control in the public arena which precluded all but a select few from peering beneath the surface to view his closely-guarded temperament and sensuality. While Preston cannot be described as a fully introspective being, a good deal of the commentary he shared about himself over the course of his lifetime points to a man who was more keenly aware of the inner workings of his psyche than he ever dared to consciously acknowledge.

It is a daunting endeavor to attempt to fully understand the life of a man who was so utterly dynamic, charismatic, and larger-than-life both as an actor and as a human being. Preston gave few in-depth interviews and left a mere smattering of telltale clues for any biographer to follow on the winding trail to reconstruct the intricate jigsaw of his life. Robert Preston will continue to live on in his films and forever be remembered as *the* Music Man, but his superlative talent and life story have been hidden away for far too long.

WAITING IN THE WINGS

As World War I raged in Europe, and the Spanish Flu global pandemic swept across the United States leaving death and devastation in its wake, the Newton Hospital just outside of Boston erected tents to tend to the influx of injured soldiers and those who fell victim to the influenza epidemic. Before the dawn of the Jazz Age, that same hospital would welcome the future silver screen and Broadway star Robert Preston.

The attraction between Preston's parents, Newton natives Frank Wesley Meservey (pronounced "Mez-*er*-vay"), known as "Doc," and Ruth Rea, began in 1917. In September 1917, seventeen-year-old Doc was employed as a garment worker when he and the ebullient, twenty-two-year-old Ruthie made their way to the altar. Standing 4'11," the diminutive Ruth was petite yet vivacious, while her strapping beau boasted a muscular 6'1" frame.[1]

Doc was born in November 1899 and raised in Newton, Massachusetts along with his older sisters Margaret and

Coralie. Their father Wesley, an electric car motorman, had been born in Maine as had generations of his French Huguenot ancestors. Wesley, in poor health as a result of arteriosclerosis, died in March 1918 at age 52, two months before the birth of his famous grandson. Doc's mother, the former Isabelle "Bella" Ross, hailed from Nova Scotia, Canada. She was a second-generation Canadian; both her maternal and paternal grandparents had emigrated from Scotland to Nova Scotia.

Ruth Rea, also a native of Newton, Massachusetts, was born in June 1895, the oldest of her parents' six children. Ruth may have been the valedictorian of her high school class, but didn't consider herself too good to participate in a few school hijinks. When she and a few male students were caught smoking cigarettes and dispatched to the principal's office, the boys were quickly accused of corrupting "little Ruthie." Ruth promptly dispelled the falsehood by informing the principal that she "was the one who brought the cigarettes."[2] Ruth's mother and father were both born to Irish immigrant parents. Her father, John Lewis Rea, was born in Charlestown, Massachusetts and her mother, the former Agnes Frances Hayes, was born across the border in Newfoundland, Canada. Agnes subsequently emigrated to the United States with her family in 1884 at age 11. Once married, Agnes Hayes Rea assumed the role of family matriarch and became the driving force behind her clan; she was the iron fist in a velvet glove who would eventually orchestrate the family's move to the West Coast and decisively impact the fate of her progeny.

Doc Meservey and Ruth Rea made the decision to elope in the fall of 1917. Although Massachusetts allowed for marriages for men as young as fourteen and women as young as twelve, marriages in which the males were under age twenty-one and females under age eighteen were considered underage marriages and required written parental consent to authorize the nuptials. Instead of marrying in their home state of Massachusetts, Doc and Ruth traveled forty-one miles north to the town of Hudson, New Hampshire where they applied for a marriage license on September 17, 1917. Electing to be less than truthful, Doc and Ruth each listed their age as twenty-one on the license application. To complete their derring-do, the couple waited the requisite five days and were married by Reverend R. J. Honeywell, pastor of Hudson's Methodist Episcopal Church, on September 22, 1917. If authorities had discovered that the couple misrepresented their ages on their marriage license, the underage nuptials could have been voided or annulled by a court of law.

The newlyweds returned to Massachusetts and settled into married life in a walk-up apartment on Lincoln Street in the Boston suburb of Newton Highlands; the groom celebrated his 18th birthday two months later on November 22. Future *Music Man*, Robert Preston Meservey, was born eight and a half months later on Saturday, June 8, 1918, at Newton Hospital. Sometime after Ruth Meservey entered the hospital to deliver her child, her labor pains came to an abrupt stop. The hospital staff responded swiftly by inducing labor, and the infant, Robert, entered the world with his umbilical cord wrapped around his neck.[3] Any hint of crisis was averted when the child's tangled cord, a phenomenon that can constrict blood flow during contractions, was quickly unlooped to relieve any compression. Despite the delivery room drama, Ruth's son was born robust and healthy. Within months, the child's blue eyes were framed by a mane of wavy brown hair.

Ruth Meservey, who planned to name her son Robert, acknowledged that it was a family matriarch who demanded the child be given the name "Preston." In a weakened postpartum state, Ruth did not possess the strength to debate the name issue with her relative, yet she instinctively knew the moniker "Preston Robert" did not ring right for her child. Ruth's family was unaware the child's legal name had been recorded as Robert Preston Meservey, since he was always called Preston Meservey by family and friends during his formative years.[4]

As a young child, Preston possessed limitless curiosity and the indefatigable energy of a whirling dervish. Ruth Meservey often marveled at her first-born son's boundless spirit and determination, declaring him to be the most independent child she had ever seen.[5] By 1920, the Meservey family had moved into a rental property located at 65 Williams Street, and Doc secured employment as a clerk with the American Express company. A second son, Frank Wesley Meservey, Jr., was welcomed into the family on April 12, 1920.

When Preston was two years old, his parents packed up their small family and headed west to California along with Ruth's parents and siblings. Preston recalled his maternal grandmother, Agnes Hayes Rea, as a "strong matriarchal type" who made the unilateral decision to relocate her entire family to Los Angeles in a bid to improve the health of her husband, John.[6] Agnes held the misguided belief that the dry California climate might provide a cure for her husband's advanced tuberculosis.

To accommodate her multi-generational family, Agnes Rea purchased a large, old white frame house in the Latino neighborhood of Lincoln Heights, one of the poorest sections of East Los Angeles.[7] The house, located at 412 N. Lincoln Park Avenue, served as a home base to eleven people: Agnes and John Rea; Doc and Ruth Meservey; Preston and his younger brother, Frank Jr.; the Rea's sons John R. Rea (b. 1898) and Robert Walker Rea

(b. 1905); and three daughters, Kathryn Frances Rea (b.1899), Florence Agnes Rea (b. 1903), and Marion "Naomi" Rea (b.1912). Doc Meservey accommodated his mother-in-law's request to move west since "it didn't matter to him where he worked. To him, a job was a job."[8] In reflecting on his formative years growing up in Lincoln Heights, Preston recalled,

> The neighborhood was predominantly Mexican, and when I started going to school there, I found I was the only white American. I was also younger than the other children in my class . . . it made a listener out of me. I hung around bashfully, listening to what everybody else said, and I've been a very careful listener ever since.[9]

Even though they were ensconced in an immigrant neighborhood, the Rea/Meservey household clung to their New England traditions. Agnes Rea regularly prepared oyster stew and other traditional New England fare, but grandson Preston preferred the savory ethnic food served by his neighbors.[10]

Doc Meservey secured gainful employment as a clerk in the shipping room of a Los Angeles garment manufacturer and enjoyed a brief stint with the Hollywood Blues of the Pacific Coast League as a baseball player. Ruth Meservey managed the record department of the Platt Music Store in Los Angeles, whose clientele included film stars and Hollywood executives.

Ruth, a "tiny little dynamo" with black hair, who always wore "very classic, bright red lipstick,"[11] regularly contacted her celebrity customers to share insider information about anticipated albums that meshed with their musical preferences. Although there were limited career options for women of that era without college educations, Ruth was "absolutely brilliant," and those in her orbit had no doubt she would have pursued great and interesting things if she had been born at a later time.[12]

Preston described his large, extended family as "fluid," noting that those in the household "came and went as [they] pleased" and maintained their own schedules.[13] The move west to Los Angeles did not significantly prolong the life of Preston's maternal grandfather, John Lewis Rea, who succumbed to pulmonary tuberculosis on May 28, 1924, at age forty-eight.

As a child, the energetic Preston displayed an amazing gift of imagination that would fuel his creativity as an adult. The scope of her son's imagination often flummoxed Ruth. On one occasion when he was about seven years old, Ruth called Preston inside for dinner, but the boy failed to respond. When Preston eventually made his way inside, Ruth queried him about his unresponsiveness to the dinner call. Preston turned to his mother and matter-of-factly explained, "I'm not Bob, I'm Mickey Mack McMichael."[14] A highly gifted child with a vivid imagination, Preston would routinely project himself into imaginary situations. Frank Meservey Jr., Preston's younger brother, when interviewed about what his famous older brother was like as a child, recalled that Preston possessed, "a sort of way of living within himself," noting that he once found his brother "alone in the backyard, standing on two planks, waving a pole and talking to himself. He told me to go away. He was exploring the upper Amazon."[15] In point of fact, as children the Meservey brothers were extremely close and maintained a strong brotherly bond throughout their lifetime.[16]

Given his prowess and passion for baseball, Doc worried whether his left-handed, eldest son could excel at the game and began to coach Preston to become ambidextrous. Doc's strategy was simple but quite effective: he would regularly take Preston for walks along the beach and alternate throwing one pebble left-handed and one pebble right-handed and had Preston do likewise.[17] The pebble-pitching tutorial was a success; Preston was not only able to play baseball effectively with either hand, but he was also able to adapt the ambidextrousness to his advantage in his later stage work.[18]

Preston's personality was an enigma almost from the moment he sprang from his mother's womb. His disposition was a study in contrast: he was at once a child with limitless energy and imagination, yet also devoured life by standing still. When Preston became mesmerized by a person, group of people, or element in his environment, he wanted nothing more than to thoroughly absorb the experience. In these instances, he would stand aloof and channel his energy into observing and quietly listening to the rhythm, mannerisms, cultural nuances, and language of the life swirling around him.

Preston, often hailed as "Pres" by family and friends, was enrolled in elementary school at a young age, making him younger than the other children in his class.[19] He enjoyed listening to the Latin music that floated through his ethnic neighborhood and quickly developed an affinity for music. At age seven, Preston embarked on a four-year course of piano lessons and his family purchased a second-hand, upright piano for seventy-five dollars on which he honed his musical skills.[20] Preston also learned to play the trumpet, saxophone, and harmonica without formal lessons, yet his musicianship leaned more in the direction of showmanship than musical precision. Ruth Meservey readily acknowledged that although her son could play no instrument correctly, he "could get music out of anything."[21] Rounding out his musical skill set, Preston would listen intently to the phonograph records his mother brought home from the music store, including those of John Barrymore reciting passages from Shakespeare plays.

Privy to insider information about local plays through her work at the music store, Ruth Meservey began taking eight-year-old Preston to see area theatrical productions. Ruth quickly recognized her son's inherent talent and used every contact at her disposal to guide and promote his success. In addition to being a member of the audience, Preston was also cast in small roles in plays that were sponsored by the local Episcopal Church thanks, in part, to his mother's encouragement. By age ten, Preston's interest in all things theatrical led to his regular attendance at movies and Vaudeville shows.[22] His role as a passive Vaudeville spectator soon evolved into active participation on the main stage when a local Vaudeville producer entered Ruth Meservey's store to purchase music. The producer was on a mission to find a child who could portray a younger version of himself in a Vaudeville sketch. Ruth wasted no time in suggesting her son for the role, and he was hired on the spot.[23] It was Preston's appearance in this production of *Carney from Killarney* that led to a steady stream of other acting opportunities.[24]

Preston also participated in pageants at the Hollywood Bowl and acted in anarchist plays at the radical, leftist Jewish Forum.[25] Even at a young age, Preston did not concern himself with the content of the material he was asked to perform or the venue in which it was presented; what was important to him was the quality of his work. One play, *He is the Greatest*, sponsored by the Jewish Forum, embodied Preston's approach to his nascent craft as evidenced by his commentary on the matter:

[It was] a play about a modern-day Robespierre . . . the play was so far to the left that it was practically anarchistic, but I never asked who was behind it, or even who had written it. My only concern was that my part, that of a young anarchist, was good and I was allowed to play it.[26]

Preston initially played juvenile roles but was quickly tapped for young adult parts and "got the reputation in Los Angeles of being a child actor who could be trusted."[27] In reflecting upon his youthful forays on the stage, Preston indicated that a future film career never crossed his mind, despite the plethora of film crews that regularly shot movie scenes in the Los Angeles area.[28]

Many of Preston and his younger brother Frank's extended family members were heavy drinkers.[29] The extended family, as well as Preston's parents, worked outside the home and contributed to the financial security of the household. When Preston was thirteen-years-old, an unfortunate tragedy shook the family. Preston's aunt, Naomi Rea, only six years his senior, died unexpectedly at age nineteen. Naomi succumbed to suppurative peritonitis and empyema on August 27, 1931, as a direct result of a botched, self-induced abortion.[30] Her grief-stricken mother arranged for funeral services for her youngest child at the Episcopal Church located at the corner of Sichel and Altura Streets in Los Angeles,[31] followed by burial at Grand View Memorial Park in Glendale.

By the time Preston was fourteen, he moved with his parents and brother into a house located in an immigrant Italian neighborhood of Los Angeles. Preston quickly immersed himself in the sights, sounds, food, and traditions of his new neighborhood, embraced his newly adopted *paisan*, and learned to play the guitar. He intermingled freely with his neighbors, closely observing and developing an appreciation for their language, food, and ethnic traditions. Preston was able to master the neighborhood Italian dialect and gain a rudimentary knowledge of the language by joining his neighbors as they sang classic songs from their favorite operas.[32]

The fall of 1931 marked the beginning of Preston's high school career as a member of Abraham Lincoln High School's Winter Class of 1935. The school, located in East Los Angeles, suffered extensive damage during Preston's sophomore year as a result of the 6.4 magnitude Long Beach earthquake that caused widespread destruction within Southern California in March 1933. The high school was partially closed to students after an engineering assessment concluded that many of the school's buildings, including the auditorium, music, library, and English buildings, were in danger of sliding down the hill. To keep the curriculum on schedule, school officials erected tents on the front lawn of the campus as temporary classrooms. Only small groups of students were allowed back into the school building over the next year.[33]

High school was not particularly easy for Preston, who was known both as "Preston Meservey" and "Duke" to his classmates. His high school yearbook notes that he was involved in the school's French club, varsity baseball team, football team, and was a yell leader who led his fellow students in a series of hurrahs during athletic and other school events.[34] His aptitude for mathematics, and geometry in particular, was nonexistent. After flunking geometry twice, Preston learned he could sideline the class and gain the necessary credits toward graduation by participating in the school's drama program.[35]

English class provided Preston an opportunity to express his flair for the dramatic. He competed in acting out passages from Shakespearean plays, and his stellar soliloquies as Julius Caesar, Polonius, and Hamlet earned him the title of "champ of the school" for three years, as well as the right to compete against similar title-holders from other Los Angeles high schools.[36] Preston's English teacher, Mr. E. J. Wenig, also served as the school's drama coach. Wenig, a Shakespeare enthusiast, instinctively recognized his pupil's raw talent and convinced the fresh-faced Preston to join the school's Dramatics Club. Wenig became a mentor to Preston and soon tapped the fourteen-year-old to play the title role in the high school's production of *Hamlet*.

During his high school career, Preston played Hamlet and Julius Caesar on several occasions, thus becoming thoroughly enamored with acting in the process. He was quickly elevated to the school's Play Production Class, a select group of students chosen by Wenig to serve as the casting pool for all the school's plays and stage productions.

Abraham Lincoln High School's 1935 yearbook identifies Preston Meservey as an "outstanding actor."[37] In his senior year, Preston starred in the school's production of *Trial by Jury* as the judge and capped his high school drama career by receiving high acclaim for his role as the ill-fated Prince Hamlet. In reflecting upon his decision to become involved in high school dramatics, Preston acknowledged that it was his role as a thespian that allowed him to stand out among his peers:

> When I acted, I was immediately good at it. I didn't go through any of the tortures of doing something I didn't like . . . what I assume is that as part of the social life in high school, I wanted to be as big a man on campus as I could. I found

I could do it in the theater, that my name that way would come to be as well-known as that of captain of the football team.[38]

Sixteen-year-old Preston, now determined to be an actor, graduated from Abraham Lincoln High School in late January 1935 as a member of the Winter Class. Even amid the Great Depression, E. J. Wenig remained determined to help his talented, young protégé gain additional acting experience and theatrical exposure. Preston recalled that Wenig "took me down to the Musart Theater where Patia Power, Tyrone Power's mother, was recasting her Elizabethan repertory company."[39]

Helen Emma Reaume Power, the ex-wife of actor Tyrone Power, Sr. and mother of actor Tyrone Power, Jr., was a talented stage actress who adopted the stage name "Patia Power" (pronounced "*PAY*-sha"). In addition to her background as a Shakespearean actress, Patia was a skilled drama teacher and voice coach who managed a small Elizabethan repertory troupe in the Los Angeles area beginning in the mid-1930s.

Unaware of his age, Patia Power gave the sixteen-year-old his first big break by casting him in the title role of *Julius Caesar* in her touring stock company. Preston was later tapped by Power to play the role of Mercutio in the troupe's production of *Romeo and Juliet*. Citing financial difficulties, Patia's repertory group folded six months after Preston's addition to the troupe. He was "left with seven dollars as his final week's pay"[40]—the amount that reflected his share of the troupe's ticket receipts.

The Great Depression exacted a toll on Preston's family, just as it did on millions of other American households struggling through the lean years of the 1930s. The Meservey family hit a rough financial patch when Doc lost his job at the garment factory. Preston, seemingly oblivious to the seriousness of his family's economic situation, acknowledged that "it never entered my head even then that I could do anything but act."[41] Doc eventually secured work with the W.P.A., installing high tension electrical lines in San Bernardino at a much lower pay rate.[42] Preston soon realized he needed to step up and assist his family to stay afloat financially. With the help of his high school football coach, Jim Tunney, Preston secured a job as both a morning janitor and an afternoon parking attendant at the nearby Santa Anita Racetrack in Arcadia. The racetrack, which opened in December 1934, regularly attracted silver screen stars and movie moguls to its grandstands. Several prominent members of the Hollywood community also owned horses that raced at the park. Preston's two seasons of employment at the track provided him with income and valuable connections that would further enhance his nascent acting career. Reflecting upon that time in his life, Preston recalled,

> I became a clean-up man at Santa Anita Park, picking up cigarette stubs and sweeping the aisles in the mornings, and parking cars for the patrons in the afternoons. I got ten dollars a week, plus tips. Will Rogers would always give a good tip, and Clark Gable was always a cinch for fifty cents. That was big money in those days, and the other parking attendants would fight with me to get him. He always flipped the coin to me.[43]

On occasion, Preston and his co-workers would get lucky and find a winning race ticket that had been mistakenly discarded in the trash. It was a practice that got Preston temporarily fired; the racetrack preferred to retain the winnings for all non-claimed tickets rather than provide a payout to an industrious employee.[44]

It was during this time that Preston began smoking unfiltered cigarettes, a habit he continued throughout the remainder of his life. At age eighteen, after two seasons at the racetrack, Preston became acquainted with co-workers who possessed acting talents similar to his own. Since he believed the best way for a budding actor to learn how to act was simply to act in as many theatrical productions as possible, Preston began to join his co-workers when they auditioned for plays at the Pasadena Community Playhouse on Sunday evenings.

The Pasadena Community Playhouse, now the State Theater of California, was founded in 1917 by the director, actor, and author Gilmor Brown. The Playhouse was originally opened in a former burlesque hall on North Fair Oaks Avenue in the quiet, upscale town of Pasadena. This clap-trap building featured a shallow stage, squeaky wooden floors, and uncomfortable seating for patrons. Gilmor Brown launched a massive fundraising drive to build a new, state-of-the-art theater complex in Pasadena. This fundraising drive garnered enough funds to allow Brown to construct a magnificent complex at 39 South El Molino Avenue, which opened in May 1925.[45]

The theater operated at a fast pace and produced new plays every two weeks. A large complement of local residents, as well as amateur and semi-professional actors, comprised the cast pool for the theatrical productions. Unlike Hollywood's venues located just sixteen miles to the south and east, the Pasadena Playhouse served as a training ground for would-be thespians by allowing them to perform before a live audience. In her book *Playhouse*, author Diane Alexander revealed that once silent movies became passé and actors were needed for the new genre of sound-oriented motion pictures known as the "talkies," the "Playhouse became a veritable treasure trove for the studios, now frantic for theater-trained actors."[46] During the decades of the 1930s and 1940s, it was common practice for the Playhouse to be "regularly monitored by agents, producers, and casting people with an unquenchable thirst for new faces [and] new stars."[47]

Casting directors needed actors to both fill the roles on the Playhouse's three stages and to replace the ongoing exodus of players who were continually recruited by Hollywood. The Pasadena Playhouse found a way to attract new talent for its acting pool by holding weekly Sunday night readings. These Sunday night readings were crowded events attended by "hundreds of people from Pasadena and the surrounding communities" who gathered at the Playhouse "for a chance to read for the many productions being cast."[48]

Preston attended the infamous Sunday night readings at the Pasadena Playhouse, and the eighteen-year-old was given the opportunity to read for Thomas Browne Henry, a Playhouse director. The impressive reading led to the budding actor being cast in a series of parts in Playhouse productions. Preston, viewed by his fellow actors as the crown prince of the Playhouse stage, quickly became an established mainstage actor and appeared in over forty-two Playhouse productions between 1936 and 1938 including: *Troilus and Cressida* (June 15-20, 1936), *Pericles* (June 29-July 4, 1936), *Coriolanus* (July 6-11, 1936), *Cymbeline* (July 27-August 1, 1936), *Ulysses Sailed By* (December 14-19, 1936), *The Chalk Circle* (December 29, 1936-January 9, 1937), *Murder in the Cathedral* (February 9-20, 1937), *Montezuma* (June 28-July 3, 1937), *Night Over Taos* (July 12-17, 1937), *The Girl of the Golden West* (July 26-31, 1937), *The Amazing Dr. Clitterhouse* (October 4-16, 1937), *The Admirable Bashville* (December 6, 1937), *Tom Cobb* (December 23, 1937), *Idiot's Delight* (February 1-12, 1938), *Knights of Song* (March 1-19, 1938), *Merrily We Roll Along* (May 3-14, 1938) and *Star of Navarre* (May 31-June 11, 1938).

Preston proved a quick study and rapidly emerged as a rising star and repertory actor at the Pasadena Playhouse. He was assigned various parts in a series of plays featured in the 1936 Midsummer Drama Festival at the Playhouse featuring the dramas of William Shakespeare.

Preston received favorable reviews for his role as Lysimachus, the Governor of Mytilene, in *Pericles*. In his review of the play, Vernon Young, the *Arcadia Tribune* theater critic, noted "the best single performance was given by Preston Meservey" and despite Preston's limited time on stage, "he helped to revive our flagging interest in the play's dénouement."[49] Cast as the First Roman Citizen in *Coriolanus*, Preston won critical praise by "again prov[ing] himself one to be watched" [50] and quickly became one of the young male actors whose acting ability was promoted by Gilmor Brown. His meteoric rise from apprentice actor to lead actor at the Playhouse resulted in his being cast in major roles on the Playhouse's Main Stage and Playbox.[51]

Preston met fellow Playhouse actress and future wife, Catherine (Kay) Feltus, in February 1937 when they acted together in the Playhouse production of *Murder in the Cathedral*. The actor performed in several plays with Catherine before he finally mustered enough courage to ask her out; the couple's first date took place on July 4, 1937.[52] Catherine was aware Preston "was a pretty shy guy"[53] and was pleasantly surprised that he somehow managed to ask her on a date. For Catherine, this date marked the inception of an all-consuming relationship and eventual marriage, marked by periods of instability and separation, that endured until Preston's death some fifty years later.

Three years Preston's senior, Catherine was born Catherine Jewel Feltus on January 18, 1915 in Bloomington, Indiana. Her father, Roswell "Roy" Feltus, was a member of a prominent Bloomington Family; his well-to-do father, Henry, owned the Feltus Printing Company which published the *Star Courier*, a Democratic party newspaper.[54] Roy caught "circus fever" at a young age and eventually held managerial positions with several American circus companies, including Ringling Brothers and Barnum & Bailey Circus. He later became co-owner of the Shipp & Feltus Circus in 1907, a troupe that primarily toured South America, Central America, and the West Indies. The Shipp & Feltus circus was the first of its kind to introduce the phenomenon of the American circus to the Southern Hemisphere.

Roy married the former Margaret Olive Leffler on November 24, 1909; the couple soon became members of the progressive Trinity Episcopal Church in Bloomington.[55] Their first daughter, Virginia Margaret, was born in Santiago, Chile in December 1912 while the circus was on tour in South America. The couple's second daughter, Catherine, was born in Bloomington, Indiana in January 1915 during a hiatus in the circus's touring schedule.

Circus life required Roy and his wife to put in many hours on the road, and Catherine and her sister often experienced unavoidable separations from their parents. When her parents were traveling with the circus, Catherine and her sister, Virginia, resided with her maternal aunt, Ida Jewel, and her husband, Robert Harper Harris. Mr. Harris owned the Harris Grand Theatre in Bloomington and the family lived in an apartment adjoining the theatre.[56] Catherine was twelve years old when her forty-five-year-old mother died on June 26, 1927 from breast cancer that metastasized to her spine. Roy Feltus remained a widower for slightly less than four years before taking another bride, providing sixteen-year-old Catherine with a stepmother when he wed Grace Rhorer in April 1931.

Catherine developed into a young adult whose sense of self was defined by excellence and achievement. Due in part to her childhood experiences, Catherine became the proverbial shining star who worked diligently to excel in each of her undertakings. Her determination and brilliant focus led to an unending stream of success, awards, and newspaper stories in the *Indianapolis Star* that publicly chronicled her numerous achievements.

After graduation from Bloomington High School, Catherine enrolled at the University of Indiana in Bloomington in the fall of 1932. She was a go-getter who became quite active in campus life; she pledged to the Kappa Kappa Gamma sorority and was later appointed rush captain. With a family that encouraged theater performance,[57] Catherine's decision to pursue collegiate dramatics was a matter of course. The University Theater was established in 1933, and Catherine played the title role in the theater's first production of *The First Mrs. Fraser.*

Catherine continued to play an active part in the University Theater, claiming the lead role in several campus productions including *The Only Girl (1933), Little Women (March 1934),* and *The Merchant of Venice (November 1934).* She also served as the theater department's first teaching assistant and was one of the founding members of the Indiana University Players.[58] In addition to her busy campus social calendar, Catherine was fiercely dedicated to academic excellence and was elected to Phi Beta Kappa in her junior year. She continued to pursue excellence and recognition and was rewarded for her efforts by being named the Outstanding Senior Coed of Indiana University in May 1936 and winning the university's Arbutus beauty contest in 1934.

A photo of Catherine as a co-ed was published in the University of Indiana's Class of 1936 yearbook. The image is of a young, modest, Midwestern woman sporting a Mona Lisa smile which exudes mystery and charm. The white lace shawl collar on her black dress demurely frames her oval face as does her brown hair, parted neatly down the middle and gathered at the nape of her neck.

Catherine graduated with honors from Indiana University in 1936 with a Bachelor of Arts degree in speech. She spent a brief time post-graduation working as an assistant to a speech instructor in Indiana while appearing in local plays. In 1937, she decided to relocate to Los Angeles to enroll as a student in the Pasadena Playhouse School of the Theater and pursue a professional career as an actress under the stage name Catherine Craig. As a member of the Playhouse's acting troupe, Catherine and Preston Meservey were cast together in a handful of productions sponsored by the Pasadena Playhouse.

While a student at the Pasadena Playhouse, Catherine first became aware of her husband-to-be when she saw a play performed on the Playhouse's laboratory stage in which a young actor performed the role of a smart-aleck butler. Her first impression of her fellow thespian was negative as she found his onstage demeanor to be "quite rude."[59] Catherine searched for the actor's name in the program and found the role of the butler was played by Preston Meservey.

The next play offered on the laboratory stage was *Ulysses Sailed By* featuring an outstanding performance of a kind and gentle padre. When Catherine learned it was Preston Meservey who played this role, she immediately recognized he was a phenomenal actor.[60]

In February 1938, Preston was tapped to play the lead role of unscrupulous, song-and-dance-man Harry Van in the Playhouse's production of *Idiot's Delight*. The Pasadena Playhouse, with its proverbial finger on the pulse of Broadway, produced Robert Sherwood's 1936 Pulitzer Prize-winning play a year before Metro-Goldwyn-Mayer released a movie of the same name with Clark Gable in the title role.

Preston found the perfect showcase for his talents in *Idiot's Delight*. In addition to his stellar performance, Preston's uncanny luck manifested itself at this critical moment in his fledgling career.

Two separate narratives exist, perhaps not mutually exclusive, that claim to establish how Preston achieved his entrée into motion pictures. *The Los Angeles Times* ran a story in August 1938 claiming that Ruth Meservey asked Everett Crosby, a regular customer in the music store where she worked and brother of legendary crooner Bing Crosby, to preview one of her son's performances at the Pasadena Playhouse. It was reported that Everett and Bing were impressed by Preston's talent and had the actor sign a managerial contract with the Crosby Agency.[61]

The story widely and often told by Preston, however, is that it was Sidney Justin, a Paramount attorney, Pasadena resident, and frequent patron of the Playhouse, who caught Preston's stage performance and recommended him to Paramount producer Harold Hurley. Much to the attorney's frustration, Hurley dismissed his entreaties. After seeing Preston again in the Playhouse's production of *Knights of Song* in March 1938, Justin once again voiced his endorsement of Preston with the Paramount brass but his recommendation fell on deaf ears.[62]

Preston's performance in *Knights of Song* was serendipitous. The Playhouse was on the verge of the opening of *Knights of Song*, a play based on the lives of Gilbert and Sullivan, when legal troubles threatened to sideline the production. On the night of the play's dress rehearsal, the Actors Equity Association ordered Earl Gunn, the actor playing the part of Gilbert, out of the production due to a jurisdictional dispute with the Playhouse. To save the production, the critical role of Gilbert needed to be recast in a hurry, and Preston Meservey was asked to step into the part on opening night.[63] Playhouse actress Lenore Shanewise recalled it was Preston's girlfriend, Catherine, who prepared him for the last-minute role and "cued him hour after hour," and it was this relentless preparation that allowed Preston to shine on opening night.[64] In addition to coaching the frenetic rehearsal, Catherine presented Preston with an enameled, tin four-leaf clover for luck. He kept the amulet in his pocket during his performance in *Knights of Song* and carried it with him as a good luck charm throughout his acting career.[65]

According to Preston, it was Sidney Justin's relentless advocacy that finally resulted in his big break at Paramount Studios. Impressed by Preston's May 1938 performance in *Merrily We Roll Along*, Justin once again approached Harold Hurley about the potential film protégé. Perhaps realizing that Sidney Justin was determined and implacable, Hurley finally capitulated and agreed to offer Preston a screen test.[66]

Unlike most screen tests that were relatively brief, Preston's was surprisingly extensive. Director Robert Florey enlisted veteran actor J. Carrol Naish to read opposite Preston. Naish, an established Hollywood star, was well-known for playing the role of black-hearted villains in numerous movies. For this screen test, Preston was asked to perform two contrasting scenes, one from *The Last Mile* (1932) and the other from *Idiot's Delight*.[67]

Preston realized the screen test was a do-or-die opportunity for his acting career. Although he ultimately benefited from director Florey's unexpected beneficence, he never forgot the trepidation he experienced during this audition:

> I didn't look forward to the test—to facing that big glass eye [of the camera]. I tightened up, just thinking about it. But Florey rehearsed and re-hearsed me. By the time we went into the actual test, I was loosened up, relaxed. And Florey did an unheard-of thing. He shot two thousand feet of film. That gave me a break. After he had cut out the bad moments, he still had some good moments left—enough to make a showing as a test.[68]

In the first portion of the screen test, Preston was asked to read the part of Killer Mears in *The Last Mile*; it was a role "that had 'star' written into it."[69] The successful screen test landed Preston a six-month contract with Paramount Studios, including options, and a starting salary of one hundred dollars a week.[70] The timing of Preston's screen test was nothing less than fortuitous; Robert Florey, who was in the process of casting a new movie, needed a young actor to play the part of a sailor in his production. Preston, tapped for the plum role in Florey's film, thus began his motion picture career with Paramount Studios.

RIDING THE B TRAIN
THROUGH TINSELTOWN

n late summer 1938, Robert Preston Meservey signed with Paramount and experienced the full star treatment given to all new protégés in the studio's stable of actors. The first order of business for the Paramount casting department was to change their young star's name. The executives thought it best to eliminate the surname of Meservey from Preston's professional moniker and bill the newest actor on their lot simply by his first and middle name: Robert Preston. Given the paternalism of the 1930s studio system and the nineteen-year-old's eagerness and naiveté, Preston acquiesced to the new "stage name," but continued to use his given name, Robert Preston Meservey, in his private life, on his bank checks, passport, draft card, and all other important identifying paperwork.

In addition to the name change, the studio brass at Paramount decided that Preston too closely resembled a truck driver with his stocky 5'11" build and shock of wavy brown hair. Someone floated the idea of raising Preston's forehead to change his look, and the hair on his lower forehead region was shaved and plucked to provide him with the illusion of a higher brow. Preston indicated the recessed hairline somewhat minimized his thick mane "so people wouldn't think I was wearing a mop on my head,"[1] but the alteration to his hairline was brief in duration. While Preston was on loan to Universal Studios for *Beau Geste* in 1939, one of the studio's directors, Frank Lloyd, noticed Preston's unusual hairline and inquired, "What happened to your hair?" Lloyd clued Preston in that the elevated hairline "changed his looks too drastically,"[2] and suggested he should "let [his hair] grow back and . . . wear a toupee in the front"[3] in the interim. Taking the director's advice to heart, Preston allowed his hair to grow back in and maintained his natural hairline for the rest of his life.

Impressed by Preston's initial screen test, director Robert Florey selected Preston for the cast of his upcoming picture *King of Alcatraz* (1938). Preston played a crew member on a passenger ship that had been commandeered by an escaped convict; his character and another crew member ultimately hatch a plot to overpower the convict and rescue the ship's passengers. In addition to Preston, the movie's cast included Gail Patrick, Lloyd Nolan, Harry Carey, J. Carrol Naish, Anthony Quinn, Dennis Morgan, and Richard Denning. *King of Alcatraz*, which debuted in October 1938, was lauded by *New York Times* film critic Frank Nugent as a "trim melodrama" and a "fresh and remarkably diverting film." Nugent went on to praise the "soundly in-character performances by Lloyd Nolan and Robert Preston as the scrapping ship's wireless men."[4]

As a member of Paramount's regular stock company, Preston was assigned to two other movies, *Illegal Traffic* (1938) and *Disbarred* (1939), in rapid succession. Preston played the role of government agent Charles Bent Martin in the *Illegal Traffic* crime drama. His character was tasked with exposing the flagrant corruption and nationwide racketeering masterminded by a transport company. The film, released on November 3, 1938, also starred J. Carrol Naish, Mary Carlisle, and Judith Barrett. Preston once again collaborated with director Robert Florey on *Disbarred,* one of the few films in the actor's career in which his character "got the girl." Preston assumed the role of Bradley Kent, an honest assistant district attorney, who railed against a disbarred lawyer and his underworld connections. Sidney Toler, Otto Kruger, Gail Patrick, and Helen MacKellar rounded out the cast of the January 1939 film.

Preston, still reeling from his spate of good fortune, was grateful for the confluence of support and mentorship from the key industry players who paved the way for his entrée to Paramount Studios. His comments to the press reflected his continued amazement at "how everybody seems to take me under wing."[5] A convergence of timing, talent, persistence, and good luck ultimately led to Preston's debut in films. Initially, it was Paramount attorney, Sidney Justin, who lobbied relentlessly for Preston's screen test and who finally convinced producer Harold Hurley to make it happen. Director Robert Florey went out of his way to shoot a 2000-foot screen test to portray Preston in a flattering light, and actor Lloyd Nolan not only promoted Preston to Paramount brass, but also taught him how to pitch his voice while acting in a film.

Paramount Studios hired Preston to join their stable of stars but soon realized they had no real idea of how to utilize the talent of their ruggedly handsome actor. As a film personality, Preston was an enigma. His background as a classically trained Shakespearean actor prepared him to successfully step onto a film set well-rehearsed for any role. Central Casting at Paramount quickly realized Preston's animal magnetism might be a bit too sexually charged in a romantic lead role. The press noticed, too, and reported that Paramount's new star exuded "sex-appeal, virility, and an excellent voice."[6] Throughout his acting career, female co-stars described Preston as oozing sensuality—a trait that only intensified with age. As a case in point, Barbara Cook, Preston's co-star in the 1957 Broadway production of *The Music Man*, described him simply as "pure walking sex."[7]

Although Paramount offered Preston a contract and immediately put him to work, the studio faced a dilemma as to the movie vehicles that would be most appropriate for their newest talent. Paramount ultimately chose to safely relegate Preston to B-movies and westerns playing supporting or villainous roles. Although Preston yearned to be cast as a romantic lead in A-list productions, the studio continued to assign him roles that thrust him into a typecasting rut and threatened to define him as an actor for a lifetime. During this nascent phase of his career, Preston accepted the studio's paternalistic directives and rarely made waves over the direction of his life's work.

As a young film actor, Preston was dedicated to his craft: he meticulously memorized scripts and flexed his ability to portray the full range of human emotions. Although Preston arrived on the set prepared to execute the script du jour, he willingly pivoted in a new direction on the whim of the director. The actor was not known to complain on set, even when expressly invited to do so by a director; he maintained restraint, seeing himself as an essential part of the cast needed to produce a high-quality motion picture. Preston's charm, professionalism, and affability led those "who shared a stage or movie set with him" to declare that he "was the best person to work with."[8] Film audiences "[felt] his energy seething just below the surface,"[9] especially in those movie roles that constrained Preston from exercising his full potential as an actor.

The actor continued to reside with his parents and younger brother in a modest home at 236 S. Crescent Drive in Beverly Hills during the first few years of his Paramount contract. A pragmatist who remained low-key about his star status, Preston did not acquire a new wardrobe or a fancy car, but instead chose to bank his earnings. He elected to hand over his paychecks to his mother, Ruth, who would provide him with an adequate allowance before investing the remainder of the funds in annuities.[10]

Preston's big break came at age twenty in 1938 when, without warning, he was summoned to the office of famed director Cecil B. DeMille and offered the role of rascal Dick Allen in *Union Pacific* (1939). Preston acknowledged this first encounter with DeMille was the closest he would ever come to heart failure, recalling he "went weak in the knees when Mr. DeMille calmly announced he wanted me to play alongside Barbara Stanwyck, Joel McCrea, Lynn Overman, and Akim Tamiroff."[11]

Cecil B. DeMille was a renowned Hollywood director and a legend in his own time. During the early years of films, DeMille produced and directed over 90 silent movies before making a successful transition to sound pictures and becoming the master of epic and spectacle films. At the time *Union Pacific* was filmed, DeMille was a force majeure in Hollywood. The director came to prominence with éclat as a result of painstakingly crafting his public image. In private, he was a staunch political conservative with a storied reputation for tyrannical behavior on his movie sets.[12]

Filming of *Union Pacific* began in October 1938 with scenes shot on location in California, Utah, and Council Bluffs, Iowa. Preston, eager for feature film success, readily accepted the free-flowing advice from DeMille. To mature the actor's twenty-year-old face for his role, DeMille instructed Preston to grow some facial hair. Preston complied and within days had sprouted a narrow-gauge mustache.[13] In addition, the director presented Preston with an unloaded Derringer pistol and instructed him to acclimate himself to the weapon so he could realistically brandish it in the film.

A visibly anxious Robert Preston arrived on the set of *Union Pacific* ready to work with DeMille. The actor acknowledged he would never forget that first day on the set and recalled,

> It was the toughest sequence in the entire script and I couldn't understand why Mr. DeMille wanted ed to shoot it first, me being so jittery and more apt than not to set the whole company off on the wrong foot when the cameras began to grind. Somehow, I managed to go through my part well enough to satisfy Mr. DeMille. The reason he selected the toughest sequence first, he explained to me when he finally okayed the shooting, was because he knew I was as high-strung as a symphony fiddle string, a state of mind and of nerves demanded of me by the sequence, and he was afraid I'd never be able to whip myself into this particular tension later on.[14]

The role of Dick Allen also required Preston to be able to realistically perform card tricks during critical scenes in the film. DeMille hired a magician to teach Preston some sleight of hand to allow him to realistically portray the character, but the star had difficulty with the maneuvers and was unable to perform the card tricks with the ease required by the script. After a few weeks of futility, Preston suggested to the director that the card tricks should somehow be spliced in and DeMille "went right through the ceiling."[15] Preston doubled down on the card practice to the extent that he was eventually able to provide a realistic performance.

Preston played directly opposite Barbara Stanwyck in *Union Pacific*. He quickly developed an affinity for the actress known as "Missy" to her friends and came to adore her. Preston appreciated Stanwyck's easy-going nature, lack of pretension, professionalism, and generosity toward her fellow actors. She was the role model against whom he measured each of his future co-stars. Preston acknowledged Stanwyck, "was the first big star with whom I worked, and later, when I got involved with others who were selfish or put on the big star act, I didn't get bugged because Missy had shown me that all stars aren't like that."[16] For the rest of his life, whenever the name Barbara Stanwyck was mentioned, Preston effusively sang her praises and would declare, "she's the most helpful, the most sincere, and the kindest woman I've ever met."[17]

While in rehearsal for *Union Pacific*, Stanwyck mentored Preston by helping him portray realistic tableaus of physical intimacy on the screen. On one occasion, "Stanwyck pulled him toward her, pressed her body against his and said, 'the difference between Lunt and Fontanne [the famous theatrical husband-and-wife acting team] and the leads in a high school play is just as simple as this.'"[18] Stanwyck shared another piece of valuable piece of advice: she warned Preston to "only read the bad things about yourself. Believing in the good notices gives an actor ideas of grandeur that's bad on him and his friends–if he keeps them."[19] Stanwyck, who converted to Roman Catholicism at the time of her marriage to her first husband, Frank Fay, gave Preston the gift of a silver St. Genesius medal. Since St. Genesius was the patron saint of actors, the medal was meant to serve as a guide for Preston's destiny. He cherished Stanwyck's gift and acknowledged he had not "stepped on a stage or in front of a camera without wearing the St. Genesius medal . . . if he was the patron saint of actors, she, in my opinion, is the patroness."[20] Preston revered his *Union Pacific* co-star, but his relationship with the film's director could not be similarly described. In *Empire of Dreams*, a biography of Cecil B. DeMille, author Scott Eyman reveals the director was the ultimate authority on his film sets, meticulously overseeing each phase of film production. It was a common occurrence for the dictatorial DeMille to launch into a brutal tirade over the smallest issue, a tactic he artfully used to impose dominance and control over the actors and the stage crew.[21] It didn't help that Preston, a self-described Democrat,[22] abhorred the politics of the politically conservative DeMille.

Union Pacific ultimately overshot its eighty-two-day schedule by eleven days and ended up $161,139 over budget.[23] Once all filming for *Union Pacific* was complete, Preston, who also was hailed on the Paramount lot as both "Pres" and "Bob," became the target of DeMille's narcissistic machinations. To promote its new blockbuster epic, Paramount Studios scheduled a series of movie premieres that involved the transcontinental transportation of the movie's cast by train. To orchestrate this rolling publicity tour, Paramount "rented a dieselized electric train that towed an old steam locomotive behind it. When the entourage got within a couple of miles [of a publicity stop], they'd travel the last leg on the old train."[24] DeMille, who needed to introduce Preston during the tour's whistle stops, summoned the actor to his private car as soon as the train departed from Los Angeles. The director, who knew nothing about Preston, began peppering the young star with questions about his professional acting background. Preston obligingly provided an outline of his work at the Pasadena Playhouse and enumerated the three B-level Paramount films in which he was featured before being cast in *Union Pacific*. Unimpressed, DeMille began questioning Preston about his non-acting work experiences. When Preston revealed he had previously "worked as a member of the cleaning crew and as a parking attendant at the Santa Anita racetrack, DeMille seized upon this information as a way to take credit for Preston's discovery."[25] The director proceeded to concoct a self-aggrandizing story and introduced Preston "for the next 57 cities as the boy he found parking cars in the parking lot at Santa Anita."[26] Preston was complicit in this charade until he was able to extricate himself from DeMille's grasp several years later. He acquiesced to DeMille's fabricated story of his discovery, explaining that, "nobody argued with DeMille, demon that he was. He took me under his wing, and when DeMille did that, you were putty in his authoritative hands. You became as much his property as his puttees or his megaphone, to be done with as he saw fit."[27]

Paramount Studio pulled out all the stops for DeMille's new film by sending the cast of *Union Pacific* on a fifteen-day cross-country train junket "described as Hollywood on Wheels."[28] The first stop on the *Union Pacific* publicity tour was the movie's April 1939 premiere in Omaha, Nebraska. The tour and premiere were timed to commemorate the 70th anniversary of the joining of the Union Pacific and Central Pacific railroads at Promontory Point, Utah. As the publicity tour continued across the country, the train made stops in various cities along the route to allow the stars of *Union Pacific* to make public appearances and promote the film. The train also made a stop in Bloomington, Indiana on May 12, 1939, at which time Preston received an on-board visit from girlfriend Catherine Feltus's parents, sister, and aunt.[29]

Since the time of their first date in July 1937, Preston and Catherine Feltus continued to be an item. Before landing his contract with Paramount, Preston was short on cash and unable to squire Catherine to dinner or "to the Grove or the Trocadero."[30] Most of the time, all he "could do was take her for a walk in the park."[31] Catherine would regularly invite Preston to her apartment to share a meal, and the two would "spend long hours listening to the radio and reading plays aloud to each other."[32] To Preston, Catherine Feltus was the total package: attractive, intelligent, articulate, talented, capable, and poised. He was utterly smitten with her, but at age twenty lacked the emotional maturity and financial security to tie the knot. During a November 1938 interview with a nationally syndicated reporter, Preston was queried about his love life. The actor readily volunteered he had been dating Catherine for the past year and a half and proudly shared, "She's from Indiana. A Phi Beta Kappa, no less,"[33] but appeared taken aback when asked if he and Catherine planned to marry. "Well, well I hadn't thought much about that" responded Preston, adding, "but it's a good idea to look forward to."[34] When Preston secured his contract at Paramount, Catherine was performing with a stock company in San Francisco, and the two maintained a long-distance romance. By the time *Beau Geste* was released in July 1939, Catherine had followed Preston to Paramount Studios as a contract player under the stage name of "Catherine Craig." Although the Hollywood rumor mill had Preston romantically linked to a string of starlets, it was Catherine who accompanied him to the premiere of *Beau Geste*. During a September 1939 interview with a fan magazine, Preston confirmed he had been dating Catherine for the past two years, but added the two had no "definite step"[35] planned for the foreseeable future.

Preston had been tapped to play the youngest of the three ill-fated Geste brothers in the epic movie *Beau Geste* (1939). The film, a virtual remake of the 1926 silent film by the same name, began production in January 1939 near Yuma, Arizona with director William "Wild Bill" Wellman at the helm.

William Augustus Wellman was a no-nonsense director with a reputation for wild personal behavior. Wellman, aptly nicknamed "Wild Bill," hailed from Newton, Massachusetts— Preston's hometown. He had been an all-star high school athlete who was ultimately cut from the hockey team when the school's headmaster caught him and a fellow student "dangling an arrogant schoolmate by his heels from a second-story window."[36] Wellman reacted to his suspension from team sports by dropping a stink bomb from a second-story window onto the head of the school's headmaster.[37] When the stunt abruptly ended Wellman's high school career, he trailed off to join the French Foreign Legion during World War I, and later served as a daredevil aviator in the Lafayette Escadrille Flying Corps, a unit comprised of American pilots. A serious plane crash broke Wellman's back in two places and ultimately relegated Wild Bill to the sidelines. The collateral damage done when the control stick of the plane was forced through the roof of Wild

Bill's mouth necessitated that a silver plate be inserted into his skull.[38] Wellman received the Croix de Guerre for gallantry under fire and was discharged from the Corps in March 1918. Soon thereafter, Wild Bill Wellman returned stateside and secured a low-level job at Goldwyn Pictures. He steadily worked his way up the ladder of the film industry, directed his first film in 1923, and eventually became an Oscar-winning screenwriter/director with a no-nonsense reputation.

Preston had an "inside track" with the director since his father and Wellman had attended high school together in Newton, Massachusetts. Preston knew all the outrageous stories circulating about Wellman were true since his father had confirmed them all.[39] Wellman razzed Preston mercilessly on the set, insisting on calling him "Meservey" throughout the entire production of *Beau Geste*.[40] On one occasion, Preston checked the next day's production schedule and call sheet and, realizing he would not be required for any scenes, decided to stay up playing poker until the wee hours of the morning. The all-nighter left Preston bleary-eyed and unsteady by sunrise. When Bill Wellman learned that Preston was sleep-deprived after a night of gambling, he "hurriedly rearranged the shooting schedule to have Bob do the scene in which he carries first, Gary Cooper, then Brian Donlevy, into the desert fort."[41] Although running on empty, Preston successfully completed the scene in one take, a feat that surprised both himself and Wild Bill Wellman.

The plot of the film focused on the lives of the three adopted Geste brothers who joined the French Foreign Legion to salvage their honor after being accused of stealing a valuable gem belonging to their adoptive parents. While in the Foreign Legion, the brothers engaged in battles with Arab aggressors and endured sadistic cruelty from their superior officer. In the A-list epic that featured adventure, a foreign locale, and a Viking funeral, Preston played the role of the youngest brother, Digby Geste, who "got to play a bugle and die in the end."[42] The other two Geste brothers, Beau and John, were played respectively by Gary Cooper and Ray Milland. The film also featured performances by Brian Donlevy, Susan Hayward, Albert Dekker, and J. Carroll Naish.

Paramount Studios built an entire desert city nineteen miles west of Yuma, Arizona to serve as the set for *Beau Geste*. This special set consisted of roads, 136 tents to house 1,000 men, mess halls, and a movie theater. No women were allowed on location; wives or girlfriends of the cast and crew had to stay at a hotel in the town of Yuma.[43]

To provide some distraction from the harsh desert heat, Wellman "supplied a large comfortable bus that left the location after dinner on the weekends bound for the only whorehouse in town."[44] Preston participated in these excursions, recalling, "We used to get the cafard, we'd go crazy, and we would go into the little Mexican border towns at night for a little relaxation."[45] Preston, among those who visited the brothels with Wellman and company, was astonished by an incident during one such soiree that confirmed all the stories he had ever heard about Wellman. The incident unfolded when a group from the film set "were in a whorehouse in Mexico—Bill and I, Gary Cooper, Ray Milland, and J. Carroll Naish," when a threatening-looking man in a black leather jacket ambled over to their table and they "all got ready for trouble." The burly guy immediately zeroed in on Bill Wellman and announced he had served as Wellman's aviation mechanic during World War I. The man proceeded to reach into his jacket pocket and produced worn photos of several of Wellman's plane crashes. It was at that point that Preston and his fellow actors, "knew that stories about Bill's exploits were not apocryphal; that the silver plate in his head that made him crazier than he was to begin with was real."[46]

The shooting schedule for *Beau Geste* was exhausting, and the extreme desert heat and constant sandstorms sent several members of the cast and crew to the Yuma hospital. To boost morale, Wellman decided to take the entire company on a three-day vacation to Mexico. The decision created an atmosphere of contentment on the set and "better attitudes for the work ahead."[47] The film, which wrapped production in April 1939, significantly elevated Preston's star status.

That summer when actor Jon Hall became sick, Preston was cast opposite Dorothy Lamour in the South-Sea thriller *Typhoon* (1939). The technicolor film, the first in Preston's career to provide him with equal billing on the marquee, also precipitated a romantic crisis for the actor. The working relationship between Lamour and Preston was initially tenuous at best, with the two stars acknowledging that they "disliked each other on sight."[48] Preston signed on to the film harboring some preconceived notions about the exotic Lamour, assuming she was a snooty, stand-offish actress who "goes around dripping glamour all over the place."[49] The initial tension between the two actors was palpable but quickly dissolved once Lamour reacted to Preston's on-set wisecracking with hearty laughter.[50]

By the time she was cast in *Typhoon*, Dorothy Lamour had garnered fame as the sarong-wearing South Seas heroine in several tropical-themed films including *The Jungle Princess* (1936), *Hurricane* (1937), *Her Jungle Love* (1938), and *Tropic Holiday* (1938). As an actress, Dorothy Lamour was known both for her sultry beauty, flowing brown tresses, scanty sarong costumes, and for being "the most down-to-earth actress in the business."[51]

Dorothy was born in New Orleans in 1914; her parents divorced when she was a mere infant, at which point she was effectively abandoned by her father.[52] As a fatherless daughter, young Dorothy craved stability, even as she daydreamed about becoming a famous singer. Seventeen-year-old Dorothy's dreams materialized when she was discovered in 1931 by bandleader Herbie Kay and immediately signed as the female vocalist for Kay and his orchestra. Lamour and Kay decided to marry while they were on tour in 1935. Dorothy eventually made her way to Hollywood in 1936 where she was immediately signed by Paramount Studios. The couple maintained a long-distance marriage until Kay filed for a fast-track divorce in April 1939. Unbeknownst to Lamour, Herbie Kay had already selected his next wife and remarried not long after the ink on his divorce papers was dry.[53]

During the filming of *Typhoon*, Preston maintained his relationship with Catherine Craig; he called her regularly, and the two occasionally spent time together when permitted by Preston's filming schedule. Preston's relationship with Catherine became strained when the Paramount publicity machine kicked into high gear and began promoting a Preston-Lamour romance. In her memoir, *My Side of the Road*, Dorothy Lamour explained that "in those days publicists used to love to match-make the stars, and start new 'romances' with each new movie," noting that the ads for *Typhoon* "didn't miss anything: Red Lips, White Arms, Black Pearls, Tidal Wave, Forest Fire, a Tornado of Tropic Love! And the gossips thought it was real."[54]

What began as a publicity romance quickly developed into a genuine, off-screen romantic relationship. Preston's relationship with Dorothy Lamour would mark the first time he waffled in his commitment to Catherine Craig, but it would not be the last. Newly single, Dorothy Lamour was in search of a serious, monogamous relationship. She acknowledged that "at first Bob and I laughed off the romance rumors, but pretty soon we became genuinely attracted to each other and began to date seriously."[55] The couple fanned the flames of gossip by regularly appearing in public together and giving interviews to fan magazines. Dorothy described her blossoming relationship with Preston in detail when interviewed by *Modern Screen* magazine for their article, "Lamour's in Love:"

> If I feel like being crazy, it's okay with Pres, and no questions asked. There are times when he feels like being crazy, too, so he understands. That's one of the nicest things about him. He understands without a lot of explanations . . . he knows the whole story of why Herbie and I divorced, but he doesn't talk about it, and I don't either. At first, we used to go to nightclubs, because he thought I wanted to, and I thought he wanted to. Personally, I didn't care if I ever saw another nightclub. One evening he said, 'How'd you like to go see some friends of mine? They have a little place down at the beach.' I said I'd love it. We never went to a nightclub again. We go to visit his friends or we go horseback riding. When we have free time, we pile into the car and drive a hundred and twenty-five miles to San Jacinto to play the marble machines. Nobody bothers us there; it's nice to get away from people who are sure to stick you in a gossip column the next morning. If we have

an afternoon off, we sometimes drive to Santa Barbara for a hot dog sandwich.[56]

During his teenage years, Preston lived in an Italian-American neighborhood and acquired the cultural habit of assigning nicknames to those in his sphere as a term of endearment. Dorothy Lamour was no exception; Preston quickly began referring to her by the affectionate nickname "Pete." Dorothy acknowledged to the press, "He never calls me Dorothy. It's always 'Pete.' No reason . . . I think it's cute."[57]

The plot of *Typhoon* required both Lamour and Preston to be costumed in a version of the sarong. Preston was mortified by his costume, recounting that Dorothy "wore a sarong, and I had to wear one, too. It didn't feel right. It embarrassed me."[58] The costume department designed a male version of the sarong for Preston that would cover his mid-section, since it was taboo to display one's navel on film during that era.[59] Preston was so revolted by seeing himself in the sarong that he became physically ill during the movie's premiere and his younger brother "had to help him to the men's room."[60] As much as he hated the sarong, Preston acknowledged he had received the most fan mail for *Typhoon*, more than for any other movie prior to 1962.[61] The plot of *Typhoon* required Preston and Lamour to share the screen with a chimpanzee who had a mind of his own. Preston ended up in the hospital for two weeks when he attempted to rein in the chimp's aggressive behavior toward Dorothy Lamour. When the animal grabbed Lamour, causing her to scream for help, Preston rushed to her side but was instead rendered unconscious by the chimp.[62]

At this juncture in her life, Dorothy Lamour's long-standing medical issues with her tonsils had reached a point where she needed to take action. Just as she had resigned herself to a tonsillectomy, she was offered a plum dramatic role in the film *Johnny Apollo* starring opposite Tyrone Power. Preston read through the script with Lamour and encouraged her to accept the film role and delay her tonsillectomy until the filming of *Johnny Apollo* was complete.[63] *Johnny Apollo*, with Lamour in the role of Lucky DuBarry, began production on December 4, 1939.

Preston was photographed at Lamour's twenty-fifth birthday party on December 10, 1939, the only other attendees being her mother and her manager. The couple's relationship advanced to the point where they exchanged Christmas gifts. Lamour revealed to the press that she "bought Pres a wrist watch, and he gave (her) a beautiful French evening bag, white brocade, with a little baguette clasp."[64] In February 1940, publicity engagements necessitated Lamour's travel to the East Coast. Preston followed close behind and the inamorati were photographed together in New York's Grand Central Station on February 10; the photo's caption, "Dorothy Lamour with boyfriend Robert Preston," confirmed the relationship status of the celebrity pair. Another photo of Preston and Lamour was taken in New York City on Valentine's Day 1940 in Lamour's dressing room at the Paramount Theatre. The publicity information which accompanied the photo indicated the two stars admitted to "keeping company," with Preston declaring, "if it could be worked out, we'd love to be married."[65] The Preston-Lamour relationship was recognized by Hollywood insiders as serious, so much so that *Radio and Television Mirror* magazine alerted their readers to "look for Dorothy Lamour and Robert Preston to elope at any moment."[66]

Catherine Craig was distressed over the newspaper and fan magazine stories that touted Preston's romance with Dorothy

Lamour; she had been cautioned by friends that Preston would naturally gravitate toward big-name actresses now that he achieved some success in Hollywood. After each new headline, Preston would wire a jittery Catherine to assure her that their relationship remained on solid ground.[67]

The time had finally arrived for Lamour to proceed with the tonsillectomy surgery. She was joined by Preston before a pre-surgery trip to Florida that had been arranged to calm her nerves, yet she remained "fearful that the throaty huskiness of her voice would disappear along with her tonsils."[68] Lamour's tonsils were successfully removed at the Manhattan Eye, Ear, and Throat Hospital in New York City on March 9, 1940[69] without causing any impairment to her voice or vocal cords.

Dorothy Lamour was acutely aware Preston had not ended his relationship with Catherine Craig, and she was frustrated with Preston's inability to fully commit to their relationship. In need of a "good long rest,"[70] a hiatus to disengage from the triangulation, and allow some time for new orthodontics to straighten her smile, Lamour embarked on a trip to Hawaii with her mother on April 18 aboard the *S.S. Lurline*. Preston, away on location with another film project, was not at the dock to wish Lamour a bon voyage. The actress, who had experienced abandonment early in life in addition to the disappointment of a divorce, simply desired to give love and be loved in the context of a committed relationship. Before she departed for Honolulu, Lamour gave an interview in which she made clear that "Bob was a grand person" but "he couldn't make up his mind"[71]about the future of their relationship. Preston contacted Lamour a few times during her stay in Hawaii, but when she arrived back on the mainland on May 9, Lamour publicly announced the end of her engagement to Preston. She went out of her way to swoon over a relationship with an unnamed Army Air Corps captain she met during her Hawaiian vacation in her interview with reporters, but refused to disclose the mystery man's identity.[72] The story of a new vacation romance may have been proffered by Lamour to maintain control, signal to Preston that her exit from the romantic triangle was permanent, and apprise the press that the Preston-Lamour romance was kaput.

Perhaps in an attempt to save face and to reassure Catherine of his devotion, Preston told reporters that he and Lamour had merely been friends, and announced he was in love with Kay Feltus (Catherine Craig). Hollywood gossip columnist Sheilah Graham was convinced that Preston's protestations were disingenuous and called him out in her column: "Personally, I remain skeptical, if the guy goes out with one girl [Dorothy Lamour], no matter how definitely he says he's in love with another."[73]

The end of the Preston-Lamour romance appeared to be a win-win situation for all involved: Lamour extricated herself from a relationship on a fast track to nowhere, Preston was no longer required to juggle two women, and Catherine got her man. The proverbial skies remained calm until a scoop about the demise of the Preston-Lamour relationship was leaked to *Movie Mirror* magazine. The sensational revelations led to the front-page headline, "Why Dorothy Lamour Lost Robert Preston," and an accompanying story that painted Lamour in an unflattering light while portraying Catherine as the wholesome, girl-next-door. The story contained alleged insider details of the Preston-Lamour relationship that demeaned Lamour by asserting she embodied an excitement that "is exhausting and has no substance."[74] Conversely, Catherine was lauded for her sweet, charming, and lady-like disposition. The article concluded that Preston had chosen Craig over Lamour after "a lot of inevitable contrasting and unavoidable weighing of values."[75] Lamour was justifiably incensed by the defamatory article. An item in Louella Parsons's gossip column revealed, "Dorothy Lamour is hopping mad and spent the week-end huddling with her lawyer over what legal steps she could take about that fan mag story, 'Why Dorothy Lamour Lost Robert Preston.'"[76] Preston stopped seeing Catherine Craig for a short time after the article's publication, suspecting she was the source of the *Movie Mirror* story about the Preston-Lamour-Craig romantic triangle.[77] The article was soon relegated to the dustbin of Hollywood history, and Preston resumed his relationship with Catherine.[78] The actor also addressed the issue in a subsequent interview in which he acknowledged dating Catherine Craig while he was also simultaneously involved with Dorothy Lamour. Preston also revealed Dorothy "was plenty burned up"[79] over his comments to the press, especially the denial that he and Lamour ever contemplated thoughts of marriage.[80] Realizing the studio planned to team him up with Lamour in future film projects, Preston managed to smooth things over with her to the point where the two former lovers were able to maintain a professional friendship.

Dorothy Lamour set the record straight on her relationship with Robert Preston both in her 1980 memoir *My Side of the Road* and in a 1982 interview with *People* magazine. In her memoir, Lamour spoke wistfully about Preston, recalling, "He was a wonderful man and we considered marriage several times, but it never seemed to work out."[81] She also acknowledged the relationship was often on-again-off-again, an aspect that did not go unnoticed by the Hollywood press: "The press had us breaking up and making up for most of the time we were together—and that was true. He wasn't quite *The Music Man* then, but we did make beautiful music together and I have fond memories of our relationship."[82] During an interview with *People* magazine in 1982, Lamour again addressed the tenor of her relationship with Preston. When queried as to whether she had been involved in any serious relationships with any Hollywood leading men, Lamour responded in the affirmative with only one name, "Yes, with Robert Preston."[83]

By July 1940, twenty-two-year-old Preston had been involved in a dating relationship with Catherine Craig for three years, notwithstanding his relationship with Dorothy Lamour. When queried by the press about his relationship with Catherine, Preston acknowledged, "A fellow in pictures doesn't have a chance to really propose or win a girl decently. There's too much opportunity for misunderstandings over things that are not your own doing. That's why, all this last year I've been urging Kay to marry me—before something more serious comes along and breaks us up."[84] With the "get-women-to-work" war effort a few years in the offing, Preston, not unlike many other men of his generation, expected his future wife to fill the traditional role of housewife. Although his own mother worked outside the home, Preston expected his future wife to "get up with me for breakfast . . . I eat a whale of pancakes, fruit juice, two or three glasses of it, and eggs, and bacon and sausages and toast and jelly. This may sound old-fashioned, but I admire domesticity and virtue in a girl."[85]

The actor was again teamed with Dorothy Lamour and Preston Foster in the southeast Asian melodrama, *Moon Over Burma* (1940). The Louis King film, which explored life on a teak plantation in the jungles near Rangoon, was panned by New York Times film critic Bosley Crowther.[86]

Preston's film career was chugging along, just not in the direction he envisioned. Cecil DeMille tapped Preston to play the role of Constable Ronnie Logan in his technicolor thriller *North West Mounted Police* alongside Gary Cooper, Madeleine Carroll, Paulette Goddard, and Preston Foster. The film plot centered on a group of Royal Canadian Mounties stationed in the Canadian northwest who were entrusted with the protection of white settlers amidst a revolt organized by a band of native Indians. Preston's character became involved in a relationship with a half-breed woman (Goddard), but he predictably died before the end of the film. Preston viewed the role in *North West Mounted Police* as simply another regurgitation of his past screen incarnations—he was playing the same character over and over again in a typecast, cookie-cutter fashion. The actor had the temerity to voice his displeasure to DeMille, who saw no issue with Preston replaying familiar roles. The annoyed director retorted by asking, "What's the matter? It's the same part you had in *Union Pacific*, isn't it?"[87] DeMille, who had come to believe his self-concocted story of Preston's "discovery," proceeded to lash out at the actor, exclaiming, "You ungrateful son-of-a-bitch, if it weren't for me, you'd still be parking cars at Santa Anita."[88]

In early November, Catherine Craig received a new contract from Paramount Pictures and a few days later, Preston and Catherine decided to elope to Las Vegas. On Friday November 8, the pair made the four-hour drive northeast to Las Vegas, and the Acme News Bureau snapped a photo of the couple as they departed Los Angeles for Sin City. The photographer from Acme's Los Angeles Bureau revealed Preston had proposed to Catherine Craig by telephone two weeks before the wedding while he was in Chicago for the premiere of *North West Mounted Police*. Once in Las Vegas, Preston and Catherine headed toward the now nonextant Hitching Post wedding chapel on

South Fifth Street. The standard fee for a wedding at the chapel was twelve dollars; this entitled the couple to a marriage license, the services of a minister, and a cozy living room setting to be used as the venue for the ceremony.[89] Hitching Post Chapel proprietor, Halley Stewart, recalled,

> The doorbell rang and I opened it, there was Robert Preston stealing a kiss from Catherine Craig. Robert Preston was nervous as hell. Jumpy. My wife and I put him at ease. He turned out to be one swell person, sweet and sincere. The wedding ring used in the ceremony was 80 years old and had been handed down to Catherine Craig.[90]

The wedding ceremony was conducted by the Reverend Berkley Bunker with Mr. and Mrs. Halley Stewart, serving as witnesses.[91] The couple's Clark County marriage license lists the age of the groom, Robert Preston Meservey, correctly as age twenty-two. The bride, just as the groom's mother had done twenty-three years before, misrepresented her age on her marriage license. Catherine listed her age as twenty-three when she was in fact twenty-five years of age; she would turn twenty-six just two months later.

The ink on the marriage certificate was barely dry when gossip maven Louella Parsons received a long-distance telephone call alerting her to the Preston–Craig elopement.[92] Newspapers across the country immediately blared headlines, "Robert Preston Weds," "Hollywood Couple Wed in Las Vegas," and "Bob Preston Elopes." The couple's trip to the altar was quick and without a honeymoon. Preston and his new wife returned to Los Angeles the same evening, since the actor was expected on the set of the new Paramount film *New York Town* (1941) on Monday, November 11. The newlyweds "settled down in a big Brentwood house located at 436 N. Bristol Avenue that boasted a swimming pool in the back yard and nothing but a bed and a card table inside."[93] The home, previously owned by Tarzan actor and five-time Olympic gold medalist Johnny Weissmuller, was constructed in the classic Spanish-style and was framed by a porch and a generous expanse of lawn. The property also boasted a ten-foot-deep pool originally built to accommodate Weissmuller's passion for competitive swimming.

In *New York Town* Preston played Paul Bryson, Jr., a wealthy client of a photographer portrayed by Fred MacMurray. Preston's character did survive to the end of the film, but ultimately "lost the girl" to Fred MacMurray. The movie was filmed within a month and a half, with production complete by late December 1940. Other actors with principal roles in the film included Mary Martin, Victor Ballard, Akim Tamiroff, and Lynne Overman.

Paramount then decided to loan Preston to Universal Pictures to star opposite Loretta Young in director Frank Lloyd's western film *The Lady from Cheyenne* (1941). The film began production in January 1941 in Mojave, California where an old-west town set had been constructed as the backdrop for the story. The plot of the film centered around property schemes in the fledgling Wyoming town of Laraville and the political promotion of the state's bill for women's suffrage. By 1941 Loretta Young was an established, glamourous Hollywood star who "struck fear in the hearts of studio heads, producers, and directors."[94] Young received superstar treatment on the set, which included her insistence on a change to the film's title. Preston understood that "The story was originally called *Cheyenne,* but Loretta had it in her contract that she had to have the title role,"[95] thus the movie was renamed *The Lady from Cheyenne*. For Preston, Loretta Young fell short of the star-ideal established earlier in his career by Barbara Stanwyck. According to the actor, Young was preoccupied with her wardrobe and camera angles to the extent that she "worked with a full-length mirror beside the camera [and] I didn't know which Loretta to play to—the one in the mirror or the one that was with me."[96]

Preston was next tapped for the murder mystery-cum-courtroom drama *Night of January 16*[th] (1941), which was loosely based on a play authored by objectivist philosopher Ayn Rand.

The film, directed by William Clemens, also featured Ellen Drew and Nils Asther. Drew's character is accused of murdering her boss, and Preston's character attempts to prove her innocence. The casting for Preston's role, Steve Van Ruyle, was fraught with signing issues. Paramount Studios originally contracted with Twentieth Century Fox to use Don Ameche in the film and eventually sued Ameche for $170,000 when the actor refused to accept the role.[97] The studio's other attempts to cast the role included overtures to Fred MacMurray, Melvyn Douglas, Ray Milland, and Brian Donlevy before offering the part to Preston. Much to her consternation, Ayn Rand's objectivist philosophy was completely sanitized from the movie's final script. Rand responded by distancing herself from the film and declared in an interview with Rex Reed that she "had nothing to do with the screen adaptation. There is nothing of mine in that movie except the names of some of the characters and one line of dialogue: 'The court will now adjourn until ten o'clock tomorrow morning.'"[98]

During the next year and a half, Preston was cast in a succession of war films: *Parachute Battalion* (1941), *Pacific Blackout*

(1942), *Wake Island* (1942), and *Night Plane from Chung-King* (1943) and made a brief cameo appearance in *Star Spangled Rhythm* (1942). The actor's frustration was heightened when he was offered a series of movie roles that he considered inadequate and not reflective of the range of his acting ability. Many of the scripts made their way down the Hollywood food chain of leading men to him simply because everyone else had rejected them. Although the scripts he received were often not to his liking, Preston remained a consummate professional and provided a superlative performance in each film. Even in those movies that were panned or given a lukewarm reception by critics, Preston consistently received accolades for his acting ability.

In the early months of 1941, Preston was offered a minor supporting role in Cecil B. DeMille's film *Reap the Wild Wind* (1942). The film's powerhouse cast included Ray Milland, John Wayne, Paulette Goddard, Raymond Massey, Lynne Overman, and Susan Hayward. The story, centering around the antebellum shipping trade in the south, featured shipwrecks, stormy seas, a killer octopus, and lots of fighting between testosterone-fueled sailors. Preston portrayed Dan Cutler, the brother of ruthless salvage profiteer King Cutler and secret paramour to Susan Hayward's character, Drusilla Alston. As in many of Preston's film roles, he died by the end of the movie, succumbing to a gunshot fired by his cutthroat brother. Production for the sea epic concluded by the end of August 1941.

Catherine Craig's acting career continued but was limited to minor, often uncredited, roles in forgettable B-movies produced between 1940 and 1941, including *Manhattan Heartbeat* (1940), *Doomed to Die* (1940), *Murder Over New York* (1940), *Las Vegas Nights* (1941), *One Night in Lisbon* (1941), *West Point Widow* (1941), *Nothing but the Truth* (1941), *Among the Living* (1941), and *Louisiana Purchase* (1941). On the home front, Preston and Catherine were looking forward to the expansion of their family with the proud father-to-be announcing the news of Catherine's pregnancy in the September 1941 issue of *Photoplay* magazine.[99] Sadly, the pregnancy was ectopic and non-viable.[100] Catherine survived the ectopic pregnancy, a dangerous condition in the 1940s that carried with it a substantial risk of maternal death and impairment to a woman's fertility, and the medical crisis "sort of threw water"[101] on the couple's hopes of conceiving a biological child. Following Preston's return from service in World War II, he and Catherine announced plans to adopt a war orphan from Belgium.[102] In an interview with Hollywood gossip columnist Sheilah Graham, Preston acknowledged he still hoped to have his own biological children, noting, "everyone tells me that one of the best ways to have a child of your own is to adopt a child first."[103] The adoption of a European war orphan did not materialize, and the couple remained childless for the duration of their marriage.

In late October 1941, Preston began work on *This Gun for Hire* (1942). When he initially signed on to do the film, Preston was contracted to play the male lead. Although director Frank Tuttle intended to cast Preston in the role of Phillip Raven, the film's cold-hearted killer, he was convinced by Alan Ladd's wife and agent, Sue Carol, to cast her husband in that role.[104] Preston was asked to play opposite Ladd in his screen test for *This Gun for Hire* at a time "when we didn't know we'd both be in the same movie," adding, "but he was obviously going to have the role— even without the test."[105] The diminutive Ladd had attempted to break into motion pictures for close to a decade without success after working every angle, including performing as an extra, enrolling in drama courses, and relentlessly hounding the studio casting offices. His luck miraculously changed when he met, and later married, former silent film star Sue Carol, who began acting as Ladd's talent agent. When Carol secured "an attentive ear"[106] prior to the commencement of filming *This Gun for Hire*, Alan Ladd's career was launched. In addition to Preston and Ladd, the movie's main cast included Veronica Lake, Laird Cregar, and Tully Marshall.

The plot of the film-noir thriller centers around a professional killer (Ladd) who seeks revenge upon Willard Gates (Cregar), a Nitrochemical Corporation executive who solicits his services and then double-crosses him by placing the police on his trail in an attempt to silence him. The film's parallel subplot involves Veronica Lake's character, Ellen, acting as an undercover agent to gather information about Gates to help the U.S. government foil Nitrochemical's plans to sell toxic gas to the Japanese. Although Robert Preston's name was billed above Alan Ladd's on the film marquee, Ladd's performance, coupled with his heart-throb looks and on-screen chemistry with Veronica Lake, eclipsed Preston and pushed him into a supporting role to the new star. Preston, playing the role of Veronica Lake's detective boyfriend, gave Lake her first on-screen kiss.[107] Both Preston and Lake realized that Frank Tuttle was on a mission to make Alan Ladd the primary focus of the film. Preston was practically "wiped out"[108] of the film's major scenes, and Veronica Lake, irritated because she "was the star of the picture," came to believe Tuttle was using her "mainly for decorative purposes"[109] and turning the film into a vehicle to promote Alan Ladd. *This Gun for Hire* marked the first appearance of Veronica Lake and Alan Ladd together as a screen couple. Standing five-foot, one-inch tall, Lake was one of the few actresses in Hollywood the five-foot, four-inch actor did not have to stand on a crate to kiss in a love scene.[110]

Like many Hollywood actors, Preston answered his country's call to service in World War II. He initially attempted to enlist in the Marine Corps Aviation unit in June 1942 but was turned down.[111] On October 29, 1942, Preston was inducted into the U.S. Army at Fort MacArthur in San Pedro, California as a private under his full name, Robert Preston Meservey,[112] and was initially sent to Florida for an assignment as a G.I. physical instructor. Always one to see the humor in situations, Preston mused he "had the feeling that World War II started only to get me away from Cecil B. DeMille."[113]

Preston refused to settle for the status quo and enrolled in the Army Air Force Officer Candidate School in Miami, Florida in November 1942 as a way to work his way up the military ranks. One of his fellow classmates, Hollywood director Joshua Logan, recalled that Preston was "a magnificent soldier" who possessed a "healthy, bawdy sense of humor but his dedication to duty was unseducible."[114] Preston, assigned to the 555th Bomb Group, landed in England in October 1943.[115] By April 1944, he advanced to the rank of First Lieutenant in the Army Air Force in the 386th Bomb Group as a combat intelligence officer, coaching aviators in the Marauder group on "what to expect from the Germans in way of opposition."[116]

Preston was subsequently stationed in France and Belgium and continued to brief "B-26 and A-26 pilots heading for missions over Germany"[117] while also participating in "bombing runs over Germany and France."[118] Preston's exemplary leadership earned him the rank of Captain while serving as an S-2 intelligence officer in Combat Intelligence for the Ninth Air Force.[119]

Preston appeared briefly in the short military propaganda film *Wings Up (1943)*, produced by the United States Office of War Information. The purpose of the film, narrated by Clark Gable—then a Captain in the Army Air Force—was to promote the U.S. Army Air Force Officer Candidate School in Miami, Florida to would-be enlistees. The film outlined the rigors of the twelve-week officer training course, noting that only 23 of every 1,000 men in the United States armed services would qualify to enter the Officer Candidate School.

In a 1945 letter home to Catherine, Preston described the bathing rituals of his Army Air Force group stationed in France. Each Wednesday evening was "shower night" for the men, a ritual carried out with military precision. Preston related, "Ten men shower every five minutes. First the shower is turned on for exactly one minute. We all get wet and soaped. Then, exactly two minutes later, the shower is turned on again for a final two-minute spray."[120]

Soldiers who wished to bathe any other day of the week were relegated to taking a spit-bath using their steel helmets as basins for soap and water.[121]

At the end of the war in Europe, twenty-seven-year-old Preston was stationed in St. Trond, Belgium with the 386th Bomb Group. By August 1945, he received a citation for distinguished service and had accumulated a sufficient number of discharge points to allow him to muster out of military service. Preston was one of 418 soldiers who arrived stateside on August 10, 1945, and disembarked the *Conrad Weiser* at Pier 16 in Staten Island, New York.[122] He was initially dispatched to Fort Kilmer, New Jersey before being transferred to California where he was processed through the Santa Ana army separation center and honorably discharged.[123]

In the interim, Preston's younger brother, Frank, initially tried his hand in films, landing a few minor roles as an actor and as a stand-in for his brother before opting to operate a local beer distributorship. At age twenty-three Frank married the former Florence Vacca, a beautiful twenty-one-year-old of Italian heritage and fellow graduate of Abraham Lincoln High School, on October 22, 1942. The couple made their home in Glendale and added a son and a daughter to their family during the late 1940s and early 1950s. Frank served his country during World War II, as had Preston; their father, Doc, also chose to enlist as a member of the Navy Seabees.

Preston returned to Hollywood and attempted to restart his film career after three years of military service. Once back in Hollywood, Preston made the disillusioning discovery that no one in the film capital had noticed his absence, noting, "The first time I was out in civilian clothes, I went to a party that Veronica Lake was throwing and no one even knew I'd been gone. I was disgusted."[124] By December 1945, Preston found himself at loggerheads with Paramount over his contract, and gossip columnist Louella Parsons was quick to report there was "trouble brewing between Robert Preston, war hero, and Paramount."[125] Preston, through his agent, filed suit against the studio, which planned to add his three years of military service to his existing contract. The actor, who was not paid by the studio during his years in the service, demanded that he be given a contract commensurate to the one provided to Army Air Corps veteran Jimmy Stewart and Navy vet Henry Fonda.[126] Although Paramount gave Preston a better contract, he realized he "was still going to play the lead in all the small pictures and the heavy in all the big ones."[127]

On the home front, Robert Preston and Catherine Craig maintained a modest lifestyle. Catherine resumed her acting career while Preston was away at war.[128] Once Preston returned home from his deployment overseas, the couple decided that Catherine would continue her acting career at Paramount "as long as their domestic happiness" was "not interfered with"[129] or until such time a child was added to their family. In an interview with the *Los Angeles Times*, Preston and his wife confided they lived without servants "or other fancy trimmings"[130] and expressed their intention to continue to do without the extravagances typically associated with the Hollywood lifestyle. Preston perceived his marriage as even-keeled and without the "Hollywood clashes of temperament"[131] that doomed other career couples in Tinseltown. He realized it was not uncommon for other Hollywood pairs to "breakup over such things as 'who makes the coffee this morning'" but believed he and Catherine were "immune"[132] to any such ego-driven gamesmanship within their marriage.

Preston returned from the military a different man. "I matured while I was away," he observed, adding, "before that, I'd been a kid."[133] His first film following his military discharge was a loan-out to United Artists for *The Macomber Affair* (1947) in April 1946. The film, starring Robert Preston as Francis Macomber, Joan Bennett as his shrewish wife, Margot, and Gregory Peck as a professional safari guide, Robert Wilson, tells the story of a wife's infidelity and treachery toward her faint-hearted husband during the society couple's safari adventure in Africa. The movie's hunting scenes were filmed in East Africa; during the final hunt, Margot Macomber, with a gun raised to shoot a buffalo, kills her husband instead.

The movie, based on a story by Ernest Hemingway, significantly detoured from the author's narrative. The script was altered to depict Gregory Peck's character in a more favorable light and negatively twisted Hemingway's original depiction

of Francis Macomber. After Macomber's death, the film de-
parts from the original story such that the changes "violate
the mood and meaning of Hemingway's characterizations."[134]
The altered storyline sentimentalizes the relationship between
Robert Wilson and Mrs. Macomber when, in fact, Hemingway's
story makes it clear Wilson views her as a harridan who merely serves as a convenient sex partner. *The New York Times* review of *The Macomber Affair* criticized the film's alteration of
the original Hemingway story, noting the "contrived conclusion that the guide has fallen in love with the dame and that
possibly the shooting was accidental is completely stupid and
false. It is plainly a sentimental fixture which has no place in
the film."[135] Some critics thought that Peck and Preston should
have exchanged roles, observing that, "tall, clean-shaven and
very American, Peck looked more like a wealthy socialite, while
Preston, shorter, with a close-cropped mustache, resembled the
Wilson of the story and even the young Hemingway himself."[136]
Despite the studio's changes to the Hemingway tale, Preston
"had the richest role and received superlative reviews."[137]

In early 1946, Cecile B. DeMille offered Preston the part of
the villain in his film, *Unconquered* (1947), which was slated to
begin filming in late July. Preston had already appeared in three
DeMille films and was all too aware that the only difference
between his roles in each movie was a change in uniform.[138]
Preston bemoaned DeMille's tendency to typecast actors and
use them repeatedly in similar movie roles; he felt pigeonholed
by the characters he portrayed in DeMille films and did not wish
to work with the director again. In addition, Preston harbored a
negative opinion of DeMille's personality and directing ability
and suspected "the only man DeMille ever envied was Hitler . . .
it's no secret how I felt about him."[139] Preston rejected the role

in *Unconquered* and realized the only way to convince DeMille of his need to break away from playing the "heavy" in movies was "to walk out of his office."[140] The actor's refusal of the part in *Unconquered* gave rise to the enduring wrath of DeMille, and the insulted director never spoke to Preston again.[141]

Preston's role in *The Macomber Affair* marked the beginning of the end of his professional association with Paramount Studios. Although he was featured in "another clutch of movies," he "was still dissatisfied."[142] Preston was well aware that twelve years into his contract with Paramount, he had "gone about as far as they were going to let me go in that town. You reach a certain spot in your career, and that's where they're going to keep you. If you haven't made it really big, you're not going to . . . I could play the lead in all the small pictures, and the villain in all the big ones, and that was it. That was as far as I could go." [143] Preston expressed frustration at the pecking order for film roles at Paramount that tended to place him at the bottom of the heap, explaining:

> A producer with a script would look over the Paramount list of leading men. Then he'd submit it to, say Fred MacMurray. It wasn't for Fred, so he'd pass it on to Ray Milland. Down the line it would come. Alan Ladd was next. He'd dump it in my lap. I would turn to get rid of it, but there was never anyone behind me. I lived in all the B pictures and died in all the A's. I got the girl in the B's and the fella in the A's.[144]

It was during this period of frustration with his film career that Preston was able to achieve a level of professional satisfaction by performing on the stage. He became one of the founding members of Eighteen Actors, a professional acting group composed of other Pasadena Playhouse alumni and their wives. In addition to Robert Preston and Catherine Craig, the acting troupe included Dana Andrews and Mary Todd, Victor Jory and Jean Innes, Byron Foulger and Dorothy Adams, Don Porter and Peggy Converse, Morris Ankrum, Charles Lane, and Moroni Olsen.[145]

In August 1947, Preston and his wife had the opportunity to act together for the first time in the production of *Girl of the Golden West,* with Catherine in the title role and Preston playing the mysterious stranger.[146] The group operated out of a building in Pasadena that had been donated to them by the state of California and scenically overlooked the Rose Bowl. Eighteen Actors used this setting on the weekends to stage "serious plays for serious playgoers."[147] Audience attendance was by subscription only. Each of the plays ran for four consecutive weekends and helped keep the movie-actor cast "gym-trained in the theater."[148] Each of the actors received the Equity minimum of $40 a week for their performances, and their paychecks were promptly donated back to the Eighteen Actors group.[149] Preston revitalized his interest in the stage through participating in the troupe and continued his participation in Eighteen Actors during the remainder of his time in Hollywood. It was this creative outlet that "undoubtedly influenced Preston's decision two years later, to switch to the stage full time."[150]

From a young age, Preston continually challenged himself as an actor and used each role to hone his deftness as a performer on stage and screen. Although the roles undertaken by the actor during his Pasadena Playhouse years, on-screen at Paramount, and as a member of Eighteen Actors were diverse and demonstrated the wide range of his acting ability, Paramount never really grasped the talent they had in Preston and continued to relegate him to B-movies.

Eloquent, highly energized, charismatic, intelligent, and cognizant of his acting ability, Preston possessed both an acute self-awareness of his innate gifts and unrecognized talent. After some conscious and subconscious introspection, he publicly declared that successful actors possess both a high IQ and emotional immaturity,[151] and sustain an "insatiable appetite for praise and approval" similar to that of "a child constantly seeking praise and approval from his elders."[152] He discounted the suggestion that actors seek to escape reality through their characters, insisting instead that the prime motivation for actors is their "need for acclaim from their fellow man."[153]

While under contract with Paramount, Preston had continued to be assigned to a series of bad guy roles that under-utilized his talent and he faced a catch-22 situation: act in predictable roles in B-movies or not work at all. Preston did manage to refuse a few particularly cringeworthy roles, but was warned by a Paramount executive, "Next time you turn down a script, we'll drop your option."[154] The actor waited to be cast in the right part, but no such roles were forthcoming from the studio.

Preston was then cast in *Wild Harvest* (1947), a film that reteamed him with both Alan Ladd and former flame, Dorothy Lamour. Lamour, now married to advertising executive William Ross Howard III and mother to an 18-month-old son, found herself cast in a romantic triangle involving her "old beau Robert Preston."[155] Preston's brother, Frank Meservey, began his short-lived acting career by serving as a stand-in for his brother in the film.[156] The plot of *Wild Harvest* which centered around the business of wheat farming and a romantic rivalry among friends, required Paramount to recreate an actual wheat field on one of the studio's soundstages to supplement on-location filming.

Wild Harvest marked the fourth film pairing of Robert Preston and Alan Ladd; the two men had become friends, but it was not a close relationship.[157] Lamour noted Ladd needed to stand on three planks when acting in scenes with Preston; Ladd's diminutive stature also became the focus of an incident at a cast party held at a local bar. Lamour wrote in her memoir, *My Side of the Road*, that when a burly interloper entered the bar and became unruly, Ladd promptly asked the man to leave. Rather than acquiescing to Ladd's request, the rowdy gent responded by calling the actor "Shorty." In an attempt to short-circuit certain trouble, Preston quickly diffused the situation by locking the man's arms behind his back. Lamour speculated that the troublemaker "may have heard of Bob's exploits as a heavyweight in the service. In any case, he cooperated in his fast trip to the door."[158] *Wild Harvest* also effected a professional reunion between Preston and actor Lloyd Nolan; the pair had previously worked together in Preston's first film, *King of Alcatraz,* in 1938. Preston's character in *Wild Harvest,* "Bashful" Jim Davis, sported a false tooth and this attribute became problematic during filming. During each of the movie's major fight scenes, one of the other actors invariably knocked the tooth out of Preston's mouth. Each time Preston's prosthetic tooth became dislodged, filming was abruptly halted so crew members could crawl around on all fours in search of the wayward incisor.[159]

Preston's last film while still under contract to Paramount, *Whispering Smith* (1948), was a technicolor western that also featured Alan Ladd. Once again, Preston was cast as the film's arrogant villain, for whom Ladd's character serves as the heroic foil. Preston became unnerved when Ladd's wife and agent,

Sue Carol, lobbied for a change in the script that would benefit her husband at his expense. When Preston objected to the proposed script changes, Carol insisted the changes were needed for Ladd to receive good reviews from film critics who did not take him seriously as an actor. Never one to take things lying down, Preston reminded Carol that she and Ladd had elected to sustain Ladd's heartthrob status rather than pursue serious roles, adding, "I get good reviews from the critics. Laddie gets five thousand fan letters a week. That's the choice you made."[160]

Despite his good movie reviews, Preston was frustrated by Paramount's lack of responsiveness to his need for expansive roles and hungered for more. He was confident in his ability as an actor but recognized that "the roles that you did were the roles that the studio wanted you to play."[161] The actor believed his chances of landing more expansive roles could be accomplished by being a free agent. By the fall of 1947, Preston was tired of being tethered to a paternalistic studio and wanted out of his contract with Paramount. He approached the Paramount brass about tearing up the contract he had originally signed in 1938, but his entreaties were initially met with resistance. The major stumbling block to Preston's freedom was then-studio chief, Henry Ginsberg, who refused to let Preston out of his contract.[162] Ginsberg, who became the head of production and hatchet man at Paramount in 1944, was described as a wretched human being with a penchant for doubletalk.[163]

Preston ultimately prevailed and secured his release from his Paramount contract with the assistance of powerful gossip columnist, Louella Parsons. Preston approached the gossip maven at a Hollywood party and shared his plight about being unable to secure a release from his Paramount contract. Parsons took the tidbit of information she received from Preston and used it to foster discomfort and fear within the Paramount hierarchy by accusing them of abusing a war veteran. Preston was released from his contract when Parsons ran with the story the very next day with "a headline about Paramount being mean to a returned war hero . . . [and] the front office got the shakes over that kind of publicity."[164] Although Preston credits Parsons with using her considerable clout to free him from Paramount, he did acknowledge the studio may have been inclined to nullify his contract—which paid him more money than Alan Ladd for playing the rapscallion in Ladd's movies—noting it would be less costly for Paramount to hire him back to work on a film on a per-picture basis.[165]

In his December 11, 1947 *Hollywood Wash* column, Hugh Dixon reported that Preston and Paramount were parting company.[166] Newly emancipated from Paramount and the studio-system's patriarchy, Preston and his wife traveled to New York to celebrate a white Christmas in the Big Apple.[167] Despite feeling stymied by the paternalism of the studio system, he had not formulated a strategy for career success as a free agent once he parted ways with Paramount.

Preston was uncertain as to the best way to proceed and described himself as being like "a bird who has lived so long in a gilded cage that he doesn't know how to fly out by the open door."[168] Although he left Paramount in search of a career in film that would showcase his full potential as an actor, his next few films as a free agent—*Blood on the Moon* (1948) for RKO, *Big City* (1948) for MGM, and *The Lady Gambles* (1949) for Universal—were not much of an improvement over his film roles at Paramount.[169]

He then landed a role in Walter Wanger's technicolor melodrama *Tulsa* (1949), along with Susan Hayward and Pedro Armendáriz. *Tulsa*, the story of an Oklahoma girl who initially battles oil tycoons only to become one herself, was the third movie in which Preston was cast with Hayward. Although Preston was well-regarded in Hollywood for his affable personality and professionalism on-set, he held no admiration for the talented Susan Hayward and once told an interviewer, "Anything I have to say about Susan Hayward you couldn't print,"[170] joking he would rather leave the acting profession than work with her again. Neither polished nor polite,[171] Hayward was unable to "keep her roiling emotions under control"[172] on or off set, often using her tongue "as a whiplash."[173] Preston, who was cast as Hayward's love interest in the film, found her ill-tempered. Other actors similarly found Hayward unpleasant to work with and, despite her box-office draw, the studio brass "disliked her attitude so much that they deliberately kept her in second-rate movies"[174] for years.

Catherine Craig continued to be featured in small, often uncredited, roles in a steady string of B-movies, including *Incendiary Blonde* (1945), *You Hit the Spot* (1945), *Love Letters* (1945), *Duffy's Tavern* (1945), *The Stork Club* (1945), *The Bride Wore Boots* (1946), *O.S.S.* (1946), *The Strange Love of Martha Ivers* (1946), *Monsieur Beaucaire* (1946), *Cross My Heart* (1946), *The Perfect Marriage* (1947), *Seven Were Saved* (1947), *Sweet and Low* (1947), *The Pretender* (1947), *Variety Girl* (1947), *Albuquerque* (1948), *Appointment with Murder* (1948) and *El Paso* (1949). *No Man of Her Own* (1950) was Catherine's last film.

In 1950, Catherine made the decision to forgo any future film roles and instead dedicated herself to the full-time role of Mrs. Robert Preston. Acknowledging that Preston "acts well enough for two,"[175] Catherine chose to become an invisible partner in a two-person-single-career marriage in order to fully support her husband's acting career and, from that point forward, fulfilled her need for professional achievement through the accomplishments of her husband. Preston was on board with his wife's decision to focus on the couple's marriage; he viewed Catherine's decision as fulfilling a prescribed marital dynamic in which "someone has to be a giver and someone a taker"[176] confessing, "I am a taker who married a giver."[177]

The fate of Preston's emergent métier in Hollywood mirrored the career trajectory of fellow Paramount star, Paulette Goddard, who likewise found herself on the receiving end of Cecil B. Demille's vindictive animus. Like Preston, Goddard starred in several movies directed by DeMille and was similarly recycled as a standard character in his films. After Goddard was pressed into service for yet another of DeMille's films, *Unconquered* (1947), a conflict erupted between the actress and director on the set. DeMille's high regard for Goddard quickly dampened, leading "some observers [to] believe that DeMille's lasting enmity helped short-circuit her career."[178]

As a free agent, Preston plodded along with roles in two westerns: RKO's *Best of the Badmen (1951)*, filmed during August and September 1950, and Benedict Bogeaus's *My Outlaw Brother* (1951), filmed in early November 1950 at Estudios Tepeyac in Mexico City. He then played the role of a father to a young boy in *When I Grow Up* (1951), a Horizon Productions venture that was filmed from late November to mid-December 1950 at California Studios. Cognizant of the myopia of Hollywood's star system and the make-or-break power of directors and producers, Preston decided to accept a role in the British film, *Cloudburst* (1951), and took a needed timeout from Hollywood as 1950 came to a close.

BROADWAY FEVER

With the decade of the 1950s underway, Robert Preston faced a conundrum: he was incredibly confident in his acting ability but stymied by getting the Hollywood film industry to recognize it. Even if the studio brass did not fully appreciate his talent, Preston was well regarded by his peers and was appointed to fill a vacancy on the Screen Actors Guild board in 1950; the plan was for him to serve until the next annual election in the fall of 1951.[1] As a matter of personal preservation, Preston upheld his own simple philosophy that allowed him to continue acting and stay relevant: "Keep moving, keep working. You may not always be in the right place at the right time, but if you are some place, your chances are better than if you are no place."[2]

Although Preston prided himself on being a working actor and preferred to have several projects in his career pipeline at any given time, he was acutely aware he might not be able to count on Hollywood as a steady source of employment and financial security. He hedged his bets by forming a production company that would allow him to independently produce films, should the well of acting roles run dry. Preston and his agent, Lou Rantz, filed the required legal paperwork to establish Cayston Productions, named in honor of Preston's wife, Catherine Craig.[3] Preston and Rantz acquired two stories, a radio script and a play, and were pressing Paramount for the rights to a baseball-themed project titled *The Sun Field*.[4] Cayston Productions ultimately failed to produce its acquired scripts or any other film prospects and eventually disappeared into the dustbin of Hollywood history.

To expand his financial portfolio, Preston invested some of his acting revenue in a new housing project located just outside Los Angeles, but an issue with television reception almost derailed the success of his investment shortly after the construction of the first few homes. Since television was the new medium for 1950s America, it was important for homeowners to be able to watch their favorite TV shows from the comfort of their living rooms. When Preston became aware prospective buyers were hesitant to purchase homes in the development due to concerns about antenna signal issues, he sprang into action and "solved the problem by calling in TV technicians for a survey to assure prospective buyers they would be able to see their favorite shows, no matter what the atmospheric conditions."[5] At about the same time, Preston garnered compensation and national exposure by promoting Schenley whiskey on billboards and in print advertisements that appeared in major newspapers across the country.

Catherine remained her husband's stalwart supporter and confidante. She knew instinctively when her husband required soothing, admiration, attention, or a reality check, and offered him a safe haven in which he could display his temperamental side—a side which Preston kept carefully hidden from the outside world.[6] The fact that Catherine was "not the nagging type"[7] was simply icing on the cake. Preston and Catherine celebrated their tenth wedding anniversary in November 1950 and gave the impression of the perfect Hollywood couple. The marriage had not produced any biological children in the aftermath of the devastating ectopic pregnancy in 1941, and by January 1951, Catherine was thirty-six years old. Although the age of first-time mothers has steadily increased since 1950, thirty-five was viewed as advanced maternal age in the early 50s, with a woman's last, not first, birth typically occurring around age thirty-five. The couple exhausted "every test possible"[8] to assist in their quest to conceive a child, although assisted reproductive technology such as ovarian stimulation drugs and IVF treatment was not yet available to couples facing infertility in the 1950s. For some couples of the era, the issue of infertility was omnipresent as a silent yet ticking time bomb within the relationship. The inability to conceive was often devastating for women in the mid-twentieth century and men sometimes found themselves torn between the subconscious desire for fatherhood, love for their spouse, and the reality of an infertile marriage.

By 1950, Preston's frustration with his professional and personal life was palpable. Although he managed to continue as a working actor in Hollywood, leading roles appeared to be out of his reach. He maintained high standards for himself with a reputation as an actor who arrived on each movie set familiar with the script and the extraordinary ability to memorize and regurgitate lines on cue. With his expressive energy and ability to successfully film many of his scenes in a single take, most directors viewed Preston as film-industry gold. However, the glamorous world of Hollywood is a people-centered industry in which relationships are key to success, and Preston was notoriously reclusive. Rather than immerse themselves in the Hollywood scene, Preston and his wife kept to themselves and often went so far as to avoid answering their phone to elude distracting, disruptive, and time-consuming calls.[9] In pre-1950s Hollywood, star billing may have eluded Preston for a variety of reasons: film financiers may have insisted on other actors whom they viewed as box office gold, a director/producer had a stronger social connection to another actor, another actor better fit the look and demeanor of a particular film role, or another actor cast in the film—with power and influence in the industry—preferred to work with an actor at or below their level who proved less threatening to their ego.

Weary of the fickleness of Hollywood, Preston quickly seized the opportunity when offered the starring role in the British film, *Cloudburst* (1951). Although he was well aware the film's producer was seeking "a second-rate Hollywood name to strengthen the box office appeal" of the movie,[10] Preston hoped a brief hiatus from Hollywood would generate a much-needed change in his acting fortunes. Just before Preston and Catherine departed for New York over the weekend of December 23rd, gossip maven Sheilah Graham found the actor "popping with good spirits"[11] when she encountered him at Lucey's Restaurant in Los Angeles. Preston told Graham he was looking forward to filming *Cloudburst* in England and expected to begin filming *The Four Poster* with Evelyn Keyes once he returned stateside.[12] *The Four Poster* project ultimately fell through, but Preston would go on to star in a stage version of *The Four Poster* some sixteen years later, retitled as the smash Broadway musical, *I Do! I Do!*. Robert and Catherine flew to London during the first week in January 1951, just before the commencement of filming for *Cloudburst* on January 8.

The psychological drama *Cloudburst* was produced by Executive Films, Ltd. and filmed in January and early February 1951 at Bray Studios in England. Preston played the role of John Graham, a World War II veteran skilled in espionage who methodically avenges the death of his pregnant wife after she is mowed down by a mysterious speeding car. He was impressed by the English cast of the film, which included Elizabeth Sellars, Colin Tapley, Sheila Burrell, Harold Laing, and Mary Germaine, most of whom were stage-trained actors who actively worked in the London theater.[13] Preston was amazed by the versatility of the English actors who were able to transition from working on a movie set during the day to acting on London's West End stages in the evening. He recognized the proximity of the movie studios and theaters in London allowed actors a large degree of professional flexibility, and he was "green with envy."[14] Preston was nonplussed that the center of the film industry in California and the stages of Broadway were separated by thousands of miles, a geographic chasm that forced actors to choose between the stage and the screen rather than affording them the ability to participate in both genres simultaneously.

The movie stint in England helped Preston gain more confidence in himself as an actor,[15] and it was at this point in his career that he began to seriously contemplate making the leap from Hollywood to Broadway. On his way back home to California following the filming for *Cloudburst*, Preston made a stop in New York City. He was drawn to the vibrancy of Broadway and had the incredibly good fortune to run into actor/director José Ferrer. Ferrer, who was starring in the Broadway revival of *Twentieth Century* at the Fulton Theatre, desperately needed a replacement to allow him to travel to Hollywood for a film project. Ferrer not only had the main role of Oscar Jaffe in *Twentieth Century*, but also served as the play's producer and director. He opened *Twentieth Century* on Broadway on December 24, 1950, but by the spring of 1951, Ferrer had bigger fish to fry. He had received the Academy Award for Best Actor in March 1951 for his portrayal of Cyrano De Bergerac in the film of the same name and was anxious to return to Hollywood to begin filming the romantic comedy *Anything Can Happen* (1952). Ferrer's *Twentieth Century* co-star Gloria Swanson—who had previously played the Academy Award-nominated role of Norma Desmond in *Sunset Boulevard*—decided to exit the show along with Ferrer, fearing she would be unable to carry the show without him.[16] Swanson quickly returned to Hollywood and was offered the role of Ann Haven in the romantic comedy *3 For Bedroom C* (1952).

Robert Preston viewed his meetup with José Ferrer as fortuitous and was so anxious to land the role in *Twentieth Century* that he told Ferrer, "Here's a paper napkin . . . let's sign a contract right here and now!"[17] Preston was immediately stricken with Broadway fever and viewed the role in *Twentieth Century* as a springboard to a future Broadway career. He was grateful for having been given the chance to join the cast of *Twentieth Century* without an audition and recalled,

> I was going to do something, but I didn't know how. For the position I was in then, it wasn't easy, because you couldn't go begging, and no one was going to ask you to audition, so how the hell could I do it? It was a little like sneaking in the back door.[18]

Ferrer also quickly signed English actress Binnie Barnes to replace Gloria Swanson in the role of the temperamental film star, Lily Garland, allowing both stars to exit the production simultaneously.

Preston briefly returned home to Catherine in California, but the couple parted ways as he flew east to star in *Twentieth Century*. Preston longed to showcase his acting talent in diverse roles and was fed up with the stagnation he had experienced in Hollywood. He was determined to start his career anew on Broadway, but Catherine was not on board.[19] In reflecting upon this period in his life, Preston recalled he knew he "had to get away,"[20] and ventured east—alone—in March.

Catherine vigorously denied any hint of separation to gossip columnist Louella Parsons. Parsons perpetuated the denial in her May 2, 1951 newspaper column by assuring readers there was no truth to the rumors of discord in the Prestons' marriage, insisting that "Bob is just going East for a Broadway show."[21]

Once in New York, Preston received yet another unexpected role from actor Ralph Bellamy. Bellamy, who starred as detective Mike Barnett in the hit CBS television series *Man Against Crime,* was in desperate need of a temporary replacement for his character to allow him to take a much-needed summer vacation. Preston recalled Bellamy approached him and said, "Come on the show with me. I'll introduce you as my younger brother, Pat, and you can take over for six weeks while I take a break. I've done 82 shows without a week off and I'm going crazy."[22] Preston accepted the temporary role on *Man Against Crime* but realized that, depending on the future run of *Twentieth Century*, he might be required to juggle simultaneous appearances in the play and on a live television show.

On June 2, 1951, Preston made his way to 210 West 46th Street in Manhattan to watch José Ferrer's last performance in *Twentieth Century* at the Fulton Theatre. By observing Ferrer as the larger-than-life, bankrupt Broadway impresario, Oscar Jaffe, Preston was immediately struck by the cold, hard reality that he would be limited in the changes he could bring to the role:

> I realized that he was a powerhouse in the role, and that there were certain things he had established in the part that I couldn't change. I had to play almost an imitation of him, because the others in the cast were so dependent on every little thing he did. If I had changed things, it would have thrown the whole show off. My main obligation was to see to it that the audience was entertained.[23]

Preston and Binnie Barnes made their Broadway debuts in *Twentieth Century* on Monday, June 4, 1951. From his first night on stage, Preston put his own subtle spin on the role of Oscar Jaffe. A review of the play and its new cast in *The Brooklyn Daily Eagle* described *Twentieth Century* as "still a lively, entertaining show, though not to the same degree."[24] Although Preston received favorable reviews, one critic observed that "while Ferrer leaned backward in the role, Preston crouched—ready to pounce."[25] Although the actor's Broadway debut went better than expected, he was aware,

> Everyone expected me to be lousy in my first stage appearance on Broadway. People were saying, "Who does Preston think he is? Just another B-picture leading man trying to rejuvenate a

sagging career." Well, the critics came and reviewed the show, and I got good notices.[26]

By the following week, *Twentieth Century* was struggling
under the weight of its substantial operating costs and rumors
swirled about the play's imminent closure. The play limped
along for another week and was finally shuttered on June 30.
Because Preston began his live television performance as Pat
Barnett on *Man Against Crime* on Friday, June 29, the curtain
time for *Twentieth Century* on that evening was delayed from
8:30 p.m. to 9:00 p.m., with the actor's first appearance on stage
conveniently delayed until 9:10 p.m. to allow him to perform on
television as well as at the Fulton Theatre.[27] Despite the closure
of *Twentieth Century* after just two weeks on stage, Preston was
determined to remain in New York to forge a new career on
Broadway. He knew he could easily return to Hollywood and
earn a decent salary in the same old B-movies, but "money was
never that important"[28] to him. Preston instead opted to remain
in New York and reinvent himself as a Broadway star.

As *Twentieth Century* headed toward its final curtain call,
Preston continued to sub for Ralph Bellamy in the role of Mike
Barnett's younger brother, Pat, on *Man Against Crime*. Bellamy
and Preston appeared together in the episode which was televised on June 29 to establish the premise of Preston's recurring role over the next five episodes of the CBS program. In the
July 6 episode of *Man Against Crime* titled, "A Model Murder,"
Preston's character exposed a phony illustrator bent on murdering a beautiful model and making it appear like a suicide.
One TV critic pronounced the role of Pat Barnett was "played
very convincingly by Robert Preston" to the extent that "the
continuity of the show isn't lost and the viewer hasn't the sense

of the usual loss with a substitute."[29] The episode on July 13, titled "Secret Crime," centered around Pat Barnett's encounter with a secret society dedicated to committing the perfect crime. A case of mistaken identity became the thread that tied the whole mystery together. Commentary published in *The Atlanta Constitution* made the observation that Preston "appears to be equally 'at home' in the star spot."[30]

When Preston initially arrived in New York in March 1951, he found his way to 10 East 60th Street, the Copacabana Nightclub, to see famed songstress Peggy Lee's show. Preston and Lee had encountered each other a year before in Las Vegas when Preston caught Lee's performance in the Copa Room at the Sands Hotel. In her autobiography, *Miss Peggy Lee*, Lee describes the immediate and powerful sexual chemistry that overwhelmed her during her initial conversation with Preston,

> When I first saw that face, I knew it meant trouble, but I also knew there was no choice . . . He said, "Hello, I've been looking for you." And I swear I answered, "Where have you been?" I didn't and I don't say things like that to perfect strangers. But I did this time . . . I could see by his look that we both had a problem.[31]

At the time of her sexually-charged encounter with Preston in Las Vegas, Peggy Lee was married to guitarist Dave Barbour, with whom she was still very much in love. Lee was, however, quite impressed when Preston told her that he and his fellow World War II servicemen stationed in Europe regularly listened to her jazz and blues music and believed she was a Black chanteuse. He acknowledged the faux pas to Lee, confiding, "Can you imagine what a surprise it was to see this blonde Scandinavian walk out when they announced you?"[32]

Peggy Lee had soared to stardom by 1941 as a sultry jazz and blues singer with Benny Goodman's Orchestra. An accomplished singer, actress, and composer, Peggy had been raised by a cruel stepmother following the unexpected death of her biological mother when she was four years old. Life with a battle-axe stepmother who abused her and made her feel unloved and unwanted[33] left Peggy craving love and attention, and the neglect and abuse spawned a life-long fear of being alone.

Peggy Lee's silky, come-hither voice and palpable charisma garnered her several hit songs while singing for the Goodman Orchestra, including *Let's Fall in Love, We'll Meet Again, Why Don't You Do Right?* and *On the Sunny Side of the Street.* By 1952 she had already recorded three hit albums as a solo artist. While with the Goodman Orchestra in the 1940s, Lee established a friendship with Tommy Dorsey crooner, Frank Sinatra, that would endure a lifetime. Sinatra's friendly relationship with Lee was not entirely platonic;[34] he was very protective of Peggy, showered her with his largesse,[35] and spent countless hours in-person and on the phone listening to her problems.[36]

Lee met her first husband, Dave Barbour, during his stint as a guitarist with the Goodman Orchestra. At age twenty-three and two months pregnant, Lee married Dave Barbour on March 8, 1943; their daughter, Nicki Lee Barbour—Lee's only child—was born in November of the same year. The marriage began to unravel due, in large part, to Barbour's heavy drinking and alcohol-fueled binges.[37] Although Lee loved her husband, she found it increasingly difficult to live with him and felt alone in the marriage.

Deeply insecure and not one to ever be alone,[38] Lee quickly set her sights on Robert Preston as the new romantic focus in her life. In her autobiography, Lee recalled when she and Preston saw each other again after her Copacabana performance in March 1951, sparks flew when Preston asked to take her home,

> If it hadn't been snowing, we probably would have been riding in a hansom cab or something that lovers in New York do, but it was snowing, and we didn't want to miss the beauty of the snowflakes settling on our faces. We walked all the way home, not even aware of the cold. Certainly not *feeling* cold. He took me to the lobby and, wisely, said goodnight there. The emotion between us was so strong it held us in that special, wonderful spell that can't bear to be broken.[39]

Following their encounter at the Copacabana, Lee and Preston quickly began a whirlwind romance that was punctuated with numerous fits and starts—a pattern reminiscent of Preston's prior relationship with Dorothy Lamour. The relationship was on-again-off-again to such an extent that it was often difficult for their fans, the press, and the public at large, to maintain a pulse on the status of the star-crossed romance.

Now ensconced in a relationship with Preston, Lee moved forward with divorce action against her husband. She initially considered a fast-track divorce in Las Vegas, but ultimately filed for the dissolution of her marriage in Santa Monica, California on May 15, 1951.[40] Preston and Lee soon became regulars on the frenetic New York Café Society scene and their liaison made national headlines. Noted Broadway columnist Dorothy Kilgallen remarked that since filing for divorce, Peggy Lee had "found something new to sing about—Robert Preston," and on May 28th the songstress was spotted "crooning to him, ever so softly, at a corner table at Gogi's Larue."[41] Lee acknowledged her relationship with Preston was intense, one in which they shared "pure joy and tears and laughter."[42] She recalled,

> The two of us went to the races and baseball games. We went to the opening nights of *The King and I* and *South Pacific* and *My Fair Lady*. We dined at Danny's Hideaway almost every night and the others we went to the Drake and listened to Cy Walter. Night after night we would finish our evening with a few sets at the Embers and listen to Joey Bushkin or Erroll Garner or Red Norvo. We drove to the country and found little out-of-the-way places, and we fed the ducks on the river at Westport.[43]

By the end of May 1951, Robert Preston and Peggy Lee were identified as a "new duo," and Preston's separation from his wife was publicly acknowledged.[44] On July 15, a house photographer at Manhattan's Stork Club photographed Preston and Lee dancing cheek-to-cheek.[45] The caption that accompanied the published photo suggesting the pair was bound for the altar was supplied by Peggy Lee.[46] As her relationship with Preston continued, Lee came to believe Preston was her soulmate, and she pressed him to divorce his wife.

In the meantime, Catherine Craig kept busy in California. She was cast in a minor role in *Susan and God*, a stage play starring Joan Bennett with performances at the La Jolla Playhouse between July 17 and July 22, 1951. Owing to the constant drip of information from gossip columnists in every major newspaper, Catherine was all too aware of her husband's relationship with Peggy Lee. Despite the hype of the Preston-Lee romance, Catherine made the painful decision that marriage to Robert Preston was worth enduring the hurt and humiliation created by his new relationship. Despite the noise in the press, Catherine remained steadfastly confident in her relationship with her husband, and her instincts both guided and steadied her through Preston's liaison with Peggy Lee. The woman who willingly chose to sacrifice her career on the altar of her husband's success knew him all too well. Patience and perseverance emerged as Catherine's long-term strategy and she was able to take a small measure of comfort in knowing that no other woman could ever secure the same level of importance in her husband's life.

Preston was beguiled by Peggy Lee, a celebrity who was sultry, exotic, exciting, bursting with sexual energy, and driven to achieve success. A man without children of his own, Preston actively nurtured a father-daughter relationship with Lee's seven-year-old daughter, Nicki. According to Lee, Nicki quickly bonded with Preston, and he provided the child with the consistent attention she desperately craved from a parent. Lee accepted that Preston set aside one evening a week to provide Nicki with his undivided attention:

> The two of them had the most charming arrangement . . . every Tuesday was their night out, and I was not allowed to go. They went to places like the Plaza or the Tavern on the Green. They rode in hansom cabs and . . . came home laughing and

singing. He would carry her piggyback up and down the stairs.[47]

On the eve of his appearance in the July 20 episode of *Man Against Crime*, Preston announced his intention to marry Peggy Lee as soon as Ralph Bellamy returned from his European vacation.[48] Preston, who planned to marry Lee in Greenwich, Connecticut, had already presented her with a ring on May 26 for her thirty-first birthday. The ring was an "antique wedding band—a hair ring in which he placed a lock of his hair"[49] intertwined with several strands from her platinum blonde mane. On July 31, gossip maven Louella Parsons provided her readers with a read-out of the temperature of the Preston-Lee relationship by proclaiming, "Yes, they're better than hot."[50]

When Ralph Bellamy returned from Europe, Preston headed west to California on August 11 to discuss a divorce settlement with his wife. An article in the Hollywood newspaper, *Valley Times*, reported Preston planned to discuss a property settlement agreement with Catherine as he believed their marital separation to be final.[51]

Broadway columnist Dorothy Kilgallen reported in her column on August 16 that the formal announcement of the Prestons' divorce would pave the way for Robert Preston's marriage to Peggy Lee.[52] In a subsequent column on August 22, Kilgallen announced Peggy Lee continued to see-and-be-seen in New York City during Preston's trip to California, but that her escorts were mere music publishers who were "not calculated to make Bob jealous."[53]

Although Preston may have intended for his trip to California to focus on a divorce settlement, no such settlement was reached. Rather than dissolving their marriage, the Prestons initiated a reconciliation. Peggy Lee was devastated when Preston informed her that he had "offered to give up everything he had ever made," to secure a divorce, but his wife "told him that wasn't enough."[54] In his biography of Peggy Lee, author James Gavin indicates Preston told Lee that divorce was "impossible" since his wife "was Catholic and would never agree to it."[55] It is not known whether a rejected Peggy Lee manufactured the story of Catherine Craig's Catholic faith to save face or if Preston misled his paramour, but Catherine Craig was not a Roman Catholic. Her parents were lifelong congregants of the Trinity Episcopal Church in Bloomington, Indiana, a church in which funeral services for her father, Roy Feltus, were held in 1954.[56]

Preston arrived in Miami on Sunday, August 26 to begin rehearsals at the Roosevelt Playhouse for the stage play *Detective Story*[57] with his wife in tow.[58] Earlier in the year, Preston was tapped to play the role of Detective McLeod in the Miami production of *Detective Story,* a role Ralph Bellamy had made famous on Broadway some years earlier. Preston had eight days to rehearse *Detective Story* before its premiere at the Roosevelt Playhouse on Tuesday, September 4. Opening in December 1949, the Roosevelt Playhouse was a small Miami theater that featured screenings of Hollywood movies and hosted live stage plays. Performances of *Detective Story,* a stage play about the inner workings of a New York City police squad room, were presented Tuesday through Sunday at 8:40 p.m., with extra matinee performances featured at 3:00 p.m. on Saturdays and Sundays. The weekend prior to opening night, Preston participated as a guest on the popular Miami teenage broadcast, *The Youth Roundup Speaks,* and provided autographs to fans before the start of the broadcast. A large group assembled to hear Preston being interviewed in person and many disappointed fans were turned away due to lack of space.[59] Sighs and swoons from teenage fans were audible as Preston was interviewed by Janice Pape of St. Mary's School.[60] When asked about his personal life, Preston told fans he was "married to the beautiful actress, Catherine Craig"[61] without revealing any hint of the recent marital separation. On September 11 newspapers confirmed the Robert Preston-Catherine Craig reconciliation.[62] Not surprisingly, Preston received rave reviews for his performance in the scheduled two-week run of *Detective Story*,[63] which concluded on Sunday, September 16.

The Prestons' reconciliation was short-lived. It was not long after Preston returned to New York with Catherine that he resumed his relationship with Peggy Lee. In her autobiography, Lee recounted going into shock over the separation from Preston.[64] She purposely began dating to alleviate her inconsolable heartache, and on one such outing she ran into Preston "at Danny's Hideaway, our place, and he was with [his wife]." Lee observed Preston "couldn't bear to see me with another man" and his wife "saw his grief and left for California that night."[65] Preston then began actively "searching for a fall show" to keep him on the East Coast near Peggy Lee.[66] In mid-October, columnist Al Salerno reported that despite their "denial of romance, Robert Preston and Peggy Lee see a lot of each other and are so lovey-dovey."[67]

Preston next appeared in a *Lux Video Theatre* television production of *Café Ami*, a drama centering on an American serviceman during the Allied occupation of Europe and a mysterious German girl. Maria Riva, Rod Steiger, Walter Matthau, and Susan Wayne rounded out the cast of the show. Toward the end of October, both Dorothy Kilgallen and Hedda Hopper reported that Robert Preston and Peggy Lee had resumed their relationship.[68] By the first week of November, friends of Preston and Lee informed Louella Parsons that "Peggy Lee's next [husband] will be Robert Preston," and confirmed that Preston's reconciliation with his wife "didn't take."[69]

On November 24, Preston appeared as the guest performer on the TV series *Your Show of Shows*, hosted by comedians Sid Caesar and Imogene Coca, and by December 5, Preston had reconciled, yet again, with his wife.[70] The reconciliation occurred just prior to the December 6 airing of the *Schlitz Playhouse* television production of *The Nymph and the Lamp* in which Preston appeared alongside actress Margaret Sullavan. However, as 1951 came to a close, Preston was once again back in the arms of Peggy Lee. It was noted that Preston, who began sporting a rather unattractive beard, shaved off the facial hair at the urging of his paramour.[71] As the new year of 1952 dawned, Peggy Lee remained madly in love with Robert Preston. She sought the security of marriage, but instead found herself in a relationship that resembled an on-again-off-again emotional roller-coaster punctuated with magnificent highs and devastating lows. To say that Lee was distressed by Preston's romantic lability would be an understatement.

A curious incident occurred late in January 1952 when Preston became the victim of an organized, mob-like attack by a group of men on a mission. On Sunday, January 27, Preston was enjoying a meal with a friend at a Broadway restaurant when he was approached by a gang of five to six men who suddenly began taunting him with remarks like, "You think you're better than I am."[72] Following the ominous encounter, Preston paid his check, exited the restaurant, and was accosted by the same group of goons as he attempted to enter his friend's car. Before Preston could reach the vehicle, one of the men hit him in the head from behind. In recounting the attack, Preston indicated the same man "dodged behind a telephone pole and rolled an ash can at [him]."[73] It was at that point that the man Preston later identified as lightweight fighter, Joseph Scarlato, attacked him from the other side. Within seconds, Preston found himself on the ground being violently kicked in the head and face by Scarlato.[74] The manner in which Preston was roughed up smacked of retaliatory violence unleashed to settle a score, respond to an insult, or send a message. The underlying motive for the assault was unspoken and unexplained since Preston had no previous dealings with his attackers.

Preston sustained a bruised face, lost three teeth, and required twenty stitches in his lower lip as a result of the unprovoked attack. After filing a complaint against twenty-five-year-old Scarlato, who was subsequently arrested, Preston appeared in New York Felony Court on January 31 to describe the attack in which Scarlato was identified as one of Preston's attackers, but "not the ringleader."[75] Magistrate Phillip R. Thurston held Scarlato over on $1,000.00 bail pending trial in a special session court on a simple assault charge.[76] Preston informed the court he had not sustained any permanent injuries "except for the three missing teeth which would be replaced"[77] in time for an upcoming television appearance.

Preston regularly appeared on live television shows and specials throughout 1952. He was featured in an episode of *Footlights and Kleiglights* along with Ben Grauer, appeared in the *Lux Video Theatre* episodes of *Kelly* on February 2 and *Happily, But Not Forever* on September 22, as well as in the *Pulitzer Prize Playhouse*'s presentations of *The Jungle* on April 9 and *Curtain Call* on June 20.

In February, it was formally announced that a limited, two-week revival of *The Male Animal* would be featured at New York's City Center theater from April 30 to May 11. The play's producers arranged for Elliott Nugent to reprise this role as Tommy Turner that he previously performed on Broadway.[78] Actress Martha Scott was hired for the role of Tommy Turner's wife, Ellen, and Robert Preston rounded out the main cast in the role of former university football hero Joe Ferguson. The comedy, directed by Michael Gordon, focuses on the travails of English professor Tommy Turner during the weekend of Midwestern University's big football game. The professor runs into trouble when he reads controversial material to his students as an example of noteworthy writing. Facing possible dismissal by the university's board of trustees, Turner is further vexed by the return to campus of former football hero Joe Ferguson for the big game. Ferguson, who is recently divorced, attempts to woo back his former college girlfriend, Ellen, who is now married to Turner.

There is a strong possibility that Preston made a short trip to Los Angeles in early March, before the debut of *The Male Animal*, perhaps in an unsuccessful bid to convince Catherine to agree to a divorce. On April 30, *The Male Animal* opened at the New York City Center theater to good reviews, and Preston was hailed as "just about perfect" in his portrayal of Joe Ferguson.[79]

Preston identified Michael Gordon as one of the directors from whom he learned the most. He was impressed with Gordon's technique, noting the director "got boff laughs by cutting the small ones. We were playing that big barn, the City Center, and you've really got to be on your toes with the comedy timing there, because the laugh rolls up to the third balcony and then rolls back down at you."[80] Gordon also taught Preston a lesson about the importance of attitude in acting, a lesson he continued to draw upon through the remainder of his acting career,

> Mike was the original camp counselor of the Group Theater, and though he puts it down by saying things like "pull your adjustments closer together" instead of telling you to pick up your pace, there is a great deal of the true Method in the way he works. I remember once I was supposed to be on the witness stand in one scene, and I had to say something like, "Well, we went across the street and had some chop suey." At the end of the day, Mike asked me, "Pres, how do you feel about chop suey?" I said, "I don't know. I don't think I've ever had any." And he said, "You've got to have some sort of attitude toward it. You can't just say 'chop suey,' so will you please come up with something? I don't care if you love it or hate it, but please have some sort of attitude toward it, will you?" And it's stayed with me to this day. Of course, it's true; you cannot say anything without having some sort of an attitude toward it. [81]

Just as Preston and Peggy Lee had "rekindled their flame at the Embers"[82] nightclub in New York City, Lee departed for a brief gig at Ciro's nightclub in west Hollywood. Preston was immersed in gearing up to perform in his second Broadway play while Lee was taking steps to advance her career.

In April 1952, Warner Brothers announced it would produce the remake of the 1928 film *The Jazz Singer*. The studio originally planned to feature Danny Thomas and Doris Day in the movie's primary roles, but Day opted out of the film.[83] At the urging of studio head Jack Warner, director Michael Curtiz headed to Ciro's nightclub to evaluate whether Peggy Lee was suitable for a role in *The Jazz Singer*. Curtiz caught Lee's sold-out performance at Ciro's and was impressed by her "laser-beam focus" and "low burning intensity."[84] As Curtiz watched Lee perform, he found himself under the spell of both her "quiet but hypnotic sex appeal" and her face which became "radiantly beautiful as she sang."[85] With no time to lose, Curtiz approached Lee backstage to request that she audition for the role of Judy Lane in *The Jazz Singer*. Lee was given a two-reel screen test in which she answered questions about herself, sang a few songs, and did a cold reading of a dramatic scene.[86] Warner Brothers immediately signed Lee for *The Jazz Singer* after observing an unmistakable spark of talent in the songstress.[87]

Peggy Lee was a peerless jazz and blues singer, recording artist, and songwriter who was thrilled about the possibility of making her mark in Hollywood as an actress. The happiness of the sultry, sensual entertainer was at its zenith when she was able to professionally capture the spotlight on center stage, wherever that stage may be. It was no contest: Lee inevitably gave priority to her career over her personal life, despite the fact she was a needy woman who required the constant presence of a man in her life. Lee's professional aspirations came into conflict with Preston's—it was unimaginable that Peggy Lee could nourish Preston's career when she was all too focused on her own.

As besotted as Preston was with the exotic Lee, he also maintained a strong, emotional connection with his wife. Catherine Craig remained very much in love with her husband; she knew what made him tick and understood that what he needed to flourish was *her*. Catherine had no control over her husband's relationship with Peggy Lee other than to refuse to cooperate with any proposed divorce action. She wisely recognized the restoration of her marriage boiled down to a waiting game— and there was never any doubt that Catherine planned to out-wait Peggy Lee.

By May, *The Male Animal* became such a hit during its two-week run at the New York City Center theater that producer John Golden made the decision to move the play to the Music Box Theatre on Broadway, and "offered everyone new contracts commensurate with their screen earnings."[88] Although Preston hoped to continue with *The Male Animal*, he had made a previous commitment to return to Hollywood for a film.[89] At this important juncture in his career, the actor reverted to habit and instinctively turned to his wife for advice and guidance. When Preston reached out to Catherine in California, she volunteered to read the scripts of his upcoming films and report back to him.[90] After reading the scripts, assessing their quality, and making a determination whether they would boost Preston's career, Catherine called her husband and proffered the following advice:

> You stay in *The Male Animal*, because these [film] scenarios are just a lot more of what you've been doing too long. And there aren't parts like Joe Ferguson growing on trees. I'll pack our belongings and join you [in New York] in a week.[91]

The studio released Preston from his film obligations, and he continued with his stage role in *The Male Animal*. The play was featured at the Music Box Theatre from May 15, 1952 to

January 31, 1953, although Preston withdrew from the play in mid-December 1952 to pursue other opportunities.[92] Catherine arrived in New York as promised by June 10, 1952; Dorothy Kilgallen reported in her newspaper column that the Prestons had "kissed and made up—again."[93] The reconciliation had not yet completely solidified since, by mid-July, Ed Sullivan reported Preston was long-distancing with Peggy Lee while she was in Hollywood preparing to film *The Jazz Singer*.[94]

Production of *The Jazz Singer* began in Hollywood on August 1. Around the same time, Preston and Catherine moved into an apartment in the cozy, affluent enclave of Sutton Place on the East River in New York.[95] The couple maintained their home in California[96] which was turned over to Preston's parents for their use. By August 12, the Prestons' marital rapprochement had been reforged, and columnist Dorothy Kilgallen reported the "reconciliation is solid" and "the Peggy Lee thing is all over."[97] Kilgallen credited Preston's success in *The Male Animal* as the catalyst that "helped to patch up his marital rift."[98] Peggy Lee was crushed by Preston's decision to reconcile with his wife. Unable to accept that "another man walked out on her," she told her friends that she had simply "sent him home to his wife."[99]

A month prior to Preston's departure from the cast of *The Male Animal*, his most recent film, *The Bride Comes to Yellow Sky* (1952), was released on November 14. The western was part of a composite double feature of two short films entitled *Face to Face* (1952), which also included *The Secret Sharer* (1952) starring James Mason. The plot of *The Bride Comes to Yellow Sky* was based on a short story of the same name by author Stephen Crane which follows the impending showdown between the local Marshall and Scratchy Wilson, the town's aging, drunken gunslinger. The film, in which Preston played the lead role of Marshall Jack Potter, received positive reviews in *The New York Times.*[100] In a twist of cosmic serendipity, *The New York Times*' review of *The Jazz Singer* (1952), starring Preston's former flame Peggy Lee, was also featured on the same page as the review for *Face to Face.*

Preston enjoyed a brief stint on television as the co-host of *Anywhere, U.S.A.*, a medical drama miniseries launched in December 1952. The purpose of the series, hosted by the Health Information Foundation, was to increase the American public's awareness of advances in medical science and health issues and stressed the importance of regular physical exams. Preston and his co-host, Eddie Dowling, narrated medical dramatizations which highlighted new therapies for injuries during the half-hour show which aired weekly on Sunday evenings through January 1953. Preston then had the opportunity to serve as the guest host of an episode of *Your Show of Shows*, the popular, live 90-minute variety show featuring comedians Sid Caesar and Imogene Coca, in January 1953.

During the first week of January, Preston began rehearsals in New York for an hour-long live episode of *Robert Montgomery Presents* that would be featured on CBS television on January 19, 1953. In the season four episode titled "Maggie Pack Your Bags," Preston played the role of retired ex-army intelligence officer Jeff Frazer who resides in Mexico with his second wife Maggie, played by Margaret Hayes. The plot of the episode centered around an unexpected visit to the Fraziers by Jeff's son from his first marriage, now serving in the military, and an army general who both attempt to coax Jeff back into military service and disrupt his blissful life with Maggie.

New York movie critic Dorothy Masters published an in-depth interview with Robert Preston in the *Daily News* on March

1 in which he mused about his film career and indicated he had no intention of "burying his initiative, signing a long contract and settling for studio handouts"[101] in Hollywood. Masters was so impressed by Preston's personality, talent, and intellectual acumen that she concluded, "The movies haven't done him justice."[102]

Preston was Broadway bound once again in the spring of 1953. He had been selected to star as the high-pressure public relations man, Peter Hogarth, in Richard Condon's *Men of Distinction*. The comedy was written with lightning speed by Condon; it was a satiric roman à clef based on the scandalous 1952 Jelke trial that generated a rash of headlines in New York newspapers.

The Jelke trial exposed the travails of a scion of a wealthy family, Minot "Mickey" Jelke, who allegedly used income from prostitutes to supplement his paltry trust fund income. Mickey Jelke was raised in the affluent Chicago suburb of Lake Forest, Illinois, the grandson of oleomargarine titan John Faris Jelke, and was already ensconced as a member of the social register at the tender age of twenty-three. Mickey subsisted on a meager trust fund stipend of two hundred dollars a month while he awaited the $5,000,000 family inheritance he would receive on his twenty-fifth birthday. To generate extra cash while awaiting his payday, Mickey and a press-agent friend allegedly pimped out would-be models and actresses to entertain high-profile clients for a fee. Suspecting Jelke was the mastermind of a call-girl operation, the district attorney obtained a court order to wiretap his telephone. The DA gleaned enough incriminating evidence from the wiretap to raid Mickey's New York apartment and secure his arrest, with every salacious detail of the sensational Jelke trial chronicled in the headlines of the New York newspapers. Mickey Jelke was ultimately convicted for inducing, enticing, and procuring women for prostitution and served twenty-one months of a two to three-year sentence.[103]

Originally, the two producers of Men of Distinction, Chandler Cowles and Martin Gabel, planned to have acting roles in the comedy, but Gabel decided such a dual role would be too much for him.[104] The ink on the script barely had time to dry before the producers had assembled a cast, and rehearsals began the week of March 9. Prior to opening at the 48th Street Theatre on April 30, the play was showcased for four nights in New Haven, Connecticut and two weeks in Philadelphia, Pennsylvania.[105]

New York theater critics provided favorable reviews for Preston's performance as Peter Hogarth, noting that he "ably conveys the strait-laced hypocrisy and conniving geniality of the public relations man."[106] However, the harsh reviews of the play itself by New York theater critics led to the closing of Men of Distinction after just four performances. John Chapman from the Daily News described Men of Distinction as "a desperate, tasteless, and witless comedy" with a plot that is "plain punk as it flounders through a seedy intrigue,"[107] and other critics found Condon's play about the seamy side of New York's café society to be "too unpalatable"[108]for a Broadway audience.

Following his performance in the ill-fated Men of Distinction, Preston busied himself for the remainder of 1953 by acting in live television productions for Lux Video Theatre, Plymouth Playhouse, and The United States Steel Hour. To provide programming options for viewers in the early days of television, the networks added several series featuring live plays and dramas of adapted works to their weekly line-up of broadcasts. These live, dramatic performances were noted for their high level of production and presented quality entertainment within the constraints of a live broadcast. Extensive training and experience were required of actors who would be expected to rehearse for two weeks or less and then perform on live television. Given the demands of live television, the television networks needed to hire seasoned actors who could learn the roles and provide a flawless performance with only a modicum of rehearsal.[109] Veteran actress Angela Lansbury, who similarly appeared in these television productions, described the lucrative work on live network television as "quite a workout and exhausting."[110] Lansbury mused, "An awful lot of actors took to the bottle because you came out of those shows and you were a wreck just trying to remember your lines, get onto your mark, and get out of the way of the cameras. It was a rat race—it was exciting, but it really knocked the stuffing out of you."[111]

Preston was delighted to perform on live television since the genre was similar to a live theater production—a venue in which he flourished—and provided him with an opportunity to work with a diverse retinue of accomplished actors. In May 1953, Preston was featured in a *Lux Video Theatre* production on CBS of *The Betrayer* alongside Richard Carlyle, Grace Kelly, Bruce Gordon, Louis Lytton, and Doris Rich. He next appeared in the comedy *Baby and Me* on ABC's *Plymouth Playhouse* in mid-June. Preston and fellow cast members Janis Paige and Stanley Praeger portrayed family members who experienced unexpected change when the daughter of the house won a beautiful child contest.

By 1953, the Prestons' marriage was solidly back on track. Catherine, playfully nicknamed "Catita" by her husband, was by now firmly transplanted in New York City. She busied herself by doing all the housekeeping and decorating the couple's Sutton Place apartment with her chic hand-made curtains and quilts. Preston made time to appear with his wife in a limited theatrical performance of *Bell, Book, and Candle* at the Myrtle Beach

Carolina Circle Theater located in the ballroom of the Ocean Forest Hotel in Myrtle Beach, South Carolina. *Bell, Book, and Candle* opened on June 20 for a one-week run—the first play to be featured in the theater's eleven-week theatrical series for 1953.[112]

Preston returned to live television in August on CBS's *Medallion Theatre*. The episode, *The Quiet Village*, written by Rod Serling of *The Twilight Zone* fame, featured Rod Steiger as a ruthless director out for the scalp of a down-on-his-luck actor played by Preston. A few weeks later in early September, Preston teamed up with Madeleine Sherwood for *The Boys on the Corner*, a teleplay featured on CBS's *Danger* series. Preston's final live television performance of 1953 was in an episode of *The United States Steel Hour* entitled *Hope for a Harvest* which aired on November 10. The episode centered on the lives of an impoverished farm family that were reinvigorated when a member of the family returned home from Europe after a lengthy absence. Fay Emerson, Sophie Treadwell, and Dino DiLuca were also featured in supporting roles in the television drama.

As 1953 drew to a close, Preston received an offer to perform on Broadway with Celeste Holm in Fay and Michael Kanin's new romantic comedy, *His and Hers,* to be directed by Michael Gordon. The play told the story of a divorced couple who collaborated to write a play with an eye toward remarriage should the play prove a success. The play initially opened off-Broadway for a two-week engagement at the Cass Theatre in Detroit and was met with dismissive reviews by local theater critics. While performing in Detroit, Preston sat for an interview with John Gardiner of Ontario's *Windsor Star* newspaper. Preston made an indelible impression on the seasoned reporter who effusively praised him for being an "excellent actor," and extolled his admirable qualities of "magnetism, forthrightness, and sincerity of purpose based on a firm structure of intellectualism."[113]

Cognizant of the deficiencies in the play's plot and dialogue which earned the lukewarm reviews of theater critics, Preston acknowledged to Gardiner,

> We knew we had a problem, part of which was to convince the playwrights that *His and Hers* needed revision—lightening up. This has been done. Our new first act is a beauty and we have no apprehension whatever as regards our Broadway opening. Our analysis of the shortcomings of the play was confirmed by audience reaction. We have ironed out all the snags and are thankful we were given the opportunity to do so.[114]

Gardiner cited Preston as professing a fondness for the stage over film, preferring the instant gratification afforded by the theater: "There is a danger . . . in becoming lazy in filmdom. It's a nice life, you meet nice people—but the real reward in stage work is when you can feel and hear an audience's appreciation."[115]

The production of *His and Hers* moved to the 48th Street Theatre in New York City in early January 1954, and made its Broadway debut on January 7 to lackluster reviews. *The New York Times* theater critic Brooks Atkinson found the play mediocre at best and compared the plot to "a romantic story . . . in a slick magazine" that is "the epitome of mediocrity," and he went on to chastise director Michael Gordon for directing *His and Hers* "with all the dexterity of a B movie."[116] Celeste Holm was celebrated as looking "dazzling and successful"[117] in her wardrobe designed by Oleg Cassini, with Preston lauded as act-ing "with a good deal of lightness and spontaneity" as a "first-rate comedy player in or out of *The Male Animal.*"[118] Despite the stellar performances by Preston and Holm, the deficient script and uninspired stage direction doomed *His and Hers* to limp along through seventy-six performances before ultimately go-ing dark on March 13, 1954.

Even though the previous play directed by Michael Gordon failed miserably, Preston signed on to appear in the cast of yet another Gordon production, this time in a Julian Funt play en-titled *The Magic and the Loss.* The script of *The Magic and The Loss* highlighted a family drama involving a 1950s divorced, Manhattan career woman striving to advance herself on the job while juggling a new romance, an ex-husband, and an unhappy adolescent son. Uta Hagen, Charles Taylor, Danny Dennis, Edith Meiser, and Lee Bowman rounded out the production's ensem-ble. The play, scheduled to open on Broadway at the 49th Street Theater on April 9, 1954, was previewed on the road at the Nixon Theatre in Pittsburgh, Pennsylvania beginning on March 29. The production then moved on to the Parsons Theater in Hartford, Connecticut on April 5 before heading to Broadway.

The play received less than favorable reviews on its Broadway debut. *Time* magazine characterized *The Magic and The Loss* as an "unharmonized play" and identified "too many problems" with the script "for it to focus quite tight or reverberate on the stage.[119] Brooks Atkinson of *The New York Times* praised Preston's performance, noting the actor was "at the top of his form" but panned the production as a "private problem play" which "never moves outside a circumscribed area of private concern." Atkinson went further by pointing out the play "is like a case history on child psychology," and it was "difficult to feel much more than a detached respect and occasional sympathy for the characters on the stage."[120] The troubled play, unable to attract an audience, closed on May 1 after a mere twenty-seven performances.

On the heels of the closure of *The Magic and The Loss*, Preston made three television appearances in April and May, the first of which was in an episode of the *Campbell Summer Soundstage* on NBC entitled "Al Toolum and His Buddy Leo." The teleplay, which aired on April 30, included Leo Durocher and Van Dyke Parks in the cast. Preston next appeared in the May 11 episode of ABC's *The United States Steel Hour.* The drama, *The End of Paul Dane*, also featured fellow actors Warren Stevens and Teresa Wright. He then joined Jake LaMotta and former first-daughter Margaret Truman a few days later to dish out some comic relief in a live episode of NBC's *The Martha Raye Show* on May 15.

While he waited for another Broadway show, Preston headed to Philadelphia to star in the play *Boy Meets Girl* at the Playhouse in the Park from July 12–18. On hand in Philadelphia to observe Preston's rehearsal and performance was New York theatrical producer Kermit Bloomgarden. Preston's versatility impressed the producer. The encounter proved to be fortuitous for both men as evidenced a few years later when Bloomgarden signed on to produce *The Music Man* on Broadway. During the sold-out performance on July 14, almost 1100 theatergoers were dismissed ten minutes before the final curtain due to a violent storm with torrential rain that battered the tented playhouse. It was reported by *The Philadelphia Inquirer* that "the tent—a new one erected only last Saturday night—was torn in several places" as a result of the storm.[121] Preston remained in Philadelphia to appear in the Playhouse in the Park production of *Front Page* during the week of July 19.

In late summer, Preston signed on to appear in *The Tender Trap*, another play directed by Michael Gordon. Preston's castmates included Ronny Graham, Parker McCormick, Julia Meade, Kim Hunter, Janet Riley, Jack Manning, and Joey Faye. The central plot of the comedy featured Charlie Reader (Graham), a Manhattan bachelor with the remarkable ability to juggle a parade of girlfriends without having to say "yes" to marriage. After Charlie's married childhood friend, Joe McCall (Preston) pays a visit, the bachelor runs into trouble when he simultaneously gets engaged to two women. Written by Max Shulman and Robert Paul Smith, *The Tender Trap* opened on October 13 at the Longacre Theatre to mixed reviews. Drama critic Brooks Atkinson of *The New York Times* noted that although the audience at the Longacre "laughed consistently,"[122] the playwrights had crafted the play "with more desperation than humor,"[123] and their miscalculation resulted in an inferior quality play. Despite his overall disappointment with the play, Atkinson hailed Preston as an excellent actor and a "blustering, persuasive comedian" who is "always good company in the theater, and a tower of strength in any faltering play."[124] The *Time* magazine review of *The Tender Trap* similarly found the play to be "unsatisfying," noting the script "lacks the right touch and tone."[125] Despite the lukewarm reviews, *The Tender Trap* managed to limp along through 102 performances before eventually closing on January 8, 1955.

Preston was back on television on ABC's *The United States Steel Hour* on January 18, appearing in the episode, "The Bogey Man," with his former *His and Hers* co-star Celeste Holm. The actor also appeared in several other teleplays during February and March. The first of these appearances was in a February 24 *Climax!* episode titled "The Box of Chocolates," based on an adaptation of Anthony Berkley's mystery, *The Avenging Chance*. Preston co-starred with Pat O'Brien and old friend Victor Jory in the program about an unpopular columnist who becomes involved in a murder after receiving a box of chocolates with an accompanying note requesting that he sample the candy. Twelve days later Preston was featured on *The Elgin Hour's* production of *Crime in the Streets*. On March 17, the actor appeared in the role of Phil Baxter in the *Lux Video Theatre* production of *It Grows on Trees* along with a large supporting cast. The telecast, based on a 1952 film of the same name, was a fantasy-comedy about a down-and-out couple who faced ethical dilemmas after discovering two lucky trees in their backyard sprouted money.

Preston once again found himself on Hollywood's radar. Harry Cohn, president and production director at Columbia Studios, believed Preston was perfect for the role of churlish cavalry officer Colonel Frank Marston in the upcoming film *The Last Frontier*. Columbia sent Preston the script for the western, but he was uninterested in the role since, "It was just the sort of thing [he] had gone to Broadway to get away from."[126] The role of Colonel Marston was not quite a villain, but Preston was aware that Victor Mature had been cast as the hero of the film. Undaunted by Preston's rejections, the studio continued to try to change his mind about accepting the role. Exasperated by Columbia's refusal to take "no" for an answer, Preston finally provided the studio with an outrageous salary demand he knew would be prohibitive and thus put an end to their unending entreaties. Surprisingly, the role of Colonel Marston remained uncast up until the day before the film crew was set to leave for location in Mexico. At the last minute, Preston received a call from his agent informing him that his salary request for *The Last Frontier* had been accepted by Columbia Studios. Harry Cohn had begrudgingly capitulated to Preston's salary demands and instructed the film's producer to "pay the blankety-blank what he wants."[127]

Filming for *The Last Frontier* took place in central Mexico, forty miles southwest of Mexico City near the country's second-highest peak and stratovolcano, Popocatépetl. The terrain was selected to replicate Wyoming in the 1860s during the conflict between the United States Army and the Sioux tribe. Preston played the role of embittered army officer, Colonel Marston, who is determined to teach the Sioux and their leader Chief Red Cloud a lesson. Anne Bancroft was cast in the role of Corinna Marston, the long-suffering wife of the Colonel; her raven hair was dyed blonde to emphasize her role as a fair-haired, civilized woman. Victor Mature played the role of Jed Cooper, a macho, uncouth Wyoming fur trapper who is attracted to the Colonel's wife. The film, directed by Anthony Mann, also featured Guy Madison, James Whitmore, Russell Collins, and Peter Whitney. At one point in the script, Preston's character is slated to accidentally fall into a bear trap and is forced to plead with Victor Mature's character to rescue him. Following his scripted tumble into the bear pit, Preston recalled a makeup mishap that resulted in him being dirtied up quite a bit more than he expected:

> There was a scene in the film where I fall in a bear pit and plead with Vic Mature to help me out. Anthony Mann was directing this scene and he stopped the cameras after I made my tumble into the pit, head-first. Peering down at me, Tony yelled at the make-up man, "His face isn't smeared up enough for the scene. Put some dirt on it." One of the Mexicans who had helped dig

the pit was curiously looking on. He didn't understand English too well and before any of us knew
what was happening, he scooped up a shovel full
of dirt and threw it right in my kisser. My first
reaction was to crawl out of the pit, without Vic's
help and murder the guy. But I must say he did a
swell makeup job with that shovel.[128]

Preston delivered a standout performance as the complex,
single-minded army officer with a brutish personality. The
film, however, received a thumbs down from film critic Bosley
Crowther of *The New York Times*. Crowther panned the film and
opined that moviegoers who paid to see the film did not receive
a "decent deal" since "the story is so disordered and the color
photography is so deliberately dim that the whole thing is thoroughly obscurist."[129]Although Preston acquiesced to Columbia
Studios and appeared in *The Last Frontier*, he did not make an
attempt to see the movie once it was released by the studio.[130]

Once filming for *The Last Frontier* was completed, Preston
once again headed back to television. In April, he appeared
with Myrna Loy in *General Electric Theater's* telecast of *It Gives
Me Great Pleasure* hosted by Ronald Reagan, and was then featured in *Kraft Theatre's* teleplay *Drop on the Devil* airing on NBC
in June.

Preston was thoroughly enamored with the Broadway stage
and desired to perform in all genres of theater work. Aware that
some of the most popular Broadway shows of the day were musicals, he decided to pursue vocal training. After appearing in
The Tender Trap, but before signing on to star in *The Hidden River*
in 1956, Preston contacted Broadway's most successful vocal
coach, Herbert Greene, and began studying voice. These lessons

occurred sporadically whenever both Greene and Preston "had a little spare time,"[131] but the actor "didn't stay with it too long."[132]

In August, Preston was cast in the role of cuckolded husband, Gil, in the Broadway production of *Janus*. The storyline of the comedy, slated to open on Broadway in late fall, centered around a married woman who engages in a secret affair by spending each summer with her paramour. Two other actors had already been signed to appear in *Janus* in late May: Claude Dauphin would play the lover, Denny, and Margaret Sullavan would play the role of Jessica, the housewife living a double life.[133] Sullavan was a brilliant, tough-as-nails star of stage and screen who had a reputation for being temperamental, volatile, and intimidating. The actress once publicly doused her ex-husband, Henry Fonda, with ice water after he complained to a fellow actor about Sullavan's refusal to contribute to a collection for Fourth of July fireworks.[134] On another occasion, the high-strung actress impulsively broke a mirror over the head of her manager before a matinee performance of *The Voice of the Turtle* in the early 1940s, then sent her maid to find out if he was still planning to have dinner with her later that evening.[135]

While preparations for *Janus* were underway, Preston, never one to pass up an acting opportunity, was featured on NBC in the September 12 episode of *Robert Montgomery Presents* titled "Woman in the Window." The episode was based on the J. H. Wallis novel, *Once Off Guard*, about a college professor who is beguiled by a painting of a beautiful woman. When Preston's character and the mystery woman finally meet, she invites him to her apartment for a drink and murder.

Rehearsals for *Janus* began in early October 1956. The Playhouse in Wilmington, Delaware hosted the initial four-day preview of the play beginning on October 19. A review of the Wilmington production of *Janus* found the play to possess "a cast that is letter perfect for the script,"[136] and Preston was identified as "a master of the comic situation as the shipping tycoon whose interrupted trip lands him squarely in the center of an unexpected romance."[137] The next stop on the road to Broadway was the Forrest Theatre in Philadelphia. A review of the production by *The Philadelphia Inquirer* found Margaret Sullavan to be "charming, breathless, and droll in her performance" and identified the male cast members as standout performers. Preston, playing the deceived husband, was lauded for "keeping ahead of the plot's extravagances with his combination of explosive outrage and introspective humor."[138]

Janus finally opened on Broadway at the Plymouth Theatre on November 24 to mixed reviews. One critic compared the plot of *Janus* to chiffon pie: "fluffy but not very filling. Pretty on the outside, but tasteless when you dig in."[139] Sullavan, Dauphin, and Preston were lauded in *The New York Times* for giving "hilariously professional performances" in a "wild and enjoyable" play, and Preston was additionally praised for acting with "bluster and comic earnestness" in a role that was "ideal for him."[140] Although *Janus* was favorably received by audiences, Sullavan began to exhibit a troubling labile mood that quickly became a cause for concern amongst the cast and crew. They were "shocked to witness lightning-quick changes in [Sullavan's] demeanor once she stepped off the stage," and "many were amazed that she held up during the performance as, off-stage, she looked as if she was suffering greatly from mental anguish."[141] Sullavan's unhappiness was palpable and it didn't help that Preston's role in *Janus* eclipsed her own. Actor and director Harold J. Kennedy noted the lack of *esprit de corps* between Sullavan and Preston and observed,

> Maggie was the undisputed box office draw and I don't think Bob cared for that and Bob had the unquestionably show-stealing part and I know Maggie didn't care for that. At the end of one of their little 'discussions,' Bob said: "Let's leave it this way, Maggie. You keep bringing them in and I'll keep on entertaining them.[142]

In his book, *The Season: A Candid Look at Broadway*, author William Goldman recounts Preston's working relationship with the mercurial Margaret Sullavan. Although Preston graciously did not identify Sullavan by name, the identity of the mystery actress is unmistakable:

> A long time ago I was supporting a lady, I won't tell you who, it doesn't matter. We were rehearsing a play, and it went happily until opening night, when a scene we had together turned out to be funnier than she thought, and more than that, the laughs seemed to be coming on my lines . . . I was surprised when I found out the next day that the scene was being severely cut. Do I have to tell you I wasn't happy? And neither was the producer, who naturally wanted the scene to stay but didn't want his star quitting either. I went to see her, and we talked about the scene. I tried to tell her that although people were laughing on *my* lines, they were really laughing at *our* situation: it

was both of us that they were enjoying. "I don't care," she said. "I don't care what you say. I hate those lines—they're *your* goddamned laughs."[143]

Sullavan, increasingly unhappy that Preston received the lion's share of audience laughter during nightly performances, effectively cut him dead.[144] If Sullavan experienced angst over his performance in *Janus*, Preston believed "that became her problem, not mine. If she was unhappy, I'm sorry. Onstage or on the set, you're there to solve difficulties, not to make them."[145] A month into the Broadway run of *Janus*, Sullavan alerted producers that she planned to exit the play at the end of her contract in April 1956, giving them sufficient time to find a bankable actress as a replacement for her role.[146]

While performing nightly on Broadway in *Janus*, Preston also found time to appear in a December 11 television episode of *The Alcoa Hour* on NBC entitled "Undertow." He was paired with Teresa Wright as a military captain and his hardworking wife living in Nova Scotia with their two sons. It is only when the family experienced a near-tragedy that they were able to break through their emotional walls and reveal their true feelings.

The actor was also tapped to narrate *Sentinels in the Air*, a short documentary film about the United States Air Force Reserves Defensive Early Warning Line. The film showcased various phases of Air Force training and highlighted the important role of Air Force personnel in protecting the nation against potential enemy attacks. The short documentary film, produced under the RKO-Pathe banner, was released to the public on February 10, 1956. At the same time, Preston also appeared in *Long After Summer*, an episode of *The Alcoa Hour* which told the story of a Cape Cod sculptor who befriends his teenage, orphan housekeeper.

In the shadow of Sullavan's imminent departure from *Janus*, Alfred De Liagre, the play's producer, called Claudette Colbert one evening and managed to persuade the actress it would be a "lovely gesture" if she agreed to replace Margaret Sullavan "who was quite ill." Colbert agreed to fill in for Sullavan for a short stint beginning the first week in April through the first full week in June.[147] Modifications to the script were planned by the play's author to suit Colbert's acting style.[148] Colbert had to learn Sullavan's part quickly; she was only allowed twelve rehearsals before her Broadway debut in the role, with each session lasting only four hours.[149] Margaret Sullavan's final performance in *Janus* took place on April 1, 1956, with Colbert replacing her the very next evening.[150] About a year after her exit from *Janus*, Sullavan suffered a nervous breakdown after disappearing from a scheduled CBS television program. The troubled actress spent a year in a private sanitarium in Stockbridge, Massachusetts,[151] and later died from an overdose of barbiturates on January 1, 1960.[152] In reflecting on his collaboration with Sullavan some twenty years later, Preston remarked that acting is "often a cynical business that can leave performers burned out, bitter, and broke," adding, "I know a lot of people in this business who go crazy . . . I was in a play once with Margaret Sullavan and she hated performing so much I often wondered why she did it."[153]

When drama critic John McClain reviewed Claudette Colbert's performance in *Janus*, he found the actress "charming" and her stage presence "beguiling."[154] Colbert was successful in *Janus*, so much so that Alfred De Liagre attempted to persuade her to continue in the play beyond the eight weeks of her contract. Colbert declined the offer as she had promised her husband, Dr. Joel Pressman, professor and chief of the division of head and neck surgery at UCLA, that she would bow out of the production in two months.[155] Unable to extend Colbert's contract, De Liagre hired comedienne Imogene Coca to assume the role of Jessica in the romantic comedy. Although Coca received favorable reviews from the New York theater critics for her performance, *Janus* closed on June 30, 1956 after 251 performances.

At this juncture in his career, Preston had appeared in several Broadway productions and developed a reputation as an illustrious stage actor and a consummate professional.[156] One playwright considered Preston a dream to work with and recounted the actor's refreshing demeanor during a pre-Broadway preview of a play:

> We were dying out of town, it was miserable, and the leading lady was a bitch on wheels, but Bob just went about his business. You've got to work with him to know what it's like. He is this oasis, and you know you'd die without him.[157]

When the syndicated newspaper comic strip *Tales from the Great Book* was produced as a record by RCA/Victor in July, Preston lent his distinctive voice to narrate a portion of the album. The two-record set of Bible stories was conceived by illustrator John Lehti as a way to bring the moral values of the Bible into American households via LP recordings. Each record in the set featured twelve minutes of recording per side. The tracks were meticulously designed to "lend excitement to the experience of listening"[158] by having organ music played in the background throughout the readings in addition to the occasional punctuation of other dramatic sound effects. In *Tales from The Great Book* Volume One, actor Joseph Cotten tells the story of Moses. Preston narrates the story of Joshua through four separate stories, "Spies in Jericho," "Joshua Crosses the Jordan," "The Battle of Jericho," and "The Ambush at Ai." Volume Two of the recording featured the story of Joseph as told by Brian Aherne and the Story of Abraham narrated by Ronald Reagan. Once complete, *The Tales from The Great Book* LP was released in October 1956.[159]

In step with his liberal leanings, Preston eagerly supported a Democratic fundraising effort that involved the production of a long-playing record. The album, titled "The Democratic Party: The History, the Campaigns, the Presidents, the Music," was produced in August 1956 by Marvin Frank and narrated by Henry Fonda. Preston was featured on the recording as the voice of Thomas Jefferson, William J. Bryan, and John W. Davis. The album also featured David Wayne as the voice of Stephen Douglas, Grover Cleveland, and the Clerk of Congress; Myron McCormick as the voice of Andrew Jackson, Horace Greeley, and James A. Cox; Arthur Kennedy as the voice of Martin Van Buren, Samuel Tilden, and Woodrow Wilson; Clarke Gordon as the voice of Lewis Cass, James Buchanan, Alton B. Parker, and Franklin Pierce; and Martin Gabel as the voice of James Polk, Horatio Seymour, Winfield Hancock, and Alfred E. Smith. In addition, recordings of the voices of Franklin D. Roosevelt and Harry Truman were showcased on the album, as was Adlai E. Stevenson's acceptance speech at the Democratic National Convention on August 17, 1956.

In early September, the New York *Daily News* and other news outlets reported that Preston had been tapped to play a major role in Ronald Alexander's play, *Bon Voyage*, about the adventures of an American couple and their two twenty-something daughters on a European vacation.[160] The play, eventually re-titled *Holiday for Lovers*, premiered at the Longacre Theatre on

Valentine's Day in 1957 with Don Ameche instead of Preston in the cast.

The actor's talents were showcased on various television programs during the last quarter of 1956. On October 3rd, Preston appeared as army officer Captain Walner in the *20th Century Fox Hour's* production of *Child of the Regiment.* The storyline centered around the adoption of a Japanese orphan by the captain and his wife and the ensuing racial intolerance from a commanding officer that threatens to derail the captain's army career. Four days later, Preston was featured in an episode of the *Goodyear Playhouse* entitled "Missouri Legend" portraying the dual persona of Jesse James and Thomas Howard. The episode chronicled the last days of notorious bank robber Jesse James, who was known to his fellow Missouri natives as Thomas Howard. Less than two weeks later, Preston appeared on CBS in "The Midas Touch" on *Climax!* The October 18 episode involved the owner of a mine who traveled to a South American town to investigate the death of his brother during a tragic cave-in.

In late October, Preston signed on to appear in the Broadway production of Ruth and Augustus Goetz's play *The Hidden River.* The play, co-produced by Martin Gabel and Henry Margolis, was a dramatization of Storm Jameson's 1954 novel of the same name. Preston was to play the role of Jean Monnerie, the elder brother who runs the family vineyard in post-war France's Loire Valley with his younger brother, Francis. The mystery-melodrama focused on identifying the betrayer of a World War II French resistance fighter killed by the Nazis before the action of the play begins. Prior to the start of rehearsals, Preston guest hosted two episodes of *Playhouse 90* on CBS: "Eloise" on November 22 and "Confession" on November 29. Although rehearsals for *The Hidden River* began on December 2, Preston made time to appear in "Made in Heaven," an episode of *Playhouse 90* that aired on December 9. In "Made in Heaven," the actor was teamed with his *Janus* co-star, Imogene Coca, to tell the story of a married couple who became embroiled in an argument after returning home from a cocktail party. The marriage unravels when the couple's argument escalates, resulting in a marital separation and the romantic pursuit of fellow party guests.

Rehearsals for the cast of *The Hidden River*—which also included Peter Brandon, Lili Darvas, David King-Wood, Jack Bittner, Gaby Rodgers, and Tonio Selwert—continued through December. The play opened at the Shubert Theatre in New Haven, Connecticut to good reviews on Wednesday, January 2, 1957 and closed four days later on Saturday, January 5. The play then moved to its next venue at the Walnut Theatre in Philadelphia for a two-week run beginning on January 7. Theater critics in Philadelphia responded with good reviews and lauded Preston's performance. Henry Murdock with *The Philadelphia Inquirer* noted, "Robert Preston wins high stature as an actor as a man who has a stern decision to make."[161]

Having grossed $14,000 during the two-week preview in Philadelphia[162]—an equivalent of approximately $141,000 in 2022 dollars—the producers advanced *The Hidden River* to Broadway, opening at the Playhouse Theatre on January 23, 1957. Although the play opened to enthusiastic reviews from both John Chapman of the *Daily News* and Brooks Atkinson of *The New York Times*, *The Hidden River* closed on March 16 after just 61 performances, having grossed approximately $19,000 of revenue per week from New York audiences.[163] The play's closure was baffling to some in the theater industry since *The Hidden River* was "performed by an expert cast," received favorable reviews, and its serious subject matter was "sufficiently appealing not to discourage the public."[164] However, the producers of *The Hidden River* were keenly attuned to the cold, hard truth of Broadway in the late 1950s: it was the ultimate consumer's market. Broadway playgoers at that time, with an appetite for quality entertainment, had so many outstanding theatrical choices that nothing less than a smash hit would do.[165]

During his stage run in *The Hidden River*, Preston appeared in *The Animal Kingdom*, an episode of *The Alcoa Hour* airing on NBC on February 17. The episode, an adaptation of Philip Barry's stage play of the same name, also featured an ensemble cast including Alan Hale Jr., Joanne Linville, Paul McGrath, Meg Mundy, and Mary Welch. Preston starred as a man with a suspicious wife, a mistress, and a choice to make between the two women in his life.

Preston remained busy with television appearances over the next several months as he waited for his next Broadway role. The actor accepted an opportunity to appear as a panelist on an episode of the popular game show *What's My Line?* on March 17 alongside panel regulars Arlene Francis, Dorothy Kilgallen, and Bennet Cerf. Preston was introduced to the dais by Arlene Francis as "a distinguished actor who has given one of the most beautiful performances this year in play called *The Hidden River*." The panelists attempted to identify the occupations of Miss Toni West, a female judo instructor, and Mr. Mike Finnyham, a hotel bellhop in Chicago, along with mystery celebrity guests Dr. Norman Vincent Peale and Judy Holliday. A week later on March 24, Preston appeared in an *Omnibus* presentation of *The Fall River Legend—The Trial of Lizzie Borden*. Preston's role was that of Lizzie Borden's attorney; his character presented a defense against the charges that Lizzie perpetrated the ax murders of her father and stepmother. Other members of the cast included Katharine Bard, Richard Kiley, Margaret Hamilton, Christopher Plummer, and Lois Bolton.

In June, Preston appeared in the live television drama, *Nothing Personal*, featured on NBC's *Kraft Theatre*. Preston co-starred with Nina Foch in this tale of a married couple who find themselves on the brink of divorce after fifteen years of marriage. The couple, who meet up one last time to divide their marital possessions, end up rekindling their romance by the end of the story. The episode's supporting cast included Sue Randolph, Marcel Hillaire, and Jack Weston. Another member of the cast, making his acting debut in *Nothing Personal*, was Mary Martin's son, Larry Hagman. *The Philadelphia Inquirer*, which panned John Whedon's lackadaisical script, praised Preston and Foch for their acting chops while noting that Hagman's appearance established little more than "he's a tall and personable young man."[166]

It was later that month when Preston learned he might be asked to audition with director Morton DaCosta for a role in a new Broadway musical written by Hollywood songwriter Meredith Willson. As soon as the actor received a copy of the available music, he went to work perfecting a performance of the most difficult segment of the score. As he honed his rendition of "Ya Got Trouble," Preston moved forward with plans to appear in an off-Broadway production of *Inherit the Wind*.

THE HAPPIEST ACTOR
ON BROADWAY

n the early 1950s, composer Meredith Willson began drafting
a musical based on the recollections of his youth in his hometown of Mason City, Iowa; that musical would later become
the "valentine to America"[1] known as *The Music Man*. Willson
began his career as a flutist for John Phillip Sousa's band before
moving on to play with the New York Philharmonic Orchestra.
He extended his talent to songwriting and arranging music
and signed on as a musical director for a variety of radio and
television shows in the 1940s. Recognized as a capable song-
smith, Willson went on to earn an Academy Award nomination
for Best Original Score after composing the music for the 1940
Charlie Chaplin film *The Great Dictator*. On the heels of this
success, Willson was tapped to arrange the music for the score
of William Wyler's movie, *The Little Foxes*.

The plot of *The Music Man* begins in the summer of 1912
and tells the story of Harold Hill, a silver-tongued traveling

salesman who poses as a music professor and promises to establish boys' bands in towns across the country. Not only are Hill's academic credentials entirely bogus, but so is his musical ability—he is unable to read or play a note of music. When Hill disembarks from the train in River City, Iowa, he uses his charm and a fast-talking sales-pitch to convince the citizens that a boys' band will keep the youth from becoming morally corrupt at the town's pool hall. While Hill easily bamboozles the townsfolk, the unmarried town librarian and music teacher, Marian Paroo, discovers evidence of Hill's deception and plans to expose him to the town elders. Marian scuttles the exposé when she recognizes her withdrawn, lisping, younger brother, Winthrop, is looking forward to playing cornet in the band. In addition to his positive influence on Winthrop, Hill becomes a catalyst for transformative change among the residents of River City. Harold's plans to take the money and run are thwarted when he develops feelings for Marian. He ultimately declines the opportunity to flee River City when his deception is exposed by a rival traveling salesman. Hill is ultimately discovered, arrested, and brought before a mob of angry residents in the town gymnasium. Marian rushes to Harold's defense when the mayor suggests he should be tarred and feathered. The mob frenzy is quelled when uniformed members of the boys' band enter the gymnasium and Hill manages to have the band eke out a tune. By the musical's denouement, Harold is transformed into a respectable citizen through Marian's love and is accepted by the River City townsfolk.

Willson took several years and over thirty revisions to complete *The Music Man*, for which he wrote more than forty songs. While shopping around for a producer for his musical, Willson was impressed by Kermit Bloomgarden's remarkable record of theatrical hits and recognized *The Music Man* would benefit immensely from the "Bloomgarden touch."[2] After numerous revisions to the score, Willson and his wife, Rini, arranged to audition their concept for *The Music Man* before Bloomgarden in December 1956; the Willsons were ecstatic when Bloomgarden agreed to produce the musical. Prior to his collaboration with Willson, Bloomgarden had enjoyed a string of successful productions on Broadway including *Deep Are the Roots* (1945), *Another Part of the Forest* (1946), *Command Decision* (1947), *Death of a Salesman* (1949), *A View from the Bridge* (1955), and *The Most Happy Fella* (1956). Once on board with *The Music Man*, Bloomgarden quickly secured Morton DaCosta as the musical's director. DaCosta, known as "Tec" (pronounced "*Teak*"), quickly focused on pulling together the cast and crew for its stage production. In short order, the Buffalo Bills barbershop quartet was added to the cast along with soprano Barbara Cook for the role of Marian Paroo, the town librarian. Howard Bay was tapped to handle the set production and lighting for *The Music Man*, Raoul Pene du Bois would serve as costume designer, and Onna White was hired to plan the choreography. Moving forward with lightning speed, Kermit Bloomgarden secured the Majestic Theater in New York City and selected December 19, 1957 for the musical's Broadway debut.

The process of casting the lead role of Harold Hill became such a complicated undertaking that the principals jokingly concluded that the only person who could convincingly play the role was Ethel Merman.[3] Comedian Milton Berle was interested in the part as was *The Honeymooners* actor Art Carney.[4] The list of other song-and-dance men who were considered for the role of Harold Hill included Danny Kaye, Dan Dailey, Ray Bolger, Phil Harris, and Gene Kelly. Although Ray Bolger was interested in the part of Hill, he "wanted fifteen minutes in the musical's second act to do his own thing."[5] His demand for a personal routine was ultimately a dealbreaker for Willson. In June 1957, with frustration mounting over the need to find the perfect Harold Hill, Bloomgarden pointed out to DaCosta and Willson that the man selected for the role must be a top-notch actor, and suggested that the right actor could be taught to sing, dance, and move.[6]

Kermit Bloomgarden had seen Robert Preston perform in *Boy Meets Girl* at the Playhouse in the Park in Philadelphia, and Tec had likewise seen Preston perform in a few off-Broadway shows. Both men believed that Preston possessed the energy to project himself as larger than life in the role of Harold Hill.[7] Tec then approached Meredith Willson and suggested that they "ought to talk to Bob Preston about playing Harold,"[8] but Willson remained hesitant. He had only seen Preston in a smattering of B-movies and once on Broadway in a serious role in *The Hidden River*, and wondered if Preston possessed the joie de vivre and energy required to portray Harold Hill convincingly.[9]

Tec wasted no time in arranging for Preston to audition before himself and vocal coach Herb Greene in New York City.[10] Preston found the role of Harold Hill "very comfortable to fit into," noting that after the roles he played as a child, *The Music Man* "seemed simple and easy to do."[11] To immerse himself in the role of Harold Hill, Preston selected the most difficult song in the show, "Ya Got Trouble," to rehearse for the audition.

Impressed by Preston's performance, Tec arranged for the actor to audition for Kermit Bloomgarden the very next day.[12] Blown away by Preston's audition, Bloomgarden arranged for Preston to reprise his performance for Meredith Willson; it was forty-eight hours after the audition with Bloomgarden that Preston, accompanied by the producer, found himself on a plane bound for California to perform for Willson.[13]

Willson was immediately impressed by Preston's breezy, confident manner and recalled his first encounter with the charismatic actor:

> "Hi," Robert Preston says . . . as he precedes Kermit through our front door. "Bob is my name."
>
> "Meredith," I says. "Never did figure out a very good nickname for that." "Yeah. Meredith. That's a tough one. Wouldn't dare shorten it to Merde, now would we? No nickname, huh? Gotta work on that. Shall we get acquainted now or later?"
>
> "Whatever you say," I says.
>
> He took off his coat, walked over to the piano. I gave Kermit a fast hello, hit an upper octave E-flat and Robert Preston disappeared into Harold Hill with *Ya Got Trouble, friend* . . . and that was it.[14]

Preston's rapid-fire performance of *Trouble* was a show-stopper and won him the coveted role of Harold Hill. With his first song-and-dance gig securely in his back pocket, Preston moved forward with his commitment to star in *Inherit the Wind* at the Grist Mill Playhouse in Andover, New Jersey. The play, which had closed on Broadway just two weeks earlier, was slated to open at the Playhouse on July 15 for a six-day run. The cast of *Inherit the Wind* included Robert Emhardt and Alan Hewitt, with the latter reprising his Broadway role in this production. Preston's wife, Catherine Craig, was part of the forty-member supporting cast of the play that featured Preston as Clarence Darrow and Emhardt as Williams Jennings Bryan.[15]

Preston next appeared on CBS in an episode of *Climax!* titled "Trail of Terror" along with Diana Lynn and a large ensemble cast. Preston was cast in the role of Lieutenant Hogue, a police detective investigating the apparently motiveless murder of a young doctor. The plot thickens when Hogue learns that before his death, the victim had been trying to contact the relatives of a patient who died of a rare disease.

In mid-August, it was announced that Barbara Cook and Robert Preston would play the lead roles in *The Music Man* and Morton Da Costa would direct the Broadway musical.[16] Columnist Leonard Lyons gleefully reported Preston would "at last" be shaving off the mustache he had sported for many years after discovering "the mustache gave too much tension to [his] upper lip" while singing.[17]

The cast of *The Music Man* was complete when auditions for the dancers and singers took place during the week of September 5 at the Imperial Theatre. Rehearsals for *The Music Man* began on October 9. Preston's musical co-star, Barbara Cook, praised the actor's stamina and team-building ability, noting he was "a great team leader . . . he really did spark the company . . . the company adored him and he was very, very easy to get along with."[18] When Preston began rehearsals, he wore sneakers and moved "like a man who is always just on the verge of getting out of town." In the process of transitioning to dress rehearsals, Preston realized, "It was obvious that I couldn't wear sneakers on the stage, so we had a couple of dozen pairs of thin-soled, light leather shoes made up. They have the feel of sneakers and gave me the same sort of pussy-foot prance."[19] Preston's metamorphosis into Harold Hill was dizzying. Since he would shoot on and off the stage like a bullet, the actor incorporated this light-footed behavior into his performance after he found himself, "rehearsing the acting on one floor of the rehearsal hall, the singing on another floor, and the dancing on another floor. I was always running up and down stairs and I got the idea that [Harold Hill] was always running to catch a train."[20]

The first New York rehearsal of *The Music Man* on a real theater stage took place on the New Amsterdam roof on 42nd Street, with a live audience run-through of the musical held at the Barrymore Theatre on 46th Street.[21] The audience for this event was not only comprised of family and friends, but included a collection of prominent producers, writers, critics, and other industry influencers. Although the run-through was greeted with thundering applause by the audience, Willson, DaCosta, and Bloomgarden realized the true test of the musical's success would manifest itself during *The Music Man*'s four-week preview in Philadelphia.

The Music Man opened on Monday, November 18 in Philadelphia's Shubert Theatre. The audience, as would every *Music Man* audience from that day forward, burst into rhythmic applause when "Seventy-Six Trombones" was played during the finale of the show.[22] The musical was well received on opening night with "enthusiasm and applause," and the audience response was believed to "augur well for the success of this new musical."[23] In praising Preston's performance as Harold Hill, theater critic Henry Murdock described him as "a veritable Gilbert and Sullivan patter man" who gave "the best performance we have ever seen him give, musical, movie, or otherwise."[24]

The score and scenes of *The Music Man* were continually changed during the musical's run at the Shubert Theatre. The scene involving Harold Hill and Marian Paroo in the River City Library had its ending re-written five times, yet the actors were instructed to revert to the original ending just before the Broadway premiere in New York.[25] By opening night, not only did the cast not remember what the original ending was, but there was zero time to rehearse it. This uncertainty and pressure could have easily tested Preston's temper, but he remained calm through it all and performed the scene flawlessly.[26]

Preston's co-star, Barbara Cook, marveled at his even-tempered and convivial disposition, noting he "was such a consistently pleasant person to work with throughout the long and frequently trying rehearsal period. No matter how well a company gets along together, there's bound to be some point at which somebody screams and hollers. Yet with all the demands on him at rehearsal, Bob never blew his top."[27]

Preston's search for perfection was in overdrive during the previews in Philadelphia as well as during *The Music Man*'s Broadway run; this modus operandi underscored his reputation for "working his tail off and never causing trouble, in good times or bad."[28] Recognizing that an actor could easily flub musical lyrics, Preston ensured he never found himself in such a predicament by repeating all of his lyrics to himself, over and over again, so that it became impossible for him to make a mistake.[29] This incredible personal discipline guaranteed Preston's success in his first musical role.

Disaster befell the production in Philadelphia when Preston's voice suddenly went mute. Meredith Willson believed Preston's vocal cords became strained due to the actor's tendency toward excessive chattiness. In his book about the making of *The Music Man*, titled *But He Doesn't Know the Territory*, Willson described Preston as "a big talker" who "loves to talk about a role and the intricacies, gradations and subtleties lurking therein . . . he likes to get unwound from a performance by sitting around later that same night talking about it, and how late he'll set there and talk depends on how late you'll set there and listen."[30] Willson's wife Rini, a Russian-born soprano, knew Preston lacked significant vocal training and warned the actor that he needed to occasionally rest his strained voice. Preston cavalierly dismissed her concerns insisting, "Don't worry Rinitchka, my voice is made out of rawhide. It'll stand the gaff—always has."[31] Until it didn't.

During the final Saturday matinee prior to the last week in Philadelphia, Preston managed to push through the score until his voice completely gave out, much to the shock of the musical's cast and crew. The actor was immediately dispatched back to his hotel and bombarded with doctors, compresses, sprays, and mandated voice rest, in addition to every other known remedy of the day. Without much warning, Preston's understudy, Larry Douglas, was pressed into service and had to perform the role of Harold Hill on Saturday evening with less than three hours of rehearsal.[32]

Preston remained in bed until Monday when he returned to the theater just before curtain time. Meredith Willson marveled at Preston's fortitude and his determination to reclaim the stage. He recalled seeing the actor in his dressing room about a half-hour before curtain time when Preston grabbed an atomizer and squirted the contents down his throat before "brazenly looking [Willson] in the eye" and confidently vocalizing "Mi-mi-mi!"[33]

The Music Man completed its run in Philadelphia on December 14, and the cast and crew made their way to New York. The musical's Broadway debut at the Majestic Theatre on December 19 was greeted by an enthusiastic audience and critical acclaim. Brooks Atkinson, the theater critic from *The New*

York Times, gave the musical a proverbial thumbs-up and raved that Preston, in the role of glib Harold Hill, "could hardly be improved upon."[34] Preston moved onstage with effortless grace and displayed unparalleled vitality and charm. Critics quickly realized that Preston's portrayal of the smooth-talking con man could never be replicated; Preston would remain the incomparable, inimitable embodiment of Harold Hill and would forever be recognized with "Seventy-Six Trombones" as his signature song. Theater critics also found it incredible that Preston's talent had been allowed to languish as a second-string Hollywood leading man for nearly two decades prior to his role in *The Music Man.*[35] Even Wolcott Gibbs from *The New Yorker* magazine lavished praise on Preston, noting the actor possessed "two top things demanded by the stage—infallible technique and a unique personality—and these, in combination with a wonderfully picturesque role, make his performance one of the season's memorable events."[36] Forty-year-old Preston, who sang unpretentiously and glided tirelessly through scene after scene as Harold Hill,[37] was soon recognized as the number-one performer on Broadway; he had finally received his due after working countless years in Hollywood and on Broadway. The critical acclaim Preston received for his portrayal of Harold Hill reinforced his long-held belief that both the Paramount Studios naysayers and Cecil B. DeMille had grossly underestimated his talent. DeMille and Preston had not spoken for the last ten years of the director's life, since the actor "simply had no respect for the man and [he] let him know it."[38] It gave Preston immense satisfaction to know that "DeMille lived long enough to know that [he] played Harold Hill."[39] With his success in *The Music Man,* Preston realized he had at long last "arrived" in the eyes of Broadway and Hollywood elites, and his contentment was reflected in the sign that he hung on his stage-left dressing room door: *The Happiest Actor on Broadway*.[40]

Preston's stunning performance as Harold Hill caused the proverbial scales to fall from the eyes of those in the entertainment industry; Hollywood honchos would never again view Robert Preston in the same light. Meredith Willson acknowledged that Preston's role in *The Music Man* released the actor "from the wrong identity he had been strait-jacketed in throughout the greater part of his career."[41] Willson was dumbfounded that Hollywood studios kept Preston "chained to roles that not only obscured his true abilities but showed him . . . in complete and unfortunately, highly successful juxtaposition to everything his great gifts clamored to really reveal."[42] Preston was equally impressed by Willson, noting, "the world of Meredith Willson is a beautiful world. I've never talked politics with him, but my guess is that he's a Republican who thinks Democrats are pretty nice people."[43]

The role of Harold Hill was physically strenuous and thoroughly exhausting. Preston was cognizant that the character must continuously "hold the stage, because if he doesn't, it's really not all [that] much of a show."[44] The role kept Preston running from one side of the stage to the other, and for this reason, every night was like opening night.[45] Thick makeup needed to be applied to Preston's face before each performance since he was in constant motion on stage and perspired heavily. He acknowledged, "I sweat so much in this role that any other makeup wouldn't last through two scenes of the show;"[46] and arranged for his theater-dresser, Jimmy Davidson, to "stand ready in the wings with a Turkish towel for [his] exits during a performance."[47]

Preston was described by the cast and crew of *The Music Man* as a gifted and tireless professional and the catalyst that maintained the musical's equilibrium. Actor Iggie Wolfington who portrayed Hill's former partner-in-con, Marcellus Washburn, indicated Preston was irreplaceable: "How good was Bob Preston? I'll tell you. He wasn't out often and his understudy was good, but whenever Bob was out, I would walk around the stage and felt like I was following a suitcase. It just was never the same," adding, "Bob Preston *was* Harold Hill. I feel sorry for anyone else who has to play that part."[48] Barbara Cook likewise lavished praise on her co-star and described him succinctly as "a force of nature." She believed Preston's greatest asset was his sex appeal. Aware that Ray Bolger had been considered for the role of Harold Hill, Cook observed, "but [Ray] wasn't sexy, and I think Harold Hill has to be sexy. Robert Preston was a very sexy guy, I'm telling you."[49] Cook inherently understood that,

> The key to the role of Harold Hill is that he has to be sexy as hell, and one of the things that made our production of *The Music Man* work so well was that Bob Preston was an extremely sexy guy; you could really imagine that the whole town— men, women, dogs, cats, and sheep—could have fallen in love with him.[50]

Although very happily married at the time, Barbara Cook recognized that in addition to his cat-like moves onstage, Preston's casting as Harold Hill "worked because Bob Preston was pure, walking sex–and, my God, he was great in that role."[51] Cook adored Preston, appreciated their wonderful working relationship, and felt safe with him onstage.[52]

Preston's persona was the glue that fostered cohesiveness among the cast and crew of *The Music Man*. Actor Iggie

Wolfington observed that "in each performance, there must be an outpouring of warmth and happiness to envelop the entire theater, and Bob is what makes it happen. We all catch the spirit and get the lift from him. I play most of my scenes with him, and it's like jumping on a cloud."[53] Comedienne Helen Raymond who played the role of Mayor Shinn's wife, Eulalie, proffered another explanation for the cast's affection toward Preston. She was quick to point out that "Bob is entirely without the star complex. He not only doesn't resent you getting laughs but he helps you get them."[54] Patti Mariano, one of the young performers in *The Music Man* cast, likewise attested to Preston's character and thoughtfulness. Mariano recalled Preston "had Piper-Heidsieck champagne for everyone's birthday on the bandstand after the show. There was a little ginger ale for the children. There were paper cups and everybody had a toast to whoever's birthday it was. Everyone's birthday–he didn't miss a one."[55]

Following the successful Broadway premiere of *The Music Man*, Meredith Willson presented Robert Preston with a gold cigarette lighter.[56] To capitalize on the show's success, the original *Music Man* cast album was recorded immediately after the show opened on Broadway. Although the album "ranked at the top of the charts for twelve weeks, won the Grammy Award for Best Cast Album, and sold one million copies while remaining on the charts for nearly five full years," the cast only "received two weeks' salary for recording the album, but never one cent more."[57] Barbara Cook realized Preston, who was not a trained singer, possessed excellent rhythm and pitch and "developed a very effective manner of speaking/singing his songs, à la Rex Harrison in *My Fair Lady*;" he also moved onstage like a trained dancer, although he had no formal dance experience.[58]

Despite their close working relationship, Cook came to know Preston as an extremely private person who could talk about every subject under the sun, yet reveal nothing about himself:

> Bob presented a very interesting dichotomy–very gregarious, seemingly open, but at the same time extremely private. Each night before the show began, he would come into my dressing room and we'd talk about the day–politics, what was happening in the world, a great one-on-one conversation. And yet, after each of these encounters, he would leave and I felt as if I didn't really know him at all.[59]

Preston and his wife, Catherine, continued to maintain a modest lifestyle in their unpretentious Manhattan apartment. Catherine decorated the flat with the same type of Early American décor and chintz-covered furniture that she used to stylize the couple's California home. Catherine's oil painting of the couple's Brentwood home was hung directly above a bright red sofa on a dark green wall of the living room which also featured Catherine's hand-made draperies and pillows.[60] Catherine's portraits of Preston as Harold Hill in *The Music Man* and as Jean Monnerie in *The Hidden River* were hung in the master bedroom. In addition, the apartment was also home to a pair of canaries that had been gifted to Preston on the night of *Music Man's* Broadway premiere along with a pair of ballet slippers and the message, "Don't just stand there—sing!"[61]

Catherine basked in the ethereal glow of her husband's success during this high point in their lives. She was described by Barbara Cook as a beautiful, sweet woman with a motherly presence who engendered a calm in those in her sphere.[62] Catherine, who readily acknowledged her husband had become the focal point of her life, insisted on doing all of the housekeeping herself, preferring to "live [her] own life" on her schedule rather than be regimented by maids.[63] Her almost slavish devotion to her husband became the hallmark of her existence built entirely around Preston's schedule and needs. Catherine's flair for the domestic extended to her role as Preston's stylist. She took great care to purchase all of her husband's clothes, and her fashion sense and attention to detail paid off when Preston was named as one of the ten best-dressed men of the year.[64]

Catherine knew all too well that her husband's role in *The Music Man* was a strenuous one, and she made every effort to "take all the pressure off Bob"[65] by serving as her husband's buffer and emotional firewall to the outside world. She provided a safe place for her husband to fall, express the frustrations and disappointments he would never think of airing on the job, and endured his temperamental side. Preston took great pains to comport himself in a calm, professional manner during stressful situations on a stage or movie set, yet readily acknowledged he was "not afraid to show [his wife] a side that I won't show to other people."[66] Catherine, for the most part, tended to take the intricacies of her husband's personality in stride. At other times, however, Catherine found herself unable to identify the origin and depth of Preston's emotional frustration:

When he's in a play, you know what the tensions are, and I feel it's best to let him get rid of them somewhere. Quite often, there's nowhere else. We do go around a bit then . . . that I understand.

Sometimes, though he's temperamental and I don't understand.[67]

Preston maintained a regimented schedule while performing in *The Music Man*. His preferred evening meal consisted of steak, potatoes, and a salad, and Catherine had his supper on the table promptly at 5:30 p.m.[68] She would then drive her husband to the Majestic Theatre each evening and return just before the final curtain to pick him up after each performance. The traffic cops, who quickly came to recognize Catherine and her chauffeuring schedule, generously allowed her to wait at the curb until Preston exited from the theater each evening.[69] On nights when Preston chose not to hold court at Sardi's bar, the couple would return straight home and enjoy a late meal that was both substantial and "a little different."[70] Catherine, who was an accomplished cook specializing in Italian and Jewish cuisine, developed several sauces and signature recipes that rivaled those of professional chefs.[71] Evenings would wind down with the couple watching *Tonight Starring Jack Paar* on television or spending time in their study working on jigsaw puzzles.[72]

Preston appreciated his wife's devotion and confirmed she was his only extravagance. The actor's indulgence of his wife was on full display when Catherine arrived for an interview with *The Indianapolis Star* wearing a luxurious, full-length mink coat. When asked by the interviewer if she had received the coat in celebration of her husband's success in *The Music Man*, Catherine demurred, noting she received the gift a few years earlier during her husband's stint in *Janus*. Catherine, well aware of a fur coat's shelf life, told the interviewer, "I understand a mink coat is to last ten years, so that means there will have to be another hit when the time expires."[73]

The Music Man continued to delight Broadway audiences while boosting Preston's stature as a versatile, accomplished actor. *Time* magazine reported that the musical continued to be "the toughest ticket in town" seven months into its Broadway run, with New York natives and visitors alike swarming "the box office at every performance." The success of *The Music Man* was lucrative for its producers who were able to net $19,000 in clear profit from the gross weekly ticket sales of $70,000.[74] In addition, the producers reaped the proceeds from twenty different *Music Man* recordings and albums as well as from the sale of sheet music for "Seventy-Six Trombones" that was purchased by brass and marching bands across the country.[75] As a further measure of *The Music Man*'s success, the show's cast album went on to capture the first Grammy Award for Best Original Cast Album in 1959 and spent 245 weeks on the Billboard chart.

The Music Man received nine Tony Award nominations for the 1957-1958 Broadway season, though a strike against the local CBS station in New York precluded the television broadcast of the Tony Awards program. The black-tie awards ceremony was held in the Grand Ballroom of the Waldorf Astoria Hotel in midtown Manhattan on April 13, 1958, and featured a reception, dinner, and dancing to the music of Meyer Davis. Preston emerged as a star of the Broadway stage upon receiving the Distinguished Musical Actor Tony award for his portrayal of Harold Hill. In addition to Preston, Barbara Cook took home a Tony award for Distinguished Supporting or Featured Musical Actress, David Burns won for Distinguished Supporting or Featured Musical Actor, Herbert Greene was recognized in the Conductor or Musical Director category, and *The Music Man* beat out *West Side Story* in the race for Best

Musical. As a further measure of its success, *The Music Man* was named the Best Musical of the 1957-1958 season by the New York Drama Critics Circle.

In light of the smashing Broadway success of *The Music Man* and the popularity of its cast album, it was no surprise that a screen adaptation of the musical was an inevitability. Bing Crosby and Frank Sinatra, both of whom had their eye on the screen role of Professor Harold Hill, separately approached Meredith Willson and Kermit Bloomgarden about obtaining the film rights to the musical[76] without success.

Preston had established himself as a major Broadway star and a recognized performer by September 1958. The musical's staying power was evident when tickets for the show were still being sold through June 1959. While Preston was starring in the runaway Broadway hit, television networks around the country began to televise his old movies. Preston, now a seasoned actor, bemoaned the revival of his films from the late 1930s and 1940s noting, "I've never made a movie I'm ashamed of, but I think it's unfortunate they're on television. You're not seeing me, you're seeing a 20-year-old boy who became me."[77] Despite Preston's reticence about televising his prior filmography, the small-screen exposure boosted his star status and ensured his continued Broadway success; he began receiving fan mail from admirers who viewed his films on television and now planned to see him in-person on stage.[78]

Preston had been portraying Harold Hill on stage for a year-and-a-half by June 1959 when a pregnant Barbara Cook left the musical after recognizing the pregnancy was affecting her singing voice.[79] Cook indicated that before she departed from the show, Preston insisted on changing their dance routine to protect against any injury during her pregnancy:

He was so happy [for me], but he was also afraid. We had little lifts when we danced, and after a month or so [Preston] said he wasn't going to do them. So, we sat out the dance a little longer than the other couples.[80]

Audiences continued to flock to see *The Music Man* even after Arlyne Frank was added to the cast to fill the role of Marian Paroo. Although Preston had not tired of *The Music Man*, he did not plan to stay with the show indefinitely. It was in mid-1959 that Preston began dropping hints about his exit from the musical, telling one reporter that he was "under contract until November 30 and will want to stay on unless there are a couple of things that seem irresistible."[81]

After nine years in New York, Preston considered the state his new home, noting he and his wife had gained "more and closer friends than we ever did at any other period in our lives."[82] It was at this time that Preston and Catherine decided to put down permanent roots in the east and purchase a home. Since he and Catherine were "the kind of people who have to look at water," the impetus to purchase property was spurred by new construction near the Prestons' Manhattan apartment. The couple had resided in an apartment overlooking the East River for almost a decade, but when a taller apartment building was constructed across the street that blocked their view of the river, they moved out.[83] After searching for a perfect location that featured waterfront views and proximity to Manhattan, Preston and his wife purchased a 150-year-old remodeled carriage house on two-and-a-half wooded acres at 370 Grace Church Street in Rye, New York on June 1, 1959. Preston projected that the large house, which overlooked Long Island Sound, would take at least a year to be completely furnished. Catherine was aware the new home provided her husband with "the kind of outlet he needs" in a climate that showcased the four seasons–a feature Preston loved but was unable to enjoy in California.[84]

Preston began the daily commute from his new home in Rye to the theater district in Manhattan, confessing, "I love the commuting. I drive in and out every night. On the way in, I begin to gear up for the show. Coming home, it's a great way to start to relax."[85] He was unfazed by the thirty-two-mile commute, pointing out,

> Why, in California you have to drive that far to get a sandwich. I clip the hedges and mow the lawn and Catherine is wonderful at gardening and such. I like the small-town atmosphere about it all. The milk truck driver and the garage man will stop by and pass the time of day.[86]

Both Preston and Catherine became hands-on homeowners in their newly adopted, conservative suburb; he regularly used power tools for domestic projects while Catherine rolled up her sleeves to paint walls with a roller.[87] Preston, who built chairs by hand in an old cow barn he converted into a tool shed, would regularly take outdoor showers by hanging a hose over an apple tree, since "there's a lot of privacy when leaves are on the trees."[88] He took an active role in maintaining the outdoor aesthetic of his home and became an avid gardener in the process,

> I love all of it, the planting and the weeding and mowing the lawn, trimming the hedges. I'm also Rye's actor. They don't encourage that sort

of thing, really, but they tolerate me. They even overlook the fact that I'm a Democrat.[89]

Preston and Catherine's nephew, Charles Leinenweber, recalled when he visited his aunt and uncle at their home in Rye, the house "didn't have much in the way of furniture."[90] Although the home lacked a traditional dining room table, it did feature an octagonal poker table on which Catherine would spread a tablecloth to normalize the table's odd-shaped contours.[91]

Despite the rigors of *The Music Man*, Preston found the time in late October 1959 to star with Claudette Colbert in a television adaptation of *The Bells of St. Mary's* on CBS. Preston, as Father O'Malley, and Colbert, as Sister Mary Benedict, reprised the roles originally performed by Bing Crosby and Ingrid Bergman in the 1945 film of the same name. Preston took pride in being an active, working actor and believed actors needed to take work whenever and wherever it was available. He explained to syndicated reporter Margaret McManus that he,

> . . . never accepted the theory that actors must necessarily have long periods of unemployment. There is always work somewhere. It may not be in the movies or on Broadway, maybe it's a little theater group in York, PA. But better to work in York, Pa, than not to be working at all. You have to go out after work. Parts will not pursue you. Just the opposite."[92]

The actor's diligent work paid off financially and earned him $200,000 a year ($1.9 million in 2022 dollars). For all his monetary success, Preston and his wife opted to save the bulk of his income rather than indulge in a splashy lifestyle.[93]

The Music Man showcased Preston's versatility as an actor, and Hollywood immediately took notice. By 1959, studio heads began wooing the actor for upcoming film roles, and in December of that year, Jack Warner announced Preston had been signed to star in the screen adaptation of William Inge's play, *The Dark at the Top of the Stairs* (1960), to be directed by Delbert Mann[94] with a cast that included Dorothy Maguire, Eve Arden, Angela Lansbury, Frank Overton, Lee Kinsolving, Shirley Knight, and Robert Eyer.

Preston acknowledged his decision to appear in the Warner Brothers film was a calculated one, since he believed the studio would be purchasing the film rights to *The Music Man*.[95] The actor was astounded when he initially read the script for *The Dark at the Top of the Stairs* and realized the opening scene was a candid bedroom tableau featuring the central married characters. He questioned Delbert Mann about the sequence, noting the censors "never used to let anything get by [like] this before."[96] Prior to the 1960s, movie and television studios had been reluctant to depict married couples in the same bed; Ozzie and Harriet as well as Nick and Nora Charles in the *Thin Man* films were regularly seen settling down for the night in separate twin beds.

The play, on which the film is based, recounts the story of Rubin Flood (Preston), a middle-aged traveling harness salesman in the 1920s who is frustrated by financial troubles, the loss of his job, and his passionless marriage. Rubin's wife, Cora (Maguire), who is dissatisfied with her life, alternates between living vicariously through her teenage daughter, Reenie (Knight), and smothering her younger son, Sonny (Eyer). Reenie becomes involved with Sammy (Kinsolving), a Jewish cadet attending the nearby military academy, and the two come face-to-face with bigotry when they are asked to leave a friend's party at a local country that does not allow Jewish members. A despondent Sammy summarily attempts suicide, is hospitalized, and eventually succumbs to his injuries. Cora, jealous of her husband's friendship with Mavis (Lansbury), a local hairdresser, visits Mavis' salon posing as a customer. Mavis assures Cora her relationship with Rubin is platonic, but advises her not to resist her husband's romantic overtures. Rubin lands a new job as a salesman for an oil drilling equipment company and receives an apology from his now-contrite spouse. The film ends with Rubin sending his son and friend off for an afternoon at the movies before he heads upstairs to join his wife in their bedroom.

The five-year hiatus since the release of Preston's last film, *The Last Frontier*, had finally ended. Filming of the Inge classic was scheduled to begin in January 1960; Preston was scheduled to exit *The Music Man* on January 9, 1960 after a two-year stint portraying Professor Harold Hill, and Eddie Albert was named as his successor on December 18, 1959.[97] Albert's contract to headline in *The Music Man* was scheduled to end in June 1960.

At the same time Preston's role in *The Dark at the Top of the Stairs* was publicized by Warner Brothers Studio, Jack Warner announced the studio had acquired the motion picture rights to *The Music Man*. Acquisition of the film rights proved to be a hot commodity in Hollywood with every motion picture studio actively vying to acquire the property. Although no price tag was released at the time, it was later learned that the film rights to *The Music Man* were purchased for $1,000,000,[98] one of the most expensive payouts for a theatrical property in that era.[99]

When filming began for *The Dark at the Top of the Stairs*, director Delbert Mann made the decision to employ the same unorthodox rehearsal technique for this movie that he had successfully used when filming *Marty* in 1955. Mann required the actors to complete an initial run-through of the entire movie script and then rehearse the script on stage before the same scenes would be memorialized on film.[100] Preston was delighted that Mann chose to direct the film by rehearsing the entire cast in sequence and allowing the actors to be able to understand their characters before the actual filming got underway. Once the cameras started to roll, Mann maintained a continuous stream of action and allowed the actors to feel confident in their performances.[101] As the movie entered production, an actor's strike loomed on the horizon. To avoid any substantial filming delays resulting from a strike, Warner Brothers Studio decided to embark on a rigorous seven-day-a-week filming schedule to complete the film before the March 7 strike deadline.[102]

Being back on a movie set made Preston feel as if he were starting his movie career all over again, although he was no longer the greenhorn he was when he appeared in his first films prior to World War II.[103] The actor credited his years of experience on the stage and screen with allowing him to confidently resume his movie career:

> Even though it was years since I worked on a Hollywood sound stage and was somewhat nervous when I reported to the Warner set, I knew most of the people around me and had no qualms about facing the top brass when it came to signing a contract for a picture. Years ago, I would have been petrified, but I found myself surrounded by

familiar faces and that eased the tension even in the executive suite.[104]

Preston next appeared in an episode of the *DuPont Show of the Month* on CBS, titled "Years Ago," on April 21. The episode was an adaptation of actress Ruth Gordon's 1946 autobiographical play in which Preston played the role of Gordon's stern, independent father.[105] The teleplay, directed by Alex Segal and produced by David Susskind, also featured Sandra Church in the role of stage-struck Ruth Gordon.[106]

Eddie Albert's contract to perform in *The Music Man* ended on June 1, 1960. The producers had hired Bert Parks, best known as the host of the Miss America telecast, as a replacement for Albert. The day after Eddie Albert's departure from the show, an eleven-day, million-dollar Broadway blackout began when the Actors' Equity Association and the League of New York Theaters were unable to reach an agreement on a contract dispute.[107] Bert Parks found himself unable to rehearse for his role as Harold Hill as a result of the strike and subsequent theater shutdown. Preston came to the rescue by agreeing to return to the Majestic Theater to reprise the character of Harold Hill from June 13 through June 25 and thus allow Bert Parks enough rehearsal time to feel comfortable taking over the role.[108]

In mid-July of 1960, it was announced that *The Dark at the Top of the Stairs* would open at Radio City Music Hall in New York on September 22. The critical reviews of the film were generally positive; however, a few critics were uncomfortable with Preston's on-screen virility and the film's storyline, which showcases the then-taboo subject of marital sex. The review of the movie that appeared in the *Film Bulletin* described *The Dark at the Top of the Stairs* as an "absorbing drama with goodly shares of humor, warmth, and tragedy" and lauded Preston as bringing "dynamic surges of virility and vitality to his role."[109] Although *Variety* praised the film as "well cast and persuasively acted,"[110] *Motion Picture Daily* took critical aim at the direction of Delbert Mann, whom the publication felt "failed to draw out of some of the most vital scenes, all the urgency and pathos that [the playwright] Inge wrote into them."[111] An editorial in *Life* magazine reported that the Legion of Decency labeled 24% of the films released in 1960 as objectionable for their departure from decency and cited *The Dark at the Top of The Stairs* as a film that was tastelessly and "obtrusively sexed up."[112] *The New York Times* film critic, Bosley Crowther, appeared uncomfortable with the film's exploration of the sexual relationship between Mr. and Mrs. Flood. Crowther roundly criticized the film for starting out on a "tasteless note" with an opening scene that portrays "the intimacies of marriage with an explicitness that could make a strong man blush."[113]

Despite the priggish reaction to the film by a limited few, *The Dark at the Top of the Stairs* was voted one of the ten best films of 1960 by the National Board of Review of Motion Pictures. Actor Lee Kinsolving earned a Golden Globe nomination for his role as Sammy Golden, Delbert Mann was nominated for an Outstanding Directorial Achievement Award by the Directors Guild of America, and actress Shirley Knight received an Academy Award nomination for Best Supporting Actress for her role as Reenie Flood, plus two Golden Globe nominations for Best Supporting Actress in a Motion Picture and New Star of the Year.

Until mid-1960, it remained uncertain whether Preston would be tapped to reprise his original role of Harold Hill in the film adaptation of *The Music Man*. Although there were bigger Hollywood names who could play the role and were actively vying for the part, the show's composer, Meredith Willson, was Preston's champion.[114] Warner Brothers desired a big-name star for the role of Harold Hill and considered Bing Crosby, Burt Lancaster, Frank Sinatra, Kirk Douglas, Dean Martin, and Cary Grant as viable contenders for the part. Preston, aware that Frank Sinatra was pursuing the film role, remarked, "Frank Sinatra wanted the part badly. I for one couldn't quite picture him playing Professor Harold Hill, who certainly wasn't from Hoboken, New Jersey."[115] Preston gave "political reasons," the nature of which he was not privy to, as the basis of the Warner Brothers' protracted announcement about their decision for him to reprise his Broadway role as Harold Hill on the big screen.[116]

In her memoir, Shirley Jones, who played Marian Paroo in the movie version of *The Music Man*, recounted that Jack Warner pushed unsuccessfully to cast Frank Sinatra in the title role of Harold Hill, but that choice was a clear "no" for composer Meredith Willson. Willson made it clear to Warner that unless Preston was cast in the role, there would be no movie.[117] Jack Warner then approached another box-office megastar, Cary Grant, about portraying the starring role in the film. Grant recalled, "Jack Warner begged me to do *The Music Man* but I declined because nobody could do that role as well as Bob Preston."[118] It was widely reported that Grant, who had seen *The Music Man* on Broadway a dozen times, also told Warner, "not only will I not play it, but if Preston doesn't do it, I won't even come to see the picture."[119] Warner, a man used to getting his way, finally capitulated to Willson's demands and signed Preston to star in the film during the summer of 1960.[120]

With Robert Preston cast in the role of Harold Hill, despite the fact that he was a movie veteran and had won a Tony Award for his role in *The Music Man* on Broadway, Jack Warner was determined to cast what he considered a 'bankable" star in the role of librarian Marian Paroo. He quickly signed singer/actress Shirley Jones, who had recently won an Academy Award for Best Supporting Actress for her performance as prostitute Lulu Bains in *Elmer Gantry*, to play Marian. Warner then began filling in the remainder of the cast by recruiting actors and actresses from the Broadway production of *The Music Man* to reprise their roles on screen. Among those making the transition from Broadway to film were the Buffalo Bills barbershop quartet, Paul Ford as Mayor George Shinn, and Pert Kelton as Marian's mother, Mrs. Paroo. Warner also added some new faces to the cast including Hermoine Gingold as the Mayor's wife Eulalie Mackechnie Shinn, Ron Howard as Marian's lisping younger brother, Winthrop Paroo, comedian Buddy Hackett as Marcellus Washburn, Susan Luckey as Zaneeta Shinn, and Timmy Everett as Tommy Djilas.

What made the production of *The Music Man* unusual was Warner's selection of Morton DaCosta, who directed the musical on Broadway, to direct the film. Similarly, Onna White, the choreographer of the Broadway musical, was tapped to choreograph the film's musical numbers. With DaCosta assuming the directorial helm of the movie and White taking charge of the choreography, both the studio brass and moviegoers could feel reassured that the film version of the musical would closely mirror the original Broadway production.

Preston was comfortable reprising his role as Harold Hill on screen with Morton DaCosta in the director's chair, admitting that he "wouldn't have taken kindly to having to do [the film] with anyone else,"[121]

Any other film director would have interpreted the whole thing differently from Tec; and his interpretation, to my way of thinking, was a perfect blend of all that's best in a big-scale musical. He came to the film with the advantage of knowing the subject inside-out and backwards; the stage production was in a way a three-year rehearsal for the film . . . ."[122]

The film's estimated production budget of $4.24 million was relatively low in comparison to other musicals of that period whose production costs ranged from $5 million to $8 million.[123] Aside from the million-dollar price tag for the film rights to *The Music Man*, Warner Brothers compensated Robert Preston with a salary of $154,000 (about $1.5 million in 2022 dollars) and Shirley Jones with $105,000 (roughly $1 million in 2022 dollars) for their starring roles in the film.[124] The movie featured all but one of the songs in the original Broadway score, swapping out Marian's ballad, "My White Knight," for the newly composed tune, "Being in Love."

The fall prior to the filming of *The Music Man*, Preston hosted the *Bell Telephone Hour's* patriotic music special on NBC, *One Nation Indivisible*, on October 28, 1960. The telecast showcased classical and Broadway music and featured performances by Mahalia Jackson, Peter Palmer, Jo Stafford, Dorothy Collins, Bill Hayes, and The Dukes of Dixieland. The songs performed on the program included, "Oh, What a Beautiful Morning," "Seventy-Six Trombones," "Shrimp Boats," "A Rovin'," and the campaign medleys "Jefferson and Liberty," and "Keep Cool with Coolidge."

Seven weeks of scheduled rehearsals for *The Music Man* began in mid-February 1961, and filming commenced on April

3 in the backlot of Warner Brothers Studio where a replica of the fictional River City had been constructed.[125] It was fully expected that filming of the musical would continue through August.[126] The team from Pacific Title and Art Studio was tasked with preparing the film's opening credits using wooden marching figures and stop-animation filming to spell out the titling. Warner Brothers considered hiring the UCLA and USC bands to stage live formations on a field to accompany the film's opening credits, but the cost of this plan was prohibitively expensive. Instead, Rocco "Rocky" Longo of Pacific Title painstakingly moved wooden toys on a rubber carpet, one step at a time, to create the animated lettering for the title sequences.[127] Marching bands from UCLA and USC were ultimately hired to appear in the final scene of the movie which featured Harold Hill leading a large band through the streets of River City.

Shirley Jones acknowledged being simultaneously thrilled and nervous about playing opposite Robert Preston in *The Music Man*. Her nervousness stemmed from the fact Preston had acted in the Broadway version of the musical for two years, and she feared he would make comparisons to his Broadway Marian, Barbara Cook, and that:

> [he] might cite Barbara [Cook] and her brilliant performance in the show all the time: "But Barbara did this scene like this," and so on. But Bob was so great, so bighearted, that he never once mentioned the Broadway show or Barbara Cook to me. And his performance as Professor Harold Hill was consistently fresh and new.[128]

Filming of the musical encountered a major hiccup when Jones discovered she was pregnant with son Patrick Cassidy. Jones made the calculated decision to initially keep her delicate condition a secret. Her then-husband, singer/actor Jack Cassidy, was out of work at the time, and she feared being bounced from the film if her condition was revealed to the director and the studio. When her pregnancy became too difficult to conceal, and there were already enough scenes filmed to make her dismissal from the film untenable, Jones shared the news of her pregnancy with director Morton DaCosta. A shocked DaCosta counseled Jones to keep mum about her pregnancy and assured her that every effort would be made to conceal her condition, including the use of corsets and camera shots that filmed her from the waist up.[129] Preston made the startling discovery about Jones' pregnancy during the filming of the musical's romantic footbridge scene. Jones explained Preston was holding her extremely tight against his chest while he sang "Till There Was You" to her and kissed her passionately with his eyes closed. At that moment, the child in her womb volleyed a massive kick and "Bob practically passed out in shock."[130] Jones announced to a nonplussed Preston, "that was Patrick Cassidy"[131] as a way of informing him of her pregnancy and introducing him to her unborn child. Many years later when Preston was appearing on Broadway, Jones's then adult son went backstage to meet him. Jones recounted that Patrick, "held his hand out to Bob [and announced] 'My name is Patrick Cassidy.' Preston took three steps back [and said], 'Oh no! We've already met.' Then he gave [Patrick] a big smile."[132]

Filming for *The Music Man* was completed in August 1961; Preston's performance as Harold Hill had taken a total of 74 days to complete.[133] Preston credited Morton DaCosta's familiarity with *The Music Man* for being able to streamline the production, noting "one of the big musical sequences—the 'Ya Got Trouble' number—[was filmed] in a couple of nights instead of the nine [that were] scheduled."[134] Around this same time, MGM announced Preston had been signed to play the role of a wagon master in their upcoming film *How the West Was Won.*

During the filming of *The Music Man*, Meredith Willson became aware of President John F. Kennedy's physical fitness initiative for the nation's youth. Willson offered to compose a song, free of charge, that could be used in schools to promote exercise for school-aged children, and the resulting tune, "Chicken Fat" became the hallmark of the President's youth fitness program. Willson approached Preston about recording "Chicken Fat," and the actor donated his time and talent to the project. Capitol records provided their musicians, chorus, and recording studios to allow Preston to record the song in early 1962 with full orchestral accompaniment. The end product was a six-minute song, featuring eleven different exercises, that began:

> Touch down
> Every morning
> Ten times!
> Not just
> Now and then.
> Give that chicken fat
> Back to the chicken,
> And don't be chicken again.
> No, don't be chicken again.
> Push up
> Every morning
> Ten times.

Push up
Starting low.
Once more on the rise.
Nuts to the flabby guys!
Go, you chicken fat, go away!
Go, you chicken fat, go! . . . [135]
(Meredith Willson, "Chicken Fat")

Three million copies of the "Chicken Fat" record were provided to public schools across the United States. Some schools played the song over the public address system each morning in the 1960s and 1970s, while others used "Chicken Fat" to augment their gym class curriculum.

Preston used his voice and dramatic flair to punch up the song lyrics and help motivate students to exercise. In discussing "Chicken Fat" on his blog, Robert Elisberg points out that, "Robert Preston doesn't let up even a hiccup on this silliness for over six minutes. He puts his all into everything, absolutely everything, every second of the way"[136] and "shows how an actor can take the most absolutely, utterly, gut-wrenchingly silly piece of material and by believing in it, committing *totally* to it, 100%, and not letting up for one *single* second, turn that silliness into something rich and wonderful."[137]

Amidst his busy professional schedule, Preston and Catherine made time to make improvements to their home in Rye. One of the couple's projects involved enlarging the master bedroom to accommodate an extra-large bed. The expansion of the bedroom necessitated the removal of the bathtub from the master bathroom, a change that suited Preston just fine since the shower stall was his bathing method of choice.[138] As one year ended and a new year began, Preston faced a date book replete with back-to-back films, stage plays, and television appearances. The frenetic schedule left the actor with little downtime and necessitated regular commutes between Hollywood and Broadway.

ROLLER COASTER

T he year 1962 saw Robert Preston's career advance at a
frenetic pace with appearances in multiple motion pictures, a Broadway musical, and the long-awaited movie
premiere of *The Music Man*. Preston waxed poetic during a
February 1962 interview with Hedda Hopper when asked to
speculate on how the trajectory of his career may have been
altered had he not pivoted to Broadway. Ever the realist,
Preston mused,

> One thing my experience has taught me is that
> people get in a rut when they try to play life safe.
> My philosophy is, if something starts fraying your
> nerves, get away from it. Take a chance. If you
> fail, try again. You soon learn that nobody has to
> do anything he dislikes–except die.[1]

Now considered a hot commodity, Preston was actively
courted by Hollywood. Although he had languished in dead-end

films on the Paramount lot in the early years of his career, Preston was now bombarded with plum movie roles. With his success in *The Music Man*, he now had the luxury to be selective in his choice of film projects. One role the actor rejected was that of Senator Fred Van Ackerman in Otto Preminger's film *Advise and Consent* (1962); he instead chose to pursue the role of wagon master Roger Morgan in *How the West Was Won* (1962).

MGM began production of the blockbuster film on May 28, 1961. The movie script was formulated from a series of *Life* magazine articles in 1959 that detailed the settlement of the western United States. Studio brass determined the movie would be filmed using new widescreen Cinerama technology- a filming technique that shot scenes with three synchronized cameras that shared a single shutter.

In August 1961, Preston joined the star-studded cast that included Carroll Baker, Lee J. Cobb, Henry Fonda, Carolyn Jones, Karl Malden, Gregory Peck, George Peppard, Debbie Reynolds, Jimmy Stewart, Eli Wallach, John Wayne, and Richard Widmark, among others. The studio hired three directors, John Ford, George Marshall, and Henry Hathaway, to film separate segments of *How the West Was Won*: "The Rivers," "The Plains," "The Civil War," "The Railroads," and "The Outlaws," and projected that the film would take eight months to a year to complete.[2]

The saga of the film chronicled the trials and tribulations of the Prescott family and daughters Eve (Baker) and Lily (Reynolds) as they make their way west from New England to California. Filming of the various action segments took place on location in Battery Rock near the Ohio River in Illinois, in the Colorado Rockies, in California, on the Arizona-Utah border, in Paducah, Kentucky, and in South Dakota.

Preston spent weeks growing a beard for his role in the film but was ordered to lose the whiskers since the director wanted him clean-shaven on screen.[3] The actor appeared in the second segment of the film titled "The Plains" as rugged wagon master Roger Morgan. As Morgan leads a wagon train of pioneers westward, he falls in love with Lily Prescott to whom he proffers repeated marriage proposals. Morgan is ultimately rebuffed by Ms. Prescott in favor of gambler Cleve Van Valen, portrayed by Gregory Peck.

The cumbersome, 800-pound Cinerama camera often filmed the actors from as close as eighteen inches away. Debbie Reynolds described being filmed by the mammoth camera as a "frightening" experience, noting that "looking into a Cinerama camera from only 18 inches away throws you . . . it's like looking into the back of a giant watch. You can see the wheels going around, you can see the darn thing shifting gears."[4] Preston similarly observed that the Cinerama camera with the "see-all sweep of its lenses puts 146-degree background and action even into 'close-ups,'" joking that on occasion he had even been captured "in the picture standing *behind* the camera."[5]

Tragedy struck the cast during filming when stuntman Bob Morgan was severely injured and almost killed while filming a scene on a moving train. The accident unfolded when the chains on a flatbed car securing a three-ton pile of logs snapped and severely injured Morgan. The weight of the logs smashed and sheared off parts of the stuntman's face, and on-site rescuers had to tie his eyeballs back into place with gauze. A disfigured Morgan, who ultimately lost his left leg two inches above the knee, endured a seven-and-a-half-month hospital stay and a five-year recovery.[6]

Filming of *How the West Was Won* was completed in June 1962. The episodic western epic cost MGM $15 million to produce, a full three million dollars more than had initially been budgeted for the film.[7] The studio decided to delay the release of the film and opted to release another Cinerama blockbuster, *The Brothers Grimm*, beforehand.[8] *How the West Was Won* was initially released in London and Paris in November 1962 and premiered in the United States on February 20, 1963. Bosley Crowther, the film critic from *The New York Times*, panned the film. He described the James Webb script as "horribly written," one which produced "random episodes" and a "patchwork of Western fiction cliches."[9] Other newspaper reviews of the film proved far more favorable; regional critics recognized *How the West Was Won* as a hit in London and Paris and touted the movie as a "superb piece of entertainment."[10] The film went on to garner seven Academy Award nominations in 1964 and won three awards in the categories of Best Original Screenplay, Best Sound Mixing, and Best Film Editing.

Preston anticipated his next Broadway vehicle after *The Music Man* would be a drama, but he settled for the lead role in *We Take the Town*, describing the production as "a play that could go without music."[11] The actor hoped that his role in *We Take the Town*, a musical biography about Mexican revolutionary Pancho Villa, would recreate his Broadway success in *The Music Man*. The musical, adapted from Ben Hecht's screenplay for the 1934 film *Viva Villa!*, was Stuart Ostrow's first solo gig as a musical producer.[12] Ostrow hastily selected television director Alex Segal to direct the musical, despite Segal's lack of experience with stage or musical productions, since Preston "insisted on rehearsals beginning in a month's time."[13] According to assistant choreographer Stuart Hodes, Segal not only underestimated the difficulty of directing a Broadway musical, he quickly

removed large segments of the production and focused dispro-
portionally on minor scenes.[14]

Unlike other stage musical scores, Preston was aware the songs
in *We Take the Town* were steadfastly rooted in specific scenes,

> We have a book and set scenes. It's not one of
> those things where if a song doesn't work in
> the first act you can move it to the second. The
> songs and dances are integrated into the action.
> The lyrics all sound as if they were translated
> from Spanish.[15]

By January 1962, the casting of *We Take the Town*, which
included Preston, Mike Kellin, John Cullum, Carmen Alvarez,
Kathleen Widdoes, Romeny Brent, and Lester Rawlins was complete.[16] Ostrow considered hiring Barbra Streisand for the lead
female role, but Preston nixed the idea as he wanted "a straight
actress" instead of a singer to play the part.[17] The plotline of the
musical told the story of Pancho Villa's "swath across Mexico on
his way to its Presidency."[18] Preston grew a flowing handlebar
mustache to play the role of "the legendary Mexican caballero
who fought, drank, sang, and roared his way from an obscure
bandit to a national hero."[19] The actor portrayed Villa with just
a trace of a Spanish accent, recognizing that the audience could
only listen to so much dialect in a two-hour production.[20]

The musical's initial preview opened on February 17, 1962
at the Shubert Theatre in New Haven, Connecticut. As the lead
actor, Preston was on-stage about "ninety-five percent of the
time, singing, dancing, and generally knocking himself out."[21]
During the New Haven soft opening, Preston experienced every
Broadway actor's worst nightmare: he lost his voice. Although

the doctor ordered him to remain in bed, he ignored the advice and instead appeared at the theater wearing a bathrobe with a towel around his head to spend hours coaching the rehearsal of his understudy, Art Lund.[22] A determined Preston made a miraculous recovery and appeared on stage the very next evening,

Broadway veteran John Cullum, who played an American press agent in We Take the Town, recalled Preston "was incredibly strong on stage, nobody could take the stage away from [him]. No one could hold a candle to him when he turned on his energy."[23] Cullum established an enduring admiration for and a camaraderie with Preston while the two actors performed together in the musical. Cullum described the gregarious and amicable Preston as a man who preferred to rub shoulders with the crew, a stark contrast to how most other actors spent their off-hours. Although not an excessive drinker, Preston "hung out in bars" and liked "to hang out with the stage hands" rather than actors after the curtain went down.[24]

The musical received mixed reviews in New Haven. Barbara Comstock White, the drama critic for the Record-Journal, described We Take the Town as a musical history and a "departure from the old forms and an experiment in a new sort of musical theater;" she also observed the audience was unaware if "they were supposed to laugh at Pancho or to deplore his savagery." White praised Preston as "magnificent" in the role of Pancho Villa, acting like "a buffoon one minute, a savage the next," though she lamented "the story, like its hero, tends to get out of hand." White ended her review by warning theatergoers that We Take the Town "breaks new musical ground, and does it with a bang. You may not like all of it, but we guarantee it will keep you awake."[25]

We Take the Town likewise received mixed reviews from Theodore H. Parker, the drama critic from the Hartford Courant, who described the musical as "an odd dish of chile." Despite his tepid reaction to the production, Parker praised Preston's performance, noting that the actor gave Pancho Villa "whimsical, wistful, turns that improve on history . . . and generally provides good entertainment."[26] Parker was unimpressed with the musical's script and viewed the storyline as depicting the same old, standard, tired formula inherent to musicals:

> There are a lot of shenanigans in *We Take the Town* but not much of it goes anywhere. Most of it is a prelude to action that does not come off. Instead, it settles for the usual interludes that are the stuff of standard musicals everywhere—love interest, comic bits, schmoozy atmosphere, backdrops for songs."[27]

In a departure from his even-keeled demeanor, a frustrated Preston lost his temper with the quarreling that surfaced during the production. The actor intervened when a heated and prolonged argument erupted between the director and choreographer; he pulled no punches in telling the choreographer to "shut up" and ordering the director to "get out of the theater and don't come back until you're ready to work." Preston's intervention resulted in a mutual apology between the director and choreographer and the resumption of rehearsals.[28] In an effort to improve and salvage *We Take the Town* before it was scheduled to reach Broadway in early April, Preston insisted that the producers and director undertake the necessary rewrites and repairs to the musical. Unfortunately, Preston's entreaties fell on deaf ears since no changes were made to the script.[29] It was no surprise that the production quickly unraveled almost as soon as *We Take the Town* moved on to Philadelphia for its second out-of-town preview.

The musical's fate began a downward spiral when actress Kathleen Widdoes, who played the role of a young, aristocratic lady sympathetic to Pancho Villa, gave the producers a two-week notice of her exit from *We Take the Town* on March 14. Widdoes never expected to land the role of Teresa del Castillo in the first place since she "really [could not] sing that well" despite taking a few singing lessons. Looking ahead to her career as an actress, Widdoes predicted that *We Take the Town* would be her last musical. The actress explained she decided to exit the musical production because she "had been hired as an actress but didn't have sufficient opportunities to act."[30]

We Take the Town opened in Philadelphia on Wednesday, February 28 to less than enthusiastic reviews. Henry Murdoch, the drama critic with the *Philadelphia Inquirer*, rejected the label of "musical adventure" that had been attached to the production. Murdoch praised Preston's performance as Villa, noting that he "gives a larger-than-life size picture of the illiterate peon on the warpath with a possible core of patriotism under the tough hide of vengeance," but panned the script which "tells of the rise and fall of Pancho Villa" and "surrounds Preston with a lot of empty spaces, whirling words, symbolic attitudes, and dance rituals." Murdoch informed his readers that although Preston "tries to break through [all of this] with his natural exuberance, he cannot escape the leaden script. Nor the overall pretentiousness of the show." Murdoch strongly suggested that major changes to the script were in order, since "as the show now stands, *We Take the Town* has sort of [an] action, pause, action beat" and urged director Alex Segal to "get rid of some of the pauses" to improve the viability of the production.[31]

Jerry Gaghan of the *Philadelphia Daily News* likewise praised Preston's performance but found the script and musical score lacking. Gaghan lauded Preston's performance for creating "the sort of full-bodied characterization rarely found in the song-and-dance field. He is, in truth, the stirring, sweating, sympathetic giant who became the Robin Hood of Northern Mexico." Gaghan identified the script as historically inaccurate as a "book play" and more in line with a ballad-type vehicle for the glorification of Pancho Villa. In addition, Gaghan disparaged the score by Matt Dubey and Harold Karr as lacking any "immediately discernible hit parade material."[32]

Preston immediately went into overdrive to salvage the production that he viewed as headed for collapse and ignored the advice of *Music Man* producer, Kermit Bloomgarden, to pull out of the show.[33] After a featured actor dropped from the musical, Preston "arranged and paid for the flight of a substitute from Los Angeles."[34] An experienced director may have been able to salvage the production, but those who attended the Philadelphia preview determined that *We Take the Town* was moving headlong toward a death spiral. The atmosphere of impending doom temporarily abated when Jerome Robbins agreed to replace Segal as the musical's director. The reprieve was short-lived; Robbins collapsed during rehearsals and Preston nixed the idea of Ostrow taking the helm as the show's director.[35] Not envisioning a path forward, Ostrow closed the musical on March 17, two weeks ahead of schedule, and "threw a farewell party for the company."[36] Unable to keep afloat in Philadelphia, the production did not make its planned Broadway debut at the Broadway Theatre on April 5.

Preston, who expressed hope that the musical would be revised for a Broadway run in the fall,[37] was devastated by the abrupt closure of the production. The failure of *We Take the Town* was a professional disappointment that Preston was unable to completely shake off. John Cullum observed that Preston, who frequently referred to the character of Pancho Villa as his favorite stage role,[38] "never fully recovered from [the flop] in terms of his sense of his stage work in New York."[39]

While the actor was grappling with the collapse of *We Take The Town*, Preston's alleged niece, Tracy Palmgren Monroe, recounted that his brother Frank reportedly rekindled a relationship with his former high school girlfriend, Margaret Deming.[40] Margaret, a striking raven-haired beauty and Los Angeles area model, served as a stand-in for actress Joan Bennett in the early 1940s. Frank and Margaret had been in love as teenagers, but Margaret's parents disapproved of the relationship and took steps to end it. Frank married, had children, and settled in Glendale; Margaret married in late August 1941 and established a family in Long Beach, California. The star-crossed high school sweethearts reconnected when Margaret moved to Los Angeles for a time-out from her rocky marriage. A year later, a pregnant Margaret returned home to her husband in Long Beach prior to the birth of her daughter, Tracy, in August 1963.[41]

As Preston continued to ride his post-*Music Man* fame, he was tapped to co-host the 1962 Tony Awards ceremony with Ray Bolger. That year, the ceremony was held in the Grand Ballroom of the Waldorf Astoria Hotel in New York City, and local television coverage of the Tony Awards was provided by WCBS-TV. Bolger emceed the first half of the program in which awards for Broadway's finest talent were presented for dramatic plays; Preston served as master of ceremonies for the second half of the show during which awards were presented for musical productions. Special awards were presented to Richard Rodgers,

Franco Zeffirelli, and drama critic Brooks Atkinson who was a founding member of the American Theatre Wing. Preston concluded the broadcast with a quote about the theater from eighteenth-century English writer Samuel Johnson.

The world premiere of the film adaptation of *The Music Man* was held at 9:45 p.m. on June 19, 1962 at the Palace Theatre in Meredith Willson's hometown of Mason City, Iowa. Preston, along with Shirley Jones, Ron Howard, Morton DaCosta, Arthur Godfrey, and Hedda Hopper, arrived in Mason City on Monday, June 18 and checked into the Hotel Hanford.[42] A post-premiere 'champagne supper' was held at midnight in the Wedgewood Room at the Hotel Hanford; invited guests did not begin dining until 1:00 a.m.[43] The 'champagne supper,' hosted by Technicolor Corporation, featured a menu of Lobster Newburg and Chicken a la King a la Sherry along with Meredith Willson at the hotel's piano playing and singing tunes from *The Music Man*. Preston amused the crowd by climbing on a luggage cart and cheekily riding it around the hotel lobby.[44]

The Music Man received shining reviews from Bosley Crowther at *The New York Times*, as well as from the *Chicago Tribune*, *Variety*, and a multitude of other newspapers and trade magazines across the country. Best of all, audiences were enthralled with the film. *Variety* recognized that it was Preston himself who made the film a timeless classic,

> Warners might have secured bigger screen names but it is impossible to imagine any of them matching Preston's authority backed by 883 stage performances. His know-how in this film is as close to a tour-de-force as is likely to be seen during the calendar year. Not only does he

project verve, singing and dancing with a beguiling style of his own creation, but his acting has remarkable plausibility.[45]

Likewise, *Sight and Sound* film critic Barbara Davies similarly identified,

> The film owes its punch essentially to *The Music Man* himself, a one-in-a-lifetime performance by Robert Preston, who played the part on Broadway. Not a natural singer or dancer, he has mastered the art of appearing to be both; and his handling of the rabble-rousing, talking-to-music number "Trouble" is a brilliant piece of timing and inflexion . . . Preston's performance is a triumph of sheer professionalism: it is his film from start to finish, all two and a half hours of it.[46]

In addition to its popularity with movie audiences, the film garnered six Academy Award nominations for Best Original Score, Best Picture, Best Production Design, Best Costume Design, Best Sound Mixing, and Best Film Editing. One Academy Award was presented to composer Ray Heindorf for Best Original Score for *The Music Man*. Gossip maven Hedda Hopper was greatly displeased that the Motion Picture Academy of Arts and Sciences overlooked Robert Preston for an Oscar nomination for his role as Harold Hill in *The Music Man* and blasted the Academy in her column on March 26, 1962:

> I'm so mad I could spit! If ever there was an actor who carried a show, that was Mr. Preston. He was

only great-the picture made millions. How could they nominate an Italian (Marcello Mastroianni) whose voice had to be dubbed, and overlook Preston? Peter O'Toole was fine in "Lawrence;" so was Greg Peck in "Mockingbird." Jack Lemmon was sensational in "Wine and Roses," also Burt Lancaster in "Bird Man." But for Bob not to get a nomination is outrageous![47]

The film won a Golden Globes for Best Motion Picture in the musical category and received nominations for Best Director and Best Original Score. In addition, Robert Preston and Shirley Jones were nominated for a Golden Globe for Best Actor and Best Actress in a Motion Picture Musical or Comedy.

Even with the extensive publicity received by *The Music Man* and the film's favorable reviews by critics, the movie's box office performance proved to be a disappointment for Warner Brothers. The film grossed slightly more than $7.8 million in domestic and international theaters, leaving Warner Brothers with a profit of $3.5 million after having spent $4.24 million in production costs plus publicity expenses.[48] The return on the film did not inspire confidence that musicals were making a comeback as some in the industry had expected.[49]

It was the folksy film version of *The Music Man* that transformed Robert Preston into an "A" list star after years of languishing in "B" movie roles. It soon became evident that although other actors could and would play the role of Harold Hill on stage or film, it was Preston who created and embodied the role and would own it for all time, making it virtually impossible for moviegoers to completely accept another actor in the role without comparing their performance to Preston.

Never one to remain idle, Preston decided to pivot to motion pictures and signed on to star in a Warner Brothers comedy initially titled *Not on Your Life!* later retitled to *Island of Love* (1963). *Music Man* director Morton DaCosta was tapped by Jack Warner to produce and direct the movie that would begin filming in Greece in June.[50] At about the same time, Preston was contacted by Broadway producer Leland Hayward who urged him to accept the coveted title role in the Irving Berlin play, *Mr. President*, slated to open on Broadway in the fall. Preston not only turned down the role but likewise nixed playing the lead in a musical version of *Dodsworth*.[51]

Preston found himself able to accept a role in *Island of Love* as a result of the premature closure of *We Take the Town*.[52] It was the "zany quality" of the script that ultimately induced Preston to accept a role in the film; he found himself attracted to the script written "in the tradition of the wild kind of breakaway comedy Billy Wilder does so well."[53] Preston was eager to be featured in a comedy film and had honed his comedic skills by watching old Carole Lombard movies. He acknowledged that the secret to an actor's success in a comedy role "is to play every situation with tremendous seriousness, no matter how funny the circumstances;" noting an actor must be able to "lose his own sense of humor to make a scene play hilariously."[54] The Technicolor sequences of the film were shot on the Greek is-lands of Hydra and Spetses, and featured Tony Randall, Georgia Moll, Walter Matthau, and Betty Bruce.

The *Island of Love* plotline involves Preston as Steve Blair, a failed, slick-talking producer of bad movies who travels to Greece with his writer friend, Paul (Randall), to increase his fortunes and escape the wrath of his latest mark (Matthau). While on the island of Paradeisos, Blair invents a scheme to promote the island as a tourist destination for lovers. To bolster his plan, Blair plants bogus artifacts for an archeologist to "discover," thus enhancing the island's erotic appeal to tourists. After making a boatload of cash, Blair falls in love with Elena (Moll), the niece of his latest mark, and decides to ditch his con-man ways for an honest life. Blair ultimately winds up in jail when his deception about the island is exposed, but a local cleric redeems him by validating the existence of a real love shrine on the island. Blair's mark drops his plan for revenge when he discovers his niece is set to wed the former con man.

Filming for the production kept pace with the prescribed schedule, although the cast experienced a fair share of mishaps. While filming in Greece, Tony Randall sustained a minor head injury after being struck with a replica of a Grecian urn that was expected to crumble upon impact. The crew realized all too late that the urn had been crafted by an Athens potter who was unfamiliar with Hollywood's "breakaway" technology.[55] Scalding Mediterranean temperatures found director Morton DaCosta shooting scenes with the thermometer registering 140°F. During one blazing day, DaCosta burned his fingers when he grabbed an antique brass vase that had been broiling in the hot sun.[56] Like Randall, Preston also suffered injuries while on location in Greece. While skin diving in the Aegean Sea, the actor sustained a foot wound that bled profusely after he stepped on a sharp rock. When Preston arrived back on the Warner Brothers lot in August, he was visibly limping and surgeons were called in to lance his infected foot.[57]

Catherine accompanied Preston to Greece at the beginning of July for the filming of *Island of Love*. As a dutiful wife, she made every possible effort to remain in the background so as to not interfere with her husband's professional responsibilities.[58]

Catherine spent her days abroad washing her husband's socks, writing the letters he lacked the time to write, and dabbling in oil painting. The couple spent time together each evening after 6:00 p.m. when the daily filming was complete.[59] During a 1962 interview with the *Indianapolis Star*, Catherine disclosed that she envisioned her role as a "strong wife" who "sees that her husband gets his proper rest and health care." When questioned about her husband's career, Catherine indicated she has refrained from proffering career advice unless asked, noting the extent of her involvement in her husband's work was "sending his reviews to his mother and father."[60]

On August 12, The *Los Angeles Times* reported that filming of *Island of Love* had concluded twenty-three days ahead of schedule.[61] That same day, Preston and his wife returned to the United States on TWA Flight 845 from Athens, Greece. DaCosta, Preston, Randall, and other cast and crew members stopped briefly in New York to film interior scenes for the movie before proceeding on to Warner Brothers Studios in Burbank, California.[62] Preston's wife, Catherine, temporarily returned to the couple's home in Rye, New York, but drove out to Hollywood a week before the final filming was completed so she would be able to "ride back to New York with him."[63]

Island of Love was released in Los Angeles on June 5, 1963 and met with lukewarm reviews. Despite the film's breathtaking views of the Greek islands, the erotic Grecian statuary, and scenes of beautiful women on the beach, the New York *Daily News* awarded the film two-and-a-half stars, pointing out that Preston and Randall were unable to "get much mileage" from the gags and jokes which punctuated the film.[64] *Time* magazine described the film as a "tasteless gaffe-riot"[65] while another publication declared *Island of Love* as "short of anything special."[66]

Variety announced the movie had been panned by the National Legion of Decency; the self-proclaimed watchdog group gave the film a "B" rating for being "morally objectionable," labeled the movie as "tawdry," and declared the film's theme had been "developed in an atmosphere of vulgarity, suggestiveness, and irreverence."[67] Despite the weak reviews, *Island of Love* was the tenth most profitable film release of the year.[68] The following year, Preston filed a $64,000 lawsuit against Warner Brothers Studio, claiming he was still owed $30,000 for *Island of Love* as well as $34,000 for soundtrack recordings for *The Music Man*.[69]

During the first week in September 1962, Paramount Studios announced it had signed Robert Preston and actress Jean Simmons to star in the black-and-white film version of James Agee's Pulitzer Prize-winning play, *A Death in the Family*.[70] Both Preston and Simmons agreed to appear in the film, retitled *All The Way Home* (1963), on a deferred salary basis by accepting a share of the film's profits rather than a set salary.[71] As a direct result of the salary arrangements negotiated with Preston and Simmons, producer David Susskind hoped to be able to keep the film's budget to under $650,000.[72] Preston, in particular, agreed to accept a role in *All The Way Home* as a "labor of love."[73] The actor became acquainted with author James Agee when the two appeared in *A Bride Comes to Yellow Sky*; Agee played the role of the town drunk in the film while Preston was cast as the town sheriff.[74]

All The Way Home would be filmed under the direction of Alex Segal, who had directed Preston in the ill-fated stage musical *We Take the Town*. Rehearsals for the film began in New York during the week of September 24 at the Central Plaza Jazz Emporium on lower Second Avenue, with Segal having the cast rehearse the script before filming scenes, as if it were a stage play.[75]

All The Way Home was set to be filmed in Knoxville, Tennessee, the hometown of novelist James Agee. The film cast arrived in Knoxville on Sunday, October 7, a day before the start of production, and was feted at a dinner at the Hotel Andrew Johnson by the Hamilton National Bank.[76] In addition to Preston and Jean Simmons, the film also featured Pat Hingle, Aline MacMahon, Thomas Chalmers, John Cullum, Ronnie Claire Edwards, and seven-year-old Michael Kearney. Preston was particularly impressed by Jean Simmons whose star status and personal/professional demeanor he equated with Barbara Stanwyck's. He acknowledged that working with Simmons was "one of the happiest experiences" of his career, noting "there aren't many like her today" who are "always on time, [display] no outbursts of temperament, [and are] completely free of jealousy."[77]

One of the first orders of business on the set involved period costuming of the cast. Despite being attired in the men's fashions of the early 1900s, the director felt Preston's haircut did not look "1915 enough" for the film. To achieve a turn-of-the-century look, Preston had to submit his wavy locks to old-time hair clippers. The experience brought back memories for the actor who had not received a haircut with hair clippers since he was a young child.[78] A week into filming, the entire cast and production crew were notified they would be required to vacate their digs at the Hotel Andrew Johnson and spend the following weekend in four stationary Pullman train cars. Preston, as well as the other actors and film crew, were evicted from their hotel suites to accommodate an influx of college football fans who would be flooding into town to attend the Alabama-Tennessee football game on October 20. Preston took the disruption in stride, joking, "It'll be just like playing one-nighters at a couple of whistle stops–only without getting off the train."[79]

The film's script was based on Agee's 1957 novel, an autobiographical story that chronicled his early childhood experience with loss. The plot centers around six-year-old Rufus Follet (Kearney) who treasures the time with his father, Jay (Preston), while watching a movie, accompanying him to the neighborhood tavern, and watching trains pass through town. The relationship between Jay and his pregnant wife, Mary (Simmons), is solid, although Mary takes issue with her husband's occasional drinking and lack of religious faith. When Jay is unexpectedly killed in an automobile accident, his young son is thrown into despair. To assuage his grief, Rufus revisits the spot where he and his father spent time together train-watching. Mary Follet comforts Rufus and tells him she is expecting a child who will keep the memory of his father alive before mother and son return to the family home to face the heartache and hope of life following the tragedy.

To maintain the authenticity of the early 1900s, two steam locomotives, each over 50 years old, were brought to Knoxville from Johnson City via a network of railroads. The locomotives had to be transported to the filming location, rather than driven, as the antique locomotives lacked the necessary automatic safety equipment. The cost to transport the engines to Knoxville set back the production by $800 each way plus an additional $200 a day in rental fees.[80] The issue of authenticity also extended to the automobiles used in the film. Preston was one of the only members of the cast and crew who knew how to operate and drive the 1915 Model T Ford used in the movie. When Preston's large feet began hitting too many of the car's floor pedals, he removed his shoes to allow him to properly operate the vehicle.[81] Director Alex Segal planned to film a scene in which the Model T was parked with the engine off but with its headlights on, overlooking the fact that the vehicle was not built with a battery. Segal was not aware that electricity for the headlights on the Model T was supplied by a magneto electrical system that only operated when the engine was running, and sought to connect an external battery to the car to allow him to film the Model T with the engine off and the headlights on. Preston objected to having a modern battery hooked up to the car; he was keenly aware that antique car buffs would notice the historical inaccuracy portrayed on screen. In the end, the scene was filmed without using the car's headlights[82]

Scenes involving the funeral of Jay Follet were filmed at the local Alcoholics Anonymous chapter meeting hall that was staged to resemble a funeral parlor. Producer David Susskind was awakened early one morning at 3:00 a.m. in his hotel suite by a group of Alcoholics Anonymous members who demanded $385 for repairs to the floor of their meeting hall. The AA members contended that the film crew ruined the floor when they moved the coffin used for the visitation and funeral scenes.[83] As the deceased father, Jay Follet, Preston's role required him to spend four days lying motionless in a casket during the filming of the movie's heartbreaking visitation tableau.[84] When the actor began his climb into the coffin, the coins in his pocket began to jingle; he quickly turned to producer David Susskind and quipped, "Who says you can't take it with you?"[85] After the final editing of the film, Preston appeared lying in repose in the coffin for a total of two seconds during the funeral service scene.[86] If having to lie in a coffin for prolonged periods wasn't bad enough, the actor was injured on the set when a door jammed and a transom fell on his head and foot. Preston was whisked away for x-rays at a local physician's office and was released back to the set when it was determined that the bruise to his foot and the slight blow to his head did not constitute serious injuries.[87]

As he did with most children he encountered, Preston took a shine to Michael Kearney, the child actor who played his son, Rufus Follet, in the film. Kearney later described Preston as charismatic and outgoing in contrast to actress Jean Simmons who "mostly kept to herself" on set.[88] The bond between father and son onscreen reflected Preston's offscreen interaction with his young co-star. Kearney acknowledged that Preston "really made [him] feel like he was [his] dad, not only on the set, but also off the set."[89] Preston was generous with his time and attention to Kearney during filming, "spent time" with the young actor, and "talked to [him] even after the cameras stopped."[90] Kearney and his family continued to stay in touch with Preston for several years after the filming of *All the Way Home*. When Kearney was nine-years-old, he and his mother went to visit Preston backstage during the actor's appearance in the Broadway run of *Ben Franklin in Paris*.[91]

After scouring the Tennessee countryside and coming up empty, the film's prop department sent out a casting call in late October for live butterflies, with the compensation rate of one dollar per insect.[92] The butterfly ads paid off; over twenty-five insects were submitted by the public. Butterflies, which symbolize resurrection and rebirth, were needed for the burial scene when a butterfly was needed to land on Jay Follet's coffin and then symbolically fly out of the grave and into the sky. This particular scene was never viewed by moviegoers since all of the cemetery footage was edited out of the final version of the film.[93]

While in Knoxville, Preston was able to reconnect with fellow World War II veteran Grady Adkisson; the two men served together in the Army Air Corps in Florida during 1943. Adkisson, now Dean of Admissions at the University of Tennessee, arranged to take Preston on a hunt at a mountain game preserve in nearby Walland, Tennessee. Preston was able to bag a 180-pound Russian boar on his third shot.[94] Unable to nail the boar on his first try, his fellow hunters observed the long-time tradition of cutting off Preston's shirttail.[95] Preston made many friends during his brief stay in Knoxville and attended several sporting and social events. An article that appeared in the *Knoxville News-Sentinel* six years later revealed that Preston's name surfaced in the divorce trial of a local surgeon who accused his wife of having an affair with Preston during the Knoxville filming of *All The Way Home.*[96]

With approximately 40 percent of the film shot on location in Knoxville, the on-site filming wrapped in early November and allowed Preston to fly back to New York on November 10. The last scene of the film was shot on November 11 with Jean Simmons and Michael Kearney.[97] Interior scenes were later filmed at DuPont Studios in New York and subsequently edited into the film.

As 1962 drew to a close, Preston was signed to appear in a television special with Carol Burnett slated to air in February 1963 and was tapped to host an hour-long telecast of *Dinner with The President,* sponsored by the Anti-Defamation League of B'nai B'rith. *Dinner With the President* was broadcast to the nation on CBS from the Sheraton-Park Hotel in Washington, D.C. on January 31, 1963. The program featured a tribute to America's democratic legacy with folk music performances by Judy Collins, Lynn Gold, the Clancy Brothers and Tommy

Makem, Will Holt, Josh White, and Odetta. Judy Collins, recently discharged from National Jewish Hospital in Denver after treatment for tuberculosis, flew to D.C. to perform in the telecast.[98] Collins arrived late to the venue to find rehearsals already underway. In her book, *Sweet Judy Blue Eyes*, Collins initially misidentified Preston as Robert Ryan as the star with whom she performed at the presidential tribute. Collins corrected the error in an August 16, 2015 post on her Facebook page in which she identified Robert Preston, not Ryan, as the individual with whom she appeared in the *Dinner With the President* program.

Preston was already onstage rehearsing when Collins arrived at the Sheraton-Park Hotel. Collins, who knew Preston from New York, dedicated a passage in her book to describe her interactions with him and, in the process, provided a first-hand insight into his personality and political leanings:

> His presence dominated the room even though at that moment it was filled only with waiters and performers. [He] was an impressive man, tall and handsome, with dark hair that fell over his eyes that seemed to single me out, looking directly into mine . . . I had the feeling that [he] couldn't have cared less if the crowds had not yet arrived. He was the same in public as in private. His looks and demeanor set him apart as a star, but his smile was warm and welcoming and his politics (He was an early opponent of the war in Vietnam) were as friendly to my own as his smile. He put his arms around me in a welcoming embrace, and I felt I belonged; he was someone who made you

feel that way always, whether he was in the limelight or you were, or neither of you were. It is a
rare quality.[99]

Just before the broadcast, Preston proposed a toast to the
assembled performers, wishing them all well and "express-
ing hope that the poetry and music of the evening would help
convince Kennedy to reconsider the war in Indochina."[100] The
telecast concluded with the presentation of the America's
Democratic Legacy Award to President Kennedy followed by
the President's prepared remarks. From Collins's vantage point,
the event proved to be a great success. After the conclusion of
the telecast, all of the performers assembled in a reception line
to shake President Kennedy's hand.[101] The program was a hit
with viewers and considered a TV milestone, given the prime-
time appearance of President Kennedy[102]

The next month, Preston appeared as the sole guest in a
Carol Burnett television special. The actor received an invitation from the twenty-nine-year-old comedienne to share the
stage with her in an hour-long CBS special titled *Carol and
Company*. Since the network allowed Carol to cast the guest
stars of her choice for her first television special and, because
she was a "great big fat fan of Robert Preston," she asked
Preston to appear on the program.[103]

Burnett first met Preston in 1962 and asked her agents to approach the actor about appearing on her TV special. Burnett's
agents were meeting with Preston over dinner to discuss the
television special when Burnett unexpectedly crashed the dinner
meeting because she needed to know "if *he* wanted to work with
me," believing they needed to meet face-to-face to determine "if
the 'chemistry' was there."[104] Burnett considered it a coup for

Preston to agree to appear in her special since his television appearances were limited.[105] Truth be told, Preston was pleased to appear on *Carol and Company*. The actor's long-time friend, Henry Fonda, let Preston know he was a "mighty lucky person" to be tapped to appear with Carol Burnett," noting that he would be willing to trade places with Preston without receiving any compensation.[106] Preston wholeheartedly agreed with other actors who advised him that "working with Carol is about the best thing a person in this business can do."[107] He praised Burnett noting "she is not only a tremendous talent and remarkably warm character, but she seems to bring out the best in everyone she works with [with] no apparent effort. In fact, I sometimes think she is deliberately trying to make other people look good rather than merely concentrating on her own performance."[108]

Rehearsals for the show were held in the auditorium of the Fraternal Club in Manhattan[109] and the special aired on CBS on the evening of February 24, 1963, replacing the regularly scheduled programs *Candid Camera* and *What's My Line?* The telecast began with an opening monologue from Burnett and a musical number in which she sang "I Don't Want to be Nelson," a song reminiscent of her playing the part of Nelson Eddy in childhood skits with her cousin, who always assumed the role of Jeannette MacDonald. Burnett then introduced Preston by announcing to the television audience, "He's very sexy. He's got shoulders like Joan Crawford."[110] Burnett and Preston then launched into a series of duets including "Row, Row, Row Your Boat," "You Are My Sunshine," "Frere Jacques," and "My Bonnie Lies Over the Ocean."

When Burnett questioned Preston about why his film characters always seemed to die, the dialogue provided a segue to the actor singing a clever, satirically written solo by Ken Welch about all of the death scenes he enacted in the movies. The first few stanzas of Preston's fast-paced song went like this:

> Yes, I died a thousand deaths, drew a thousand
> dying breaths
> No one ever died as many times as I
> Die in glory, died in pain, died for love and died
> in vain
> I said 'Hello' and then—pow-pow—goodbye.
> I died all over.
> In frozen lands, on Arabian sands, in Chesapeake
> Bay, on old Broadway, in a London fog, in
> a slimy bog, and in and on and under the
> Atlantic. And the Pacific.
> And the Red Sea. And the Dead Sea. Once in a
> reservoir.
> And they killed me in various places
> In Kenya, Yika, Tahiti, Burma and Bombay.
> Also, in Amarillo and Abilene and they ran me
> down on the Appian Way in a chariot.
> Hung with a lariat by the neck until dead in Tulsa
> Died of thirst on the Oregon Trail
> Then done shot me, oh they got me right outside
> Dodge City delivering the mail.
> I died in jail.
> With a pow, pow and a bang, bang, bang
> With a 'take that,' ugh and aah.
> And a wham, bam, look out Sam, and oh no—ah!
> With a pow, pow and an e-e-e-e-h, En Garde! Ah
> ha! Ugh!

(Whistles like a bomb drop) Pow! (Breathing
   heavy)
"I love you" (Feigns dead) . . . [111]
(Ken Welch, "I Died A Thousand Deaths")

Preston compared "I Died a Thousand Deaths" to the song
"Ya Got Trouble" from *The Music Man*, noting "Trouble" was "a
little difficult," but "I Died a Thousand Deaths" was "a lot more
intricate" and downright "impossible."[112]

Preston and Burnett moved on to a sketch about a bad date
in which they portrayed a couple in the gentleman's apartment
listening to records on his stereo system. Preston's character
ignores Burnett's seductive entreaties and is more interested in
the sounds emanating from his hi-fi stereo system. He implores
Burnett to listen to his recordings of a train wreck and a firing
squad, announcing, "the great thing is you can't believe it isn't
happening right in this room."[113] The sketch concludes and the
fervor of Burnett's character wanes when Preston pours beer
down her dress. Preston found it necessary to keep his eyes off
Burnett during the sketch, aware that "she can raise an elbow
or an eyebrow and get more comedy appeal from these simple
movements than Mack Sennett got with a whole truckload of
gushy pies."[114]

Carol Burnett created her iconic character 'The Charwoman'
for the *Carol and Company* program.[115] Burnett entered the stage
dressed as a charwoman, complete with cap and ragged clothes,
and began mopping the floor. When the charwoman hears the
rhythmic beating of a drum, she begins a bump-and-grind mock
strip tease to David Rose's burlesque tune, "The Stripper," before exiting the stage. When the charwoman returns to the
empty stage, she sits on her bucket and sings the sad song,

"Nobody."[116] Preston and Burnett ended the show with a final duet, "Just Can't Say Goodbye" about the difficulties of saying 'so long' to each other and the television audience.

Most television critics around the country saw *Carol and Company* as a "highly entertaining hour."[117] Dwight Newton gave high marks to the telecast in *The San Francisco Examiner*, praising Preston as "a fine foil" for Burnett and for lending the program "added spirit and strength and charm."[118] Cynthia Lowry of the *Associated Press* described the Burnett TV special as "a sparking hour," lauded Preston's "competent presence," and declared the special as a "television treat."[119] Although *Carol and Company* generally received good reviews, Jack Gould of the all-important *New York Times* went out of his way to criticize Burnett. Gould declared that Preston "who without seeming to be really trying radiates a commanding presence and vigorous vitality . . . and such was the force of his attractive personality and magnetism that he walked off with whatever honors the evening allowed."[120] Gould snidely declared Burnett was "overshadowed" by Preston and displayed "little of the sense of intuitive timing that is the stamp of the comedienne."[121]

The next phase of Preston's life can best be viewed through the lens of a mid-life crisis. As he matured into his middle adult years, Preston achieved success and acclaim in his work, gained greater self-confidence, maintained his ambition, and continued to hone his acting skills. Despite all of the professional success, the next two years of Preston's personal life were fraught with vacillation, instability, and rapprochement with his wife.

Preston received a script for a revival of George Bernard Shaw's play, *Too Good To Be True*, in November 1962 from producers Patrizia "Buff" Cobb and Paul Vroom, and returned the signed contract by the first week of January 1963.[122] According to actress Lillian Gish, the entire cast wanted to appear in the Shaw revival and agreed to work for reduced salaries in a limited run of the play that would be featured from March to June.[123] The stellar cast composed of Preston, Sir Cedric Hardwicke, Cyril Ritchard, Lillian Gish, Eileen Heckert, Glynis Johns, David Wayne, and Ray Middletown began rehearsals under the direction of Albert Marre on February 24, 1963. Just before the Broadway opening of the play on March 12 at the 54th Street Theatre, Preston fell on the ice at his Rye, New York home and broke three ribs. Undeterred by his injuries, the actor did not miss a performance "despite the fact that his part called for him to be thrown all over the stage."[124]

Sir Cecil Hardwicke had played the lead role in the original 1932 production of Shaw's play. Preston played this part in the revival and Hardwicke instead played the character's father. Hardwicke took the role reversal in stride and, according to Preston, saw it as "a big lark."[125] Preston conveyed that "there has been nothing but calm, peace, and eager cooperation" among the actors during rehearsals and downplayed that the cast was receiving limited compensation noting, "who needs money when it's all one big love affair among us."[126]

Preston found himself drawn into a relationship with fellow cast member Glynis Johns during the rehearsal and production of *Too Good To Be True*. Glynis was a blonde, green-eyed, breathy-voiced Welsh actress who had appeared in several notable movies including *Miranda* (1948), *The Court Jester* (1955), and *The Sundowners* (1960) for which she was nominated for an Academy Award for Best Supporting Actress.

Glynis Johns was born in Pretoria, South Africa on October 5, 1923 while her Welsh theatrical parents were there on tour. Her father, Mervyn Johns, was a well-known Welsh actor and Glynis was the fourth generation of the Johns family to pursue an acting career. She began performing on stage at the Old Vic in London at age twelve and soon after made her British movie debut at age thirteen. Her acting trademark was her throaty voice which various critics described as a cross between that of actresses Jean Arthur and Margaret Sullavan.[127]

By 1963, the actress had been wed and divorced three times to actor Antony Forwood (1942-1948), Colgate Palmolive executive David Foster (1952-1956), and London businessman Cecil Henderson (1960-1962), as well as involved in a high-profile 1951 engagement to British film producer Antony Darnborough. Actor Christopher Plummer, who described Glynis as possessing "pixie charm"[128] was well aware of the actress's history with men. When sitting across the dinner table from Glynis and fellow British actress Deborah Kerr, Plummer came to the ungallant realization that "between them they'd had more lovers than Napoleon's army."[129] Glynis, who had one son, Gareth Forwood, from her first marriage, owned a chalet in Switzerland. In keeping with her somewhat ditzy persona, Glynis once parked her car in the parking lot at the Geneva airport when en route to the United States and "completely forgot about it" for the next two years until she was contacted by an airport representative who requested that she arrange to remove the car from its parking spot.[130]

Too Good To Be True previewed on March 9 and subsequently opened at the 54th Street Theatre on March 12. Glynis's role in the play involved a lot of yelling; her fellow cast members often held their breath hoping that she could finish the show without losing her voice.[131] Reviews of the play were mixed. Although Howard Taubman from *The New York Times* described the play as a "pert revival,"[132] *Time* magazine pronounced the Shaw production as "a cursedly garrulous bore,"[133] and critic William Glover declared the play "static" with an uninspired message.[134]

Glover described the revival's plot as "a rickety scaffold about a jewel robbery, fake kidnapping, and adventure in far places," concluding that the play was "an earnest try, but no show."[135]

When Preston's relationship with Glynis Johns became serious, he initiated a separation from Catherine after twenty-three years of marriage. During the week of May 6, Preston moved out of the marital residence in Rye and into a suite at the legendary Warwick Hotel in Manhattan.[136] He planned to drive cross-country to Los Angeles in June and return to his West Coast home with his parents. In the interim, Preston's parents, Doc and Ruth, visited him in New York on Mother's Day weekend. Preston arranged for his mother and father to see *Too Good To Be True* and took them out for a Mother's Day meal at Absinthe House, introducing them to the restaurant regulars as "Doc and Gertie."[137]

In an interview with columnist Earl Wilson on May 17, Preston discussed his marital separation without disclosing the reason for the split. Preston told Wilson, "How can you give a reason for a thing like this? Everybody considers it dreadful, as I do. This was one of our businesses' [sic] happy marriages."[138] The actor went on to express relief that the impending divorce would not impact any children and acknowledged, "That's one thing I'm pleased about—there are no kids involved."[139] Within a week of Preston's interview with Earl Wilson, Glynis Johns was officially signed by Walt Disney to appear in her third Disney picture, *Mary Poppins* (1964),[140] with filming to commence in June. Glynis desperately wanted the lead role in the film, but was instead chosen to play the mother of the children who would be cared for by Mary Poppins. It was reported that Glynis "couldn't hide her disappointment when Julie Andrews got the role" of Mary Poppins, but she "thought it over and agreed to do another part in the film."[141]

The producers' plans to keep *Too Good To Be True* open through the summer of 1963 collapsed. Since the contracts of the original revival cast were set to expire, they planned to replace the cast and move the Shaw play to a different theater. The plan did not materialize as "business became too unsettled" for the producers to underwrite the risk involved in extending the play's run.[142] With plans for an extended run dashed, *Too Good To Be True* closed on June 1 after ninety-four performances.

As the romance between Preston and Glynis Johns flourished, they were spotted having dinner at Absinthe House on the night the play closed and appeared "more relaxed than ever" now that their relationship had gone public.[143] A few days later, the lovebirds were canoodling at the Embers nightclub in Manhattan where they requested to hear the ballad, "What Kind of Fool Am I?"[144] The next day, June 9, Glynis flew to Hollywood to begin filming *Mary Poppins.*

Preston was interviewed by Harrison Carroll during his cross-country road trip to Los Angeles and was pressed on whether a divorce from Catherine was in the works. The conversation between Carroll and Preston is telling and suggests that perhaps Preston was having second thoughts about his relationship with Glynis. Preston told Carroll he had not been in communication with his wife since the separation in early May and surprisingly indicated that the issue of divorce would be "up to her."[145] When Preston was asked if he planned to continue dating Glynis Johns, he responded with, "I probably will."[146] Following up on Preston's comments, Harrison Carroll contacted Catherine Craig by phone at the couple's New York home. Catherine made it clear to Carroll, and indirectly to her husband and Glynis, that divorce was not in the cards: "Absolutely no divorce. We've been through this once before, if you remember. Anything else you'll have to get from Bob. The separation was his decision."[147] Broadway columnist Dorothy Kilgallen was quick to pounce on Catherine Craig's pronouncement that "there will be no divorce," pointing out that this wifely proclamation would be "enough to make a more timid girl than Glynis Johns extremely nervous."[148]

Now both in Los Angeles, Preston and Glynis began to make plans for the future. He openly discussed plans to purchase a house in Malibu once his divorce was final and the two were able to be married.[149] Preston arranged for Glynis to visit his mother, sister-in-law, and young niece to lay the groundwork for her acceptance by his family. Preston's niece recalled Glynis arrived "wearing a whole bottle of perfume" and took great pains to get on the good side of Preston's mother, Ruth, and sister-in-law, Florence.[150] Ruth, who knew her son inside and out, quickly recognized that Preston and his paramour were not well suited, and it would be only a matter of time before the relationship would fizzle. Ruth predicted to Florence, "Watch . . . give her enough rope and she will hang herself." Preston's niece indicated that in the end, Glynis "was too controlling for Pres," and within a matter of months, "boom—[the relationship] was over."[151]

Preston and Glynis continued to be spotted together in and around Los Angeles for the next several weeks. On one occasion, they dined on the Sunset Strip before venturing to Ye Little Club to catch the set of comic Dave Madden[152] and were regulars at the Tonga Lei Polynesian restaurant in Malibu.[153]

In the interim, Catherine Craig selected a quiet beach location on the East Coast and retreated there for a few weeks, taking frequent walks along the shore to collect seashells. She knew all too well that the entertainment industry was hard on marriages, with "temptation at every turn." Although

Catherine realized she "hadn't married a saint," she knew Preston's "love for her ran deep and true" and that he would eventually return to her.[154]

Glynis Johns's career appeared to be on the upswing: she was filming *Mary Poppins* and had signed on for a CBS situation comedy series. Since the conclusion of *Too Good To Be True*, Preston was "in clamorous demand for all kinds of roles–comedy, straight drama, and musicals."[155] At long last, he had achieved the luxury of being able to alternate his acting focus between Hollywood and Broadway. In addition, Preston was named chairman of the Los Angeles County annual Hope Chest campaign fund drive for research to help combat multiple sclerosis, and was slated to make personal, radio, and television appearances on behalf of the drive beginning on August 1.[156] Now residing with his parents, Preston was asked by Hedda Hopper about Doc and Ruth Meservey's thoughts concerning his marital separation. He acknowledged his parents did address the issue, noting "they occasionally make noises like parents," adding "they have every right" to do so.[157]

When the best male ballet dancer of all time, Rudolf Nureyev, performed in the United States for the first time in 1963, he stayed in the home of Hollywood publicist Rupert Allan. Preston received a highly coveted invitation to a party for Nureyev, cohosted by Allan and his partner, movie producer Frank McCarthy, at Allan's Beverly Hills home. Preston arrived at the soirée with Glynis Johns in tow, but the two left the event before dinner was served. When Hedda Hopper queried Preston about why he and Glynis were departing so early, he replied, "Too many stars around."[158] With filming for Glynis's television series scheduled to start on July 16, Preston embarked on a fifteen-city promotional tour for *All the Way Home* before the film's release later that fall.

In the meantime, Catherine used the marital separation to renew her acting career. She appeared in Jean Kerr's comedy *Jenny Kissed Me* at the Bucks County Playhouse in New Hope, Pennsylvania. The plot of the comedy centers around charming eighteen-year-old Jenny who comes to reside in the household of an elderly priest, Father Moynihan. The priest, as well as several area youths, throw their efforts into making Jenny more fashionable and attractive to young men. Jenny ultimately finds romance, but remains a simple yet attractive young woman. Theater and film actor James Daly and his children Tyne, Glynn, and Tim also appeared in the production. While appearing in *Jenny Kissed Me*, Catherine was the house guest of Mike Ellis and his wife. Ellis, the dynamic theater producer who owned and operated the Bucks County Playhouse, planned to have Catherine appear in another Playhouse production later in the season.[159] During her stint in *Jenny Kissed Me*, Broadway columnist Dorothy Kilgallen reported backstage rumors at the Playhouse suggested that a "Philadelphia gent (was) smitten" with Catherine.[160]

In mid-July, Preston let word out to the press that his relationship with Glynis Johns was solid and their "union was imminent," yet just a week later, the couple's future marriage had been placed on the inactive list.[161] Glynis filed for United States residency and citizenship, fueling speculation about a fourth trip to the altar with Preston. The actress explained that she met Preston "while working together in *Too Good To Be True* on Broadway," but rejected any notion of being a homewrecker, indicating she did not believe "there is ever any such thing as anyone stepping in and breaking up a marriage that is happy and strong."[162]

By mid-August, Preston's relationship with Glynis Johns began to unravel. On August 11, it was reported that Glynis had already been spotted dating someone else,[163] but on the very next evening, Glynis and Preston presented as a happy couple at Tracton's restaurant in Los Angeles.[164] Glynis was injured in an automobile accident in Culver City later that month and "suffered facial injuries when her car swerved out of control and hit a parked vehicle." Despite an inch-long cut on the inside of her lip, a bruised chin, and treatment for shock, Glynis was back at work on the set of her television series within a couple of hours.[165] In September, gossip columnist Sheilah Graham sounded the death knell for the Robert Preston–Glynis Johns relationship,[166] and observed Preston was "playing it safe" by continuing his residence at the Warwick Hotel until such time that Catherine could "find it in her heart to forgive him for his little fling with Glynis Johns."[167] Glynis continued to work on the *Glynis* series and had taken a year's lease on Rod Steiger's Malibu beach house.[168] The actress's fall television program on CBS, slated to air on Wednesday evenings at 8:30 p.m., premiered on September 25. The show, which centered around an attorney and his scatter-brained mystery writer wife who constantly encounter whodunit situations,[169] nosedived in the ratings and only lasted one season before being canceled by the network on December 18 after thirteen episodes. Glynis recovered quickly from the dissolution of her relationship with Preston, announcing her engagement to screenwriter Elliott Arnold in June 1964.[170]

During his separation from Catherine, Preston received an invitation to attend the wedding of Peggy Lee's daughter, Nicki Lee Barbour. Nicki retained a soft spot in her heart for Robert Preston, the man who had lavished attention on the then eight-year-old child during his relationship with her mother in the early 1950s. Nicki treasured the memories of that pseudo-father-daughter relationship and insisted on inviting Preston to be a part of her marriage celebration.

Nicki Barbour was a month-and-a-half shy of her twentieth birthday when she and her twenty-one-year-old boyfriend, Richard Foster, decided to tie the knot. The couple exchanged vows at a Catholic church in West Hollywood on September 14, 1963, and Peggy Lee held a posh wedding reception for the newlyweds in the garden of her hilltop home on Kimridge Road in Beverly Hills.[171] Preston not only accepted Nicki's invitation to be a guest at her wedding, but re-appeared on the scene and behaved "almost like a second father of the bride."[172] Preston assisted Peggy Lee with making "two five-foot-long swans with chicken-wire frames, filled with thousands of chrysanthemums and bachelor buttons for eyes, that floated on the pool during the reception,"[173] and he became a "welcome member of the wedding," even to Nicki's father David Barbour.[174] According to James Gavin's biography of Peggy Lee, the songstress, "still pined for Robert Preston [and] seeing him [again] made her all the more wistful, but she didn't let on."[175]

That same week, Preston closed a deal to appear in two Broadway shows. In the first production, *Nobody Loves an Albatross*, Preston would play a flamboyant Hollywood writer/producer[176] and the high-energy role would require him to be on stage in every scene of the performance.[177] Rehearsals for *Nobody Loves an Albatross* were scheduled to begin on November 1.[178] Preston also signed on for the lead role of Benjamin Franklin in the musical *Ben Franklin in Paris*, slated for Broadway in the fall of 1964. The script for the musical focused on the adventures of Benjamin Franklin during his stint in Paris as ambassador to France.[179]

Meanwhile, *All the Way Home* had its initial screening at the first New York Film Festival held at Lincoln Center's Philharmonic Hall; the movie was one of the nineteen films screened at the festival between September 10 and September 19.[180] Catherine, now back at the marital home in Rye, New York, attended the festival and screened the debut of *All the Way Home* on September 14. She was so unnerved by the glimpse of her husband lying dead in a coffin that she burst into tears, and called her wayward husband at the Warwick Hotel to tell him to come home.[181]

Catherine was well aware of the human frailties that vexed her husband. She was deeply in love with Preston, yet realistic about the temptations that befell actors and actresses in the entertainment industry. Catherine once told her nephew, "You are absolutely out of your mind if you ever let your husband go on a location shoot, and you don't go along with him."[182] One key to the success of the Prestons' marriage hinged on Catherine's willingness to endure tough times. Preston gravitated to exotic blondes; women so very different from his reserved, brunette wife. When a rival surfaced, Catherine instinctively knew to wait out the infatuation. When she learned of Preston's liaison with Glynis Johns, Catherine was so confident of "his return to their fold" that she clipped the daily *New York Times* crossword puzzles for three and a half months and stacked the clippings on his bedroom nightstand where he found them upon his return to the marital residence.[183] On September 27, syndicated gossip columnist Earl Wilson announced Preston had sent out "official word" that he and his wife, Catherine, had reconciled and that the couple was "very happy."[184] Two days later, Preston and his wife were spotted dining "cozily at Danny's Hideaway" in New York City.[185]

With the marital reconciliation an apparent fait accompli, Preston turned his attention to his calendar for October 1963, a month that proved to be a busy one for the actor. On October 8, Preston both hosted and performed in an episode of the premiere fall episode of the *Bell Telephone Hour* on WNBC. The hour-long program featured internationally renowned ballet dancers Rudolph Nureyev and Svetlana Beriosova performing "Black Swan Pas de Deux," the folk-singing Chad Mitchell Trio singing "Moscow Nights" in Russian, and pianist Grant Johannesen playing a Ravel piano concerto featuring the first movement of Ravel's "Piano Concerto in G." Preston explained *La Boehme* to the viewing audience before Metropolitan Opera stars Richard Tucker and Anna Moffo sang some of the opera's arias from the closing scene of Act One, and he closed the episode by singing popular tunes including "Lady Be Good," "Too Many Rings Around Rosie," "Something Short of Grandish," "They Say It's Wonderful," and "Jubilation T. Corpone."[186] The episode was well received with Preston praised for injecting "zip, movement, and excitement" into the program.[187]

The newly reconciled Prestons flew into McGhee -Tyson Airport near Knoxville, Tennessee on the evening of Wednesday, October 16 to attend the world premiere of *All the Way Home*. Robert Preston and his child co-star, Michael Kearney, were the only two actors from the film to attend the Knoxville gala. Preston and Catherine roomed on the ninth floor of Knoxville's Hotel Andrew Johnson while Kearney and his family were lodged on the twelfth floor.[188] Early the next day, the actors and local dignitaries were taken on a tour of the filming locations in Knoxville, culminating with a picnic lunch at Cades Cove.[189]

The film's producer, David Suskind, arrived in Knoxville in mid-afternoon to participate in the festivities.[190]

Before the screening, Robert Preston and Michael Kearney were made honorary citizens of Knoxville and bestowed the title of Honorary Colonel of the State.[191] The film's world premiere took place a little after 8:35 p.m. at the Tennessee Theater in Knoxville to an overflow crowd of over two hundred attendees while thousands more lined the street to witness the celebratory event.[192] The local press took note that "the always affable Preston wisecracked with his fans, signed autographs, and generally ingratiated himself with his public."[193]

All The Way Home received mixed reviews from film critics. Mike McGrady of *Newsday* characterized the movie as "no less than a two-handkerchief film." McGrady described *All The Way Home* as "unremittingly maudlin—but right on target" and praised the performances of Jean Simmons, Pat Hingle, and Robert Preston as having "never been better."[194] Similarly, film critic Kate Cameron of the New York *Daily News* described the film as one of "love and loss" designed to "touch the heart of the toughest beholder."[195] Cameron acknowledged that the film's director, Alex Segal, "had a difficult task in bringing the picture of a child's unreasoning sorrow into focus without drenching the screen in a bathetic shower."[196] Conversely, Bosley Crowther of *The New York Times* was unimpressed by the film. He contended the rewrite of the original Agee novel erased much of the "poetry and unduplicatable intimacy of Mr. Agee's particular expression." In the process of transferring the novel to the screen, it was Crowther's opinion that the script had been "completely drained of specialness."[197]

The release of the lachrymose film was additionally plagued by poor timing. The movie was overshadowed by another black-and-white film, *To Kill a Mockingbird,* which was released the same year and similarly based on the youthful experiences of its author.[198] In addition, the film's premiere in Knoxville was held thirty-six days prior to the assassination of President John F. Kennedy and opened in theaters nationwide a week after his death. Actress Jean Simmons aptly pointed out that no one "had the heart to see James Agee's little story about the death of the father figure"[199] after President Kennedy, a father of two young children, had been killed and the entire country was in mourning. Despite the mixed reviews and inopportune release of the film, *All the Way Home* was cited as being among the ten best films of 1963 by the National Board of Review of Motion Pictures.[200]

Preston and Catherine flew back to New York on October 18. Later that evening, the International Alliance of Theatrical Stage Employees (IATSE) recognized Preston's contributions to the stage, film, and television by bestowing him with the union's Fiftieth Anniversary Award that evening at a dinner held at the Americana Hotel.[201]

Under the direction of Gene Saks, the Ronald Alexander comedy, *Nobody Loves an Albatross,* began rehearsals in the hall above Ratner's Dairy Restaurant on Second Avenue in New York during the first week of November 1963. Preston had only committed to a six-month contract to appear in the play, as he already signed a contract to star in the musical *Ben Franklin in Paris* in the fall of 1964. *Nobody Loves an Albatross,* a spoof of the television industry, included characters who were thinly-veiled Hollywood stars, agents, and producers. One of the play's characters is a comedienne who owns a television studio and stars in her own TV series—a doppelganger persona for Lucille Ball.[202] Preston, in the lead role of Nathaniel Bentley, acted alongside Constance Ford, Carol Rossen, Leslye Hunter, Richard

Mulligan, Marie Wallace, Barnard Hughes, Gertrude Jeannette, Jack Bittner, Phil Leeds, Leon Janney, Frank Campanella, and Marian Winters. The two-act play is set in the living room of the slick, talentless, often-divorced television producer Nathaniel Bentley (Preston), who knows just how to wheel-and-deal and take credit for work written by ghostwriters. While parenting his young daughter, Diane (Hunter), during her summer vacation, he coolly prevaricates his way through each scene as a disarming rogue. Bentley's young daughter and his newly-hired assistant (Rosson) are the only two characters in the play who have not yet been jaded by the cynicism in the television industry. Marie Wallace, who played the role of a high-class hooker, noted Preston always made the cast feel comfortable, never wanting to be seen as the "star" but simply as a fellow actor. She recalled Preston gave an informal speech to the director and his fellow thespians on the first day of rehearsals in which he emphasized that he "was just another member of the cast," and he expected them to treat him that way.[203]

Leslye Hunter, who played Preston's young daughter, Diane, enjoyed an avuncular relationship with Preston with whom she interacted frequently. Preston's running gag involved chiding his young co-star with the refrain, "Are you a Leslye hunter? You know Leslyes are in season!" Hunter observed that Preston appeared to be continually "on" and seemed "a bit pressured to be up and enthusiastic all the time."[204]

The play was slated for three-and-a-half weeks of rehearsal in New York before an out-of-town review at the Shubert Theatre in New Haven, Connecticut. Rehearsals were suspended when President Kennedy was assassinated in Dallas, Texas on Friday, November 22. Leslye Hunter recalled the news of the assassination was conveyed to the cast by Jason Robards,

Jr. Robards, who was rehearsing another play in a different studio, rushed into the *Albatross* rehearsal space with tears on his face and announced that the President had been shot. The cast went into shock at the news, began crying, and rushed down to the restaurant bar beneath the rehearsal studio to watch the television broadcast; Preston appeared visibly shaken and upset.[205] Marie Wallace recalled the cast was rendered "stunned and speechless" after hearing Walter Cronkite announce the assassination of the President on national television. The cast was only able to participate in one rehearsal before heading to Connecticut for the play's preview opening in New Haven.[206]

Nobody Loves an Albatross opened on Wednesday, November 27, the evening before Thanksgiving, and concluded its brief run at New Haven's Shubert Theatre on November 30. Connecticut's *Record-Journal* newspaper published an unfavorable review of the play, noting that much of the jargon used by the play's characters was vernacular to TV insiders and, since most audiences would not be "hep to the lingo," the meaning of the lines would go right over their heads.[207] The review praised Preston for providing a "courageous and untiring performance" punctuated with "outrageous mannerisms," but argued the actor's talent was "too good to waste on [such] mediocre material."[208]

The production then moved to Boston for a second, longer, out-of-town preview. Upon arrival in Boston, Preston sent a gracious note to each of his fellow cast members along with gifts of champagne and flowers.[209] The Boston preview of *Nobody Loves an Albatross* opened Monday, December 2 at the Wilbur Theater to unenthusiastic reviews. Kevin Kelly's critique in *The Boston Globe* was abysmal and signaled a major overhaul was needed for the comedy. Kelly revealed "the major failing of the play . . . is its lack of definition for most of its first two acts," adding the playwright wallops theatergoers "black and blue with nothing more than sex jokes and comedy routines."[210] Despite the criticism of the script, Kelly praised Preston for providing a "vivid portrayal of an ambitious cutthroat" and creating "a complex character with startling credibility." The review aptly pointed out that *Albatross* was "not yet the play it is meant to be," warning that if the script was not retooled, it would remain "an interesting failure, a sharp comedy that misses its target for a good part of the evening."[211] The production likewise received a cringe-worthy review from Richard Andrews of *The Harvard Crimson*. Andrews declared the play "fails as a moral lesson," adding the "only thing impressive about *Albatross* is Preston's acting," since he "keeps Act I from collapsing altogether by the sheer force of his personality."[212]

Nobody Loves an Albatross ended its limited run in Boston on December 14. In response to the stinging reviews from critics in New Haven and Boston, playwright Ronald Alexander rewrote thirty-five percent of the play before the production's Broadway debut at the Lyceum Theatre on Thursday, December 19.[213] Marie Wallace recalled that "bountiful, beautiful bouquets of flowers were waiting for all the actors in our dressing rooms" on opening night and Preston "wrote a very personal note" to each of his fellow actors.[214]

Ronald Alexander's alterations to the script were successful, as evidenced by the positive commentary from the New York theater critics. Howard Taubman of *The New York Times* declared *Nobody Loves an Albatross* "admirably rises to the occasion" and described the plot as a "sharper and more ruthless account of behind-the-scenes-maneuvers in TV land." Preston was lauded as delivering "a marvelous, sustained performance" that made his character, Nat Bentley, "credible," and playwright

Alexander was given kudos for composing a "hilarious comedy with a slashing satirical edge."[215] *Albatross* also received high marks from John Chapman at the *Daily News* who remarked that "the company of 13 actors is well chosen." Chapman commended the playwright for producing a script containing "many barbed lines and . . . enough twists of plot so that the director, Gene Saks, can keep the comedy moving briskly and crisply."[216] Critics from *Time* magazine likewise gave a nod to the play, noting that Preston played his role with "prancing, gleeful guile" and was "as magnetic as sin."[217]

Just as he had during *The Music Man* and *We Take the Town*, Preston began experiencing hoarseness while performing in *Albatross*. To soothe his strained vocal cords and avoid losing his voice, the actor maintained a cup of hot water mixed with blackberry juice in the wings and would sip the sweet, warm elixir between scenes to prevent vocal strain.[218]

The revamped production inevitably experienced a few minor hiccups. Preston's performance was interrupted on December 30 by a drunken interloper who somehow managed to stagger down the aisle of the Lyceum Theatre. The inebriated man leaned against the apron of the stage and began shouting to the actor, "Preston, I can't buy tickets to your show." Preston did not react to the heckling and continued seamlessly with his lines. Although Preston maintained his composure when the interloper resumed his rantings, playwright Ronald Alexander "rushed down the aisle and led the man out of the theater."[219] During another performance of *Albatross*, an audience member interrupted the performance by shouting to the actor, "Mr. Preston, would you please sing "Seventy-Six Trombones"?"[220] Preston turned the heckler's remarks into howling audience laughter with his next line of dialogue that just happened to be, "All right, I tell you what we're gonna do, and I don't want any interruptions."[221] A few months later, an awkward situation arose when two former presidential rivals attended the same performance of the play. Both former President Harry S. Truman and former Governor Thomas E. Dewey, Truman's challenger in the 1948 election, were in the audience on April 21 to see *Albatross*. Truman was seated in the seventh row of the theater while Dewey sat two rows in front of him.[222] When both Truman and Dewey ventured backstage after the final curtain to meet Preston, a photographer captured a photo of the two political foes shaking hands while Preston stood in the center as a neutral arbiter between the two men.[223]

In April 1964, the National Association for the Advancement of Colored People (NAACP) began plans to stage a telecast to raise one million dollars to finance its civil rights efforts. A two-hour national telecast was scheduled for May 1964 to commemorate the tenth anniversary of the *Brown v Board of Education*, the Supreme Court decision that outlawed school segregation, and spur fundraising for the NAACP.[224] Federal judge Thurgood Marshall, who argued the case before the Supreme Court as chief counsel for the NAACP, would be presented the Freedom Bell Award during the program by NAACP Secretary Roy Wilkins.[225] The telecast, titled the *Freedom Spectacular*, was the largest fundraising project in the civil rights movement to date. The NAACP made arrangements for the program to be simulcast to various theaters and auditoriums in over fifty major American cities[226] on May 14 with half of the TV special originating in Los Angeles and the other half broadcast from New York City.[227]

Preston signed on to perform in the *Freedom Spectacular* broadcast along with other notables such as Sidney Poitier, Elizabeth Taylor, Sammy Davis, Jr., Richard Burton, Harry

Belafonte, Nat King Cole, Cannonball Adderley, Carolyn Jones, Burt Lancaster, Dorothy Dandridge, Garry Moore, Frederic March, Tony Bennett, Gloria Foster, James Darren, Duke Ellington, Bill Cosby, Ossie Davis, Ruby Dee, Della Reese, Agnes Moorehead, Edward G. Robinson, Steve Allen, Lena Horne, Ed Sullivan, Eartha Kitt, Gene Kelly, Ed Begley, Barbara McNair, Godfrey Cambridge, Piper Laurie, Richard Widmark, and the Lon Fontaine Dancers. Actor Burt Lancaster narrated the West Coast hour of the *Freedom Spectacular* from the Los Angeles Sports Arena, while Sidney Poitier emceed the East Coast portion of the program from New York's Madison Square Garden. Preston appeared in the New York portion of the *Freedom Spectacular* telecast and performed a new Yip Harburg and Burton Lane song titled, "Freedom Is the Word," accompanied by the chorus from Brooklyn's Midwood High School.[228] A photo taken by David Gahr of Sidney Poitier and Robert Preston during the *Freedom Spectacular* captured the two actors standing side-by-side on stage looking dapper in their tuxedos during the nationwide broadcast.

The day after the *Freedom Spectacular* telecast, it was announced that Preston had won the twenty-fifth annual drama award presented by the Barter Theater of Abingdon, Virginia for his "outstanding contribution to the theater." The Barter Prize consisted of "an acre of land on a mountainside near the Barter Theater, a Virginia ham and a platter to eat it off of."[229] A week later, Preston served as master of ceremonies alongside singer Steve Lawrence for the eighteenth annual Tony Awards. The theater awards ceremony, held at the New York Hilton on May 24th, was broadcast on local New York television station WWOR.

Having completed his contractual obligations, Preston left *Albatross* on May 30 and was replaced in the role of Nat Bentley by Barry Nelson. By the time he finished his run in *Albatross*, Preston was viewed as a "dynamic force in the theatre" and was sought by Broadway producers who knew that he could "almost guarantee the success of a show simply by appearing in it."[230]

According to Leslye Hunter, the cast of *Albatross* was unhappy about Preston's departure from the production and instinctively knew his exit marked the beginning of the end for the play.[231] The cast's premonition proved accurate; *Albatross* closed less than three weeks later on June 20 after 212 performances and failed to return its capital investment to the play's backers.[232] As a token of his appreciation, Preston gave his young co-star a magnum of Dom Perignon as a departing gift. When Hunter reminded him that she was only twelve years old, Preston instructed her to save the champagne until she was legally old enough to drink it. Hunter dutifully cracked open the champagne on her twenty-first birthday and toasted Preston in absentia.[233]

Forty-six-year-old Preston had no sooner exited his role in *Nobody Loves an Albatross* than he began preparations to portray septuagenarian Founding Father Benjamin Franklin in the musical comedy *Ben Franklin in Paris*, slated to open on October 8 at Broadway's Lunt-Fontanne Theater.[234] Preston's wife Catherine, perhaps as a presage to her future marital turmoil, expressed opposition to her husband's decision to portray the elderly statesman, but Preston. dismissed his wife's concerns and wholeheartedly embraced the role of Franklin.[235] The mature role was a comfortable one for the actor who routinely refused to play younger roles on stage or screen and preferred characters who either matched his chronological age or were older.[236]

Ben Franklin In Paris originated as a book of the same name written by playwright Sidney Michaels. Michaels later wrote lyrics to accompany the music composed by Mark Sandrich Jr., with the plot of the musical loosely based on the role Franklin played in securing French support for American independence from Britain.[237] The musical, produced by George W. George and Frank Granat, tells the story of Founding Father Benjamin Franklin, who was the Ambassador to France in 1776. Franklin traveled to the French court in Paris to secure the support of the French King for the colonial war against Great Britain. In the course of events, Franklin courts an old acquaintance, Comtesse Diane de Vobrillac, who has influence with the king. After several plot twists, the Comtesse eventually intercedes on Franklin's behalf with the monarch.

With Preston already signed to play Ben Franklin, the producers scrambled to find a foreign leading lady for the role of Comtesse Diane de Vobrillac. The producers unsuccessfully attempted to secure actresses Simone Signoret and Danielle Darrieux for the role and ultimately reached out to Ulla Sallert, the First Lady of Swedish musical theater, as a possible candidate for the Comtesse.[238] Sallert, a mezzo-soprano, was flown in from Sweden during the last week of June to audition for the role by singing a rendition of "Hello Dolly!"[239] The blonde actress who was being considered to play the role of a French countess was actually a European baroness; her 1945 marriage to Baron Franz von Lampe, a member of the peerage, allowed Sallert to move in Swedish society as the Baroness von Lampe.[240] On a tight deadline with rehearsals set to begin on July 6, the producers overlooked Sallert's thickly-accented English and selected her to portray the role of Franklin's love interest.

Forty-one-year-old Swedish opera and musical theater star Ulla Sallert was born in Stockholm in March 1923 to working-class parents. After studying at the Royal Academy of Music, Sallert was discovered while performing at the Oscar Theater. She went on to achieve acclaim in Swedish theater productions of *Kiss Me Kate, Guys and Dolls, Annie Get Your Gun, South Pacific, My Fair Lady,* and *Oklahoma!* as well as several Swedish films.[241] Ulla (pronounced 'OOH-la') wed Baron Franz von Lampe, an actor, musician, and sculptor, in 1945; the couple's only child, Thérèse, was born in 1949.

Ben Franklin in Paris went into rehearsals on schedule under the watchful eye of director/choreographer Michael Kidd.[242] Several weeks into rehearsal, Preston and Ulla Sallert "began having dinners together,"[243] and a torrid romance began between the co-stars[244] that appeared to fly under the radar of both the press and their respective spouses. The August 1964 interview Preston and his wife Catherine provided to AP journalist Vivian Brown is a case in point. The information solicited from the couple gave the impression of domestic bliss: they spoke of looking forward to celebrating their twenty-fourth wedding anniversary in November, while Preston lavished praise on his wife's gardening and culinary skills.[245]

Robert Preston was in prime physical condition in 1964 as he assumed the role of the venerable Ben Franklin. At the time, an interviewer described the actor as possessing,

> Shoulders like a lion, a flat stomach, and the levi hips and spiky legs of a horse wrangler. He enjoys a brisk walk—and keeping up with his stride when he decides to hike crosstown to the Lunt-Fontanne Theatre can be tiring. Even standing

still, with feet planted widely apart, his thumbs hooked into the pockets of his tapered trousers, he looks as sturdy as a sequoia tree —but no more rooted to the spot than a cougar.[246]

Despite his youthful virility, Preston would need to transform himself into the elderly Benjamin Franklin through the use of make-up, costumes, and wigs. A variety of wigs were tried, but none felt secure over the actor's massive head of hair. To make the wig feel more comfortable atop his head and ensure that it would not tumble off mid-performance, Preston took it upon himself to shave off all his hair to allow the wig, which showcased Franklin's receding hairline, to be glued securely to his scalp.[247] A production assistant for *Ben Franklin in Paris* confirmed that the idea of shaving off his hair was entirely Preston's, noting "nobody would have dared ask him to do it."[248] The drastic step of shearing off his hair was viewed by some as Preston's "full measure of his devotion to his profession."[249]

On August 11, just before the musical's preview in Philadelphia, the producers announced that the Broadway opening of *Ben Franklin in Paris* would be pushed back from October 8 to October 13.[250] The musical's preview opened at Philadelphia's Shubert Theatre on August 24 to mixed reviews. Henry Murdoch, the theater critic from the *Philadelphia Inquirer*, described Preston's portrayal of Franklin as "outstanding," but lamented that despite Ulla Sallert's loveliness, her accent often made her lyrics "hard to understand."[251] Jerry Gaghan from the *Philadelphia Daily News* praised Preston's persuasive performance and flag-waving curtain speech, but not much more. Gaghan expressed disappointment in director Michael Kidd's second-act opening scene, Sidney Michael's lyrics, Oliver

Smith's sets, and pointed out that Ulla Sallert's Swedish accent contributed to her lyrics being "almost unintelligible" even in the front rows of the theater.[252]

An accident sustained during the show's preview in Philadelphia allowed Preston to more realistically portray an elderly Ben Franklin. With his eyes full of soap, Preston slipped in the shower, cracking three of his ribs and fracturing three others. As a result of the injury Preston, with his taped ribs, moved more like an older Franklin. The change in Preston's on-stage agility delighted the director who proclaimed, "Now *that's* Ben!"[253]

Following the musical's final performance in Philadelphia on September 12, the production moved to its second preview venue at Boston's Shubert Theatre. The Boston debut of *Ben Franklin in Paris* on September 16 likewise met with dour reviews. Although Kevin Kelly of *The Boston Globe* praised Preston as "quite close to perfect in a musical far from it," he indicated the musical "isn't much of a show"–a sentiment evidenced by the title of his review: "A History Book Musical That Won't Make History."[254] Since the production needed re-tooling, the producers announced on September 29 that the Broadway opening of the musical would once again be pushed back from October 13 to October 27.[255]

Ben Franklin in Paris ended its Boston preview on October 3, and the production moved to New York to begin on-site previews at the Lunt-Fontanne Theater on October 7. The musical repertoire was tweaked with the addition of the Jerry Herman ballad, "To Be Alone With You," and Michael Kidd made sufficient adjustments to the production to have it running smoothly on opening night. Preston settled in at the Lunt-Fontanne and adorned his dressing room with a small sign, framed by Catherine, which declared "Security Is Knowing All Your Lines."[256]

The sign was reflective of Preston's personal mantra, work ethic, and perfectionism. In order to remain sharp and fresh while performing in a stage production, Preston would repeat all of his lyrics to himself on a daily basis as he was acutely aware,

> You can forget dialogue because you can fake it since you know approximately what the character is doing, but you can't fake a lyric. I say them over and over so that it becomes impossible to make a mistake.[257]

In reaction to the dismal Philadelphia and Boston reviews, Preston made a point to encourage the ensemble cast and crew. He attempted to elevate the deflated morale of younger cast members by advising them that "unless you want to quit, you're going to have to be here for the next two and a half hours. So why not have a ball? Enjoy it!"[258]

Ben Franklin In Paris made its long-awaited Broadway debut at the Lunt-Fontanne Theatre on October 27th, 1964. Ulla Sallert's husband and daughter flew in from Sweden for the opening night performance, and Catherine Craig was likewise in the audience to support her husband. Despite all of the tweaking and revisions to the script and score, the musical received tepid reviews from the New York theater critics. Howard Taubman from the *New York Times* lamented that the musical's plot was "predictable and commonplace" and noted the script, based on Sidney Michael's book, appears more organized than created.[259] *Time* magazine was equally caustic in its review: the musical's script was described as "synthetic," Mark Sandrich's score was pronounced "music-to-yawn-by," and Ulla Sallert's Swedish accent was viewed as "a lip reader's delight" since "baffled playgoers may feel that she is singing in tongues."[260] The review also acknowledged that "no one could coax a poor performance out of Robert Preston" and recognized Preston would be the only one capable of saving the show "if there is one to save."[261]

The review provided by John Chapman of the *Daily News* was less dour: he described the musical as a perilous Broadway undertaking that was carried off with considerable charm. The review acknowledged Preston was "the perfect choice" for the role of Benjamin Franklin, adding that if Preston "can't make it run, nobody else can."[262]

A picture snapped by a photographer with the New York *Daily News* during the musical's opening night party captured Ulla Sallert, husband Baron Franz von Lampe, and Catherine Craig seated together at a round banquet table. By the expression on her face, it appeared Catherine had become aware of the intensifying relationship between Miss Sallert and her husband. The photographer captured Catherine looking to her right and directly at Ulla; her discerning, woeful gaze resembled how one might look while witnessing an impending train wreck, yet be powerless to stop it.

The New York *Daily News* reported that Preston moved out of his marital home in Rye, New York and into a suite at the Warwick Hotel in Midtown Manhattan on Thursday, November 12.[263] By November 17, Preston's affair with Ulla Sallert exploded onto national headlines with articles announcing, "Ben Franklin Preston Counsels Wife to Fly Kite & Dates Ulla," "'Franklin' Has Actress on String," and "Robert Preston Separation From His Wife Told."

Preston's friends dismissed his liaison with Sallert as the actor simply "having another fit of restlessness."[264] However, it was hard for friends to overlook the very public nature of Preston's relationship with Sallert. Preston was comfortable attending the *Poor Bitos* opening night party on Saturday, November 14 with Sallert on his arm and publicly dined with Sallert and her teenage daughter, Thérèse, in a Manhattan restaurant the very next evening.[265] Meanwhile, Preston acknowledged to reporters that he and his wife had once again separated, insisting "this time it's final." He also vigorously insisted that the origin of the marital schism was not in any way related to Sallert.[266]

Sallert made headlines of her own on November 19 when she publicly announced her plans to end her nineteen-year marriage to Baron von Lampe. Like Preston, Sallert maintained her decision to divorce her spouse had "nothing to do with the separation of Preston from his wife."[267] The actress, who revealed she and her husband had been separated for six months in 1963, explained the couple decided to move forward with a divorce when her husband traveled to New York to see the Broadway opening of *Ben Franklin in Paris*.[268] Baron Von Lampe returned to Sweden and initiated divorce proceedings while the couple's daughter remained in New York with her mother. The Swedish court moved swiftly, and the marriage between Sallert and the Baron was dissolved within a few short months. In the interim, Sallert remained in the United States and focused on "looking for the right school in Connecticut" in which to enroll her teenage daughter.[269]

Frenzied New York newspapers and tabloids chronicled Preston's separations and reconciliations with his wife during the Broadway run of *Ben Franklin in Paris*. Headlines blared the latest on the on-again-off-again trajectory of the Preston-Sallert relationship, one that clearly replicated the predictable, unstable pattern of the actor's past extramarital liaisons.

Preston's relationship with the Swedish soprano was on full display when the two appeared together on the November 28 episode of *American Musical Theatre*, a CBS television program hosted by Earl Wrightson. Preston, sporting a bald head, was questioned about his decision to shave off his hair to replicate Franklin's receding hairline. The actor made a point of identifying a parallel in his roles in *The Music Man* and *Ben Franklin in Paris*, pointing out that Harold Hill and Ben Franklin were both great salesmen–noting that Franklin, unlike Hill, "was on the up and up"[270] as he was promoting the American colonies to France. When Wrightson inquired whether the actor preferred to perform in motion pictures or on the Broadway stage, Preston acknowledged, "It's marvelous to have a choice," but admitted he preferred acting in the theater because "it's more fun" and an actor "can continue to grow in a role"[271] on the stage, a phenomenon that is not possible in film. Ulla Sallert was introduced by Preston during the second half of the program before Donald Pippin, the musical director for *Ben Franklin in Paris*, joined Preston and Sallert for the interview. Pippin recounted Sallert's musical audition in which she sang "Hello, Dolly!" in Swedish–a revelation that prompted Sallert to launch into a few bars of the iconic tune. The final segment of the program featured Sallert serenading the audience with two songs from *Ben Franklin in Paris*, "Look for Small Pleasures" and "How Laughable It Is."

Although Preston had high hopes for the success of *Ben Franklin in Paris*, the musical's 1964 launch suffered from bad timing and fierce competition from such successful Broadway shows as *Funny Girl*, *Fiddler on the Roof*, and *Hello Dolly!*[272] It has been suggested that the producers selected the wrong year to open the show since "the competition in 1964 left no room for Preston or his show to breathe, much less catch fire."[273]

To promote the show and boost lackluster ticket sales, Preston performed a scene from the musical on the December 13 episode of *The Ed Sullivan Show*.[274] Preston and members of the musical's cast entertained viewers with a rousing rendition of the song "Half the Battle," a tune designed to bolster the Franklin family's spirits after learning that British forces captured his adopted hometown of Philadelphia during the war for independence.

Preston and Sallert continued their romantic relationship while performing together on stage. Sallert, unfamiliar with the American press, was unnerved by the newspaper headlines that linked her name to Preston's; she was accustomed to the Swedish press who were "tactful of the private life of stars."[275] Moreover, Sallert was mortified to be portrayed as *the other woman*. In an interview in the *Detroit Free Press*, Sallert insisted her impending divorce did not involve Robert Preston, adding the Swedish press were well aware that she and Baron von Lampe had been separated for six months in 1963–a fact rarely mentioned by the American press.[276] The gossip about the pair on the Great White Way was no less harsh. Gossip columnist Walter Winchell overheard a contingent of Broadway actors discussing the Preston-Sallert relationship at a local eatery just before Christmas 1964. While one diner pointed out this would be Ulla Sallert's first divorce, Patsy D'Amore jokingly noted, "You've gotta say one thing for Robert Preston, every time he leaves a wife it's the same one!"[277]

Jabs from the press were unmerciful. Preston was publicly excoriated by Watson Crews, Jr. of the New York *Daily News* for his recent extra-marital relationships with Glynis Johns and Ulla Sallert. Crews lambasted Preston's pattern of separations from his wife, noting that, "these days, it seems, whenever he plays opposite anybody near his own age who has the tiniest bit of gleam in her eye, he gets a bad case of the 20-year itch and wants to shuck off his marital yoke."[278] Although Preston openly acknowledged a previous separation from his wife in 1963, he chastised the press for making "it look as if another woman was involved, but that simply was not true."[279] Crews, clearly skeptical of Preston's demurral, remarked that the actor's behavior exhibited a clear pattern: after a few dates with Ulla, Preston was "back at the Warwick Hotel, [in] the same hostelry into which he stormed when it simply was not true about Glynis."[280]

Much to Sallert's chagrin, Preston briefly reconciled with his wife Catherine after tragedy struck the Meservey family in mid-February. Preston's forty-three-year-old sister-in-law, Florence Meservey, had been hospitalized at the Glendale Sanitarium following a January 12 automobile accident at the intersection of Verdugo and La Canada Boulevards in Glendale, California.[281] When Florence died unexpectedly during her hospital stay on the morning of February 14, gossip columnist Hedda Hopper spoke to Preston's mother, Ruth, about the loss of her daughter-in-law. Although the cause of Florence's sudden death was unknown, Ruth recounted that on the morning of her death, Florence "got up, washed her hair, got a violent headache, and died."[282] Catherine immediately flew out to California to "pull things together" for the family,[283] and the tragedy became a catalyst for a brief reconciliation between Preston and his wife.

The marital reconciliation left Ulla Sallert the odd-woman-out in the very public romantic triangle. Sallert, who remained very much in love with Preston, continued to perform in scenes with him in *Ben Franklin in Paris,* and the awkward situation intensified her misery. To protect herself and limit her vulnerability, Sallert and Preston did not speak to each other except during their scenes on stage.[284] Sallert's mother traveled from Sweden to New York to visit her daughter during this emotionally charged period.[285] The actress, who acknowledged to the New York press that her romance with Preston was "all over," was labeled a "poor loser" by columnist Dorothy Kilgallen for characterizing her paramour's decision to reconcile with his wife as "running home to mama."[286]

After three weeks back home with his wife, Preston conceded the reconciliation "didn't work," and by April 7, newspaper headlines once again heralded Preston's intention to divorce Catherine and marry Ulla Sallert.[287] Preston and his wife acknowledged "the finality of [their] marriage"[288] in the waning days of March. Another separation ensued with Preston's moving back into the Warwick Hotel and an announcement that the break with his wife "was final."[289] Sallert was "shaken" yet ecstatic when Preston "came back after three weeks and asked me to share his life with him," adding, "I was happy because I love him and I've never stopped loving him."[290] Toward the end of April, newspaper headlines reconfirmed Preston's intention to marry Sallert once his twenty-five-year marriage to Catherine was dissolved. Despite his plan for a trip to the altar with his co-star, Preston conspicuously acknowledged that he and his wife had not yet discussed or settled the terms of their divorce.

By the end of April, it became increasingly clear that lagging box office sales could no longer sustain *Ben Franklin in Paris,* and the show closed on Saturday, May 1 after seven months and 215 performances. The musical managed to endure as long as it did due to the advance ticket sales to theatergoers who liked the idea of Preston playing the role of Benjamin Franklin.[291]

As she had in the past, Catherine remained steadfastly opposed to divorce. According to her nephew, Catherine was very far-sighted and knew what it was that she wanted out of life. Being very steady in her own right, she was very much Preston's bedrock and remained confident that her husband would never permanently abandon their marriage.[292] The future of the actor's relationship with Ulla Sallert was in flux by the time of the last performance of *Ben Franklin in Paris*. Preston had not formulated a backup plan or calculated his next move when his wife chose to stand her ground. As he had during prior relationships with Peggy Lee and Glynnis Johns, Preston vacillated between his devoted wife and his paramour, but he ultimately opted to retreat back to the safe harbor of married life with Catherine. Once back in Rye, Preston focused on trying to regrow his hair for his upcoming series of television specials.[293] Sallert, now divorced, forsaken by her lover, and out of work, returned to Sweden with her daughter.

Preston (seated, left) as Tom Cobb starring in *Tom Cobb* (December 1937) at the Pasadena Playhouse. *The Pasadena Playhouse archives.*

Preston in the role of Count De La Mole in *Star of Navarre* (June 1938) at the Pasadena Playhouse. *The Pasadena Playhouse archives.*

Catherine Craig in 1946. *John Springer collection/Corbis Historical via Getty Images.*

Robert Preston and Barbara Cook at the piano during rehearsal for the stage production of *The Music Man* (1957). *Photo by Friedman-Ables @ The New York Public Library for the Performing Arts.*

Preston, as Harold Hill, with Shirley Jones on the set of *The Music Man* in April 1961. *AP Images / Harold Filan.*

Robert Preston and Christopher Walken in the stage production of *The Lion in Winter* (1966). *Photo by Friedman-Ables @ The New York Public Library for the Performing Arts.*

Mary Martin and Robert Preston in rehearsal for the stage production of *I Do! I Do!* (1966). *Photo by Friedman-Ables @ The New York Public Library for the Performing Arts.*

(L to R) Preston, Neva Small, Bernice Massi, and Gene Saks during rehearsal for *The Prince of Grand Street* (1978). *Image Courtesy of Neva Small.*

Ruth and Doc Meservey
(Fall 1967). *Photo Courtesy
of Tracy Palmgren Monroe.*

Preston with *The Prince of
Grand Street* assistant musical
director David Krane (1978).
Image Courtesy of David Krane.

Doc Meservey and Tracy
Palmgren Monroe (circa 1977)
seated on the diving board of
Preston's Brentwood home. *Photo
Courtesy of Tracy Palmgren Monroe.*

Preston autographing a youthful poster of himself at the at the American
Cinema Awards on December 14, 1984. *AP Images / Liu Heung Shing.*

Preston and Catherine
at the Thalians Gala
(November 1984).
*Image: Ralph Dominguez/
MediaPunch
/IPX/AP Images.*

ROARING BACK

Aware that *Ben Franklin in Paris*'s dismal box office sales
signaled the production's death knell, Preston inked a
deal in April 1965 to serve as the host for a series of six-
hour-long television specials titled *This Proud Land*. The objec-
tive of the hour-long color telecasts, sponsored by the DuPont
Corporation, was to explore and showcase various regions of
the United States. Not intended to be a docudrama, the focus of
the series would be the people and places in six regions of the
United States: East, South, Midwest, Great Plains, Southwest,
and Far West. ABC planned to televise a segment per month
beginning in November 1965, with the filming of the series to
commence in early June. *This Proud Land* would be produced
by Phil D'Antoni and Norman Baer, veterans of the television
special genre. D'Antoni and Baer had previously collaborated
on producing three other television specials: *Elizabeth Taylor in
London, Sophia Loren's Rome,* and *Melina Mercouri's Greece*.[1]

The producers, who were given free rein to design the format
and flow of the specials, had no intention of producing a travelog

or documentary. Instead, D'Antoni envisioned *This Proud Land* serving as a "voyage of rediscovery" that would allow viewers to "see each portion of the country with fresh eyes, as though we were looking at a foreign land."[2] It would be in this way that the specials, written and directed by Academy Award-winning director Ernest Pintoff, would unveil the strength and richness of the United States to its citizenry. Viewers would be provided the opportunity to "see the places and people that create the special character of each region," and to "celebrate the joys and wonders of America with humor, affection, and pride."[3]

Preston was enthusiastic about serving as the host of the series and viewed the gig as "the greatest thing since the paid vacation"[4] and an opportunity for him and his wife to tour the country.[5] He envisioned his role not as a host, but as a guide "visiting one sixth of the country at a time and talking to the people there for the people in the other five-sixths of the country."[6]

The actor regularly appeared in television drama specials in the 1950s and early 1960s while performing on Broadway and actively sought out such opportunities as a way to refresh himself during a long Broadway run.[7] Preston shied away from acting in a full-fledged television series, observing that actors who did tended to disappear into their characters and lose their personal identities.[8] Described off-stage as a powerhouse of a man and great conversationalist by director Ernest Pintoff, it was noted that *This Proud Land* would be the only type of television series "that could interest Preston, an alert man with a wide range of information and a voracious newspaper reader."[9] Preston learned quickly during filming that the use of the word "television" was magical and would open doors and garner cooperation from politicians, celebrities, and everyday folk in every location.[10]

The filming of the separate segments moved quickly. By August 25, three of the six episodes were completed and Preston had logged over 10,000 miles in travel. It was expected that Preston and the film crew would travel another 25,000 to 30,000 miles before filming was completed sometime in mid-October.[11] Rain plagued the filming of the episodes, so much so that Preston joked, "We're rainmakers. Everywhere we've been . . . it has rained," adding that his "most useful wardrobe item has been a trench coat."[12]

Preston and a seventeen-man crew began filming the first segment in Boston on June 2, 1965.[13] The first episode of the series titled "The Wild, Wild East" aired on November 9 at 10:00 p.m. Eastern Time on ABC. "The Wild, Wild East" provided highlights of the Eastern portion of the United States, a panorama of picture-postcard scenery, and interviews with distinguished personalities identified with the region. The episode showcased lobster fishing in Maine and presented a panorama of the Connecticut countryside along with filming a farm, complete with a covered bridge, owned by Harwinton farmer John J. Schibi.[14] A tableau of Boston Common, Harvard Yard, and an appearance by Harvard dean John Monro were showcased in scenes of Boston. Independence Hall in Philadelphia was also featured, as well as the Capitol, White House, and Lincoln Memorial in Washington, D.C.

New York was featured heavily in this episode of *This Proud Land*. A segment at the United States Military Academy in West Point included interviews with former President Dwight Eisenhower and General Omar Bradley. The former president both reminisced about his days at West Point and emphasized the importance of the military academy to the nation. Eisenhower asked Preston off-camera, "Son, haven't we met before?" to which Preston cheekily replied, "We have never met before. The last time you spoke to me was on D-Day. I was one of the boys."[15]

A whirlwind tour of New York City included a chat with comedian Louis Nye at Shea Stadium, the showroom of famed fashion designer Norman Norell, a visit with singer-composer Paul Anka in his Manhattan office to discuss pop music, an appearance by actor-comedian Parker Fennelly as folksy character Titus Moody, interviews with architect Walter Gropius about his vision of a ribbon city (modernist architecture) and composer Aaron Copland about jazz music, a look at famed photographer Jerrold Schatzberg at work with fashion models, and a chat with Ivan Karp, the director of New York's Castelli Gallery. The episode also included an interview with actor Peter Falk on a Bronx street location that would become the setting for his upcoming night-time TV show.[16] In addition, a Connecticut to New York commuter train was featured along with scenes from New Jersey, Maryland, and Delaware.

Some television critics opined that an hour-long program was insufficient for an incisive exploration of the important cities of the East but agreed that the show might act as a catalyst to motivate Americans to explore this area of the country. Television critic Allen Rich noted that the first episode of *This Proud Land* provided "a welcome respite from the nothingness of the current [television] season,"[17] and declared Preston as the perfect choice to narrate the specials:

> Preston's narration varied between contemporary evaluations and historic facts about the areas visited. No happier choice of a guide would have been possible, for he invested his narrative with his own particular brand of virility.[18]

This Proud Land had significant competition for viewership of the first episode. CBS decided to air their own television special, *The National Citizenship Test*, to vie for ratings in the same time slot. As fate would have it, neither program aired in the northeast on the evening of November 9 as a result of a massive East Coast power failure[19] which thrust thirty million Americans and 80,000 miles of the northeast into darkness. ABC did not make plans to re-air the program locally in the East.[20]

Preston was uncomfortable with "The Wild, Wild East" being selected as the first episode for broadcast in the *This Proud Land* series, confessing that since the episode was the first one filmed by the producers, the crew, and himself that "we didn't know what we were doing."[21] He believed the series should have started with an episode such as "The Big Sky Country" which showcased a different region of the nation not as well-documented as the East."[22]

The second installment of *This Proud Land*, titled "Big Sky Country," aired on December 18, 1965 and explored the Great Plains and Rocky Mountain states of Kansas, Nebraska, North and South Dakota, Montana, Utah, Idaho, Colorado, and Wyoming. Highlights in Kansas included an interview with novelist A.B. Guthrie, a visit to the famed Menninger Clinic in Topeka for a chat with Dr. Karl Menninger, a conversation with a modern Kansas wheat farmer, a visit to Mt. Rushmore, and a reenactment of a shoot-out staged by residents of Abilene on an old movie location.[23]

While in Colorado, Preston visited with *Bonanza* alumnus Pernell Roberts at a local ranch. Roberts recited a Native American warrior's surrender for viewers and sang a pair of cowboy ballads, "Strawberry Roan" and "Doney Gal." In addition to observing Montana gold prospector Earl Lutzenhiser in a panning area near Helena, the episode featured the Little Britches Rodeo in Littleton, Colorado, the Air Force Academy in Colorado Springs, a jazz concert by Stan Kenton and his orchestra at Denver's Red Rocks Amphitheater, and cattleman Bob Johnston riding herd on his 102,000-acre modern cattle ranch.[24] Other highlights included actress Laraine Day describing her Mormon childhood to Preston as they visited an old mining camp revamped into a modern discotheque, Mildred Dunnock reading Willa Cather's words from *O Pioneers!*, The Mormon Tabernacle Choir singing, "Give Me Your Tired, Your Poor," an interview with a Black Hills Sioux chief Iron Shell, Basque shepherds demonstrating how their European ways endured in America, and a performance of "Seventy-Six Trombones" by the Rosebud Sioux at the Cheyenne Frontier Days Festival.[25]

By mid-December 1965, Preston had regrown his signature thick head of hair that had been shorn off for his role as Ben Franklin. A man who relished both knowledge and interactions with people, Preston expressed fascination and awe for the cities, towns, and residents he encountered during his tour of the "Big Sky" states,

> There's something basically romantic and fascinating, and exciting about the West . . . you go out there and you hit the little cities . . . and you talk to those people and you'll have your faith renewed in this country . . . I thought I knew this country well, from all the years I've been touring with plays. I didn't know it at all. I knew Chicago, Boston, Detroit, Miami, Washington D.C . . . I had not discovered Abilene."[26]

TV critics generally viewed the "Big Sky Country" episode far more favorably than they had "The Wild, Wild East." However, Barbara Delatiner from *Newsday*, an unabashed detractor of the series, complained the episode was overly "concerned with the trivia at the expense of the important" and felt the producers failed to "capture the beauty of the area," and "its diversity in both geography and population."[27]

The third episode, "The Sun Country," took viewers on a tour of the southwestern states of Texas, Oklahoma, Arizona, and New Mexico. Broadcast on January 26, 1966, the special opened with a Pueblo elder speaking these words in his native Tanoan language with Preston providing the translation:

> When these mountains were young, the land was nobody's land. Then it was our land. Now they say it is everybody's land. But all the time it really belongs to the Sun.[28]

"The Sun Country" explored the rugged, picturesque section of the country and illustrated the contrast between the old west of yesteryear and the modernization of the region. Actress Greer Garson, a Santa Fe resident, showcased the city's annual Fiesta commemorating the arrival of the Conquistadors. Viewers were given a glimpse of the majesty of Arizona's Superstition Mountains while Preston related the legend of the Lost Dutchman Mine. Other highlights in Arizona included a visit to Frank Lloyd Wright's Gammage Memorial Auditorium on the campus of Arizona State University in Tempe and a stop at the popular retirement community of Sun City.

A foray into Texas included a tour of the Southwestern Historical Wax Museum in Dallas to view legendary figures of the past. Former Vogue model and fashion authority, Pamela Tiffin, displayed the latest in fashions typical of the new Southwest with help from designers and models at the Apparel Mart in Dallas. The singing duo Homer and Jethro provided their rendition of "Home on the Range," and ancient cliff dwellers and their underground burial chambers were showcased in Puye, New Mexico.[29] Highlights in Oklahoma included the National Cowboy and Western Heritage Museum in Oklahoma City and a visit to the Will Rogers Memorial in Claremore.

Terry Shain of The Boston Globe echoed the opinion of most television critics in stating that the third installment of *This Proud Land* was the best to date. Shain complimented the producers for artfully interweaving fascinating legends and colorful stories with prosaic activities and for relying on visual descriptions rather than commonplace interviews.[30]

By the time filming of the third episode of *This Proud Land* was complete, Preston was being wooed back to Broadway. Producers for James Goldman's play, then titled *A Day in The Life of Henry II*, sought Preston for the title role of King Henry II of England. Preston tentatively agreed to star in the play, scheduled to open on Broadway in the spring of 1966, provided that a suitable actress could be found to portray the role of Henry's wife, Eleanor of Aquitaine.[31]

Preston began filming the fourth installment of *This Proud Land* in September which explored "The Way-Out West." The episode, broadcast on February 25, 1966, concentrated on California and Washington state. Scenes of San Francisco featured the city's famous cable cars and visits to Telegraph Hill, the San Francisco Ballet, and the 'hungry i nightclub' in the North Beach neighborhood. Author William Saroyan was on hand at Fisherman's Wharf to discuss the national influence of San Francisco.[32]

Halfway between San Francisco and Los Angeles, Preston visited Hearst Castle in San Simeon, the estate of publisher William Randolph Hearst, and chatted with the mogul's grandson John Hearst, Jr. In the Los Angeles area, baseball legend Willie Mays talked baseball, actress Lee Remick and silent film star Francis X. Bushman reminisced about Hollywood past and present, a group of Italians were filmed playing bocce ball, and excursions to Malibu and Chinatown were part of the itinerary. Appearances by former presidential press secretary Pierre Salinger, actor John Astin, and eccentric Professor Irwin Corey also punctuated the segment.[33]

The scenic views of Sequoia and Yosemite National Parks and the Santa Lucia Mountains were captured by the camera in addition to various bucolic scenes in Washington state. Preston made visits to the Seattle monorail and the Space Needle, explored pleasure boats on Puget Sound, and trekked to Mount Rainier with Jim Whittaker, the first American to climb Mount Everest.[34]

Reviews for this installment of *This Proud Land* were generally positive. Cynthia Lowry of the Associated Press deemed "The Way Out West" the best episode in the *This Proud Land* series. She described the segment as "exciting, always interesting, and absorbing" and as accurately capturing "the manners and mores of westerners, their way of life, [and] the individualism marking what was aptly termed 'the last frontier.'"[35]

Preston was pleasantly surprised by his tour through the American South during filming of the fifth episode of *This Proud Land*. Both he and the series producers made the decision to save filming in the South until last since they were uncertain about what they could expect to encounter in the region. Preston disclosed,

> We had no intention of delving into the problems
> of the South, but in the back of everyone's mind
> was the question: how the hell do you do the South
> without calling attention to the problems?[36]

However, he readily acknowledged the crew encountered fewer issues in the South than they had in other regions of the country.[37]

The episode, aptly entitled "The South," featured visits to Florida, Georgia, Kentucky, Louisiana, Tennessee, and South Carolina. During the episode which aired on March 31, 1966, Preston guided viewers through various scenes of the southern United States from antebellum plantations to modern, bustling cities. Scenes featured in Atlanta, which comprised the bulk of the segment, included Mayor Ivan Allen unveiling the new Atlanta-Fulton County Stadium erected for the Braves and the Falcons sports teams, the first day at a recently integrated school, Peachtree Street and the Atlanta skyline, the nation's longest runway at the Atlanta Municipal Airport, and a display of the Civil War Battle of Atlanta at the Atlanta Cyclorama & Civil War Museum.

A visit to Tennessee featured the Jubilee Singers from Nashville's Fisk College singing a calypso song, Eddy Arnold recording "Anytime" in a barn retrofitted with the latest electronic equipment, a performance by Roy Acuff at The Grand Ole Opry, and a tour of Andrew Jackson's Hermitage home where the love letters of Rachel and Andrew Jackson were read aloud by actress Joan Fontaine and actor Richard Kiley.

A stop in Miami included a visit with comedian Myron Cohen at Miami Beach's Eden Roc Hotel and an interview with Dr. Paul Unger, the chairman of the famed Miami Heart

Institute. Bourbon Street, Jackson Square, and mansions in the Garden District were showcased in New Orleans, and Preston was treated to a typical New Orleans breakfast at the famed Brennan's Restaurant. A Charleston Street singer and trips to Catfish Row and Fort Sumter were featured in South Carolina. In addition, well-preserved antebellum homes were filmed in Natchez, Mississippi, and the majesty of thoroughbred horses were captured at Calumet Farms in Kentucky.

The final episode of the *This Proud Land* series was "The Surprising Midwest," which was broadcast on April 25, 1966. Preston traveled through Illinois, Indiana, Michigan, Minnesota, Missouri, and Wisconsin and visited various cities, farms, and Great Lakes seaports.

The hometown of late composer Cole Porter was visited in Peru, Indiana with Preston gleaning insights about the renowned symphonist from his aunt, Mrs. Edwin Miller. In Missouri, Preston showcased the bustling cities of Kansas City and St. Louis and made a stop at Mark Twain's boyhood home in Hannibal.[38] Moving on to Illinois, Preston interviewed Chicago architect Bertrand Goldberg, the designer of Marina City, filmed the vibrancy of Chicago, and visited Lincoln's stomping grounds in New Salem. Highlights of the visit to Michigan included a Polish wedding in Hamtramck, a spotlight on jazz by the Dave Brubeck Quartet and Bertrand Vidal, and a look inside Detroit's automobile factories.[39]

Preston visited the City of Sauk Centre in Minnesota, the birthplace of author Sinclair Lewis and the inspiration for his novel, *Main Street*, the bustling seaport of Duluth, and enjoyed a chat with Dr. Tyrone Guthrie, the founder of the Tyrone Guthrie Repertory Theater in Minneapolis. In Wisconsin, Preston visited Green Bay to see the Green Bay Packers in action and interviewed coach Vince Lombardi. A mishap occurred while Preston and the filming staff were in Green Bay when a crew member lost a camera that was being used in the series's production. The actor explained that the camera had been "in a canoe with [him] and something happened, and it's [now] at the bottom of the bay."[40] Preston also made a trip to nearby Wequiock Park to view the memorial to French missionary Jean Nicolet and spotlight his exploration of the Great Lakes area and Wisconsin in 1634. Also featured in this episode was the academic work being undertaken at three midwestern public universities: The University of Illinois in Champaign-Urbana, The University of Wisconsin in Madison, and The University of Michigan in Ann Arbor.[41] While some television critics praised the *This Proud Land* series, others accused ABC of succeeding in "making each show worse than the last."[42]

By the time the second episode of *This Proud Land* was broadcast on ABC in December 1965, Preston was looking forward to his professional calendar for 1966. Noel Willman had been hired in October to direct *The Lion in Winter,*[43] and it was announced on December 2 that English actress Rosemary Harris had been signed to play the female lead in the Broadway production.[44] Just nine days later, Preston was offered the male lead opposite Mary Martin in *I Do! I Do!*, the musical version of the two-character play *The Four Poster* to be directed by Gower Champion.[45] Meanwhile, the actor who had shaved his head bare for his previous Broadway incarnation as Ben Franklin was now letting his mane and his beard grow unchecked to immerse himself in his next role as a medieval monarch. Hair, or the lack of it, was a non-issue for Preston who believed that "if a few strokes of the razor one way or the other can enhance a character even by a hair's breadth, it's all to the good."[46]

The lovely, talented, and Tony Award-winning actress Rosemary Harris began her acting career in England performing at the Old Vic and the British National Theatre paired with Sir Laurence Olivier, Richard Burton, and Peter O'Toole. Producer Moss Hart brought the actress to New York in 1952 where she made her Broadway debut in the role of Mabel in the short-lived play, *The Climate of Eden*. Harris appeared in several films and television productions in addition to plays in London and five other Broadway productions between 1956 and 1965. She had been appearing in the Lyceum Theatre production of *You Can't Take It With You*, directed by her husband Ellis Rabb, when she exited the play to begin rehearsals for *The Lion in Winter*.

Rosemary Harris revealed Katherine Hepburn was the first choice of the play's producer, Manny Azenberg, to play the role of Eleanor of Aquitaine on Broadway. Azenberg initially offered the part to Hepburn, but she declined the role because her inamorato, Spencer Tracy, was not well at the time. Harris saw herself as the lucky recipient of Hepburn's decision to forgo the role on Broadway.[47]

In addition to Preston and Harris in the lead roles, the cast also featured Christopher Walken, Suzanne Grossman, Dennis Cooney, James Rado, and Bruce Scott. Rosemary Harris revealed the name of the play was changed from *A Day in the Life of Henry II* to *The Lion in Winter* when the producers concluded that "the average Broadway audience wasn't going to be particularly interested in going to see a play about somebody they didn't know anything about."[48] Interestingly, director Noel Willman had just returned from England where he had had a huge success directing Paul Scofield in *A Man for All Seasons*. Harris recalled Willman's recent triumph had an impact on the change of title for Goldman's play,

The powers that be sat around the table and some-body made the connection of what season would the play reflect? It would be winter. What about a lion in winter instead of a man for all seasons? So that's how the play came to be called *The Lion in Winter*. It never would have been called *A Lion in Winter* if it hadn't been for Noel Willman having just directed *A Man for All Seasons*.[49]

Harris viewed the change of the play's name as rather un-fortunate, especially in light of the devastating review of the Broadway production by *The New York Times* in March 1966. Harris speculated that if the play's original title had been re-tained, theater critics may have recognized the play for what it was: "witty and funny–it wasn't to be taken seriously."[50]

The plot of *The Lion in Winter* is rooted in historical fic-tion and involves a Christmas gathering in 1183 of the duplici-tous family of King Henry II of England (Preston), his wife Eleanor of Aquitaine (Harris), and their three power-hungry sons, Richard (Rado), Geoffrey (Cooney), and John (Scott) in his castle in Chinon, France. The young King of France, Philip II (Walken), visits the family to secure the fate of his sister, Alais (Grossman), who is Henry's mistress while also betrothed to Henry's son, Richard. Eleanor, who had been imprisoned by her husband for the past ten years, is temporarily released from bondage to join the Christmas gathering. Despite the machina-tions contrived by King Henry, Eleanor, their sons, and Philip of France, no resolution is reached as to who will succeed Henry on the throne of England.

Rehearsals for *A Lion in Winter* commenced on January 10[51] at an abandoned theater in Spanish Harlem.[52] During the first-day reading of the script, the actors were feeling their way through their performances with an eye toward improvement. Preston, however, "arrived with this great performance as though he had prepared the play beforehand" and demonstrated exactly how he would execute his stage performance.[53] After four weeks of rehearsals, the cast was ready to preview the production at the Colonial Theater in Boston. Performances in Boston began on February 7 and were scheduled to last three weeks.

The Lion in Winter was the first major Broadway role for Academy Award-winning actor Christopher Walken who was tapped to play young King Philip of France in the play. Before landing the role in *The Lion in Winter*, the youthful Walken had appeared in Broadway musicals as a dancer or in the chorus. Walken understood his role in the play was a pivotal one for his budding career and credited Preston for being supportive when the producer planned to axe him from the production during the play's preview in Boston:

> I had a scene with Preston. I played the French king and he and I had a confrontational scene where I had to offer him a goblet of wine. I remember I was so nervous that my hand was shaking and I was spilling the wine. They were going to fire me. The producer took me out after the show one night in Boston and said, "You're a nice guy and everything, but it's not working out." I knew what it was. I was just terrified. I asked if he could give me three days to pull myself together and he agreed.[54]

It was then that an unusual thing happened—Preston made a point to take Walken aside for a pep talk and to offer encouragement. Walken acknowledged he would never forget that Preston encouraged him to trust his own talent,

> He sat down with me and was extremely sup-
> portive. He would see me standing in the corner
> before the show going over my lines and work-
> ing myself into a frenzy. He told me, "You *know*
> your lines, you don't have to do that. Just relax
> and come out on stage and do what you do." I was
> okay after that. If it hadn't been for his support
> and encouragement, I might have ended up back
> in the musical theater. He was a great actor and
> a great man and he was very good to me. I will
> always be grateful to him.[55]

Walken noted that Preston was powerful onstage and completely embodied the "lion" persona in *The Lion in Winter*. He
described Preston as possessing "that alpha thing" with regard
to his powerful presence and command of the stage, noting the
star possessed "the same kind of thing that Olivier had–that
great actor thing."[56]

The Boston preview of *The Lion in Winter* was met with
harsh reviews, especially against playwright James Goldman's
script. *Boston Globe* theater critic Kevin Kelly lamented that
Goldman created characters with human characteristics who
behave "like perfectly chiseled pawns on a playwright's chess-
board" but were remote and farcical rather than appearing as
authentic human beings.[57] Kelly identified the specific failure
of Goldman's script was that it was written in a way that prevented the audience from connecting with the tangled web of
emotions presented in the play.[58] Goldman was also admonished

for miscalculating some of his writing, causing two moments of high drama in the production to end up "leveled by the humor thudding against them like a wrecker's ball."[59] On the positive side, Kelly identified Preston as "perfect as Henry" and Harris as "superb" as Eleanor.[60] Timothy Mayor of *The Harvard Crimson* was not as kind. He delivered a scathing review that pointedly declared the play as "inadequate" and downright "bad."[61]

The preview closed in Boston on February 26, and the production moved to New York where it opened at the Ambassador Theatre on March 3 to mixed reviews. *The Lion in Winter* received positive reviews from Jack Gaver of United Press International, Walter Kerr from the *Herald Tribune*, and Douglas Watt from the *Daily News*, but received negative reviews from William Glover of the Associated Press and Stanley Kauffmann of *The New York Times*.

Rosemary Harris was aware *The New York Times* held more sway and power with the theater-going public than any other newspaper. She was also keenly aware that Stanley Kauffmann had been installed as the interim theater critic at the *Times* between January and August 1966–the time frame in which *The Lion in Winter* made its Broadway debut. When Kauffmann's review suggested that the production "never really shakes or concerns" the audience and declared Goldman's characters are "recognizable but not affecting; his drama is discernible but not gripping,"[62] Harris immediately recognized the review was the "death knell" for the production.[63] Although the actress conceded that "Stanley Kauffmann and the *Times* is all that mattered in those days," she nonetheless remained "cross and angry" with Kauffmann for not recognizing *The Lion in Winter* as a classic.[64] Kauffmann's review in *The New York Times* had a devastating effect on ticket sales. Harris recalled,

When Stanley Kauffmann's review came out in the *Times*, that killed us dead. And we struggled on for about three months. We talked about giving up our salaries to try and help the production, and Pres was wonderfully practical. He said, "Well, you can do what you like, but I'm not giving up my salary because I know it won't make the jot of difference. I've done this before. I've been round the block and it doesn't help at all."[65]

Despite Preston's admonition, Harris decided that doing something to save the production was better than doing nothing. The actress recalled she and another cast member were both earning $1,500.00 a week, and they agreed to individually give up a thousand dollars of their weekly salary to help keep the play afloat. Despite these valiant efforts, Harris acknowledged, "Pres was absolutely right, because it didn't make a jot of difference."[66] *The Lion in Winter* closed on May 21, 1966 after only 92 performances.

Notwithstanding the short run of the play, the 1966 Tony Awards nominating committee selected Rosemary Harris as a nominee for Best Actress in a Play. Noel Willman was also nominated in the category of Best Director of a Play. The twentieth annual Tony Awards was held in the Rainbow Room in New York City's Rockefeller Center on June 20, 1966. The afternoon awards ceremony was hosted by George Abbott and Ginger Rogers and broadcast on local radio station WCBS. Although Noel Willman lost his Tony bid to director Peter Brook for *Marat/Sade*, Rosemary Harris won the Tony Award for Best Actress in a Play for her outstanding portrayal of Eleanor of Aquitaine in *The Lion in Winter*.

The film version of *The Lion in Winter* was released in late October 1968 with Peter O'Toole in the role of King Henry II. Katherine Hepburn had been offered the film role of Eleanor of Aquitaine, which Harris acknowledged was "right and proper because it should have been her role on Broadway in the first place."[67]

Preston's personal life experienced both highs and lows during the next few months. It was in 1966 that Preston's forty-six-year-old brother, Frank, was diagnosed with malignant lymphoma and began an extensive course of treatment for the disease.[68] On a happier note, Preston and Catherine made the decision to sell their home in Rye, New York and move north to Connecticut. On June 28, 1966, the couple purchased an eight-acre estate featuring a ten-bathroom Tudor-style home, a small private lake, a greenhouse, and a swimming pool on Dublin Hill Drive in Greenwich. Once the property transfer was complete, Preston, Catherine, and Boy, the couple's Golden Retriever, moved into the Connecticut home. Their house in Rye remained on the real estate market and was not sold until almost a year later in June 1967.

Preston planned to take a respite from the stage following the disappointing run of *Ben Franklin in Paris*, but he soon discovered that even the best-laid plans often go awry. It was producer David Merrick who initiated plans to develop a musical adaptation of Jan de Hartog's two-character play *The Fourposter*, which he retitled as *I Do! I Do!* When Gower Champion was tapped to direct the proposed musical, his first order of business was to suggest Mary Martin and Robert Preston for the lead roles and to contact Tom Jones and Harvey Schmidt, composers of *The Fantasticks*, to write the book and score for the production.[69]

The plot of *I Do! I Do!* centers on the marriage of the musical's characters, Agnes and Michael. The story chronicles the ups and downs of the couple's marriage from their wedding night in the early 1900s, to the birth of their children, Michael's success as an author, his midlife crisis and extramarital affair, and concludes with the pair as empty-nesters who, after fifty years of marriage, decide to downsize to a smaller home. The action unfolds in the confines of the couple's bedroom on a set featuring a large four-poster bed.

Although Mary Martin had agreed to play the role of Agnes in *I Do! I Do!,* Merrick and Champion were unable to secure Preston for several more months. After Preston turned down the role of Michael four separate times, Gower Champion gave up on securing the actor for the musical.[70] Martin was aware that Preston had just completed *The Lion in Winter* and was hesitant about jumping into another Broadway production.[71] It didn't help that the actor was also recuperating from a recent eye injury: the retina of Preston's eye had been scratched by a low-hanging tree branch while he was walking his dog near his Connecticut home.[72] Some in the press speculated Preston was discouraged by his reception in *The Lion in Winter* and the failure of the production–the third such box office dud since his Broadway success in *The Music Man.*[73] The actor confided to friends that he planned to take a vacation from the stage, explaining, "I think that Broadway has had enough of me for a while, and that I've had enough of Broadway. I hope a vacation will be helpful on both sides."[74]

Champion set out to secure a replacement for Preston and auditioned Howard Keel for the role opposite Mary Martin. Martin, who was present at the tryout, acknowledged Keel could act and had a beautiful voice but recognized he was no Robert Preston.[75] Martin had fond memories of working with Preston when the two co-starred alongside Fred MacMurray in the film

New York Town (1941). The actress was beginning to waver in her commitment to the production, telling Champion she desperately wanted to play the role of Agnes in *I Do! I Do!* but only opposite Robert Preston.[76] It was later that evening that David Merrick announced to a delighted Martin and Champion, "I've got Bob Preston."[77] After twelve refusals, Merrick had somehow managed to secure Preston for the musical.[78] Merrick wasted no time in making his casting coup official in the press; the New York *Daily News* featured the story "Robert Preston Says I Do, I Do" in its June 20 issue.[79]

Five weeks of rehearsals for the musical began in late August 1966 at the 46th Street Theatre in New York.[80] The production was grueling for the two middle-aged stars as the musical broke existing precedent by using only two characters—no chorus line, or singing ensemble.[81] Despite the endurance required for her role, Martin found the rehearsals invigorating,

> Our entire rehearsal time was like a three-way tennis game, a love match. Bob would suddenly do something which Gower and I loved. Gower would think up something we couldn't wait to try. I stayed awake nights dreaming up things to please them. I can't ever remember having such concentrated fun while working.[82]

The script required at least one of the actors to be on stage at all times during the two-hour production. Unlike other musicals, there was "no supporting cast, no big production numbers, [and] no chance to vamp while somebody else took over,"[83] thus requiring Martin and Preston to maintain incredible stamina during each performance. To add to their stress, the two actors were not only portraying characters on stage, but were also aware they were playing theatrical versions of themselves, an approach built into the script by Jones and Schmidt and high-lighted by Champion's staging.[84]

Mary Martin wore six different wigs and had fourteen costume changes during the musical, with every wardrobe change made to the beat of the music.[85] Her quickest wig change was accomplished in five seconds and her longest costume change had to be completed in one minute and fifty-two seconds.[86] Preston, who was likewise required to make quick wardrobe changes, worked with his dresser Jimmy Davidson for hours to be able to get in and out of costumes to the tempo of the music.[87]

Given the immense trust and chemistry between the two stars, Martin and Preston were uncomfortable with the thought of performing with understudies if either of them was unable to be on stage for a scheduled show. David Merrick concurred; he realized ticket holders would be flocking to *I Do! I Do!* to see Mary Martin and Robert Preston on stage, not their understudies. Merrick established a "no understudies" policy: if either Martin or Preston could not perform for any reason, that performance would be canceled and ticket holders would receive a raincheck for a future performance.[88]

The production then headed to Boston for an initial three-week preview. The first public offering of *I Do! I Do!* was featured at Colonial Theater on September 26. Samuel Hirsch, the drama editor from *The Boston Herald,* shared positive feedback about the musical with his readers, noting that "Mary Martin and Robert Preston are in love with this charming cameo of a musical and show it. Their acting makes the evening confetti-bright."[89] Hirsch did notice that some strain was evident during the early part of the production around the smoothness of costume changes.[90] *Boston Globe* theater critic Kevin Kelly provided a favorable review of the show. On the positive side, Kelly praised Preston and Martin as being "superb" and gave a thumbs-up to both the score and to director Gower Champion. Although Kelly characterized the production as "quietly entertaining and solidly well done," he also highlighted the musical's shortcomings. Kelly perceived the production as saddled by "a few lapses and one or two ragged exits" and viewed the "Thousands of Flowers" scene toward the end of the show as being "oddly out of place."[91] Gower Champion was shaken by the criticism, believing the musical "bombed in Boston" when rumors began circulating that the show was "a disaster."[92]

Mary Martin's health issues were responsible for the cancellation of five performances between October 6 and October 9. The press was told the performances were suspended after Martin injured her left foot during a rehearsal on October 6. However, David Kaufman's biography of Martin indicates the actress actually experienced a severe case of gout that required a brief hospitalization.[93]

The Boston preview concluded on October 15 and the production made its way to the National Theatre in Washington D.C., where it opened on October 19. Former First Lady Mamie Eisenhower attended a show at the National Theatre and made her way backstage to congratulate Martin and Preston on their performances. When Mary Martin brought Mrs. Eisenhower into Preston's dressing room for an impromptu meet-and-greet, the ladies were surprised to find the actor sans trousers. Preston quickly dressed and Mrs. Eisenhower extended her husband's regrets for being unable to attend the show.[94]

The theater critics in the nation's capital reacted slightly better to the musical than did their counterparts in Boston, but not by much. Louis Cedrone, Jr. from *The Evening Sun* described *I Do! I Do!* as "charming but slight." He noted the musical picks up toward the end of the first act with a succession of four "solid songs," but characterized the songs in the second act as being only "very good off-Broadway."[95] Although R.H. Gardner from *The Baltimore Sun* told readers that the tone of the musical was "at times a little too cute" for his taste, he went on to praise the unusual two-person cast format as an "extraordinary accomplishment" on behalf of the show's director.[96] The review by Cecil Smith that appeared in *The Los Angeles Times* caused great angst for David Merrick and Gower Champion. Although Smith recognized that "much of the charm and the touching humanity of the show is in its simplicity," he also made clear that "after an enchanting first act, the musical finds itself with nowhere to go."[97]

Dismayed by the critical reviews of the musical in both Boston and D.C., an anxious David Merrick demanded that changes be made and brought in a series of songwriters, including Jerry Herman and Jule Styne, to make improvements to the show.[98] Realizing that the musical needed additional tweaking, Gower Champion asked Merrick to extend the preview period for an additional three weeks. Merrick agreed with Champion's assessment and booked the Shubert Theater in Cincinnati to provide the director additional time to work on the production.[99]

When the Washington preview concluded on November 5, the cast and crew relocated to the Shubert Theatre in Cincinnati, where the show ran from November 9 to November 26. Due to the strain of the performance schedule on the musical's two middle-aged actors, the number of weekly performances in Cincinnati was limited to a total of seven, with a matinee offered only on Saturdays.[100] Mary Martin recalled that although the production originally scheduled six nightly performances plus two matinees a week, that timetable brought both Martin and Preston to the breaking point.[101] Preston acknowledged that "by Saturday night we were playing on sheer nerve. On Sunday I had to stay in bed all day to recover. I couldn't enjoy the day off."[102] Since both Preston and Martin agreed to take a percentage of the show's weekly gross in lieu of a fixed salary, the reduction in performances per week resulted in a significant downgrade in their wages. Preston viewed the loss of compensation as necessary to protect the physical and mental stamina of the costars, noting that without the pared-down performance schedule, "we wouldn't have lived to enjoy the money."[103] Offstage in Cincinnati, the two stars could get punchy; the hijinks included Preston getting Martin rip-roaring drunk the evening *Life* magazine took a photo of the duo in their first act pajama costumes.[104]

The preview performance schedule in Cincinnati prevented the cast and crew from returning home for the Thanksgiving holiday, so Gower Champion arranged for a dinner at the hotel for the entire cast and crew where each table received its own turkey. Although *I Do! I Do!* featured only two actors on stage, the musical was supported by a crew of ninety, all of whom participated in the Cincinnati Thanksgiving feast.[105]

Two songs and reprises were eliminated from the show and four more were added during the musical's run in Cincinnati,[106] causing E.B. Radcliffe of *The Cincinnati Enquirer* to declare *I Do! I Do!* a "fine show."[107] By November 8, *I Do! I Do!* was declared the Broadway season's hottest ticket, having amassed a million dollars in advance ticket sales.[108] Gower Champion's request for an extension following the Washington D.C. preview paid off; by the time the musical completed the three-week tour in

Cincinnati on November 26, it was properly tweaked, tuned, and ready for Broadway.[109]

I Do! I Do! opened at the 46th Street Theatre on Broadway on December 5, 1966, two weeks later than had been originally scheduled, as the musical required an extended two-month try-out period to iron out all the kinks.[110] The opening night party for the musical's debut was held in the swank Rainbow Room at Rockefeller Center. Attendees at the black-tie bash were entertained by the fancy footwork of the famous dancing duo Gower Champion and his soon-to-be ex-wife, Marge.[111] The theatrical reviews of *I Do! I Do!* were generally favorable. *Life* magazine described the musical as "a love duet to a happy marriage," hailed Martin and Preston as "magnificent,"[112] and compared the actors to party hosts who "knock themselves out to give everybody a fine time."[113] John Chapman of the *Daily News* lauded the show, noting "the opening night audience was thoroughly devoted"[114] to the musical. The staff at *Time* Magazine believed the musical primarily owed its success to its two stars who were "charmers of seismic force and theatrical perfectionists." *Time*'s review went on to point out that Preston "hisses energy" and is "as restless and agile as a panther" on stage.[115]

Two critical reviews of the musical were less than glowing. Walter Kerr of *The New York Times* described the musical's content as "barely passable, a sort of carefully condensed time capsule of all the cliches that have ever been spawned" about marriage. However, he did describe Martin and Preston as "a handsome couple," and noted that Preston was "at his untouchable best when the show asks him to be pompous and blissfully obtuse."[116] Although Cecil Smith of *The Los Angeles Times* noted that *I Do! I Do!* "provides a completely enchanting evening" for audiences, he also carped that the musical arrived on

Broadway "after a lengthy tour during which authors Tim Jones and Harvey Schmidt and director Gower Champion were supposed to do a great deal of fixing it up. I saw the show a couple of months ago in Washington and I can't say that what they have now is different than what they had then."[117]

As he did in all of his appearances on the Broadway stage, Preston never offered theatergoers a walk-through performance in *I Do! I Do!* He consistently brought opening night energy to every scene, and he enthusiastically bounded across the footlights to fill the audience with the joy of the moment. The performances also benefited from the fact that Preston and Martin were fond of each other and shared mutual respect, admiration, and trust. Beyond this, Mary Martin was appreciative of Preston's considerateness. Martin was well aware that Preston was partial to Italian food loaded with garlic, and this was the culinary fare that he would often consume before their evening performances. Since the musical required the actors to "kiss about every fifteen seconds through the entire performance," Martin was grateful that Preston would always bring her "a tiny taste of his Italian dinner before we went on. Hence no problem while kissing."[118]

Although Mary Martin enjoyed an outstanding professional relationship with Preston and was thrilled to work with him[119] during the run of *I Do! I Do!*, she was acutely aware he was a private man. The script of the musical required the two actors to engage in bedroom scenes during each performance. Martin acknowledged that as a result of all the close contact,

> You get to know somebody pretty well. Bob never missed a performance, never admitted illness, never let me down. We loved working together.

He was the oboe, I was the violin. But I was more
baffled by him than anyone I'd ever known. We
rarely talked outside the theater. I was never in
his house.[120]

As Broadway audiences flocked to see *I Do! I Do!*, the musical's exhausted co-stars found the performance schedule to
be grueling. Preston and Martin originally had a "gentleman's
agreement" to do seven performances per week, including a
Saturday matinee as long as they were physically able to do so.
However, after the first six months of the musical's Broadway
run, Martin and Preston made the mutual decision to break
their agreement and eliminate all matinee performances from
the schedule.[121]

The first nationally televised Tony Awards ceremony took
place on March 26, 1967, just a few months following the
Broadway debut of *I Do! I Do!*. Martin and Preston were chosen to co-host the telecast in which they performed the duet,
"Nobody's Perfect," from their musical.[122] Preston snagged
the Tony Award for Best Actor in a Musical, beating out fellow nominees Jack Gilford (*Cabaret*), Alan Alda (*The Apple Tree*),
and Norman Wisdom (*Walking Happy*). Although Mary Martin
was nominated for Best Performance by a Leading Actress in a
Musical for her role as Agnes in *I Do! I Do!*, it was Barbara Harris
who took home the award for her role as Eve in *The Apple Tree*.
Despite her Tony loss, Martin was ecstatic about Preston's win,
exclaiming, "I was so happy for Robert. I love him dearly," and
"the most meaningful Tony Award ever received by anyone"
had been bestowed upon Preston during the 1967 telecast.[123]

The specter of illness and exhaustion continued to weigh
heavily on Mary Martin during the musical and, before long,

the rigors of a two-person play began to exact a physical toll on the actress. On May 11, 1967, Sam Zolotow reported in *The New York Times* that there had been no performances of *I Do! I Do!* in the past three days and performances would be suspended "until Miss Martin recovers from a virus infection affecting her nose, throat, larynx, and vocal cords."[124]

Toward the end of 1967, when *I Do! I Do!* was closing in on one year on Broadway, Mary Martin convinced Preston to take the musical on a national tour beginning in April 1968. The proposed fourteen-month coast-to-coast tour would involve performances in twenty-seven cities across the United States. Martin acknowledged the rapport she enjoyed with Preston was the impetus for the tour, adding, "I've never known anyone who was such a perfectionist. We've never ad libbed. I loathe people who do. We go together like an oboe and a violin."[125] Preston was on board with Martin's suggestion of a national tour of the musical. A mutual friend of the two actors pointed out that "professionally, Mary and Bob are married."[126] Preston concurred with that assessment, noting that "whatever Mary does, I do! Mary and I are crazy about each other. We breathe together. It's a tough show to do, but going it with Mary, it's not as tough as it would be with somebody else."[127]

Mary Martin's contract to perform in *I Do! I Do!* concluded on December 6, 1967, at which time she left the show for some well-deserved time off, and Preston likewise made his exit from the production. The musical continued on Broadway until June 15, 1968 with Martin and Preston replaced by Carol Lawrence and Gordon MacRae.

Shortly after completing her Broadway stint in *I Do! I Do!*, Mary Martin was admitted to the hospital and underwent a hysterectomy. Since the national tour of the musical was set to commence in April, Martin made every effort to recuperate from her surgery as quickly as possible.[128]

The year-long national tour of *I Do! I Do!* kicked off on April 4, 1968 at the Auditorium Theatre in Rochester, New York. This initial stop on the tour was followed by performances in Indianapolis and Minneapolis, before spending two months each in Los Angeles (April 29 to June 22) and San Francisco (June 25 to August 17).[129] Preston continued his life-long habit of cigarette smoking on the road, with his latest puff of choice being king-sized Viceroy filter-tips.[130] Accompanying Preston on the nationwide tour was his wife, Catherine. Mary Martin's husband and manager, Richard Halliday, likewise accompanied his wife on tour. Martin indicated the two couples enjoyed each other's company and "had a marvelous time all over the country both on and off stage."[131] The tour continued with week-long performances in Portland, Oregon; Vancouver, British Columbia; Seattle, Washington; San Diego, California; Denver, Colorado; and Phoenix, Arizona. Martin indicated as the tour continued,

> Bob and I were both coming apart at the seams, but we didn't know it. Bob began catching colds, which he never acknowledged, and having troubles with his voice. I had diverticulitis and didn't know it.[132]

Preston and Martin continued to appear in the show during stops in Kansas City and St. Louis, Missouri; Omaha, Nebraska; St. Paul, Minnesota; Milwaukee, Wisconsin; Memphis Tennessee; and Dallas, Texas. It was while the show was in Dallas that Mary Martin became ill.[133] Despite not feeling well, Martin continued to perform as the musical traveled to Houston, Texas;

Oklahoma City, Oklahoma; Hershey, Pennsylvania; Baltimore, Maryland; and Detroit, Michigan. It was during performances at the Fisher Theatre in Detroit that the tour came to a screeching halt in February 1969 when Martin was hospitalized for an intestinal infection. Given the seriousness of Martin's condition, the remainder of the Detroit shows were canceled. Preston and his wife returned to their home in Greenwich, Connecticut where he continued to keep tabs on Martin's recovery. The actor expressed the intention to resume the musical tour if and when Martin was given the green light to do so by her medical team.[134] Despite Preston's the-show-must-go-on attitude, he acknowledged he would have no regrets about ending the tour having been in the production for a year on Broadway and almost a year on tour.[135] Truth be told, both Preston and his wife Catherine "disliked hotel living," a lifestyle that was de rigueur while on tour.[136]

Both Martin and Preston were aware that the final segment of the *I Do! I Do!* tour loomed ahead: a one-week appearance in Columbus, Ohio, two weeks at the Shubert Theater in Philadelphia, and the final five-week leg of the tour in Chicago.[137] All hopes of completing the tour were dashed when Martin was flown to Chicago on March 4 where she was hospitalized at Passavant Hospital.[138] Martin acknowledged the last portion of the musical tour was canceled after receiving an ultimatum from her Chicago-based physician, Dr. Edward Briggs: "If you want to live, then my word is law. Stop working."[139]

TRIUMPH AND TRAGEDY

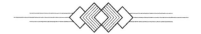

With the national tour of *I Do! I Do!* in the rear-view mirror, Preston took a step back from Broadway and Hollywood and spent the next two years enjoying a well-deserved hiatus at his estate in Greenwich, Connecticut. Gardening and woodchopping–not acting–highlighted his weekly agenda until 1971.[1] For Preston, a karmic boon unfolded when the producers of the twenty-fifth annual Tony Awards show decided the theme of the 1971 broadcast would salute the past quarter-century of award-winning musicals and hoped to feature as many of the original musical stars as possible in the program. Since *The Music Man* had won the Tony Award for Best Musical in 1958, the telecast producers reached out to Preston to inquire if he would reprise his role as Harold Hill and sing "Ya Got Trouble" during the Tony Awards tribute. Much to the disappointment of the Tony Awards production team, Preston initially declined to participate in the show. Without Preston, the producers would need to resort to Plan B and reach out to Forrest Tucker, who played Harold Hill in *The Music Man's* national tour, as a substitute performer.

Preston, fiercely protective of his portrayal of Harold Hill, quickly reconsidered his decision, wisecracking, "I'd be damned if I'd let Forrest Tucker do my role on the show."[2]

Thirteen years after his Broadway stint in *The Music Man*, Preston, dressed in a white suit and gold bow-tie, flawlessly sang the quick-tempo "Ya Got Trouble" while prancing deftly around the stage, accompanied by a chorus of singers dressed as River City residents. Watching the Tony telecast that evening was ABC Pictures executive Martin Baum, who was preparing to produce a rodeo-themed film directed by Sam Peckinpah and starring Steve McQueen. Baum, who instinctively knew Preston would be perfect for a role in his upcoming movie, *Junior Bonner* (1972), reached out to the actor with an offer to play the role of Steve McQueen's father in the film.[3] Baum was aware McQueen always surrounded himself with weaker actors and purposely cast Preston in the film to exact a stronger performance from the actor. The strategy worked and McQueen gave one of his best screen performances in *Junior Bonner*.[4] Preston's acceptance of the role of Ace Bonner officially ended his eight-year absence from motion pictures.

In the two years since the abrupt conclusion of the *I Do! I Do!* national tour, Preston had become a self-described gentleman farmer at his Connecticut estate and realized the "good life" on his farm had overshadowed the lure of stage and screen. His perspective changed when he received the *Junior Bonner* script from director Sam Peckinpah, telling Catherine, "I thought I was semi-retired, but all I've been doing was just reading bad scripts."[5] Preston knew he was "in the second awkward age of an actor. The first is in your teens, and the second when you're no longer a leading man but not yet an older character actor,"[6] but acknowledged that "there's nothing like a good script to get an actor out of retirement."[7] Moreover, Preston was looking forward to working with Peckinpah and relished being able to play the "nice salty role" of Ace Bonner,[8] a character he felt embodied "overtones of Harold Hill."[9]

The *Junior Bonner* story, written by Jeb Rosebrook, centered around the character of Junior Bonner, an aging rodeo star who drives his horse trailer from rodeo to rodeo looking for his next win, and returns home to his hometown of Prescott, Arizona to enter the town's annual Frontier Days rodeo. Flat broke, Junior borrows money to pay the rodeo entrance fees. Junior's parents are long-estranged; his mother, Elvira, has been reduced to taking in boarders and growing her own produce just to make ends meet. The family farm is being demolished by his unprincipled brother Curly, a real estate developer, to make way for a mobile home park. Curly has swindled the farmland from his father to pad his profits. Junior refuses Curly's offer to join him in selling mobile homes and instead meets up with his father, Ace, at the Frontier Days Parade. Ace is a sixty-year-old ex-rodeo star and a charismatic womanizer. With a penchant for booze and dreams of a new life of silver mining in Australia, Ace asks Junior for money to fund his trip Down Under and is disappointed to learn Junior is broke. Junior and Ace participate in the rodeo's cow-milking contest, but they lose when Ace gets tripped by a dog and spills the team's milk. The family meets up at a local bar where Ace dances with his estranged wife and Junior makes a connection with Charmagne, an out-of-town beauty with a wealthy boyfriend. Although Ace's invitation to Elvira to accompany him to Australia is met with a slap in the face, the estranged couple enjoy one last evening of connubial romance. In the bull riding event, Junior successfully rides a black bull named Sunshine, wins $950 in prize money, and uses his winnings to purchase a first-class, one-way ticket to Australia for Ace. Broke but unwilling to change, Junior drives off with his horse toward the next stop on the rodeo circuit, clearly following in the aimless footsteps of the father for whom he was named.

Preston, just twelve years McQueen's senior, was cast as his father in the film. In order to adequately age Preston to fit the role, his hair was tinted silver and skillful makeup was applied to give his face a leathery, grizzled look. In addition to Preston and McQueen, the main cast of *Junior Bonner* included veteran actress Ida Lupino as Elvira Bonner, Ben Johnson as Buck Roan, Joe Don Baker as Curly Bonner, Barbara Leigh as Junior Bonner's love interest Charmagne, Mary Murphy as Curley's wife Ruth Bonner, and Sandra Deel as Nurse Arlis. Prior to casting Ida Lupino, Preston's former *Union Pacific* and *The Lady Gambles* co-star, Barbara Stanwyck, turned down the role of Steve McQueen's mother in the film,[10] as had Susan Hayward,[11] who co-starred with Preston in *Beau Geste, Reap the Wild Wind,* and *Tulsa.* The supporting cast aside, the film was designed to showcase a different side of Steve McQueen, one quite antithetical from the roles in his previous action movies.

Steve McQueen was born near Indianapolis, Indiana in March 1930 to Jullian Crawford, a promiscuous "good-time gal"[12] and distant mother,[13] and William McQueen, a circus stuntman and absent father. McQueen endured a traumatic childhood that necessitated being taken in by various relatives when his mother would decide to disappear, as well as a step-father who brutally beat him.[14] As a youth without a stable home life, the troubled McQueen joined a violent street gang and was arrested for stealing hubcaps from pricey cars.[15] At age fourteen, McQueen was sent to Boys Republic reform school[16] where he remained until he aged out at eighteen.

With nowhere else to turn, McQueen enlisted in the Marine Corps where he served three years as a tank driver.[17] Once back in civilian life, McQueen made his way to New York where he began studying acting at the Neighborhood Playhouse[18] and the famed Actors Studio.[19] McQueen began appearing in stage productions in 1952 and in films in 1956. Many of his iconic movies were filmed between 1956 and 1971 including *Never Love a Stranger* (1956), *Never So Few* (1959), *The Magnificent Seven* (1960), *The Great Escape* (1963), *The Cincinnati Kid* (1965), *The Sand Pebbles* (1966), *The Thomas Crown Affair* (1968), and *Le Mans* (1971). By the mid-1970's, McQueen was the highest-paid actor in Hollywood.[20]

McQueen regularly used marijuana and cocaine and experimented with the hallucinogenic drugs peyote and LSD.[21] As an actor, McQueen was a nightmare for producers, directors, and other actors to work with, regularly forgetting his lines, walking off the set, being wildly argumentative, and throwing fits over the smallest issues.[22] He was also promiscuous, quick-tempered, violent, and vindictive. Envious of next-door neighbor, friend, and fellow actor James Garner, McQueen would venture out on his patio and urinate on Garner's house[23] or throw his empty beer cans onto Garner's neatly manicured lawn.[24] He behaved similarly toward another neighbor, The Who drummer Keith Moon: he twice shot out Moon's exterior spotlights in the middle of the night because they disrupted his sleep.[25] The movie-going public, oblivious to the actor's bad behavior, considered McQueen to be the coolest guy in Hollywood.

The filming of *Junior Bonner* took place in Prescott, Arizona during the town's Frontier Days Rodeo in the summer of 1971 and required seven weeks to complete.[26] Cast and crew were housed at the Prescottonian Hotel on Gurley Street. Veteran actors Lupino and Preston, old friends who had known each other since their early studio days in Hollywood,[27] maintained an open-door policy at the hotel to encourage the cast and crew to visit and enjoy a libation. Actress Barbara Leigh recalled that in the evenings, Preston and Lupino used to sit outside their rooms with their drinks and there was a lot of laughter,[28] adding it was "never a dull moment" since "when you finished partying with Robert, you floated over to Ida's for more of the same."[29]

According to McQueen biographer Marshall Terrill, Preston was very much respected by Steve McQueen.[30] However, after first meeting Preston, McQueen was concerned about the disparity in their sizes and questioned Peckinpah about Preston's height. When McQueen was told Preston was six feet tall, he insisted that Preston "wear sandals during the scenes they had together"[31] to prevent the veteran actor from towering over him on film. Barbara Leigh likewise indicated that McQueen adored Preston and emphasized he "was a true gentleman, his voice was strong" and he "took command of any scene," even those with McQueen.[32] Preston, however, recalled some tense moments on the set with McQueen:

> Steve wasn't happy. He said, "Ace has got all of the funny lines." I said, "There's not a funny line in the picture." He said, "Well, they're amusing." And I said to Steve, "Don't you realize *who* Ace is? Do you realize why he's in the picture?" [Steve] says, "He's my father." And I said, "Yeah, but the name of the picture is *Junior Bonner*. And Ace is what Junior's going to be in thirty-five years." He never bought that.[33]

Peckinpah kept the film on schedule and often reshot scenes to capture the best possible print. Preston, who had his share of retakes in the film, was asked by Peckinpah to reshoot a scene at the local bar. The actor acknowledged:

> I had a lovely, lovely speech in the bar when Ace is getting half-loaded and all the old-timers are there. Ace talked about the time that he rode the championship bull in Madison Square Garden. Oh, it went wonderful, played it beautifully. And the whole audience in the bar just ate it up. And Sam came over to me and he said, "That was good. We've got a print in case we want it." He said, "Do me a favor. Let's do one just for yourself." And I knew what he meant. Ace wasn't telling the story. He was reliving it and he didn't care if there was anyone in the bar. And I did it that way. That's the way it is in the movie.[34]

On one occasion, McQueen arrived unprepared for a scene with Ida Lupino, resulting in endless retakes, and the seasoned actress refused to continue filming until McQueen learned his lines. The scene involved Lupino, as McQueen's mother, talking to her son in the kitchen of her home over a glass of milk and a slice of apple pie. Although Lupino delivered her lines exactly as written in the script, McQueen kept changing his lines in each shot, causing all of the takes to be unusable. Lupino, who was exasperated by McQueen's lack of preparation, told the actor in no uncertain terms, "You damn well better know your lines tomorrow or you're going to eat one helluva lot of apple pie!"[35] McQueen took Lupino's admonition to heart and the scene was shot perfectly in one take the next day.[36] Preston also experienced McQueen's difficult side during a scene, filmed at Prescott's railway station, that served as a reconciliation between father and son.[37] Preston was unaware that circumstances in McQueen's past made the scene the hardest for him to film in the movie.[38] The director had already shot one take of the scene, but when Peckinpah requested a retake, Preston became frustrated when McQueen

> . . . Starts saying entirely different lines. And he would say something that I would find pretty much unanswerable. It made such little sense. Why not just take the bottle away from him . . . till he could say something I could answer? It kept rolling, kept rolling, and finally, Sam (Peckinpah) said, "What the hell are you doing?" [McQueen] said, "I'm not going to say those other lines." [Sam] said, "Well, he can't answer those crazy things that you're saying." And [McQueen] says, "Well, that's the way it's going to be. That's all, that's it." So, Sam looked at me and said, "Pres," and I said, "Sam, you've got it on the other take and you're the director." He said, "Yeah, that's right. Okay. Wrap it up." It was crazy, I never understood.[39]

McQueen initially completed that scene on the first take as dictated by the script, but he "found it difficult to do a sensitive scene with another man."[40] Unbeknownst to Preston, the train station scene evoked strong feelings within McQueen that were directly related to the painful absence of his father in his life. McQueen's emotional uneasiness surfaced in the father/son scene since Preston's "portrayal of Ace brought the emotion of father and son to absolute reality."[41] For these reasons, this was a sensitive scene that McQueen had no desire to revisit.

On another occasion, Preston remained cool when an inebriated Sam Peckinpah unceremoniously crashed a "thank you" dinner that Preston and Lupino were hosting for the hair and wardrobe crew at the nearby Pine Cone Inn. Peckinpah was miffed about not receiving an invitation to attend the dinner. Preston, Lupino, and their guests dressed up for the occasion, but Peckinpah pushed his way into the event wearing jeans and brought along two other uninvited guests in a show of power: the screenwriter and a shabbily dressed female companion. Peckinpah's behavior caused the evening to turn awkward, but rather than make a scene, Preston and Lupino kept their feelings about the incident to themselves.[42]

The filming of *Junior Bonner* was completed on August 14 and the movie was released in June 1972 with the opening night premiere held at Grauman's Chinese Theater in Hollywood.[43] It was unfortunate for *Junior Bonner* that three other rodeo-themed films, *J.W. Coop* (1972), *The Honkers* (1972), and *When the Legends Die* (1972), were also released the same summer.[44]

The critical response to *Junior Bonner* tended to skew positive. The review from *The New York Times*, proffered by Vincent Canby, noted *Junior Bonner* was a film "which looks like a rodeo film and sounds like a rodeo film, is a superior family comedy in disguise" and declared the movie was "made to order for both McQueen and Preston."[45] Kathleen Carroll from the New York *Daily News* opined that "the movie lopes along like a lovesick calf until Robert Preston and Ida Lupino appear," then the veteran actors fire up the film to "crack like a bullwhip for at least as long as they are on screen." Carroll also recognized

McQueen's role "fits him like a glove," and concluded *Junior Bonner* was "a pleasantly diverting movie."[46] Similarly, the film earned three stars out of four from *Chicago Tribune* critic Gene Siskel, who declared *Junior Bonner* was "a decent picture from a fine director."[47] George Anderson of *The Pittsburgh Post-Gazette* noted that "*Junior Bonner* is not the best film Sam Peckinpah has made, but it may be the best example of his directorial brilliance," and credited Peckinpah for taking "unexceptional material" and turning it into a film "alive with powerful, revealing scenes, truthful insights, [and] believable characters." The review also indicated that "Preston steals the picture in one of those lusty character roles for which his hearty virility is appropriate."[48] To the critics who commended Preston on his scene-stealing performance in the movie, the actor laughingly acknowledged, "Well–didn't leave my farm for nothing."[49]

On the negative side, Roger Ebert from the *Chicago Sun-Times* declared the film a "flat out disappointment," and gave the movie two stars out of four since it "simply never comes together and works as a whole."[50] *Newsweek* cinema critic Charles Michener observed that because *Junior Bonner* was the third rodeo movie to be released in a short time period, this film genre "has gone a bit stale." Although McQueen and Preston were cited as "appealing actors," they and Peckinpah were viewed as "trapped in a screenplay by Jeb Rosebrook that would break the spirit of lesser men."[51]

Despite some good reviews, the movie was considered a flop at the box office. *Junior Bonner* managed to gross $2 million worldwide, resulting in a $4 million loss for ABC Pictures; it was the only film to star Steve McQueen that lost money.[52] Preston, who was able to appreciate the irony in the situation, joked, "wouldn't you know I'd be in the only Steve McQueen movie that didn't make a nickel."[53] Despite the film's reception in 1972, *Junior Bonner* gradually transcended into an American movie classic when "virtues were discovered in the film in the 1980's that somehow previously failed to surface."[54]

Thanks to Marlon Brando, Preston found himself featured in yet another film role just a few months after the completion of *Junior Bonner*. In the fall of 1970, Broadway producer David Merrick contracted with Paramount Pictures to transform his Broadway production, *Child's Play*, into a movie. In September 1971, Director Sidney Lumet, famous for bringing psychological dramas to the screen, was selected to direct the motion picture.[55]

The plot of *Child's Play (1972)* highlights troubling events at St. Charles Catholic School for Boys. School alumnus Paul Reis returns to the school as the new physical education teacher and is reunited with his former English teacher, Joseph Dobbs. Dobbs and the school's Latin teacher, Jerome Malley, are feuding academic rivals. Malley, who is also a caretaker for his elderly mother, is feared by students for being a rigid taskmaster while Dobbs is embraced by students as a friend and advocate. When Malley begins receiving obscene mail and harassing phone calls, he assumes Dobbs is responsible for the harassment. Meanwhile, mysterious evil forces appear to be provoking students to harm and maim their classmates. The school's headmaster, Father Mozian, cancels religious services and dismisses students when a classmate is discovered stripped of his clothes and suspended over the altar in the chapel. Malley's paranoia leads the headmaster to press for the teacher's resignation. After the death of his mother, Malley refuses to resign or take a leave of absence from the school. The headmaster forces the Latin teacher's hand by showing him an obscene magazine with the teacher's name on it. Malley lashes out at Dobbs before he hurls himself off the roof of the school building in the presence of students. As the school prepares to permanently close in the aftermath of Malley's suicide, the headmaster reveals to Paul that it was Dobbs who had provided him with Malley's obscene magazine. Paul then realizes Malley's paranoia about Dobbs's knavery and deception were justified. Paul, who instructs students not to trust Dobbs after overhearing him accept a teaching position at another school, is then attacked by Dobbs's protégés. The film ends with Dobbs sitting in a dark chapel and slowly being surrounded by a group of menacing students.

Marlon Brando, Beau Bridges, and acclaimed actor James Mason were originally cast in October as the film's three main characters.[56] Merrick believed Marlon Brando would be the perfect choice to play the role of Joseph Dobbs, and Brando agreed to appear in the film if the producer found a part in the movie for his good friend, Wally Cox, of *Mr. Peepers* fame.[57]

The principal cast rehearsed in New York City for two weeks beginning in late October, and the seven-week filming schedule commenced on November 1 at Marymount Secondary School, a Catholic girls' boarding school, in Tarrytown, New York.[58] Although the action of the movie takes place in a boys' boarding school, a Catholic girls' school was instead used as the backdrop for the film since the cost of constructing a new school set would have been prohibitive.[59]

Brando began to call for dialogue changes from the moment he arrived on set, and arguments soon ensued between Brando, Merrick, and Lumet.[60] It was also reported that Brando demanded that the setting of a Catholic boys' school be changed to an orphanage and threatened to mumble his lines if his demands were not met. Merrick countered by threatening to have

Brando's lines dubbed by John Wayne.[61] Merrick gave Brando the boot after enduring two days of the actor's incorrigible behavior. The producer explained to the press that he tossed Brando from the film because the actor "wanted to make basic changes in the story and I could not accept that."[62] In the interim, Brando had informed Cox that he had been hired to play a schoolteacher in the film, but when Cox arrived on the rehearsal set, Lumet insisted that he audition for the role. Ultimately, a disappointed Cox was not cast in the film once Brando was bounced from the movie.[63] On November 2, *Variety* confirmed that insurmountable friction between Brando and Merrick resulted in the actor's replacement with Robert Preston.[64]

With a permanent cast in place, filming commenced on a six-day-a-week schedule. Lumet expected the actors on the set and ready to go at 8:00 a.m., and filming began promptly at 8:02 a.m. The cast and crew worked through until 6:00 p.m. each day, with just an hour off each day for lunch.[65] It was just a matter of days before Lumet realized he was facing a losing proposition. After viewing three days' worth of rushes, Lumet knew the story was unable to move from a stage presentation to a screen adaptation and that he was incapable of salvaging the film:

> A terrific gothic melodrama on stage had become a mundane mystery with a telegraphed resolution. It couldn't transfer to the screen–or at least I couldn't do it. What was worse, I couldn't fix it. I didn't know what the problem was, so I couldn't solve it. All I knew was that it was fake, it wasn't going to work. And I was facing seven more weeks of shooting. And worst of all was the fact that I was the director. So I couldn't tell anybody . . .

there was nothing to do but bite my lip for the next seven weeks and try to make the movie look as professional as possible.[66]

Filming for *Child's Play* was completed on December 15, 1971. The director was not quite certain as to how to end the story and filmed two different endings,[67] and this lack of certitude only added to the futility of the project.

Preston was devastated two months later when his brother and best friend succumbed to a long battle with malignant lymphoma on February 19, 1972[68]. Tracy Palmgren Monroe, Frank's alleged daughter, indicated that Frank's illness was quite long, drawn-out, and traumatic for the family.[69] Funerals were an anathema to Preston; they were rites of passage he rigorously avoided whenever possible.[70] Preston traveled to California to be with his family in their collective time of grief following the death of his brother. When the family returned to the house following the funeral, Preston appeared visibly pale and stricken by the painful loss.[71] The actor immediately returned to the refuge of his Connecticut home where he immersed himself in the solitude of outdoor chores as a way to process the agonizing loss of his brother.

Child's Play was released in theaters on December 12, 1972 to less than enthusiastic reviews. Favorable reviews included one from Roger Ebert in the *Chicago Sun-Times*, who described the film as "beautifully acted and very nicely directed," yet noted that because the movie suggests "supernatural overtones," the audience is disappointed when they are provided with "a rather conventional Freudian ending." Although Ebert recognized "the original fault [for this] lies with Robert Marasco's Broadway play," he pointed out that the problems with the play "could have been fixed for the movie."[72] Barry Westgate, the cinema critic from the *Edmonton Journal*, described *Child's Play* as "a gripping, challenging aggregation of macabre suspense, with tension very real and involving from first scene to last." Westgate declared Mason's performance to be "truly remarkable" and noted Preston was "much more controlled than is his usual style, [and] is a superb foil . . . who is so true to type that his performance engenders a kind of insidious queasiness."[73] Paul Zimmerman of *Newsweek*, however, was more critical of the film. He characterized *Child's Play* as a "mixed success" and "an absorbing film despite its disappointing ending." Zimmerman was of the opinion that the film's "real appeal is as a mystery whose twists and turns generate excitement even when they don't make logical sense." He went on to praise the performances by Preston and Mason but declared that "the character of the dimwitted gym teacher who serves as the fulcrum in this moral seesaw weakens the film's impact."[74]

Although *Child's Play* won three of the five major awards at the Irish government's Cork Film International 1973 Festival for Best Screenplay, Best Music, and Best Photography,[75] Vincent Canby of *The New York Times* declared the movie "seems just silly." He disparaged the film by pointing out that "everything in *Child's Play* seems to be rather cheaply tricky–such as the low-range photography and floor lighting designed to throw faces into eerie relief."[76] The most brutal review of the film came from Pauline Kael in *The New Yorker*. Kael pronounced the film as "disgusting" and in need of "a polished surface and suave craftsmanship." She accused the director of destroying James Mason's performance in the film, and excoriated Preston who she declared was "once a fine screen actor" but is now "ageless and painfully actorish" with a tendency to "project all over the place, even when he isn't doing anything."[77]

Prior to the release of *Child's Play*, Preston was recruited for the film version of *Mame* (1974). The Warner Brothers movie would be based on the 1966 Broadway musical comedy of the same name which starred Angela Lansbury. Desiring an actress with a box office draw for the title role, Warner Brothers elected not to ask Angela Lansbury to reprise the character of Mame on screen, but instead gave the part to sixty-one-year-old comedienne Lucille Ball.

The plot of *Mame* centers on fun-loving and free-thinking Mame Dennis who is living the high life in Manhattan during the Roaring 20s. Her life is enriched by family when her brother dies and she becomes the guardian of his young son, Patrick. Mame and her nephew quickly develop a loving bond, and she makes it her mission to fill the boy's life with adventure and a flair for living. When Mame is financially devastated by the stock market crash in 1929, she works a series of jobs to keep afloat financially and pay the salaries for her mousy secretary/nanny, Agnes Gooch, and her loyal butler, Ito. It is while working at Macy's that Mame meets southern millionaire Beauregard Jackson Pickett Burnside, who is visiting New York. When Mame and Patrick visit Beauregard in Georgia, she reluctantly participates in a foxhunt arranged by the jealous Sally Cato who deliberately gives Mame a horse who has gone mad. Despite the ill-will directed her way, Mame makes it through the hunt, finds the fox, and is discovered cradling the animal in her arms. Mame and Beauregard marry and embark on an extended trip around the world while Patrick graduates boarding school and enters college.

When Beauregard unexpectedly dies in an avalanche while skiing in the Alps, Patrick returns home to comfort his grieving aunt. Meanwhile, Mame and her actress friend, Vera

Charles, discover Agnes Gooch has never been on a date. The women initiate a makeover for Agnes, and send her out to find a man; Agnes, visibly pregnant, returns to Mame's home several months later. Meanwhile, Patrick's relationship with his flighty, social-climbing girlfriend, Gloria Upson, becomes serious. When Mame visits Gloria's family in Connecticut, she is appalled by the snobbery and bigotry of her parents. After Patrick announces his engagement to Gloria, her parents suggest that Mame should join them to collectively purchase the vacant lot next door as a wedding present for the couple. Shortly thereafter, Mame invites Patrick, Gloria, and the Uptons for dinner at her home. When Vera Charles arrives with a group of single, pregnant women, Mame announces she has purchased the property next door to the Uptons to build a home for unwed mothers. Gloria and her parents make a hasty exit, and Patrick encounters Mame's pretty new maid, Pegeen. Pegeen and Patrick eventually marry and have a precocious son, Peter. The film ends at the airport with Mame convincing young Peter's parents to allow the boy to accompany her on her trip abroad.

Although the studio suggested Rock Hudson should play the role of Mame's love interest, Beauregard Burnside, Lucille Ball vetoed the decision. Ball's preference for the role of Beauregard was Preston, whom she had admired since seeing him in *The Music Man*.[78] It was Preston whom Ball envisioned in the role of Beauregard since she "wanted someone who reminds women of Rhett Butler"[79] and knew Preston was the perfect choice to portray a dashing southern gentleman. Since Ball had the final say in all casting decisions for the film, Preston was hired in November 1972.[80] In addition to Ball and Preston, the cast of the film included Beatrice Arthur, Bruce

Davison, Joyce Van Patten, Don Porter, Audrey Christie, Jane Connell, and Kirby Furlong.

Mame was originally scheduled to begin filming in 1972 with legendary director George Cukor at the helm. The screenplay for the film, written by Paul Zindel, was based on the score Jerry Herman composed for the Broadway play. Before filming could commence, Lucille Ball broke her leg in several places during a family ski trip in Aspen. By the time Ball's lengthy recuperation was complete, Cukor had already committed to directing another film. Gene Saks, who directed Mame on Broadway, was then hired to direct the movie and Onna White, the choreographer of the Broadway production, was likewise hired for the film. Although Madeleine Kahn was originally cast by the Warner Brothers brass in the role of Agnes Gooch, Ball had final cast approval. Preston instinctively knew from the moment Lucille Ball saw Madeleine, a young, pretty redhead, that "she'd be gone by the end of the day."[81] Preston's assessment was on target; Kahn was fired and replaced by Jane Connell, the actress who previously played the role of Agnes Gooch on Broadway.[82] Ball, however, insisted that Kahn, whom she described as "too young" and "too beautiful" for the part, was not fired but quit.[83]

The rehearsals and production of Mame were marked by reported tensions on the set that were denied in print by the cast. Although the 5'7" Ball selected Preston for the role of Beauregard Burnside, she came to the conclusion that he was too short and bought him a pair of shoes with built-in lifts, which he promptly gave right back."[84] Although it was reported that a not-so-short Preston was furious and told Ball he would "wear his own elk-skin shoes on the set,"[85] Ball's "gift" was "a rude reminder that she is the boss" and he would need to "wear shoe lifts in the film."[86]

Actress Beatrice Arthur, the wife of *Mame* director Gene Saks, played the character of Vera Charles during the Broadway run of Mame and was cast in the same role in the movie. It was widely reported that the set of *Mame* was rife with tensions and disagreements between Lucille Ball and Bea Arthur. A December 1972 article in *The Hollywood Reporter* suggested that Beatrice Arthur had quit the film due to differences with Ball over her portrayal of Vera Charles and that Ball had asked Bette Davis to step into the role,[87] but both Arthur and Ball quickly went on the record to deny the rumors.[88] When Nancy Anderson of the Copley News service questioned Preston about the atmosphere on the film set, the actor insisted the rumors of friction on the set were "completely phony" and that *Mame* was "one of the few productions [he'd] been in in which everyone gets along well with everybody else."[89] However, *Chicago Tribune* journalist, Robert Kerwin, observed some troubling behavior during his visit to the *Mame* set.

Kerwin reported that Lucille Ball brought Preston with her to a portion of the *Tribune* interview but did not introduce him to Kerwin or "refer to him by name or call him by his name" and insinuated that "he's stark bald and has been wearing a wig for 20 years."[90] Kerwin observed Ball was behaving as if Preston were not present, referring to him only in an objectified way as "this" or "this role." Kerwin concluded that Preston wisely kept "his mouth shut" after hearing Ball's remarks, and came to understand that Preston was unfazed by such behavior since "he has to work with Lucy every day and wants the picture to come off the screen happy."[91]

The filming of *Mame* commenced on January 3, 1973 at the Warner Brothers Studio in Burbank, California as well as at the Disney Ranch.[92] A new song, "Loving You," was written specifically by composer Jerry Herman for Preston to perform in the film. The song was featured in a montage of honeymoon scenes in which Preston trips the light fantastic with Ball while masterfully crooning the romantic lyrics.

Mame, produced with a budget of $12 million, was completed after five months of shooting on June 5, 1973, just in time for a release during Christmas week that year.[93] It soon became apparent, however, that the film's original December 1973 release date would need to be pushed back to Easter 1974, since the film's editors found it impossible to complete a first cut of the extensive film footage by that time. The premiere of *Mame* was finally held on March 27, 1974 at the Pacific Theatres Cinerama Dome on Sunset Boulevard in Los Angeles.[94] The film debuted at Radio City Music Hall a few weeks earlier on March 7 and grossed a record $2,707,097 during its 10-week engagement in New York.[95]

The critical reception of *Mame* was mixed and included a barrage of vitriolic commentary about Lucille Ball. Many who voiced disapproval of Ball in the film were Angela Lansbury fans who believed Ball "absconded with the role that should have been Angela's."[96] In addition, the movie appeared to rankle film critics "and most of them went out of their way to be unkind."[97]

Paul D. Zimmerman of *Newsweek* proclaimed that rather than being a movie, *Mame* was "an extended award ceremony honoring Lucille Ball." He lambasted the film's attempts to camouflage Ball's age, noting that "her aging face [was] practically a blur in the protective gauze of softer-than-soft focus," and declared the film to be a "cheerful, brainless celebration of success [that] is at best, empty and a little depressing."[98] The *New Yorker*'s Pauline Kael deemed *Mame* "too terrible to be boring" and characterized the film as a "hippopotamic musical" that was blemished by Ball's "tonelessly flat" singing voice. Kael went as far as to wonder aloud whether Ball's "unfulfilled ambition to be a flaming drag queen" was the motivation for her to star in the film.[99] *The New York Times* film critic, Vincent Canby, expressed "great reservations about *Mame.*" He criticized the way Ball was portrayed on screen, observing "she has been photographed in such soft focus that her face alternately looks beatific . . . or like something sculptured from melting vanilla ice cream."[100] The *Time* review of the film was no less harsh, pointing out that "the movie spans about 20 years, and seems that long in running time." The review excoriated Lucille Ball by proclaiming that "her grace, her timing, her vigor have all vanished," and noted that close-up shots of Ball appear as though "the lens was smeared with Vaseline and shrouded in gauze."[101] A favorable review, offered by Milton Krims of *The Saturday Evening Post,* pronounced that "perfection needs no adjectives to give it greater meaning."[102]

Preston was back on Broadway at the Shubert Theater on April 21, 1974 to host the twenty-eighth annual Tony Awards along with Cicely Tyson, Peter Falk, and Florence Henderson. The theme of the show, broadcast on ABC, was "Homecoming" and featured nostalgic retrospectives of several musicals including *Over Here, George M, Raisin, A Mother's Kisses, Good News, Fanny, Phoenix '55, Seesaw, The Cradle Will Rock, Lorelei, Purlie,* as well as a medley of Broadway songs performed by Charles Nelson Reilly. At one point in the broadcast, Preston introduced Beatrice Arthur who performed "There Goes My Life" from the 1968 musical comedy, *A Mother's Kisses,* that closed out of town in Baltimore. Before he introduced Arthur, Preston publicly opined about the value ascribed to works of art and alluded to the failure of his musical *We Take the Town,*

One of the fascinating things about "works of art" is that people don't always agree that they *are* works of art. Critics don't often agree with the public, and so, in the case of painting and sculpture and music, the value of a work is frequently not recognized during the artist's lifetime. And so, it's not surprising that sometimes a theatrical work of art comes to grief. I was once in a musical that closed out of town, it was the best thing I ever did, and the music was great, but somehow or another we just couldn't get it together. [103]

In early 1974, Preston became interested in the fledgling musical, *Mack & Mabel,* a story developed by Michael Stewart with music and lyrics by composer Jerry Herman. The project, which would reunite producer David Merrick and director Gower Champion, was based on the turbulent romance of Hollywood silent film producer Mack Sennett and comedic actress Mabel Normand. Actor Jerry Orbach had originally been signed to play the role of Mack, but when Preston expressed interest in the musical, both Merrick and Champion decided that Preston would be a more bankable star in the show's title role.[104] By mid-February, Preston had been secured for the musical[105] and the search was on for an actress to fill the role of Mabel Normand.

In *Mack & Mabel,* Hollywood silent film pioneer Mack Sennett shares his ill-fated love affair with Mabel Normand with the audience while reminiscing about his past cinematic triumphs and Mabel's rise to stardom. The couple's romance crumbles, with Mabel turning to heroin and an affair with ill-fated director William Desmond Taylor, and the musical ends with Mack's announcement of Mabel's death. The action is punctuated with several memorable Jerry Herman tunes including "Time Heals Everything," "I Won't Send Roses," "Wherever He Ain't," and "Look What Happened to Mabel."

The initial sign of trouble for the musical surfaced during the problematic casting process for Mabel, which ultimately devolved into a revolving door of actresses. Rehearsals for the production began at the Belasco Theatre in New York on May 6. Marcia Rodd was initially cast in the role of Mabel but was summarily fired by Gower Champion in early May after two days of rehearsal, and was replaced by singer Kelly Garrett.[106] Champion then fired Garrett a week later after determining she could not act.[107] Bernadette Peters eventually joined the cast as Mabel four weeks into rehearsal; she arrived at the rehearsal hall joking, tongue-in-cheek, "Hi, I'm the new Mabel. The show's now called 'Mack & Maybe.'"[108] In addition to Preston and Peters, the cast was rounded out by Lisa Kirk, James Mitchell, Jerry Dodge, Christopher Murney, Tom Batten, Bert Michaels, Nancy Evers, Robert Fitch, and Stanley Simmonds.

The musical was scheduled for previews in San Diego, Los Angeles, St. Louis, and Washington D.C. before its Broadway debut on October 6. The show opened at the Civic Theatre in San Diego on June 17 and received "terrific reviews."[109] One theatergoer who saw the performance in San Diego on June 21 indicated she was "charmed by the entire production" which was "presented with a lusty bravado, ending bittersweet, but leaving the audience still 'punched up' by the Irish of it all."[110]

Mack & Mabel opened for an eight-week run at the Los Angeles Music Center on June 25. In his autobiography, Jerry Herman indicated the Los Angeles production was "even more successful" than the one in San Diego and "got beautiful notices and did smash business."[111] Herman acknowledged that although Preston "was a wonderful Mack Sennett, very strong and manly, and Bernadette Peters was absolutely exquisite as Mabel,"[112] there were "still things that were wrong with the show," including the fact that Mack Sennett and Mabel Normand "did not make the most loveable hero and heroine for a musical play."[113] Herman identified other miscalculations that led to the production's eventual undoing, specifically ending the show on a morose tone with Mabel's death,[114] and Gower Champion's decision to devote an inordinate amount of time to rewriting portions of the script that worked while ignoring others that missed the mark. The composer was further disheartened when Champion chose to focus his time on an unworkable Keystone Kops "production number than on the rest of the show." [115]

The show ended its run in Los Angeles on August 17 and moved on to a week-long preview in St. Louis, Missouri. Merrick made arrangements for the musical to be staged at the St. Louis Municipal Opera Company, a massive 11,000-seat outdoor arena.[116] In his biography of Herman, *Jerry Herman: Poet of the Showtune*, author Stephen Citron contends the enormous Opera Company venue "was a terrible mistake" that required Preston and Peters "to overplay their parts on that enormous stage, and in their overacting, they pulled the show, a simple human comedy, drastically out of shape."[117] Joe Pollak's review in *The St. Louis Post-Dispatch* was cautious; he acknowledged the show contained a few good production numbers in the second act, but noted the "story line fades, the scenes stretch forever, the pacing becomes erratic, and the ending falls flat."[118] Whatever tweaking Champion had undertaken with the musical made the show less palatable to St. Louis audiences than those in San

Diego or Los Angeles. Pollak hoped that in the month before the show was set to debut in New York that it would metamorphose into "a very good one."[119]

While in St. Louis, Preston sat down for an interview with Mimi Avins of the *St. Louis Post-Dispatch*. When queried about his success in the theater, Preston credited his sense of discipline as his primary attribute:

> You're never aware of the kind of discipline the theater demands because when you've been in it all your life; it seems there's no other way to live. There's a level of perfection beneath which you can't fall. You say to yourself one thing: forget it's my 886th performance in *The Music Man*. It's the first time those 1400 people in the audience are seeing it.[120]

Asked about the demands associated with show business, Preston indicated that for this very reason, "having no children has been, in its own way, a kind of blessing." He went on to add that in lieu of biological children, he and his wife have "had to make due [*sic*] with a lot of nieces and nephews."[121]

Once the St. Louis preview closed on August 25, the next stop for *Mack & Mabel* was to kick off the 1974-75 season at The Kennedy Center in Washington, D.C. with performances beginning on September 3. The reviews for the opening night performance were abysmal; Richard Coe of *The Washington Post* described the show as landing "on the Kennedy Center Opera House stage on Tuesday night with all the zip of a wet, very dead flounder."[122]

President Gerald Ford and his wife, Betty, were in the audience at the performance on September 4 to celebrate the tenth anniversary of the founding of the National Council on the Arts. Despite the show's flagging reviews, Ford insisted the production was "just [his] mood," said he enjoyed the dancing girls, and indicated *Mack & Mabel* was just the type of show he likes "after a hard day."[123]

Jerry Herman was troubled that, while the musical was in Washington, Gower Champion insisted that the show be torn "apart again to fix things that didn't even need fixing." The gradual and unnecessary deconstruction of the show began following the Los Angeles preview and accelerated as the show approached its Broadway debut. Even though Herman assessed that the original number was working, Gower Champion had the composer replace the Keystone Kops song "Hit 'Em on The Head" with "Every Time a Cop Falls Down." Herman viewed the changes as "a loss not a gain,' noting that such changes were "typical of the tinkering that was done on this show, which was fatally overworked on the road." Herman acknowledged that "instead of concentrating on the true weaknesses, we spent months and months working on unnecessary things." [124]

Mack & Mabel closed in Washington on September 28 and the show "limped into New York with abnormally minimal advertising and almost no promotion."[125] For Jerry Herman, the musical, which debuted on October 6 at the Majestic Theatre, was "the first and only time in [his] life, [that he] had a show open on Broadway that was *less* polished and *less* perfect than the production that had gone out of town four months earlier."[126] Opening night was marred by a near-fatal disaster that occurred while Lisa Kirk was performing in Act Two. Jerry Herman recalled that "a huge piece of scenery [that served as the backdrop for the musical number] came crashing down," and the falling lumber came very close to crushing Lisa Kirk and the dancers on stage with her. The collapse of the backdrop left the audience "absolutely stunned, they never recovered and neither did the show."[127] Preston's father, Doc, who knew Mack Sennett, was in the audience on opening night. Doc let his son know that he was "playing [Sennett] very, very well, except not mean enough." Preston, however "thought [he] was being pretty mean" in his portrayal of the silent film mogul.[128]

New York radio personality Jim Lowe attended the Broadway premiere of *Mack & Mabel* and interviewed the cast immediately following the opening night performance. Lowe told his audience,

> There was electricity in the air tonight. We're still waiting for the reviews, but I'll be surprised if they're not good because the audience just absolutely adored it. If they're not good, then there's no connection at all, no rapport between what people think and what critics write.[129]

Lowe proceeded to inform his WNEW listeners that,

> *Mack & Mabel* is a lovely show. First, it contains a stunning performance by the electrifying Robert Preston, too long gone from Broadway. As the pioneer movie producer, Mack Sennett, he moves, prances, dances, rides on camera cranes, slides down poles, and defies you not to watch him. One wonders why he hasn't done a one-man show at the Palace or Winter Garden or Minskoff-several with considerably less to offer have.[130]

Despite Jim Lowe's prediction, the opening night reviews of *Mack & Mabel* were less than enthusiastic. *The Los Angeles Times* critic, William Glover, heaped superlatives on the production and declared, "What's better than splendid—superb? Does terrific surpass enthralling? Let's not quibble. *Mack & Mabel* at the Majestic deserves all the dandy adjectives around." Clive Barnes from *The New York Times* observed that "never have so many props propped up so much show" and attributed the musical's issues to "book trouble so bad that it is practically library trouble." Barnes praised Preston for being "just the right measure of a hero" and declared he "sings . . . better than I recall, and he acts the role of a man so convincingly obsessed with his work that he can even negotiate a few lines so flat that they could make The Netherlands seem mountainous." The review acknowledged that although *Mack & Mabel* "may not win too many critical plaudits . . . it is a fair bet for a night on the town."[131] In his review of *Mack & Mabel* in the *Daily News*, Rex Reed concluded that it was "not a memorable show, but it works and it entertains and it leaves you feeling like you've been to the theater," adding that "the strong things about it outweigh the weak things going against it, and the balance makes for quite an engaging evening at the theater." Reed was impressed with Preston's performance, noting that he "sings like he's running for office; he cuts a fine, gregarious figure-eight in the acting department, and in his own chiseled, studied way, he is quite moving in the show's final scenes."[132]

Reviews of the production from other New York critics were considerably harsher. Douglas Watt, also with the *Daily News*, declared *Mack & Mabel* to be "an amiable fool of a musical so desperately anxious to tickle our funnybone and touch our hearts that it succeeds in doing neither. I spent the evening feeling sorry for it."[133] Walter Kerr suggested *"Mack & Mabel* hasn't got a story to begin with,"[134] and T.E. Kalen of *Time* magazine, whose review of the musical was titled "Reel Sad," concluded that "gimmicks aplenty and props to burn cannot keep the show from sagging."[135]

During *Mack & Mabel's* run at the Majestic, Preston continued his practice of commuting by car to and from his Connecticut home to the theater for daily performances. When not performing on stage, the actor spent time tending to his eight-acre estate. He acknowledged his wife, Catherine, "reminds me about three in the afternoon to stop working," noting that "the drive into New York is only 50 minutes; on the way in it's preparation, on the way home it's relaxation."[136]

Despite the spate of lackluster reviews, theater audiences responded with exuberance to *Mack & Mabel*. However, Jerry Herman was aware multiple Broadway-bound shows were "fighting for theater space at the time" and realized that *Mack & Mabel* was sacrificed to pave the way for a huge payday for the theater owners.[137] Before heading to Hollywood, David Merrick "left word to pull the plug" on the musical "once the advance ran out,"[138] and the show was abruptly closed on November 30 after sixty-six performances. Herman's biographer, Stephen Citron, aptly noted that,

> The musical needed rave reviews to fill a large theater like the Majestic. The show was building its audience slowly, and seemed to be getting a toehold when David Merrick abruptly decided to close it after eight weeks . . . The Shuberts, who owned the Majestic, were no help, as they had no interest in keeping *Mack & Mabel* on the boards.

They had [already] booked the theater for *The Wiz*, which, from advance reports, was a big hit.[139]

Despite its short Broadway run, *Mack & Mabel* was nominated for eight Tony Awards at the twenty-ninth annual Tony Awards ceremony in April 1975. Although *Mack & Mabel* received nominations for Best Musical (David Merrick), Best Choreography (Gower Champion), Best Book of a Musical (Michael Stewart), Best Costume Design (Patricia Zipprodt), Best Direction of a Musical (Gower Champion), Best Performance by an Actor in a Leading Role in a Musical (Robert Preston), and Best Performance by an Actress in a Leading Role in a Musical (Bernadette Peters), it did not take home any awards. Adding insult to injury, the Tony nomination committee elected not to include *Mack & Mabel* composer Jerry Herman in the Best Score category.

Less than a month after the disappointing, precipitous closure of *Mack & Mabel*, Preston found himself facing an unexpected loss during the 1974 Christmas season. On December 24, 1974, Preston's beloved seventy-eight-year-old mother, Ruth, was taken to Santa Monica Hospital Medical Center after experiencing abdominal pain. Ruth was admitted to the hospital, duct stones were determined to be the cause of her discomfort, and she was scheduled for routine gallbladder surgery on the day after Christmas. The family doctor, rather than an experienced gastrointestinal surgeon, performed the gallbladder removal surgery.[140] The procedure, allegedly botched, resulted in fatal post-surgical complications. On December 29, three days following the surgery, Ruth Meservey died as a result of cerebral and coronary thrombosis.[141] A grief-stricken Preston gathered with his father and extended family members in California following the funeral service for his mother.[142]

BOOMERANG

D uring the first half of 1975, Preston appeared in three television productions. On March 26, Preston appeared on NBC's
Bell Telephone Jubilee, a ninety-minute special billed as the
biggest television entertainment event of the year. The program,
hosted by Bing Crosby and Liza Minnelli, saluted the one-hun-
dredth anniversary of the telephone. The show featured perfor-
mances from the *Bell Telephone Hour* as well as the *Bell System
Family Theatre*, both of which had been telecast on NBC over the
past two decades.[1] In addition to a performance by Preston, the
Jubilee program also featured production numbers performed by
Julie Andrews, Fred Astaire, Harry Belafonte, Ray Bolger, Diahann
Carroll, Pablo Casals, Johnny Cash, Maurice Chevalier, Roy Clark,
Van Cliburn, Duke Ellington, Peggy Fleming, Marge and Gower
Champion, Benny Goodman, Eydie Gorme, Marvin Hamlisch,
Lena Horne, Burl Ives, The Kingston Trio, Mahalia Jackson, Joel
Grey, Steve Lawrence, Ethel Merman, Anthony Newley, Rudolf
Nureyev, Donald O'Connor, Andres Segovia, Joan Sutherland, The
U.S. Marine Corps Silent Drill Team, and Ben Vereen.[2]

In the early months of the year, Preston was approached to appear in an hour-long ABC comedy television special entitled "Happy Endings" to be broadcast on April 10. The program was the brainchild of comedian Alan King, who recruited four playwrights–Julies Feiffer, Herb Gardner, Neil Simon, and Peter Stone–to produce four original short plays, each thirteen minutes in duration.[3] King acknowledged he was only able to secure the playwrights for his production by "imposing no requirements other than a happy ending for each slice-of-life sketch."[4] The comedian, who secured Robert Moore to direct all four skits, not only acted in two of the mini-plays but also hosted the special and provided commentary to the television audience about the featured vignettes.[5] Peter Stone authored the mini-play *A Commercial Break* in which Preston was paired with actress Lauren Bacall. Alan King originally planned to act opposite Bacall in Stone's short play, but when Preston was mentioned for the role, King withdrew since "there was no comparison."[6]

The plot of *A Commercial Break* involved the sixteen-year marriage of Harry Crocker (Preston), a successful advertising salesman, and Catherine Crocker (Bacall), a consumer affairs commissioner, as they explore the rift in their relationship that developed when the couple's careers began to interfere with their marriage. The highlights of the vignette include Catherine throwing a drink in Harry's face and Harry's attempt to woo his wife by reciting "a speech borrowed from Shakespeare in which Henry V asks Catherine [of Valois] to marry him."[7] Preston and Bacall were lauded for their performances in Stone's play, but the script itself was viewed by critics as only being "so-so."[8] The three other featured mini-plays in the program included *Kidnapped* by Jules Feiffer and starring Art Carney, Elizabeth

Wilson, Lisa Rochelle, and Jimmy Fields; *Big Joe and Kansas* penned by Neil Simon and featuring James Earl Jones and Alan King; and Herb Gardner's *I'm With Ya, Duke*, starring Alan King, John Cunningham, and Nancy Andrews. Despite the notable actors who appeared in the short plays, the television special was panned by critics who suggested that "as a whole, the hour is a failure as entertainment."[9]

In June, the made-for-television movie, *My Father's House*, was broadcast on ABC, although Preston and co-stars Cliff Robertson, Eileen Brennan, and Rosemary Forsyth had filmed the TV drama over a year prior to its June 1, 1975 air date. Even though Barry Diller, the prior Vice-President of Prime-Time Programming at ABC, was verklempt after screening the movie and confided to an associate it was the best script he had ever read, the movie languished on the network's back shelf. Producer David Sontag was left to assume that once Diller departed from ABC, the new network management jettisoned the movie.[10]

The script for *My Father's House* was based on a book written by former *Life* magazine associate editor, Philip Kunhardt, and centered on the author's heart attack at age forty-one.[11] The focus of the movie, directed by Alex Segal and filmed in New York and Los Angeles, is on the character of Tom Lindholm Jr. (Robertson), a fortyish, over-pressured, magazine editor whose hectic lifestyle leads to a heart attack. During his recuperation, Lindholm engages in some soul-searching, reflects upon the fond memories of life with his father (Preston), and begins to wonder if he has chosen the right path in life. The film features numerous flashback scenes which pivot between Lindholm's youth and the present day as he recalls his happy childhood while reassessing his role as a parent to his own children. *My Father's House* concludes with Lindholm reordering his priorities and building better relationships with his wife and children.

The movie was well-received by television critics who lauded Preston's performance as "superb," and praised Robertson's acting as being "reflective" and "very fine."[12]

When he was not involved in a stage, screen, or television project, Preston enjoyed working outdoors to meticulously maintain the extensive acreage surrounding his Tudor-style home in Greenwich and spent evenings working on large, challenging jigsaw puzzles that were "laid out with surgical neatness on a table in his study."[13] The actor and his wife did not employ domestic help, except for a grounds "caretaker who work[ed] for them one day a week."[14] Preston, a self-professed "home person,"[15] was described by nephew Charles Leinenweber as extremely physically strong and powerful,[16] and the actor used his brawn to accomplish the bulk of the work required to maintain his Connecticut estate. It was Catherine who provided regular to-do lists for her husband including tasks such as sawing trees and bushes and digging holes.[17] She marveled at her husband's stamina and precision, noting that she simply had to point to a job and it was done.[18] The couple's decision to handle their own chores reflected their non-extravagant lifestyle. Although the couple's existence was simple and uncomplicated, they did own "a beautiful robin egg's blue Cadillac DeVille, the type of automobile that Hollywood actors typically drove."[19] When not appearing on Broadway himself, Preston and Catherine would regularly drive to New York City to attend Broadway plays and musicals. While awaiting the start of a production, Preston would tightly roll up the *Playbill* to form a paper ear trumpet and, just as the lights in the theater went down, would position the tube next to his wife's ear and whisper "I love you." It was a touching tradition that Preston continued until his death.[20]

The actor's hiatus from stage and screen ended in September 1976 when he signed on to play the role of eccentric Texas oilman and football team owner Big Ed Bookman in the film *Semi-Tough* (1977). The dramatic rights to the book of the same name, authored by Dan Jenkins, were purchased several years prior by producer David Merrick, who initially envisioned the story as a Broadway musical.[21] Director Michael Ritchie and screenwriter Walter Bernstein were hired by Merrick once he decided to produce *Semi-Tough* as a film through United Artists, and Burt Reynolds was hired in July 1976 to star in the film.[22] In addition to Preston, actor Kris Kristofferson, and actress Jill Clayburgh were also added to the cast in September.[23]

The plot of the pro-football comedy involves Billy Clyde Puckett (Reynolds), a running back, and Marvin "Shake" Tiller (Kristofferson), a receiver, as players on a Miami pro-football team owned by Big Ed Bookman (Preston). Bookman's daughter, Barbara Jane (Clayburgh), is a platonic roommate of both Billy Clyde and Shake. A romantic subplot develops between Barbara Jane and Shake just as Billy Clyde realizes he also has romantic feelings for the boss's daughter.

Another subplot satirizes B.E.A.T., a human potential movement similar to then-trendy EST seminars. Shake, a devotee of B.E.A.T., encourages Barbara Jane to likewise find enlightenment through the program. When Shake and Barbara Jane announce their plans to marry, a distressed Billy Clyde visits Big Ed Bookman and finds him crawling around his office on his hands and knees in keeping with Movagenics, another type of transformative new-age philosophy that promotes crawling on the floor like an infant. Meanwhile, although Barbara Jane makes an effort to understand B.E.A.T., she is unable to "get" the concept. Billy Clyde decides to attend B.E.A.T. training to debunk it. Pretending to be an adherent of B.E.A.T., Billy Clyde manages to sow seeds of doubt in Shake's mind about his decision to marry a woman who is unable to "get" B.E.A.T. During the wedding ceremony, Shake announces to Barbara Jane that he is unable to proceed with the marriage. A melee erupts in the church as Barbara Jane realizes Billy Clyde instigated the cancellation of her wedding. The film ends with Billy Clyde and Barbara Jane verbalizing their feelings for each other. Although Billy Clyde declares he is not the marrying type, he suggests that he and Barbara Jane should make plans to vacation in Hawaii.

Filming for *Semi-Tough* was scheduled to begin in Dallas in November 1976, but when Burt Reynolds experienced some unexpected health issues, the production was pushed back to early January 1977. Media outlets reported Reynolds experienced a "heart scare"[24] when it was learned he checked into Good Samaritan Hospital in Palm Beach, Florida. Reynolds's agent denied that his client experienced heart problems and instead indicated Reynolds was hospitalized due to "a chemical-glandular imbalance."[25] It was suggested that Reynolds was suffering from physical and mental exhaustion "from making movies for two-and-a-half-years with little time off,"[26] and a sixty-day regimen of rest was prescribed for the actor. Reynolds followed the medical advice and rested in Hawaii until filming resumed in Dallas on January 3.[27]

Filming began in Dallas in early January and included scenes shot at the Cotton Bowl, moved to Miami in mid-March for location shooting at the Orange Bowl, and was completed by April 6. Several pro-football players, including Ed "Too Tall" Jones, John Matuszak, Joe Kapp, and Paul Hornung, were hired to appear in action scenes to lend an air of authenticity to the film. *Semi-Tough* was released in New York City on November 18, 1977 to mixed reviews.

Vincent Canby of *The New York Times* opined that the film's screenwriter and director failed to give "dramatic structure to [Jenkins's] episodic novel," noting that "if the film's various sketch-pieces were not so funny, *Semi-Tough* would not have any story at all."[28] *Newsweek*'s David Ansen lamented that director Ritchie had taken Dan Jenkins's novel and "turned it into a send-up of the 70s fuzzy-headed quest for spiritual placebos." He also noted that "Walter Brennan's script isn't as sharp as it needs to be and Ritchie's direction lacks comic confidence."[29] Although Kathleen Carroll from the *Daily News* described the film as "wacky [and] often wildly funny," she bemoaned the film's tendency to ramble along as "Ritchie's direction is so casual and carefree that the plot tends to be overlooked until the last minute."[30] One of the film's best reviews was written by Richard Schickel from *Time* magazine who declared *Semi-Tough* "the year's most socially useful film" for its satiric take on new-age self-realization ideologies.

Schickel noted that "the movie's funniest moment" occurs when Preston's character is seen crawling around his office on all fours searching for his lost center of consciousness. Schickel embraced the comedy, which he viewed as speaking "lightly but honestly about life as it is–and what it might be–in our times," and asserted it is this quality that "sets *Semi-Tough* apart from anything else in recent memory."[31]

While appearing in *Semi-Tough*, Preston forged a friendship with fellow actor Burt Reynolds. He greatly admired Reynolds, as well as his then-girlfriend Sally Field, declaring, "What a man! Not a phony thing about him."[32] Preston was added to the group of Reynolds's friends who were invited to the star's Holmby Hills home on Saturday evenings to engage in a game of picture charades. Although Preston typically did not travel in show business circles, he and Catherine enjoyed participating in the game nights at Burt Reynolds's home, and Reynolds became one of the few celebrities that Preston and his wife socialized with in this way.[33] In his autobiography, *My Life*, Reynolds indicated that on these game nights, the guests were divided up into teams after dinner, men versus women; the teams would play a highly competitive game of charades[34] that was "fast paced and wildly animated."[35] In addition to Preston, the guest list for Reynolds's game nights often included Mel Brooks and Anne Bancroft, Ricardo and Georgiana Montalban, Esther Williams, Bette Davis, Dom DeLuise, Fred Astaire, Betty White, Orson Welles, Alan Alda, Carol Burnett, and Charles Durning, among others.[36]

On April 1, John Corry from *The New York Times* broke the news that Preston would be returning to Broadway to replace the departing George C. Scott in Larry Gelbart's farce *Sly Fox*,[37] a play based on Ben Jonson's *Volpone*. When Preston was initially approached about replacing Scott in the role of Foxwell J. Sly, he said no. However, the play's director, Arthur Penn, persuaded Preston to hold off on saying no until he had an opportunity to see the production. When Preston eventually attended a performance of the show, he instantly realized that he "could have a lot of fun in this role" and agreed to step in as Scott's replacement[38] until New Year's Eve.[39]

Preston was allowed four weeks of rehearsal preparation, ten days of which were under the direction of Arthur Penn, and first appeared as Foxwell J. Sly at the Broadhurst Theatre on May 10. The actor, who turned fifty-nine in June, effortlessly performed the strenuous dual roles of Foxwell J. Sly and the Judge in the show. The supporting cast of *Sly Fox* included Bethe Austin (Mrs. Truckle), Jack Gilford (Jethro Crouch), Bob Dishy/Geoff Garland (Abner Truckle), Gretchen Wyler (Miss Fancy), John Heffernan (Craven), James Gallery (Chief of Police), Thomas Hill (Captain Crouch), and Jeffrey Tambor/Hector Elizondo (Simon Able).

Bethe Austin recalled she first encountered Preston when she was sitting on the back staircase of the theater waiting to do her callback audition for the role of Mrs. Truckle. Austin explained, "The door suddenly opened and in walked this handsome man with thick, curly hair—it was Robert Preston. He looked at me and said 'Hello.'"[40] Austin was hired by Arthur Penn following her audition and Preston walked down the aisle of the theater to shake her hand. The actress noted from that moment on, Preston treated her like a daughter, adding "he was a fatherly kind of presence to me and treated me very much the same way."[41]

The play, set in San Francisco in the late nineteenth century, centers on the crafty and prosperous Foxwell J. Sly, who was enriched by the 1880s gold rush, and his servant, Simon Able. Foxwell, a rapacious conniver, has convinced some greedy townsfolk that he is on death's door, and three of them step forward to promise Foxwell anything he desires, in order to inherit his entire fortune. Jethro Crouch agrees to forfeit his son's inheritance in return for being named Foxwell's sole heir; the jealous Abner Truckle agrees to let Foxwell have his way with his chaste wife in order to be the sole beneficiary of Foxwell's will, while Attorney Craven defends Foxwell in court for the attempted seduction of Mrs. Truckle in return for the same promise of sole heirship. In addition, the pregnant town prostitute,

Merilee Fancy, attempts to finagle a marriage to Foxwell to gain access to his fortune. Ultimately, Foxwell J. Sly ends up bilking all three men with the help of his trusty servant, Simon Able.

Drama critics proffered lavish praise for Preston's performance. The theater critic from the *Pittsburgh Post-Gazette* gushed that Preston was "looking fit and vigorous," and noted the actor was a "splendid performer" who "throws himself into *Sly Fox* not with abandon, but with careful calculations of a seasoned actor who knows how to pace a performance."[42] The *New York Times* drama critic, Walter Kerr, likewise offered high praise for Preston's performance in the play. Kerr bluntly acknowledged that "it would take a very brave man to say that Robert Preston is playing *Sly Fox* better than George C. Scott did. I am a very brave man. Robert Preston is playing *Sly Fox* better than George C. Scott did."[43]

Other critics offered direct comparisons of the way George C. Scott and Preston handled the role of Foxwell J. Sly. Douglas Watt of the *Daily News* proclaimed Preston was "the ideal man for *Sly Fox*," noting that since Preston replaced Scott, the performance "has a better balance now that the breezily confident Preston, rather than his formidable predecessor, is manipulating the big con." Watt recognized that Preston was "delightful in buoying up a script that could . . . sag disastrously at any moment."[44] Theater critic Emory Lewis from *The Record* identified that Preston "added a raffish charm" that "immediately brightens the proceedings." Lewis expressed that, in comparison to George C. Scott, Preston was "graceful and agile in a remarkable piece of choreography," adding that "few artists on Broadway can equal his skill with deadpan humor."[45]

Preston, however, demurred to the critics' comparison of Scott's portrayal of Foxwell J. Sly to his own:

Every actor has a different approach to a part. It would be dull simply to copy someone else. George C. Scott saw Sly one way, and I see him another way. I've added more roguish wit and a dash of elegance. There are stars who refuse to assume a role they did not play on the opening night. That is nonsense. In the world of opera and ballet, that attitude just doesn't exist. Audiences enjoy watching different interpretations.[46]

As the replacement for the lead in *Sly Fox*, Preston took command of the role and ran away with it. As he had with other characters he played on stage and screen, Preston displayed an uncanny ability to connect with the emotional truth of his character to deliver a performance that allowed a deeper connection with the audience. His impressive performance in *Sly Fox* added yet another feather to Preston's theatrical cap while underscoring his versatility and strength as a performer.

Bethe Austin enjoyed working with Preston and described him as a man who was giving, open, kind, warm, charming, and who emanated "a powerful presence and charisma." Austin regularly socialized with Preston while the two were appearing in *Sly Fox*. The robust actor offered the young actress sage advice, including the health benefits of "sleeping coldly"– revealing that he preferred to slumber in a cold room. He also advised that an actor should treat the theater like a shrine and go onstage by "offering yourself on the altar of the temple of the theater."[47] Austin recounted that Preston would regularly take her to dinner at Frankie and Johnnie's Steakhouse or at Sardi's on matinee days and the meals would follow a predictable pattern:

His perfect meal at Frankie and Johnnie's started with a double negroni. Then he ordered for us— we would have a big steak. He would have a little split of Cabernet and we would have a nice hour and a half at the restaurant. After that, he would go back to the theater and take a nap, and then he would be up and ready to go onstage.[48]

Less than a month after his return to Broadway in *Sly Fox*, Preston served as a presenter at the thirty-first annual Tony Awards held at the Shubert Theatre in New York City on June 5. Without introduction, Preston glided onstage to a flourish of "Seventy-Six Trombones" and proceeded to narrate a lengthy, visual montage devoted to the adaptability of Broadway. He then presented the Lawrence Langner Memorial Award to Broadway producer Cheryl Crawford for her outstanding, distinguished lifetime achievement in the American Theatre.

While performing in *Sly Fox*, Preston reconnected with his old friend, Richard Burton. The two actors had become fast friends and cultivated a deep mutual respect while they simultaneously performed on Broadway in 1958–Preston in *The Music Man* and Burton in *Time Remembered*. During that time, Preston and several other leading Broadway actors decided to brush up on their Shakespeare by performing dramatic scenes with Burton. Preston obtained permission to use the Majestic Theatre stage as a classroom on Monday afternoons when the theater was empty and, with Burton as a coach, the actors performed scenes from Shakespeare and received the benefit of the actor's "English polish."[49] Burton was admittedly "bowled over by Preston's grasp of blank verse"[50] and so impressed with Preston's performances that he declared, "Preston is the best Shakespearean actor in America."[51] Burton also identified that Preston "could hold his own with Olivier or any of them . . . [he is] an actor of great power, with a voice like golden thunder."[52] Upon learning Burton referred to him as the best Shakespearean actor in America, Preston quipped, "I don't know if that's praise or not. How many Shakespearean actors do we have in America?"[53] Actor John Cullum, who worked with both Burton and Preston, indicated Preston "had a lot in common with Richard, because Preston could do Shakespeare as well as Richard Burton. Richard Burton said of Bob Preston that he was the only person in the world he couldn't take the stage away from."[54]

The possibility of a Burton-Preston Shakespearean collaboration began to take shape in the summer of 1977 when Richard and Susan Burton, along with Richard's daughter, Kate, attended a performance of *Sly Fox* in July. During an after-performance dinner at BackStage, Burton suggested that he and Preston should perform *Othello* and alternate the roles of Othello and Iago. According to a report in the *Daily News*, Preston reacted favorably to the idea of performing *Othello* alongside Burton and "the next morning representatives of the two men got on the phone to producer Alexander Cohen, [and] the deal for them was made."[55] It was expected that a limited run of *Othello*, headlining Burton and Preston in alternating roles, would be featured during the new Broadway season in the spring of 1978.[56] The actors' plans for an *Othello* collaboration eventually fell through, and no attempts were made to revive this synergetic Shakespearean production before Burton's death in August 1984.

While the *Othello* collaboration with Burton never materialized, Preston would not be absent from the stage for long. By

September, he was in talks with Bob Merrill to star in the musical comedy, *The Prince of Grand Street*, written by Merrill, choreographed by Lee Becker Theodore, and produced under the direction of Gene Saks. Saks was delighted when Preston agreed to play the lead role of Nathan Rashumsky, acknowledging Preston "is the only actor I know with the vitality and romantic image needed for the role."[57] In addition to Preston, the principal cast of the musical comedy included Neva Small, Sam Levene, Bernice Massi, Werner Klemperer, David Margulies, Sammy Smith, Alan Manson, Addison Powell, and Alexander Orfaly.

Merrill, the lyricist and composer of *The Prince of Grand Street*, provided an outline of the musical comedy to select guests who attended a theater party preview on September 26, 1977 at the Alvin Theatre in New York City. Merrill described the production as centering around the story of a sixty-two-year-old Yiddish matinee idol, Nathan Rashumsky (Preston), whose character is based on a blend of two bonafide stars of the Yiddish theater–Boris Thomashefsky and Jacob Adler–and who continues to play adolescent roles not appropriate to his age. The musical begins with Nathan set to play Romeo in *Romeo and Juliet*. An hour before curtain time, Nathan learns that his wife Reba has died. The tumultuous marriage had been arranged fifty years before when Nathan and Reba were teenagers in Russia. Needing to make a public show of mourning for his wife, Nathan hires a group of professional mourners. Eighteen-year-old Leah (Small), who lives with her grandfather (Levene), is among the professional criers, but she is ultimately fired for crying too loud. Nathan falls for Leah, persuades her to travel with him to Atlantic City, and the two eventually marry.

Nathan then stars in his version of the Lincoln/Douglas debates entitled "Avram Lincoln in Illinois," in which Nathan as a young Avram debates Stephen Douglas. The local theater critic Julius Pritkin (Klemperer) goads Nathan in print about his refusal to play roles suited to his age and labels him the "Huckleberry Finn of the Yiddish Theatre." Nathan, who believes that a good actor can play a character of any age, visits Mark Twain (Powell) to ask for the rights to perform *Huckleberry Finn*. Twain declines the request when he discovers Nathan plans to play the youthful role of Huck Finn. When Nathan performs *Huckleberry Finn*, without permission from Twain, he is rebuked by the theater critic for appearing clownish. Crestfallen at the review, Nathan asks Leah whether audiences see him as ridiculous for taking a young wife and performing youthful roles. Although Leah assures Nathan he is not old, she advises him to pursue a play other than *Huckleberry Finn*. Nathan, who is unable to face reality or the smallest criticism, separates from Leah and retreats to a hotel room for two months. When Pritkin visits Nathan to request his help to produce a new play at the Grand Street Theatre, the actor blames the critic for prompting his withdrawal from the theater. Nathan softens when Pritkin lavishes praise on him for his contributions to the Yiddish theater. The musical ends when Leah is summoned to the theater by a Mr. Markov, who is Nathan in disguise. When Markov questions Leah about Nathan, she confesses she still loves her husband and misses him. As Leah recognizes Markov as Nathan, he reveals he has agreed to act in a new play about a father and son who meet in paradise, but cannot make up his mind which of the two roles he wants to perform.[58]

Preston completed his run in *Sly Fox* on December 31 and was feted with a "loving farewell party" hosted by co-stars Gretchen Wyler and Jack Gilford at the Hermitage in early January 1978.[59] Rehearsals for *The Prince of Grand Street* began on February 6[60] in the Minskoff Studios on the fifth floor of the office building which houses the Minskoff Theatre.[61] On the first day of rehearsal, Preston's fellow cast members marveled at how fantastic the actor looked and even went so far as to ask Preston's dresser, Jimmy Davidson, if the star had undergone a facelift.[62] He hadn't. Readying himself to portray a Yiddish theater star, Preston announced to the assembled cast and crew with élan that this was his "last day as a gentile!"[63]

In recalling his time as assistant musical director for the show, David Krane had nothing but high praise for Preston. Krane remarked that "Bob was one of the kindest and most professional of all the stars" he had had the opportunity to work with, adding that Preston was the "first to be off book" and "head to his dressing room or private space to go over his lines" during each rehearsal break.[64]

Preston's co-star, Neva Small, began acting and singing professionally at age ten and appeared in the film *Fiddler on the Roof* as Tevye's daughter, Chava, a few years before joining the cast of *The Prince of Grand Street*. Small characterized her *Grand Street* co-star as a "charming gentleman and a lover of life" who "loved a good laugh and was a good storyteller." She described Preston as magnanimous and even-tempered, commenting that she "never saw him be moody or be a prima donna, and he was always appreciative of other people's talent."[65]

Recalling the frequent changes Bob Merrill made to the script, Small affirmed that Preston had a brilliant mind and was extremely generous as a performer:

Preston had a photographic memory. So that means that when there were changes to the script, he immediately was able to memorize them. And of course, my scenes were mostly with him and I had to study them. I don't have a photographic memory, so, I would have to knock on his door and say, "Mr. Preston, could we please run that scene?" because he had it down.[66]

Both during rehearsals and the Philadelphia and Boston previews, Preston played the role of an aging Yiddish actor without affecting an accent. Neva Small confirmed,

He played Robert Preston. When you cast somebody like that, you're casting Robert Preston. There was not a smattering of Jewish inflection . . . the Borscht Belt kind of inflection. It was always Robert Preston. He was larger than life with that great voice that would light up the stage, like he did in *The Music Man*.[67]

After four weeks of rehearsals, the production moved to the Forrest Theatre in Philadelphia for its first out-of-town preview beginning on March 7. The Philadelphia critics, believing that the musical "was pleasant, but not strong enough to carry the thin story,"[68] urged Merrill to undertake major revisions to the show. William B. Collins of *The Philadelphia Inquirer* lambasted the story, script, and casting, noting that "if the show were successful in capturing the high flavor and teeming energy of that colorful era, it would be surefire entertainment. But it doesn't; and it isn't."[69] Although the drama critic from the *Philadelphia Daily News* criticized the show as "neither important nor accurate," he predicted that once the show "undergoes the necessary repairs [during a five-week Boston run] . . . it will go on to a successful Broadway engagement. Not stupendous, mind you, but successful."[70] By March 20, the *Philadelphia Daily News* revealed that Bob Merrill was rewriting the entire first act of the show,[71] and "the cast has been called to rehearsals each day at 1:00 p.m. in addition to regular performances."[72]

While the show was in Philadelphia and in the midst of being re-written, Preston frequented Bookbinder's Restaurant, and on more than one occasion, Neva Small accompanied the actor and his valet to the Walnut Street venue for a meal. Small remarked that Preston and his trusted valet, Jimmy Davidson, enjoyed a wonderful friendship and would regularly engage in trivia banter that centered on bands and musicians of the past:

> Robert Preston was so sharp that he would say hello to the maître d' by name and some of the waiters by name. He and his valet would trade big band stories and musicians of yesteryear and they would reference them the way people do with baseball players. That kept a conversation going for a long time.[73]

The Prince of Grand Street completed its Philadelphia run on March 25. After twenty-three performances in the City of Brotherly Love, the show moved on to its second preview venue in Boston where performances commenced on April 4 at the Shubert Theatre. The opening of the preview was pushed back from March 28 to allow Merrill "to do more work on the show before exposing it to the reviewers."[74] Merrill trudged forward with major revisions to the musical to allow the show to begin previews at the Palace Theatre in New York on May 4 and proceed with its scheduled Broadway debut at the same theater on

May 11. Revisions during the Philadelphia and Boston previews included the addition of four songs—"Stay with Me," "Where Does Love Go?," "Look at Me," and a title number—and two songs, "I'm A Star" and "My Potential," were deleted.[75]

The Boston Globe raised flags in March about a "booking jam" for plays and musicals seeking a Boston preview venue; the scheduling logjam in Boston threatened to clog the flow of plays and musicals that intended to premiere on Broadway. Some shows were unable to open in Boston due to a lack of space as the calendars for the Shubert, Colonial, and Wilbur Theatres were completely booked. It was noted that some New York-bound shows would inevitably be "shut out unless [another] show suddenly cancel[ed]."[76]

Once *The Prince of Grand Street* opened in Boston, a deluge of new material continued to be added to the score, often overwhelming the performers. Through it all, Neva Small remained steady, recalling, "We were fearless. We'd get a new scene in the daytime and put it into the show that night."[77] Preston, however, journeyed into the Boston preview with some trepidation. Although he looked forward to the performances in Boston, he refused to "predict how it will go this time around," noting "if a show is going poorly, I'll never put that into words—even for myself, because I wouldn't be able to work with it afterwards."[78] Nevertheless, the actor made it clear he was unwilling to bow to all of the criticism leveled at the production thus far:

> If you're for real, you never argue with a critique. Only insecure actors do that. We're a group of veterans. We're not about to be thrown that way. The only reviews that will affect us will be the New York reviews. That's why you go on the road. You

hope to get a set of C reviews, B reviews, and A reviews–work yourself up.[79]

All of the retooling Bob Merrill did to the score thoroughly fell flat in Boston. Kevin Kelly, the theater critic from *The Boston Globe*, described *The Prince of Grand Street* as a "shloop of a musical," noting that "as written by Bob Merrill, the story . . . is a one-joke musical," adding that "the trouble is that it can't really be stretched to cover two hours' traffic on stage."[80] Kelly praised Neva Small's performance as Leah as "just plain wonderful," but criticized the production as a whole as being "pretty drab." The review contended that Preston was "pretty funny as the over-the-hill Romeo, but watching him as Huck Finn in straw hat, blond wig and overalls is painful, painful because there's not a chance for even a glimmer of dignity in Huck's adolescence, painful because the comedy is only a cartoon."[81] In his book, *Not Since Carrie: 40 Years of Broadway Musical Flops*, Ken Mandelbaum suggests that the show's demise can be linked to its failure to "come up with a plot," leaving the audience with "only the ups and downs of Nathan's relationship with his young wife, and that relationship lacked conflict or development."[82]

On April 13, just nine days after the show opened in Boston, a sheet of paper was hung on the backstage call board of the Shubert Theatre to provide notice to the cast and crew "that *The Prince of Grand Street* will close following an evening performance on April 15, 1978."[83] The closing notice, delivered after just twenty-one performances, effectively canceled the remaining two weeks of what was to be a five-week Boston preview of the musical.

The performers all knew what was coming. Rehearsals for the show ceased on Tuesday, April 11 and the next morning the

musical's director, Gene Saks, "boarded a plane and left the remaining half dozen performances behind him."[84] David Krane,
the assistant musical director for *The Prince of Grand Street*, remembers Preston's benevolence and support in the final days of
the troubled show. As a twenty-five-year-old rising composer,
arranger, and musical director, Krane appreciated that the production's musical director, Colin Romoff, provided him with
the opportunity to conduct the show's final matinee.[85] Krane
recalled that at the bows, Preston "generously came down to
the footlights with open arms and said, '*Maestro*,'" providing
Krane with his "one and only bow as conductor for the show."[86]

A complete audio recording exists of one of the final, live
Boston performances of *The Prince of Grand Street* in April 1978.
The recording reflects an impeccable orchestra performance,
solid comedic lines delivered by Preston, lyrical singing by
Neva Small, and an attentive audience that responded to scenes
and songs with enthusiastic applause and laughter in rapid-fire
fashion.[87] Some familiar with the recording have suggested that
with a little more fine-tuning, the show could have been a mod-
erate success on Broadway.[88]

John Corry from *The New York Times* provided a compel-
ling post-mortem analysis of *The Prince of Grand Street*'s premature closure:

> And now, in no particular order, the explana-
> tions for the demise: The chemistry between
> Mr. Saks and Miss Theodore wasn't right. The
> notion of modeling Mr. Preston's character on
> Boris Thomashefsky and Jacob Adler got lost (in
> one scene, for example, Mr. Preston put on over-
> alls and a straw hat and did "Huckleberry Finn,"

Thomashefsky or Adler would more likely have been doing "King Lear"). The whole notion of the Yiddish theater got lost, and the show got lost in the romance between Mr. Preston's character and the character played by Neva Small. Somehow, in the mysterious alchemy of musicals, the show looked better in Philadelphia than it did in Boston. Robert Preston isn't Jewish. Or, any of the above reasons, however you care to join them."[89]

Bob Merrill attempted to deflect blame for the show's closure away from his score and shifted the onus for the production's demise to Preston:

We had a farce being played by a serious actor. It was written for another star, not Robert Preston. He's a fine legitimate actor, but the show needed a Walter Matthau or a Danny Kaye. So, we had to retailor the show for Preston and there just wasn't enough time before we got to Boston.[90]

Neva Small was disinclined to agree with Merrill's appraisal of why the musical failed to reach Broadway. In her view, Preston was unfairly blamed for the show's closing and became the perfect scapegoat. Small acknowledged, "Some said [Preston] wasn't Jewish enough, which is so silly because they cast him in the role to begin with."[91] The actress recognized it was difficult for Preston when the show closed, noting people "usually tend to blame the star. He was miscast or whatever, but it really wasn't his fault." She speculated that the producers "just didn't have the money, so they threw in the towel."[92]

Ultimately, the show's premature closure on the road in Boston marked Preston's last stage performance and "deprived Broadway audiences of the chance to see one of their princes in his last show."[93]

A brief revival of *The Prince of Grand Street* was staged in 2003 by the Jewish Repertory Theatre in New York. Even though the revival boasted a new director and cast, a review of the 2003 show was less than enthusiastic:

> The show is seldom short of bubbling and brewing, though its aroma promises something the taste itself never quite delivers, and, despite [director Barry] Kleinbort's hard work, probably never will; while there's much in the show that's good, *The Prince of Grand Street* is not exactly a lost classic.[94]

After the collapse of *The Prince of Grand Street*, Preston was approached by CBS to star in a western mini-series based on Evan Hunter's 1976 novel *The Chisholms*. Hunter's book chronicled a Virginia family's decision to travel west over the Oregon Trail to California after losing their most fertile farmland in a legal dispute with a rival neighbor. The episodes recount the family's goal of reaching Fort Laramie, Wyoming before winter descends upon the Rocky Mountains. The long journey is fraught with disease, hardships, encounters with Native Americans, snake bites, and family drama. Preston was enticed to participate in this brief stint on television with the knowledge he would have the opportunity to work with his friend and former leading lady, Rosemary Harris. Although Preston normally made a point to avoid appearing in television movies, he agreed to play the role of Hadley Chisholm after he read the script and realized Harris would play his wife in the mini-series. In reflecting on his decision to accept a television role, Preston mused, "If you're going to have to sleep under a wagon on the Platte, you're lucky if it's with someone like Rosemary."[95]

The cast of *The Chisholms* included Preston in the role of family patriarch Hadley Chisholm, and Hadley's wife, Minerva (Harris). The Chisholm children included Will (Ben Murphy), Gideon (Brian Kerwin), twins Bonnie Sue (Stacey Nelkin) and Beau (James Van Patten), and Annabel (Susan Swift). Charles Frank, Lester Hackett, Sandra Griego, David Hayward, Anthony Zerbe, Brian Keith, Doug Kershaw, and Glynnis O'Connor also made appearances in the series.

The script for the four-episode mini-series was written by author Evan Hunter and directed by Mel Stuart. Elmer Bernstein adapted music from Aaron Copeland for the score. A sizable budget in excess of $4.5 million enabled the production team to hire a stellar cast and film on location.[96] Filming of the mini-series began on September 13 in Peoria and Springfield, Illinois, and continued in Missouri, Nebraska, and Colorado.[97]

During filming in Illinois, forty-year-old Ada Lynn Shrewsbury, a member of the Springfield theater community, was hired for a small role that included some dialogue with Preston. Shrewsbury described Preston as a "wonderful person" and a "very gracious, sweet man" who interacted with the local film extras as "John Q. Ordinary Citizen who would chit chat about this, that, and the other thing," and made the on-set work a delightful experience for the extras. At the completion of her two days of filming, Preston kissed Shrewsbury farewell, an event that the local actress admits "made [her] year."[98]

Filming around New Salem State Park continued until October 16 when the production moved to the Clayville Coach Stop at Pleasant Plains to film the remainder of the Illinois scenes.[99] By October 20, Preston and his fellow cast were filming on location in St. Louis, Missouri,[100] and by November 1 filming was underway in Scotts Bluff County, Nebraska. The ten weeks of filming required for the four episodes was completed before the end of November.

Preston enjoyed being able to act alongside Rosemary Harris and replicate the easy, onstage magic they had in *The Lion in Winter*. Since the two appeared together on Broadway in the spring of 1966, Harris divorced Ellis Rabb and married writer and North Carolina native John Ehle; the couple's only child, Jennifer, was born in 1969. Harris indicated her husband and daughter would regularly visit her on location as *The Chisholms* set moved across the country. Preston adored Jennifer and the child was equally fond of him. On those occasions when John Ehle was unable to make the trip west, Jennifer would be brought out to visit her mother on location. It was during those solo visits to the set that Preston would lavish attention on Jennifer Ehle and tell her he was her "proxy daddy."[101]

Episodes of *The Chisholms* were aired on CBS on successive Thursday evenings beginning on March 29, 1979. The miniseries was a critical success, and Preston received exceptional praise for his television performance. Lee Winfrey of *The Philadelphia Inquirer* informed the paper's readership that *The Chisholms* "has a top-notch cast, a strong script, and some of the best music written in America during this century," noting that Preston infused the role of Hadley Chisholm with "emphatic force."[102] Likewise, the *Fort Lauderdale News* described

The Chisholms as "a joy to watch" and a program that depicted pioneer life as "back-breaking but still seductive." Preston as Hadley Chisholm was deemed "absolutely perfect" in a role where he "cuts the same imposing figure as James Arness, but with more dimensionality and flair."[103]

A few months after *The Chisholms* miniseries concluded on CBS, Preston began filming *The Man That Corrupted Hadleyburg,* a short story by Mark Twain, that would air as one of eight episodes in the *American Short Story* series on PBS. Twain's story is a derisive view of American small-town life and focuses on the town of Hadleyburg, which prided itself on its reputation as a virtuous community. A mysterious stranger, who was slighted by the townsfolk in the past, rides into town with a sack of gold that he will use to expose the town's true nature.

The stranger claims that he was destitute during his previous visit to Hadleyburg, but an unidentified townsperson provided him with twenty dollars and some words of advice–an act of charity which turned his life around. The stranger sends letters to the townspeople advising them that whoever can identify themselves as the kind donor, by disclosing their past words of advice, will be given the sack containing $40,000 in gold. The townsfolk, now faced with temptation, attempt to lay claim to the gold, each asserting that he or she had helped the stranger. The machinations of the town's prominent citizens result in the town's fall from grace and its reputation in tatters. Twain's story, a test of human nature, suggested that people cannot claim to be virtuous if they have not resisted temptation.

The teleplay, directed by Ralph Rosenblum, featured Preston as the mysterious stranger, as well as Fred Gwynne (Reverend Burgess), Frances Sternhagen (Mary Richards), and Tom Aldredge (Edward Richards) in other principal roles.

The Twain story was filmed in the towns of Bethel and Royalton, Vermont in mid-August. Preston, whose feet were not shown during scenes, wore bright red tennis shoes while on the set. Preston and Gwynne were both described by Royalton residents as being "congenial," although "Preston was said to be more outgoing than Gwynne."[104] During breaks in the shooting, Gwynne whittled on a piece of wood while Preston "kept a little girl entertained with a song."[105]

Actor Brandon Maggart, who had a minor role in the *Hadleyburg* film, spent quite a bit of time with Preston off the set. Maggart indicated he and Preston formed an instant friendship, enjoying dinners together that included Maggart's then-girlfriend and Preston's wife. The actor described Preston as "the warmest person you've ever met in your life," and a man who "remembers everybody." Years after the two worked together on *Hadleyburg*, Maggart encountered Preston at an awards show and was elated when Preston went out of his way to say, "Brandon, we have followed your career and are so happy for you." Maggart confessed that Preston's words "boosted me more than the awards ceremony" adding, "I just adore that man."[106]

PBS aired *The Man Who Corrupted Hadleyburg* on March 17, 1980 as a double-feature along with a dramatization of William Faulkner's short story, *Barn Burning*, starring Tommy Lee Jones. The performances by Preston and Jones in the short-story dramatizations were deemed by critics to be "outstanding."[107]

In light of the critical acclaim received for *The Chisholms*, CBS decided to move forward and expand the mini-series into a prime-time television series starring Preston and Harris. Although Preston had no intention of appearing on a television series, he eventually relented and agreed to appear in a few

episodes of the show with the express proviso that his character
be killed off before the Chisholm family reached California:

> [The network] swore [the mini-series] was going
> to be six hours. Then they begged me the next
> year. CBS wanted six more. And they said that if I
> didn't do it, a lot of people would be out of work.
> Well, I wasn't doing anything. And the first one
> had been fun and they did shoot [the episodes]
> well. I must say it wasn't like making television.
> They shot them like a feature film. And so, we did
> the next one and I did put in that proviso [about
> being killed off] and they knew it all along . . . the
> only reason I came back and did additional [epi-
> sodes] was because of Rosemary, with the proviso
> that they kill me [off] in the last episode . . . [CBS]
> didn't write that last [episode] until they tried ev-
> ery ruse in the book to get me to sign up for more.
> So, finally, when I absolutely insisted, they wrote
> that final [episode].[108]

Rosemary Harris was aware of Preston's feelings about appearing in a television series. She knew her dear friend had
pre-arranged his exit from the show in episode five, but he had
urged her to "go on ahead [with the series] without me." She
stressed that "no one thought ill of him" for leaving the television series, and they "all missed him horribly."[109]

The filming of *The Chisholms* television series began in
early November 1979 at Fort Bentz in La Junta, Colorado with
Preston and Harris reprising their roles as Hadley and Minerva
Chisholm. Ben Murphy and James Van Patten likewise made

the transition from the mini-series to the television show. However, CBS decided to make some changes to the original 1979 Chisholm family cast and hired Brett Cullen to replace Brian Kerwin as Gideon Chisholm and Delta Burke to replace Stacey Nelkin as Bonnie Sue. The network also made changes to the directorial lineup, allowing seasoned documentary director Mel Stuart to direct episodes five, six, seven, eight, and ten, but brought in Edward Abroms (2 episodes), Sigmund Neufeld, Jr. (1 episode), and Nicholas Webster (1 episode), to direct episodes nine, eleven, twelve, and thirteen. Stuart, who had previously directed the first four episodes of the original miniseries, avoided cutting corners and insisted on authenticity.

The new episodes followed the Chisholm family on their journey by covered wagon from Fort Laramie, Wyoming to California. To provide an air of realism to the show, the producers deemed it necessary for the cast and crew to spend months on location working in weather conditions that ranged from warm winds to frigid mountain snow.[110] Temperatures on the southwestern plains of Colorado were frosty and uncomfortable for the cast and crew who were required to report to the set before sunrise. Filming was temporarily halted when a raging blizzard covered the Fort Bentz area with a blanket of snow and ice.[111]

The production moved to El Centro, California for the filming of the desert crossing sequences. Although relentless winds covered the cast, crew, and equipment with sand and dust, the mild December temperatures offered some relief from the desert heat.[112] Cast and crew then moved to the Mammoth Lakes area to film the Chisholm family crossing the Sierra Nevada Mountains into California where they worked at elevations up to 9,500 feet and in temperatures a few degrees above zero. Thermal underwear was worn by all during the filming of the mountain scenes and, when the sun began to set, battery-operated electric socks were distributed to the cast to prevent frostbite.[113]

During a press interview while on location, Preston disclosed he was anxious to return home. He spoke at length about his rugged lifestyle in Connecticut which included catching fish from his pond for meals, making the occasional foray into the kitchen to cook uncomplicated fare, pruning trees, and aging cut wood for use on the barbeque. As someone with a penchant for variety and change, Preston confessed, "I'm in love with the four seasons. I don't care how hot summer is or how cold winter is. Spring and fall are so gorgeous, especially around a place like ours."[114] In addition to the change of seasons, Preston was looking forward to working with director Blake Edwards on his new film, *S.O.B.*, which would begin filming in the spring of 1980.

Nine episodes of *The Chisholms* were aired on CBS on Saturday evenings during the first three months of 1980. The initial episode was two hours in length and contained flashback scenes to the storyline of the original 1979 mini-series; each additional episode had a one-hour run time. With Preston's character dead by the end of the fifth episode, the ratings for the subsequent episodes began to decline, and the fledgling series was ultimately not renewed by the network.

Once *The Chisholms* was off the air, Preston found himself at a dinner party with Bob Daly, then president of CBS Entertainment, and embroiled in a discussion about his decision to exit the television series:

And the first thing [Bob Daly] said to me is, "You killed what could have been a beautiful series." I said, "But how?" He said, "By not going on" . . . Jesus. I don't know, I don't think [the series] could

have gone on anyway. They tried. I could see toward the end that they were going for beating the
clock and all the rest of that. But the whole thing
was about a family trying to get to California. And
once you're there, it's just another *Little House on
the Prairie* or something like that.[115]

Preston remained confident that his exit from *The Chisholms*
was a judicious move for him both personally and professionally. He understood all too well that if the series had been prolonged, the storyline would eventually fall flat with the viewing
audience. As was his nature, Preston did not have the time or the
inclination to look back on what could have been; his eyes were
instead firmly fixed on what lay ahead: a return to Hollywood.

RETURN TO THE
SILVER SCREEN

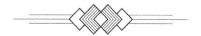

D
uring his stint on *The Chisholms,* Preston signed on to appear in director Blake Edwards's satiric film *S.O.B.* (1981)-
short for Standard Operating Bullshit-as a Hollywood
Dr. Feelgood character. The actor, who had not worked with
Edwards before receiving the script, confessed he "had no
qualms about the role" of Dr. Irving Finegarten, but he "did
about the taste of certain things the picture dealt with." Any
reservations Preston may have had about the *S.O.B.* script dissolved after he had the opportunity to view Edwards's latest film,
the bawdy, hit comedy *10.*[1] Before signing on to the Edwards's
film, Preston had not appeared in a Hollywood movie since the
release of *Semi-Tough* in 1977.

Written and directed by Edwards, *S.O.B.* is a semi-auto-
biographical account of the director's history of issues with
Paramount Studios during and after the filming of Edwards's
movie flop, *Darling Lili* (1970). *Darling Lilli* starred Edwards's wife,

Julie Andrews, and included a scene in which the actress, who maintained a wholesome public image, performed a burlesque routine. Edwards developed *S.O.B.* as a black comedy and cinematic vehicle with which to publicly dramatize the deceitful artificiality of the movie industry using satire and slapstick comedy.[2]

In addition to Preston, *S.O.B.* featured a Who's Who of Hollywood in the early 1980s including Julie Andrews, Richard Mulligan, William Holden, Robert Vaughn, Larry Hagman, Loretta Swit, Robert Webber, Marisa Berenson, Stuart Margolin, Shelley Winters, Craig Stevens, Rosanna Arquette, Robert Loggia, Jennifer Edwards, Larry Storch, and Corbin Bernsen.

The premise of Edwards's film-within-a-film plot follows Hollywood producer Felix Farmer (Mulligan) who is despondent in the aftermath of making *Night Wind*, the lowest-grossing film in history, and being abandoned by his actress-wife Sally Miles (Andrews) and their children. A distraught Farmer makes several failed suicide attempts and is finally sedated by physician-to-the-stars, Dr. Irving Finegarten (Preston). Meanwhile, a second-rate actor, Burgess Webster, falls over dead on the beach outside Farmer's home, with no one noticing the death, despite the frantic efforts of the dead man's dog to call attention to his master's demise. Snooping Hollywood gossip columnist Polly Reed (Swit) arrives at Farmer's home to follow up on rumors of Farmer's suicide attempts and encounters *Night Wind* director Tim Culley (Holden), press agent Ben Coogan (Webber), and Dr. Finegarten. Farmer botches an attempt to hang himself and crashes through his bedroom floor into the living room below, severely injuring Polly Reed and landing her in the hospital with a full-body cast.

A birthday party for actor Sam Marshall, held at Farmer's home, devolves into a debauched orgy. During the pleasure-fest,

Felix is inspired by a bare-breasted partygoer with an idea to salvage *Night Wind*. His plan involves adding a porn sequence to the film by having the squeaky-clean star, his wife Sally Miles, bare her bosom on camera. When studio head David Blackman (Vaughn) nixes the plan, Farmer offers to buy the film from the studio. Although Sally fears a nude scene will damage her image with fans, she agrees to reshoot the film with urging from her agent Eva Brown (Winters) and attorney Herb Maskowitz (Loggia). The studio decides to pursue distribution rights to the film as they realize Sally's nude scene will transform the movie into box office gold. Studio executives are denied admission to the set where the topless scene will be filmed, as is Polly Reed who arrives on location via ambulance, still sporting a full-body cast. When Sally begins having second thoughts about doing the nude scene, Dr. Finegarten administers a feel-good injection to loosen her inhibitions. Once the drugs kick in, Sally bares her breasts as the camera rolls. Blackman contacts Sally's agent to arrange for the star to sign an exclusive distribution contract with the studio. Farmer goes berserk after discovering he has been betrayed by his wife and the studio has stolen his film. He reacts by stealing a car and leading police on a wild car chase in which he crashes through a wall in Sally's home, steals his son's water pistol, and winds up at the film lab where the *Night Wind* negatives are stored.

Felix is ultimately killed by police when he is found holding a security guard hostage with the real-looking water pistol. As Sally plans a star-studded funeral for her estranged husband, Cully, Coogan, and Dr. Finegarten decide to steal Farmer's body from the funeral home and give him the Viking funeral they believe he deserves. The men replace Farmer's body in the coffin with that of Burgess Webster and use Farmer's boat to take their friend's corpse out to sea at Marina Del Rey. The trio place Farmer's body, adorned with a Viking helmet, in a rowboat, douse it with gasoline, and set it ablaze. The spectacular funeral planned for Farmer by his wife is held without anyone realizing that the producer is not actually in his coffin. Ultimately, the revised *Night Wind* becomes the highest-grossing motion picture in film history and earns Sally an Academy Award for her salacious performance.

Edwards was able to secure Lorimar Productions to produce *S.O.B.* along with an accompanying distribution deal with Paramount Studios. On March 20, 1980 at 7:45 a.m., Edwards filmed the first scenes of *S.O.B.* after eleven years of delays related to the search for studio backing and financing for the movie.[3]

Loretta Swit has warm memories of her experience on the set of *S.O.B.* where she was surrounded by "icons of [her] profession." The two-time Emmy-award-winning actress said she would visit the set to spend time with the cast even when she had no scenes to film "just to hang out with this talented, world-famous gang. It was so incredibly entertaining. It was a party-like atmosphere with all the fun and laughs" and "you didn't want to miss anything." The cast camaraderie further solidified when they gathered on weekends at the home of Blake Edwards and Julie Andrews where Edwards would run a movie and sometimes include a surprise 'take' from the week's rushes.[4] Swit, who appeared in several scenes in the film with Preston, described the actor as warm and friendly, adding that he was a gifted raconteur who loved sharing stories of his experiences in the industry:

> I felt comfortable sharing with him. My time on the set was so very special. Pres was larger than

life with his outgoing personality and his booming voice. His talent and persona brought "the
good doctor" in *S.O.B.* to life-to larger than life,
you could say. We see that gift of his in all his
work. His legacy speaks for itself.[5]

Armed with his bag of pills, vials, and hypodermic syringes,
Preston, as the jaunty Dr. Irving Finegarten, delivered lines of
dialogue with a witty tongue and philosophical eloquence. When
asked by a reporter whether his character was based on a specific
Hollywood physician, Preston indicated, "I knew one like him at
Paramount. I asked Blake, 'Is this [character] anything like X?'
'Good!' Blake said. 'Go with X.'" When queried about whether the
Hollywood orgy depicted in the film mirrored reality in Tinseltown,
Preston quipped, "They have them. They just call them story con-
ferences."[6] Having experienced his own set of issues with the
movie industry in the 1940s and 50s, Preston could easily relate to
the underlying message conveyed in *S.O.B.* and appreciated being
given the opportunity to appear in the polemical film:

> I can't tell you how much I love *S.O.B.* I love ev-
> erything about it, especially the controversy it's
> causing. I like a picture where there's no middle
> ground, and them that hates it is gonna hate it,
> which is their problem . . . I can't tell you what fun
> it is to be in a controversial picture . . . I'm really
> so pleased with *S.O.B.* that I was prepared to retire
> from films because I felt I'd never be able to top it.[7]

Preston felt a sense of gratitude toward Edwards for including him in the *S.O.B.* cast and credited the director for launching

his "third career" as an entertainer.[8] Preston abhorred type-casting, and it was the character of Dr. Irving Finegarten that provided him with the opportunity and professional latitude to demonstrate different aspects of his professional repertoire.[9]

Filming for *S.O.B.* concluded in early July 1980. When the film was released in July 1981, the critical response to the movie was sharply divided; critics tended to either love it or hate it. On the positive side, Vincent Canby of *The New York Times* enjoyed the film. Canby commented it was "difficult to remember a film as mean-spirited as *S.O.B.* that also was so consistently funny . . . the performances are wickedly right . . . [and] there's really not a bad performance in the lot." He additionally characterized the movie as "unbridled, undisguised, misanthropy."[10] Recognizing that the film gave "the profit-obsessed movie industry a mighty hot-foot," Canby also acknowledged that "sometimes there's nothing quite as exhilarating as being able to bite the hands that have fed you, but then *S.O.B.* isn't just a bite. It's a six-course meal of palms, knuckles, and fingers."[11] Dean Johnson of *The Orlando Sentinel* gave the film high marks for its "blistering hysterical performances" and viewed the film as the "tour-de-force" of the director's film portfolio.[12] Other praise for the movie came from Desmond Ryan of the Knight-Ridder News Service who noted "the film is alive with performances of withering accuracy." Ryan praised Preston as "nothing less than splendid" in his portrayal of a Hollywood quack doctor and asserted that *S.O.B.* "stands as one of the two really intelligent comedies made this year."[13] Another critic, while describing the film as Edwards's "poison pen letter to Hollywood," declared that "for all its flaws and miscalculations, *S.O.B.* might be the most intelligent film for the summer."[14] The movie was touted as "the culmination of what has always been best about Blake

Edwards: the split-second timing, the telling detail, the delicious subtle wit" by Lawrence O'Toole of *Macleans* magazine. O'Toole additionally lauded Preston's performance as the "pill-popping, booze-guzzling" doctor as being the only character in the film "who seems to truly know himself."[15]

Other film critics were brutal in their assessment of the film. Kathleen Carroll of the *Daily News* suggested that the "raucous, scathingly cynical farce" would be more aptly titled "the revenge of Blake Edwards," and determined that due to "its mostly coarse humor, *S.O.B.* tends to be an overly shrill tiresome movie."[16] Although *People* magazine panned the film, the publication noted, "the movie's only redeeming feature is the acting," adding that Preston was a "raffish delight" as Dr. Finegarten.[17] Critic Rick Brough who redubbed the movie "Standard Operational Blandness," observed that Preston "gets 75% of all the good lines" in the film. It was further noted that although "Edwards may have exorcised some of his bad Hollywood memories with this film, scream therapy isn't always good cinema."[18] Similarly, Robert Alan Ross, the film critic from the *Tampa Bay Times,* suggested that "Edwards seems confused about what type of movie he really wanted to make" and "unless he wanted a painfully disjointed collection of snide exaggerations, he didn't get what he was hoping for."[19]

Despite all the efforts by Edwards and the cast, *S.O.B.* was a box office bomb. According to IMDb, the estimated budget for the film was $12 million, but the movie's worldwide gross was only a mere $14,867,086. Paramount, the distributor of *S.O.B.,* had originally promised a publicity junket for the film.[20] The studio's marketing department sent invitations to the press as well as the film's cast, but rescinded the invitations a few days later[21] and arranged for *S.O.B.*'s release on the same weekend that Steven Spielberg's action blockbuster *Raiders of the Lost Ark* would hit theaters.[22] Citing issues of "excessive expenditures" incurred by Edwards during filming, Paramount canceled the estimated $225,000 publicity junket,[23] essentially recreating the hostile dynamic between studio and filmmaker that was enshrined in the film's script. Since the film was designed as a ferocious satire of the film industry, Edwards and the cast of *S.O.B.* viewed Paramount's lack of publicity for the film as the studio's attempt to jettison it. The director, who was in London putting the finishing touches on his next film, *Victor/Victoria*, "blew his top" when he learned that Paramount had canceled the film's publicity tour and immediately went into action to re-institute the tour at his expense.[24] Furious at the lackluster way *S.O.B.* was being distributed and publicized, Edwards– mirroring director Felix Farmer in the movie–made a failed bid to purchase the movie from Lorimar Productions, and ultimately used $200,000 of his own funds to arrange for a publicity junket for the film.[25] Six of the film's well-known cast members–Julie Andrews, William Holden, Robert Preston, Richard Mulligan, Loretta Swit, and Robert Webber–volunteered for a combination air and bus trip to seven major cities to publicize the film. The cast flew from Hollywood to San Francisco aboard two Lear jets rented from Frank Sinatra, then leapfrogged from San Francisco to Lincoln, Nebraska, New York, Philadelphia, Washington D.C., Toronto, and Chicago.[26] Loretta Swit recalled the touring actors met with the press in cozy luncheon or dinner settings where they "had an opportunity to discuss the work, the fun stories shared on the set, how it was working with Blake, and why we were meeting with the press." Swit enjoyed the publicity tour for *S.O.B.*, adding that Preston likewise "got a big kick out of it, but Pres saw the fun and humor in everything."[27]

Always one to find amusement in sticky situations, Preston referred to the traveling band of actors as "the road company of S.O.B., but with the original cast."[28] Actor Robert Webber suggested there had been "talk that the pro-Edwards performers could end up on a [Hollywood] hit-list because of their public loyalty to the director" since their participation in the publicity tour could be construed as a betrayal of Paramount.[29]

Preston won the award for Best Supporting Actor from the National Society of Film Critics for his role as S.O.B.'s sardonic Dr. Irving Finegarten, but was not considered for a Best Supporting Actor Oscar nomination from the Academy of Motion Picture Arts and Sciences.

Some critics suggested Preston was snubbed by the Academy because the film impugned the very industry that the Academy salutes on an annual basis.[30] The film itself received a schizophrenic response from Hollywood, garnering both a Golden Globe nomination for Best Director and a Razzie nomination for Worst Director (and worst screenplay) at the Second Golden Raspberry Awards in 1982.

Blake Edwards worked on finalizing the script for his new film project, *Victor/Victoria* (1982), while completing *S.O.B.*, basing the plot of the new film on the 1933 German movie *Viktor und Viktoria*.[31] The director planned to cast his wife, Julie Andrews, and Peter Sellers in the two main roles of Victoria Grant and Carroll "Toddy" Todd, but his vision for the cast was irrevocably altered when Sellers suffered a heart attack and died in July 1980.

Since Preston was so wickedly funny in the role of Dr. Irving Finegarten in *S.O.B.*, Edwards decided to cast the sixty-two-year-old actor in an even more outrageous role as the gay nightclub entertainer, Toddy, in *Victor/Victoria*.[32] Edwards

previously shared the storyline of his upcoming movie with
Preston while the two worked together on *S.O.B.* Preston recalled receiving a phone call from Edwards four months after
S.O.B. had wrapped asking, "Remember the story I told you
on the set? Well, it's a screenplay now and you're Toddy."
Preston so thoroughly trusted Edwards and was delighted to
have the opportunity to play a different character that he accepted the role and "didn't even ask to see a script" of the
film.[33] Edwards, cognizant that many actors at the time would
have turned down the role because it involved homosexuality,
recalled the phone call in which he approached Preston about
playing the role of Toddy:

> [Preston] was such a mensch. That's the only way
> I can describe him . . . I called him up and said,
> "Pres, I want you to do a film." He said "Ok." I
> said, "You're going to play gay," and he said, "Ok."
> I said, "Do you understand what I just said?"[34]

Although Edwards originally envisioned the character
of Toddy as a drag queen, Preston was able to convince the
director to allow him to "play a perfectly adjusted guy" in
the film:

> Blake and I had an understanding, right from
> the beginning, that [Toddy] was not going to be
> a "limp-wrist." But, when the moment came, he
> could do the outrageous thing a gay man will do–
> and especially with a woman. When he says to
> Julie [Andrews], "I want shoulders! Shoulders! . . .
> Tons and tons of shoulders!"[35]

The sixty-two-year-old Preston, still bursting with vim and vigor, used his energy to portray Toddy as "a very happy, well-adjusted guy" who "just happens to prefer men." He was all too aware that no one but Edwards would have thought of him as right for the part.[36] As a forward-thinking man, Preston believed that any stigma attached to playing a gay role was a thing of the past. He viewed *Victor/Victoria* as a leading-edge film that would openly feature

> A whole segment of society that's there, that's not going to go away. I wanted the gay world to like Toddy, and I played him in a way the straight world would accept. And people are people, let's not have stupid prejudices.[37]

Lorimar Productions planned to move forward with *Victor/ Victoria* and pre-production on the film began in October 1980. Two months later, however, Lorimar abandoned the project in response to serious financial losses suffered by its film division. The project was revived when MGM assumed control of the film and made the decision to shoot the movie at Pinewood Studios just outside London,[38] rather than in Paris. The sprawling Pinewood set consumed fifteen sound stages, two of which were used to construct four hundred continuous feet of 1934 Paris complete with three-story buildings.[39]

In addition to Preston and Julie Andrews, the principal cast of *Victor/Victoria* included James Garner, Lesley Ann Warren, Alex Karras, John Rhys-Davies, Norman Chancer, Graham Stark, and Peter Arne. Blake Edwards wore three hats as a writer, director, and co-producer of the film with the musical score provided by Henry Mancini and Leslie Bricusse.

The story of *Victor/Victoria* is set in Paris in 1934. British singer Victoria Grant (Andrews), unemployed and down on her luck, encounters Carroll "Toddy" Todd (Preston), a gay American entertainer, during an audition at the Chez Lui nightclub where he is employed. By chance, the two meet up at a restaurant after Victoria is evicted from her hotel room for failure to pay her rent. She asks Toddy to join her for dinner and releases a cockroach from her purse to avoid paying the dinner check. The pair manage to flee the restaurant into a stormy Paris night, and Toddy shelters a rain-soaked Victoria in his apartment. With her outfit shrunken and unwearable, Victoria dons a men's suit in Toddy's closet. Seeing Victoria dressed as a man, Toddy realizes Victoria could pose as a Polish female impersonator. He invents the name of Count Victor Breszinski for Victoria's new persona and concocts a cover story that Victor is Toddy's new lover. The ruse is successful when Toddy secures Andre Cassell (Rhys-Davies), the most successful talent manager in Paris, as an agent for Count Breszinski. Victoria, as Victor, secures a gig at an upscale nightclub as a female impersonator and her act becomes a major attraction in Paris.

When Chicago gangster King Marchand (Garner), his ditzy girlfriend Norma Cassidy (Warren), and his burly bodyguard Squash Bernstein (Karras) see Victoria's show, Marchand finds himself attracted to Victor, but is convinced the performer is not a man. Marchand sends his girlfriend packing back to Chicago and discovers Victor's true gender after surreptitiously spying on the entertainer in the bathtub. Squash and Toddy are arrested during a melee at Monsieur Labisse's (Arne) Chez Lui nightclub, but Marchand and Victor elude police and Marchand kisses Victor, who is dressed as a man. When Squash, a closeted gay man, finds Marchand and Victor together in bed, he decides to come out as gay and enjoys a fling with Toddy. Marchand and Victoria enjoy a secret romance, but maintaining Victoria's charade as a man strains the relationship. Meanwhile, Labisse grows suspicious that Victor is a fraud and hires a private detective to investigate Victor's gender.

Back in Chicago, a rejected Norma informs Marchand's business partner, Sal Andretti (Chancer), that Marchand is involved in a romantic relationship with a man in Paris. Sal and Norma travel to Paris where Sal demands that Marchand sell off his portion of the business for pennies on the dollar. Victoria saves the day, and Marchand's business interests, by revealing to Norma and Sal that she is a woman. When Cassell, Toddy, and Victoria discover that Labisse has instigated a police complaint against them for perpetrating a public fraud, Toddy substitutes for Victor in the nightclub's dressing room; the police inspector, observing that "Victor" is biologically male, drops the complaint. Victoria, now styled as a woman, surprises Marchand and Squash at their table in the nightclub. When Victor's act is introduced, it is Toddy who emerges onstage dressed in Victoria's Spanish dancer costume and performs her "The Shady Dame from Seville" song-and-dance routine. The story ends with Victoria and Marchand gleefully watching Toddy's first and final raucous impersonation of Victoria.

Preston and Catherine arrived in London in February 1981, along with Edwards and Andrews, a full month before production on the film commenced to privately rehearse the song-and-dance numbers. The actor recalled,

> We got to know who these two people [Toddy and Victoria] were . . . when you find out how a guy moves on the dance floor, you find out the way

he walks down the stairs, down the street. [Julie] never took her eyes off me. She was watching to see what fellows do. And I said, "Look, I've got to play gay. Don't look at me."[40]

With the entire cast now at Pinewood Studios, production on *Victor/Victoria* commenced on March 2. Except for the production numbers, "Gay Paree," "Le Jazz Hot," "You and Me," "Chicago, Illinois," "Crazy World," and two renditions of "The Shady Dame of Seville," the shooting schedule was kept completely in sequence with the script, which Preston acknowledged is not only "a wonderful way to work," but helped to build the relationship between Victoria and Toddy.[41]

Edwards encouraged the actors to improvise or ad-lib at will during their scripted scenes and preferred impromptu exchanges between the cast on film. Preston's first musical number in the film, "Gay Paree," was sung in the Chez Lui nightclub before "the damndest agglomeration of transvestites you've ever seen–marvelous faces."[42] Before he sang the number, Preston told the assembled audience,

This is the first time in a long career that I'm ever going to do a number in front of an audience, each of whom can do it better than I can . . . we had a lot of joking and camaraderie. So that by the time we got ready to do the scene, do the number, I could use any one of them for anything I wanted, I could touch them, get a leer from some.[43]

As Toddy, Preston thanked the audience for their applause after his performance of "Gay Paree" and threw in the ad-libbed line, "You're very kind, in fact, you're *every* kind," and Edwards left it in the scene. Realizing the demographics of the assembled audience were heterogeneous, Preston improvised the line and confessed that he could "not tell legitimately which [audience members] were male and which were female."[44]

Later in the film, Preston, as Toddy, participated in an impromptu soft-shoe routine, "You and Me," with Andrews, as Victor, at the Chez Lui. According to Andrews, the duet she performed with Preston was influenced by the Western Brothers, whom she recalled from her youth performing at the piano wearing a monocle, white tie and tails.[45] Preston indicated Edwards would not allow the two actors to rehearse the song-and-dance number since he preferred for the on-screen interaction "to be off-the-cuff, ad lib."[46] Not wanting to leave things completely to chance, Preston and Andrews "would sneak around behind the set and practice little things" to include in the scene so they "would not step on each other" while they were performing the routine.[47] On the day the impromptu scene was filmed, Edwards was able to print the first take.[48] Reflecting on the successful execution of the song-and-dance routine, Preston realized the presence of the same crowd that comprised the audience for his previous "You and Me" number was what contributed to the scene's success:

The audience was what made that number. The laughter at all our ad-libs. I said, "Taught him everything he knows" and she said, "A little bit to the left" and "Well, that was fun. Now, what do we do? You got us into this." The whole thing was right off the cuff. Except we planned one thing. And it comes from Missy Stanwyck. I made a picture with her called *The Lady Gambles*. And I had a scene in a restaurant where we're dancing and I had to say every once in a while, "Missy, you're leading again."[49]

For the final scene of the film, Preston reprises the musical number "The Shady Dame of Seville" that Andrews originally performed earlier in the story. The long Spanish flamenco-style dress worn by Andrews for her rendition of the song was the same one worn by Preston during his performance at the end of the film. The size of the costume was originally designed to fit Preston's burly frame, with a series of hooks and eyes affixed to the back of the dress to allow the material to be pulled tightly to Andrews' silhouette during her performance of "The Shady Dame of Seville." Extra black ruffles were added to the bottom of the dress to camouflage the differences in height between Preston and Andrews. Fortunately, Preston was able to execute the musical number in a single take since the dress sustained considerable rips and tears during the actor's performance.[50]

Preston confessed feeling "uncomfortable" about the final drag number in the film, as he had no idea what he would do or how he would execute the live performance:

> When they say "Rolling," you've got to do something. Well, Blake cured that by saying, "I don't know what the hell you're going to do either–do it!" And then I realized that, of course, that's it. That's the answer to it. Nobody knows what's going to happen. And the minute he said, "You're not going to pre-record it, you're going to be live," all the problems disappeared . . . every bit of the

number was an improvisation. That whole crazy ending is a real breakup. All the dancers, we just broke up and [Blake] kept [the camera] running. And the heel came off one of my shoes and that strange, crazy walk was because I didn't have a heel on that shoe. We could never have done the number again without going to wardrobe. The dress was torn in twenty different places, the wig was ruined, and my mascara was running.[51]

Lesley Ann Warren, who received an Academy Award nomination for her portrayal of Norma Cassidy in *Victor/Victoria*, shared several scenes with Preston in the film. During an interview with Tom Fitzgerald and Lorenzo Marquez in 2019, Warren confessed that Preston was her favorite co-star in the film as both were comfortable with the spontaneity and improvisation that Edwards encouraged in the cast. When it came to improvisation, Warren observed that "some of us were comfortable [with it] and some of us weren't. I felt comfortable with it and Robert did, but Julie didn't . . . Robert and I really worked well together in that way."[52]

Warren marveled at Preston's professionalism and vitality. The actress described Preston as "a consummate professional and artist, someone who really had great joy in the actual work. That sort of *joie de vivre* and bon vivant kind of attitude affected all of us around him."[53] In describing what it was like to work with Preston, Warren disclosed,

He was an absolute professional, fully prepared, and willing to sort of leap off the edge and do anything that was creative. He so enjoyed the work and didn't seem to be wound up in a particular way that actors can sometimes get when they're concerned and nervous and anxious and want to do a good job. He was very confident and very comfortable in his own being . . . he gave me courage. He really reveled in the joy of [his work] and that was contagious. He would jump in creatively to any sort of situation and circumstance and enjoy himself doing it.[54]

In addition, Warren suggested that Preston's talent benefitted from the "very alive, childlike part of him that allowed him to be such an engaging performer and actor."[55] As did many other actors, producers, and directors who worked with Preston over the years, Warren lent her voice to corroborate the observations of other entertainment professionals with respect to Preston's legendary selflessness toward his fellow actors. She affirmed Preston "was very generous as an actor" and "wanted to interact and be creative with another actor but did not crave the center of attention because he was so commanding"[56] in his performance.

Production on *Victor/Victoria* was completed on June 22, 1981, and the world premiere of the film was held at Plitt Century Plaza Theatre in Los Angeles on March 16, 1982.[57] Film critics praised the movie and Preston's performance in their reviews. Vincent Canby of *The New York Times* lauded *Victor/Victoria* as "a splendid farce" and "an unqualified hit." Canby declared that the movie's principal stars, Julie Andrews, Robert Preston, and James Garner, "each gave the performance of his and her career," adding that Preston's Toddy "is the richest, wisest, most rambunctious performance he's given since his triumph in *The Music Man*." He also asserted the film was "so good, so exhilarating . . . that Mr. Edwards is going to have a terrible time trying to top it."[58] *The Los Angeles Times* described *Victor/Victoria* as "a fresh look at sexuality" and proclaimed that "in both dialogue and deft, inventive performance, Preston's Toddy is masterful."[59] Roger Ebert of the *Chicago Sun-Times* added to the praise by describing *Victor/Victoria* as "not only a funny movie, but, unexpectedly, a warm and friendly one." Ebert also acknowledged one of the difficult roles in the film belonged to Preston "who must walk a tightrope of uncertain sexual identity without even appearing to condescend to [his] material."[60] *Variety* shared high praise for the film, declaring it "sparkling, ultra-sophisticated entertainment" and proclaiming "most impressive of all is Preston, with a shimmering portrait of a slightly decadent 'old queen.'"[61]

Preston bristled when pundits declared his role as Toddy was "the comeback performance of the decade," and offered a simple fact-check in response: "I didn't make a comeback, I never left," adding that his work in *S.O.B.* and *Victor/Victoria* was his "third stab at cinema stardom."

All the attention Preston received from his performances in the two Blake Edwards films led to an offer to star in a revival of *The Music Man*, with a guaranteed minimum payday of $2 million for his participation in a national tour. The actor swiftly nixed the proposal, pointing out that the musical's protagonist was a young man and he was now not "the right age to play Harold Hill."[62]

On October 4, 1982 Preston received an award for his portrayal of Toddy in *Victor/Victoria* at the second annual Alliance for Gay Artists Awards held at the L.A. Stage Company Theater in Hollywood. Preston took the stage to a roaring standing ovation and was presented his award by Ned Beatty and Bernadette

Peters. In his acceptance speech, Preston noted the role of Toddy "caused many of [his] acting colleagues to blanch." He additionally shared that his goal in portraying Toddy "was to play the happiness and humanity of the man. Audiences have accepted him."[63] In gratitude for the recognition by the Gay Alliance, he concluded his remarks with the playful quip, "I didn't want to play it so people would say, 'Ah, there's Robert Preston playing a gay; he's straight, of course.' I wanted people to say, 'Ah, there's Robert Preston playing a gay; he's straight of course—or is he?'[64]

Several months earlier, Preston co-hosted the thirty-ninth annual Golden Globes with actress Linda Gray. The ceremony was held on January 30, 1982 at the Beverly Hilton Hotel in Los Angeles and televised on CBS. Blake Edwards's film *S.O.B.* received a nomination for Best Motion Picture Musical/Comedy, but Steve Gordon's film, *Arthur,* captured the award instead.

In February, sixty-three-year-old Preston began filming the two-hour made-for-tv movie *Rehearsal for Murder,* written by Richard Levinson and William Link and directed by David Green. As an actor whose first love was the theater, Preston made the decision to return to the small screen after receiving fan mail which encouraged him to pursue a larger television presence[65] and, after reading the murder-thriller script, he realized it "was so good" that he had to do it.[66]

In pursuit of new pathways to channel his professional energy, Preston signed on to star in the television murder mystery, acknowledging the film was "the first mystery I've done in my life. After all these years there are still new frontiers for me . . . I'm old enough, rich enough, and I've been around long enough to do only what I want with my career."[67] Filming of the CBS TV movie, initially titled *Cold Reading,* was held at the Los Angeles Variety Arts Theater with a cast that included Lynn Redgrave, Lawrence Pressman, Patrick Macnee, Jeff Goldblum, William Russ, John Finnegan, Madolyn Smith, and William Daniels.

The plot of *Rehearsal for Murder* focused on successful Broadway playwright Alex Dennison (Preston) whose fiancé-cum-leading lady in his new play *Chamber Music*, Monica Welles (Redgrave), is found dead from an apparent suicide after receiving scathing reviews of her opening night performance. A grief-stricken Dennison suspects murder rather than suicide was the cause of Monica's death. Under the ruse of writing a new Broadway play, Dennison devises a-play-within-a-play and invites all the cast members from *Chamber Music* to an empty theater for an impromptu reading of his new script, the plot of which involves the death of a leading lady in a play. As cast members participate in the cold reading of the script that appears to re-enact the last day of Monica's life, they each find themselves uncomfortably in the role of a murder suspect. Erstwhile, a private detective (Pressman) hired by Dennison, sits in the audience to observe the suspects as well as actor Frank Heller (Russ) who was hired to play the role of Police Lieutenant McElroy. After several twists and turns, it becomes clear the scenario has been staged by Dennison and his friends for an audience of one–Monica's killer. Dennison's suspicions are validated when it is discovered Frank Heller blackmailed Welles and was responsible for her death.

Preston made the conscious choice to pattern Alex Dennison after playwright James Goldman who wrote the Broadway play *The Lion in Winter,* the drama in which Preston starred in the mid-1960s. The actor recognized that Goldman had the erudition and talent that he planned to infuse into his character.[68]

Rehearsal for Murder aired on May 26, 1982 to enthusiastic reviews. Television critic Bill Carter from *The Baltimore Sun* called *Rehearsal for Murder* a "five-course-treat" and encouraged his readers to tune into the show. Carter underscored that "the script is as carefully crafted as anything you are likely to see on television" replete with "a cast of classy pros to play the roles."[69] Dianne Holloway from the *Austin American-Statesman* boasted the movie was a success due to "a strong cast and a lot of charm." She described *Rehearsal for Murder* as "engrossing entertainment that, unlike most television movies, requires viewers to pay attention and even *think* for a couple of hours."[70] Marvin Kitman of *Newsday* also had high praise for the movie, pointing out that "the acting in this post-Shakespearean psychodrama is great. Robert Preston is marvelous as the playwright-producer who uses the theater to catch the killer." He additionally revealed the movie had him on the edge of his seat and "not slumped back sleeping, which is where [he] usually winds up during so-called TV mysteries."[71] In addition to the high marks from television critics, *Rehearsal for Murder* also earned Levinson and Link the Edgar Allan Poe award for Best Television Feature or Miniseries.

During the final days of filming *Rehearsal for Murder*, Preston made a weekend trip to New York to take part in the *Night of 100 Stars* television special held at Radio City Music Hall.[72] Over two hundred celebrities participated in the three-hour broadcast on February 14, 1982, that honored the centennial of the Actors Fund of America. The actor was featured in the segment of the show, "The Lullaby of Broadway," which served as a tribute to the actors and actresses who were a success on the Great White Way. As Carol Channing finished singing the first few lines of "Diamonds Are a Girl's Best Friend" from *Gentlemen*

Prefer Blondes, Preston glided past her and began singing several bars of "Seventy-Six Trombones" as he deftly pranced forward and backward across the stage in an homage to *The Music Man*. At the conclusion of the segment, all the Broadway performers assembled onstage for a mock curtain call. Preston took a bow with his peers as the group of Broadway veterans received a rousing standing ovation from the audience.

Preston was back on Broadway on June 6 as a presenter and performer at the thirty-sixth Annual Tony Awards. The ceremony, held at the Imperial Theatre and broadcast on CBS television, featured Preston in a tribute to composer Irving Berlin. The actor was accompanied by Inga Swenson, Pam Dawber, and Michelle Lee in performing a medley of the composer's musical scores featured in *Miss Liberty, Annie Get Your Gun*, and *Call Me Madam*. Preston also presented the award for Outstanding Performance by a Leading Actor in a Musical to Ben Harney in *Dreamgirls*.

It was in 1982, after Preston appeared in a spate of motion picture and television movie roles, that Catherine began urging her husband to relocate to California near the epicenter of film and television production, given her weariness of the winter weather in Greenwich. Preston had initially moved east in 1951 with Catherine joining him a few years later. Initially apartment dwellers in New York City, the couple moved to a home in Rye, New York, before putting down roots in Greenwich in 1966. It was no secret that the ability to experience the four seasons was of great importance to Preston, a predilection made possible with residences in New York and Connecticut. However, Preston was also acutely aware that,

> All those years we lived in the east; I had the theater. [Catherine] would come into New York on

the occasional night when something was going on. But for the most part, she was a suburban housewife and that's not what she is.[73]

After thirty years of living on the east coast, Catherine was ready for a change and understood a location near Los Angeles would allow her husband to take advantage of more film opportunities–not to mention the ability to enjoy year-round sunshine and balmy weather. Since Preston had been active in Hollywood over the past few years, Catherine strongly hinted that it would be just as easy for him to read scripts living near Hollywood as it would be in the cold winter weather in Greenwich.[74] Preston confessed he "got the message" and acceded to Catherine's wishes, acknowledging he "really [made the move] for his wife," since his life had been full with the New York theater scene, "but it wasn't [that way] for her."[75] Above all else, Preston was a realist. Although his heart belonged to Broadway, good stage opportunities had become all but non-existent over the past few years. He acknowledged that "part of the motive for the move is a certain weariness with snow; another is uncertainty about the Broadway theater scene," adding, "I'm just not sure I could be comfortable playing in front of an audience that has paid $45 a ticket" ($125.00 in 2022 dollars) to see one of his shows.[76] The couple quietly began house hunting in the laid-back, upscale community of Montecito, California in Santa Barbara County. The luxurious community, which boasts a spectacular coastline, has been a haven for celebrities and influencers in the entertainment industry.

In late November, Preston was invited to appear as a guest on *Bob Hope's Pink Panther Thanksgiving Gala* on NBC which aired on Sunday, November 21. The television special featured

Bob Hope and his guests Julie Andrews, Robert Preston, Dean Martin, Bernadette Peters, Dudley Moore, Willie Nelson, and Robert Wagner in a two-hour tribute to the twentieth anniversary of Blake Edwards's *Pink Panther* movies starring Peter Sellers. Each segment of the show was punctuated with clips of Sellers's comedic performances in the *Pink Panther* film series.

Following a short stand-up comedy routine by Bob Hope, Bernadette Peters danced alongside two male dancers clad in pink suits as she sang Cole Porter's classic tune, "Let's Misbehave." Preston was featured in the next skit with Hope, Wagner, and Martin, all dressed as football players, in a spoof on the eight-week 1982 NFL football strike. Country & Western singer Willie Nelson took the stage to sing, "You Are Always on My Mind," and Andrews followed with the country ballad, "Love Is a Place Where Two People Fall."

In a skit about Thanksgiving Dinner at the White House, Hope assumed the role of President Reagan, with Peters as Nancy Reagan, Martin as Vice-President Bush, and Wagner as OMB Director David Stockman. Preston appeared in the segment as Speaker of the House Tip O'Neill. When asked to stay for Thanksgiving dinner at the White House, Preston as O'Neill declared, "I never eat Republican turkeys–too many right wings."[77]

Dudley Moore played the theme song from the movie *10* on the piano followed by Dean Martin crooning "Just Bummin' Around." Up next were Preston and Andrews, both dressed in tuxedos, to reprise the song-and-dance number "You and Me" from *Victor/Victoria*. Following the duet with Andrews, Preston joined Hope onstage for some light-hearted banter. When Hope mentioned that Preston appeared in several potboilers in the late 1930s such as *King of Alcatraz, Illegal Traffic,* and *Disbarred*, Preston retorted, "I never knew if I was going to be shot, stabbed, strangled, poisoned, or drowned. I was a method actor. In every picture, I was killed by a different method."[78] Hope noted that Preston was equally at home on stage as in front of a camera, and when Preston was asked to identify which performance medium he preferred, the actor reiterated his preference for the stage, "Oh, working live, I think. You get that immediate audience reaction; you know what I mean?"[79] The final segments of the program featured Hope chatting with Robert Wagner and Willie Nelson singing the hit song, "Last Thing I Needed First Thing This Morning."

By November, Preston had been approached to star in the CBS made-for-television movie, *September Gun*, about an aging gunslinger enlisted to save a group of Apache children from being placed in a military compound. About the same time, the seeds of the Prestons' house-hunting came to fruition: he and his wife found the perfect property located at 1035 Fairway Road in Montecito abutting spectacular Butterfly Beach, and they made the momentous decision to give up their life in the east and move back to Hollywood. The oceanside house on Fairway Road included rights to a portion of adjacent Butterfly Beach and featured "extensive English gardens" that would "occupy [Preston's] leisure hours and those of his wife."[80] The couple purchased the Montecito house with the closing set for January 21, 1983. Although Preston and Catherine placed their Dublin Hill Drive estate in Greenwich on the market, it did not find a buyer until August 1983. The Connecticut property, consisting of two tracts of land, was eventually sold to a family from Greenwich for $795,000 (approximately $2,242,000 in 2022 dollars).[81]

The closing date on the Fairway Road home dovetailed perfectly with Preston's start date for filming *September Gun*. After packing up their Greenwich home, Preston and his wife drove west and made a lengthy stop in Tucson, Arizona where the actor would film *September Gun* from January 12 to February 1.[82]

Executive producer Hal Goodman had originally planned the made-for-tv-movie as a half-hour script for actor Walter Brennan in the 1960s. The sidelined script was eventually expanded by *September Gun*'s co-producer Ed Self to include a new storyline adding the character of Sister Dulcina.[83] The film, shot in Mescal and Tucson, Arizona, was produced by Brademan Self Productions in conjunction with Quinn Martin Productions and directed by Don Taylor. The central cast of the production included Robert Preston (Ben Sunday), Patty Duke Astin (Sister Dulcina), Geoffrey Lewis (Sheriff Johnson), Sally Kellerman (Mama Queen), David Knell (Jason, Ben's nephew), Jacques Aubuchon (Father Jerome), Christopher Lloyd (Jack Brian), Jon Gries (Brian Brian), and Clayton Landey (Boomer Brian). Although Preston had not ridden a horse for several years prior to the production of *September Gun*, his character was expected to spend a good deal of screen time doing just that. The actor acknowledged, "It's been a dozen years since I rode a horse, but it's like ice skating or bike riding. Once you get the hang of it, you don't forget."[84]

September Gun takes place in the American southwest of the 1880s and involves a feisty Catholic nun, Sister Dulcina, attempting to save a group of orphaned Apache children from being shipped off to a military encampment. Posing as local priest Father Jerome, Sister Dulcina sends word to aging gunfighter Ben Sunday that his services are needed to provide the children safe passage to a church in a Colorado mining town. The cantankerous Sunday, accompanied by his nephew Jason, reluctantly takes the job when it becomes clear that the children are in danger.

Sunday, Sister Dulcina, and the children ride off to Columbine, Colorado only to discover that the church building has been co-opted by villainous saloon operator Jack Brian and his sons Brian and Boomer. After temporarily taking up residence in an abandoned barn on the outskirts of town, Sunday and Sister Dulcina learn that Mama Queen, the resident madam and Jack Brian's mistress, has a bevy of women on the second floor of the saloon ready to entertain the saloon customers. Not wanting his booming saloon and brothel business to be jeopardized, Jack Brian kidnaps the Apache children to pressure Sister Dulcina into leaving town. Sister Dulcina receives little help from drunken Sheriff Johnson, but manages to successfully help Mama Queen, and her coterie of scarlet women, find religion. Sunday and the reformed Mama Queen take a shine to each other, while the kidnapping of the children sets the stage for a showdown between Jack Brian and Sunday. Brian's plans to have his sons ambush the gunslinger fail after he and his two sons are injured in the gun battle, and he is asked to vacate the church building.

Once the church building has been reclaimed, Sister Dulcina begins preparing the building for use as a classroom; her first order of business is emptying all the liquor bottles from the saloon. Before he and his nephew ride out of town, Sunday makes plans to rendezvous with Mama Queen in Denver the next month.

CBS broadcast the ninety-minute *September Gun* as the Saturday Night Movie on October 8 to favorable reviews from television critics. John O'Connor of *The New York Times* indicated Robert Preston and Patty Duke Astin "keep *September Gun* perking along nicely," and the movie is buoyed by "the nifty performances of Mr. Preston and Ms. Astin, supported by a good cast."[85] The *Daily Press* likewise praised the movie, noting "there's no surprises in this [show], but plenty of fun and good acting, especially by Preston and Kellerman."[86] *Newsday* declared *September Gun* as the only show worth watching for those who were not following the American League playoff games on television. Preston's performance in the movie was lauded, noting the actor "has the gift of making every line—including some decidedly banal ones—a polished gem. His energy and good will lift *September Gun* well above itself. He never falters, never fudges a speech, a gesture, a leer."[87]

Once filming for *September Gun* was complete, Preston and Catherine continued their journey west to Montecito where they settled into their oceanfront property. A few months after acclimating themselves to their new home and community, Preston crowed that his wife was "happier in Montecito than anyone you've ever seen. She's gardening twelve months a year. She says it's even fun to go to the market again. This move has revitalized our whole marriage."[88]

The Los Angeles Film Critics Association announced the winners of the best in filmmaking awards for 1982 on December 11 and honored Preston with a Career Achievement Award at the ceremony on January 13, 1983. Within days of that announcement, The National Board of Review made public that Preston would receive the Best Supporting Actor Award for his role as Toddy in *Victor/Victoria* at the Board's fifty-fourth annual gala on February 14. Academy Award nominations were released on February 18, with Preston garnering a Best Supporting Actor nod for *Victor/Victoria*. Other nominees in this category included Charles Durning (*The Best Little Whorehouse in Texas*), James Mason (*The Verdict*), John Lithgow (*The World According to Garp*), and Louis Gossett Jr. (*An Officer and A Gentleman*). It was Preston's performance in *Victor/Victoria* that finally provided him with the Oscar nomination he should have received in 1962 for his outstanding portrayal of Harold Hill in *The Music Man*.

Preston and his family were under no illusions that he would receive the Academy Award for Best Supporting Actor in 1982; they were keenly aware that Louis Gossett Jr. was the odds-on favorite to receive the Oscar for his role as Marine Corps Gunnery Sgt. Emil Foley in *An Officer and A Gentleman*.[89] When asked directly about his Academy Award nomination for Best Supporting Actor, Preston was pragmatic:

> Blake Edwards made *S.O.B.* and *Victor/Victoria* so much fun. My God, anything that was that much fun and that easy to play is not worth an award. It's like falling off a log.[90]

Victor/Victoria received seven Oscar nominations for Costume Design, Art Direction, Best Actress (Andrews), Best Supporting Actor (Preston), Best Supporting Actress (Warren), Best Original Song (Mancini/Bricusse), and Best Adapted Screenplay (Edwards). Preston and wife Catherine walked the red carpet at the fifty-fifth annual Academy Awards held on April 11 at the Dorothy Chandler Pavilion in Los Angeles. Preston sported a black tuxedo with a red pocket square and a dual-color black and red bowtie for the awards event. Catherine wore a floor-length, long-sleeved, tangerine velvet dress with an embroidered jeweled collar and a mink stole. Her modest jewelry included a thin gold bracelet, a gold and diamond pin, and small gold hoop earrings, while her long, salt-and-pepper hair was swept back in a high-rolled chignon. As anticipated, Louis Gossett Jr. won the Oscar for Best Supporting Actor for his role in *An Officer and A Gentleman*. Although *Victor/Victoria* had been nominated for seven Academy Awards, only Henry Mancini and Leslie Bricusse walked away with an Oscar for Best Original Song Score.

About a month after the Oscar telecast, Preston began filming the sci-fi adventure film *The Last Starfighter* (1984) in the role of the fast-talking, likable, intergalactic con man, Centauri. Preston confessed he agreed to play the role of Centauri to allow "all those kids who were ten when they saw me in *The Music Man* on July 4 [to] find out what I've been up to lately."[91] The action picture would be the veteran actor's final Hollywood film.

The principal cast of *The Last Starfighter* included Preston, Lance Guest, Dan O'Herlihy, Catherine Mary Stewart, Norman Snow, Kay E. Kuter, Barbara Bosson, Chris Hebert, Dan Mason, Vernon Washington, and Meg Wylie. According to producer Gary Adelson, when *The Last Starfighter* was in development, the prototype for the character of Centauri was Robert Preston in *The Music Man*. Once the script was complete and the role of Centauri needed to be cast,

> We said, "What about Robert Preston?" And we sent the script to him and he accepted. And we were so excited because that's who the character was. So that was pretty amazing for us at the time.[92]

The Last Starfighter tells the story of restless, high school teen Alex Rogan (Guest) who resides in a trailer park with his mother, Jane (Bosson), and younger brother, Louis (Hebert), and spends time playing the "Starfighter" arcade game to destroy enemy alien spacecraft. Alex hopes to move to the city with his girlfriend, Maggie Gordon (Stewart), and attend college, but his dreams of a college degree are dashed when his college loan application is rejected. When the teen breaks the record on "Starfighter," he soon discovers the game was designed to recruit fighter pilots for the planet Rylos by Centauri (Preston), an alien con-man. Centauri whisks a curious Alex away to Rylos in his StarCar vehicle and leaves Alex's android, Beta, behind so no one will realize Alex is in outer space. Once transported to Rylos, Alex becomes acquainted with the reptilian pilot Grig (O'Herlihy). He is asked to join the Rylan Star League to fend off the Ko-Dan Armada, led by the evil Xur (Snow), who intends to destroy Rylos. Alex asks to return home, Xur declares war on Rylos, and an alien assassin attempts to kill Alex on Earth, but mortally wounds Centauri instead. Alex returns to Rylos where he and Grig fight and destroy the Ko-Dan Armada with a prototype Gunstar equipped with Death Blossom weaponry, but not before Xur escapes into intergalactic space. Hailed as a hero, Alex agrees to remain on Rylos to rebuild the Starfighter fleet. Alex learns Centauri is very much alive before he makes a quick trip back to his earthly home; he informs his family that he will be returning to Rylos and asks Maggie to join him there. Louis is inspired by his brother's accomplishments and begins playing the "Starfighter" game to follow in his footsteps.

The film, produced by Lorimar Productions and distributed by Universal Pictures, began filming on May 8, 1983 in Soledad Canyon, Arizona under the direction of Nick Castle, Jr. with the movie's release date planned for the summer of 1984. According to Gary Adelson, the film had a $12 million budget, but ended up spending $13 million. He acknowledged the film "went a million dollars over, and there were many, many times during that film that we didn't know if it could be done . . . we had about seventeen months' worth of work and we had six months to do it . . . so it was a challenge."[93]

It was a daunting endeavor to film *The Last Starfighter* within a six-month time frame given the movie's groundbreaking use of computer-generated visual effects. According to David J. Hogan's article "Digital Drama in Outer Space," the film contains twenty-seven minutes of computer simulation that was used to portray alien worlds, spacecraft, and intergalactic battles.[94] To achieve the special effects, a $3 million contract was awarded to the California-based computer graphics firm Digital Productions to generate computer-generated imagery (CGI) using the Cray XMP supercomputer. The Cray XMP was a one-of-a-kind computer behemoth with the capability of generating images that would "fool you into thinking that the spaceships, planets, and terrain you're looking at are real."[95] This computer technology, relatively new in 1983, was labor-intensive and time-consuming for the software developers who were expected to meet a six-month deadline. Larry Yaeger, a software developer with Digital Productions, emphasized *The Last Starfighter* was "the first film that actually used computer graphics to portray what used to be portrayed with models and miniatures."[96]

The film's visual effects coordinator Jeffrey Okun, feared the film would not be ready within the proposed timeline. When the theater release of *The Last Starfighter* was six months away, Okun recalled he "did the math" and calculated it would take "seventeen months to complete this film."[97] The movie's creative team ultimately pushed themselves and the Cray XMP to the limit and managed to complete the film, replete with a full complement of CGI effects, on schedule.

The movie's special effects were added to its final cut once the traditional cinematography had been filmed. The need to act in a scene around unseen special effects was a new experience for Preston. A seasoned professional, Preston predictably took the new hybrid method of acting in stride, explaining that "what the actor does in a movie like this is ignore everything except playing the part. You don't even wonder what's going on in the special-effects area."[98]

The Last Starfighter was shot on a tight forty-day schedule with many of the scenes filmed at night. Lance Guest, a twenty-three-year-old actor at the time he appeared in the film as protagonist Alex Rogan, indicated the production team limited the cast to two takes of a scene with limited rehearsals[99] By serving as his rehearsal partner, the energetic, sixty-five-year-old Preston was as magnanimous with Guest as he had been with Neva Small during the preview productions of *The Prince of Grand Street*. Seeking extra time to rehearse his scenes, Guest would "knock on [Preston's] trailer door and say, 'Hey Pres, you want to run this scene?'" The amenable Preston informed the young actor that he had grown up in the theater and offered to be available to rehearse as "many times as you want."[100] Guest, who marveled at Preston's boundless reservoir of energy during the movie's night shoots,[101] recalled that,

> The cool thing about him is that he's like a really tough guy, but he never was like "No, leave me alone" . . . He was just like, "Whenever you're ready kid, let's go." So, he was really, really cool that way.[102]

Once the on-set filming was completed at the conclusion of the forty-day shoot, the tech wizards at Digital Productions began creating action scenes with computer-generated imagery and incorporating these images into the existing footage. As the

film was in the process of being edited, the director and producers decided to re-work an important sequence in the film. The
revision required Preston, Lance Guest, and Dan O'Herlihy to
return to the studio in early December 1983, along with a supporting cast of alien extras, to shoot the new footage.[103]

Catherine Mary Stewart, whose scenes were primarily shot
on the trailer park set, did not have the opportunity to meet
Preston during *The Last Starfighter*'s initial filming in the spring
of 1983. The actress did encounter Preston when the two actors
were at the studio on the same day in December to film pick-up
shots. Of her encounter with Preston, Stewart recalled, "He was
leaving as I arrived. We were introduced and he took my hand
and kissed it saying, 'It is a pleasure to meet you, Catherine.' I
literally swooned!"[104] The actress added that for her,

> It was like a dream come true. He was truly a
> movie star that kind of glowed when you were in
> his presence. He just glowed and I remember he
> took my hand and he kissed it and I was in my
> early twenties and I was like, "I'm never washing
> my hand again." He just sort of had that efferves-
> cence about him. He was a beautiful man.[105]

The Last Starfighter opened in New York and Los Angeles on
July 13, 1984 to modest reviews. Lawrence Van Gelder from *The
New York Times* characterized the film as "good-humored, bent on
action, and even touching,"[106] while film critic Roger Ebert viewed
The Last Starfighter as "not a terrifically original movie," but one
with "competent" special effects and "good" acting.[107] The review by *Time* magazine's Richard Schickel portrayed the film as
presenting the same ideas as *Tron* (1982), *E.T.* (1982), and *Close*

Encounters of the Third Kind (1977) that "people have all had just about enough of." However, Schickel praised Preston's performance in the film as the fast-talking, intergalactic con man, noting that "after almost half a century, Preston's energy and infectious pleasure in performance remain delightful."[108]

Despite the film's lukewarm reviews, Preston was nominated for a Saturn Award for Best Supporting Actor for his role as Centauri by the Academy of Science Fiction, Fantasy & Horror Films. Four other actors were also nominated in this category, with Tracey Walter ultimately winning the award for his role as Miller in *Repo Man* (1984) at the twelfth annual Saturn Awards ceremony.

The Last Starfighter proved not to be a box office success. According to IMDb, the film which cost $14 million to produce, grossed a disappointing $28,773,290. Despite the unimpressive box office numbers, *The Last Starfighter* became a cult classic among sci-fi fans and gamers, the CGI technology sparked the imaginations of budding computer engineers, and Preston's portrayal of Centauri in the futuristic classic revived his éclat while earning him a new legion of fans.

THE FINAL CURTAIN

N ever one to rest on his laurels, Preston forged ahead with
a busy schedule for the remainder of 1983 and 1984. As
a previous award recipient himself, Preston was chosen
to co-host the 1983 Alliance for Gay Artists Awards ceremony
with actress Rita Moreno. The third annual awards ceremony
was held on September 19 at the Huntington Hartford Theatre
in Los Angeles. Lynn Redgrave, Eileen Brennan, Robert
Hooks, Loretta Swit, Alex Karras, Burt Lancaster, Jean Smart,
Pat Hingle, Susan Clark, Vivian Blane, and Ted Danson were
among the stars who participated in the "well-written, well-
performed, and well-received" show.[1] The Alliance, which
provided assistance to producers "dealing with homosexual
themes," served in part to "monitor productions that focus on
gay life styles" and "eliminate homosexual stereotypes."[2] The
two productions which merited Alliance awards in 1983, the
John Sayles film *Lianna* and the Los Angeles production of
Last Summer at Bluefish Cove, written by Jane Chambers, featured lesbian characters.[3]

Later that year, the actor signed on to narrate the television documentary *Going Hollywood: The 30s,* which showcased the most glamorous era in Hollywood history and the one in which Preston launched his own film career. Preston helped present an overview of the cinematic period which included Movietone newsreels of in-depth interviews with national and world leaders, stars endorsing their own products, and Tinseltown news such as the death of Rin Tin Tin. The documentary, initially airing on The Movie Channel on April 1, 1984, showcased several notable stars of the era including John Wayne, The Three Stooges, Gary Cooper, Laurel and Hardy, Shirley Temple, Cary Grant, Joan Crawford, Boris Karloff, Clark Gable, Mae West, William Powell, The Little Rascals, Jimmy Durante, Carole Lombard, Humphrey Bogart, Fred Astaire, and Ginger Rogers. Featured 1930s movies included *Rain* (1932) starring Joan Crawford and Walter Huston; *A Farewell To Arms* (1932) headlining Gary Cooper and Helen Hayes; *Of Human Bondage* (1934) with Leslie Howard and Bette Davis; *My Man Godfrey* (1936) featuring William Powell and Carole Lombard; *Stand-In* (1937) starring Humphrey Bogart, Leslie Howard, and Joan Blondell; *History Is Made At Night* (1937) with Charles Boyer and Jean Arthur; and *Stagecoach* (1939) featuring John Wayne, Claire Trevor, and John Carradine.

Another distinguished face, that of famed director Cecil B. DeMille, was showcased advising novice actress Suzanne Emory who was unsuccessful in her attempt to break into films during the past year. Julian Schlossberg directed the hour-and-a-half-long documentary that was the first in a series of four features that explored various Hollywood themes; the three subsequent titles included *Hollywood Ghost Stories* (1986), *Hollywood Uncensored* (1987), and *Hollywood: The War Years* (1988). For

Preston, the deep dive into 1930s films highlighted the exceptional talent of actors and filmmakers of that era. An inimitable professional, he had little use for imposture both in his professional and private life, disclosing, "I don't like phonies, actors who can't act, directors who can't direct, hack politicians . . . I'm eliminating the phonies."[4]

As 1983 drew to a close, Preston served as one of the ringmasters for the *Eighth Annual Circus of the Stars* CBS television special filmed at Caesar's Palace in Las Vegas and SeaWorld in San Diego, and broadcast on December 18. Thirty television, stage, and motion picture stars performed difficult and dangerous acts during the two-hour telecast: Lynn Redgrave performed an act with Liberty horses; Judy Landers donned roller skates and spun around on a six-foot-wide platform four stories in the air; Michelle Lee agreed to be sawed in half in a torture box; Jamie Farr escaped from an enclosure with a tiger; Kari Michaelson, Peter Scolari, and Bruce Penhall thrilled the audience with a high wire act; Herve Villechaize mastered the art of fire-eating; Missy Gold, Morgan Stevens, and Tracey Scroggins performed daring stunts on the trapeze; Phyllis Diller danced with a sea lion and a walrus; Brooke Shields performed a graceful aerial ballet; Pia Zadora and Doug Barr performed an elephant act; Dean Butler took a turn at being a lion tamer; Linda Blair dodged a knife thrower; Pamela Bellwood took an exciting ride on dolphins; Judy Norton-Taylor wing-walked; Tony Curtis escaped from a mirrored crate suspended in the air; Candy Clark levitated several feet in the air; Foster Brooks played drunk during a bicycle routine; Marty Allen participated in a dog act; Tracey Gold and Andre Gower soared in an aerial performance; and Charlie Callas attempted to keep a series spinning plates aloft on spindles.

Preston's ringmaster duties for the special were shared by Louis Gossett Jr., Beverly D'Angelo, and Dottie West. The actor opened the program by sounding the ringmaster's whistle and introduced several acts during the show. At the height of the program, Preston introduced Michelle Lee as she entered an ancient execution blade box, helped her into the contraption, and kissed her hand when she exited unscathed.

The year 1984 evolved into a pinnacle year of recognition for Preston during which he received multiple honors for his talent and artistry as an actor. It was following the release of *Victor/Victoria* that the public at large recognized Preston as a Hollywood and Broadway treasure. The actor was tickled pink when an audience applauded him and his wife as they entered a theater to see a play, acknowledging to director Morton Da Costa "that's never happened before."[5]

In spring 1984, it was announced that Preston would be the honored guest at the fifteenth annual Los Angeles Drama Critics Circle Awards. The awards dinner was held on April 2 at the Variety Arts Theatre on Figueroa Street in Los Angeles. Preston was introduced as the evening's honored guest by his *S.O.B.* and *Victor/Victoria* co-star and friend, Julie Andrews, who described Preston as "a maker of magic."[6] For Preston, the event brought his long career full circle. In accepting the award, Preston stressed that his career as an actor was one in which "the rewards are so rich for a life of having fun." To the amazement of the audience, the actor revealed he was "standing on the stage right now where I made my professional debut as a child fifty years ago," and declared with plucky optimism that the ceremony marked "a good time to start looking forward to the next fifty" years of his career.[7]

Preston was then invited to co-host the thirty-eighth annual Tony Awards with Julie Andrews; the awards show was broadcast live on CBS from the Gershwin Theatre in New York on June 3. When announced as the show's host, Preston strolled to the middle of the stage amid an orchestra flourish of "Seventy-Six Trombones." He welcomed the audience and asked,

> Did you notice the music? "Seventy-Six Trombones" from *The Music Man.* I had the joy of playing that musical on Broadway for a couple of years about eighteen years ago, and I also had the added joy of making the movie of the same name. Ever since then, every time I've come out on the stage anywhere, I've been played on by that music.[8]

The actor's remarks reinforced the obvious: "Seventy-Six Trombones" had become *his* signature song, one that would be forever synonymous with him, and him alone, in tribute to his role as the iconic Harold Hill in *The Music Man.* Julie Andrews then entered the stage to the strains of "I Could Have Danced All Night" from *My Fair Lady.* Preston and Andrews reminded the audience that even though the nature of musical theater is collaborative, it is the songs that audiences remember. In addition to co-hosting the show, Preston also presented awards and participated in song-and-dance routines. He had the privilege of announcing the nominees for Outstanding Performance by an Actress in a Play and presented the Tony award to Glenn Close for her performance as Annie in *The Real Thing.* Following a quick wardrobe change, Preston participated in a musical tribute to composer Stephen Sondheim along with Carol Channing, Robert Goulet, Nancy Dussault, Tony Randall, Leslie Uggams,

Tony Roberts, Julie Andrews, Larry Kert, Robert Guillaume, and Dorothy Loudon with songs from *West Side Story*, *Gypsy*, *Anyone Can Whistle*, *Company*, and *A Funny Thing Happened on the Way to the Forum*.

After a quick change back into his tuxedo, Preston returned on stage for an ensemble musical tribute to composer Jerry Herman featuring music from *Hello, Dolly!*, *Mame*, *La Cage Aux Folles*, and *Milk and Honey*, and sang a portion of "I Won't Send Roses" from *Mack & Mabel* accompanied by Bernadette Peters who reprised "Time Heals Everything" from the same musical. Later in the program, Preston read the nominees for Outstanding Performance by an Actress in a Musical and presented the Tony award to Chita Rivera for her role as Anna in *The Rink*.

Three days after the Tony Awards broadcast Preston signed on to appear in the HBO romantic comedy movie *Finnegan Begin Again*. Mary Tyler Moore's production company, MTM Productions, had purchased the story several years prior from screenwriter Walter Lockwood. The project, which required substantial definition and revision, was eventually purchased by HBO with the stipulation that Moore would star in the production.[9]

Although Moore wanted Burt Lancaster to play opposite her as the male lead and eventual love interest in *Finnegan Begin Again*, the actor was unavailable, and on May 24, 1984 a Brooklyn newspaper announced that Jason Robards would be appearing in the HBO movie instead of Lancaster.[10] Robards abandoned plans to accept the role of Michael Finnegan once he agreed to return to Broadway as Long John Silver in the musical version of Robert Louis Stevenson's *Treasure Island*.[11] An astounded Preston, who was then chosen to portray Finnegan in the film, asked himself, "who in the world would offer a 65-year-old man a romantic lead?"[12]

Despite his surprise over being cast as Michael Finnegan, Preston acknowledged he "always felt good about playing romantic leads," confessing that even in his sixties he has "never felt more romantic in [his] life."[13] Perhaps in a case of art imitating life, Preston mused that his character, Finnegan, was not finished with life at age sixty-five and shared his views on aging:

> For myself, I've never had any mournful thoughts about aging. I once had a break after a long run in a Broadway show, and they gave my replacement a grey wig to wear. Well, until that point, I just hadn't noticed that I'd sprouted my own head of grey hair. As far as I'm concerned, it's the same face I shave every morning in the mirror. It seems I don't notice the passage of time.[14]

In addition to Moore and Preston, the other principal cast members starring in *Finnegan Begin Again* included Sam Waterson, Sylvia Sydney, David Huddleston, and Bob Gunton.

Filming took place on location in the Fan District of Richmond, Virginia, and Richmond's *Times-Dispatch* newspaper agreed to allow some key scenes in the movie to be shot in their newsroom. The movie began filming after a week of rehearsal and scenes were shot "as a theatrical film" over a period of six weeks.[15]

Finnegan Begin Again is a romantic comedy that follows widowed, mid-forties art teacher Elizabeth "Liz" DeHaan (Moore) who finds herself involved in a dead-end affair with her married, mortician lover, Paul Broadbent (Waterston). Paul, who has no intention of leaving his wife and children, strings Liz along, and the two meet for steamy trysts each Thursday afternoon in a run-down, rented room in a bad part of town. Liz encounters sixty-five-year-old Michael "Mike" Finnegan (Preston) on the city bus. Michael is a semi-retired, award-winning newspaperman who has been demoted from the city desk to answering letters for the paper's Felicity Hope advice column. He presents a buoyant façade, but is depressed over his empty marriage to his much-older wife Margaret (Sydney), who is paranoid and fragile. Michael and his wife reside in a once-magnificent home in a crumbling neighborhood; the home has become overrun with unmanageable clutter since the death of Finnegan's son at age ten. Although Michael had engaged in a brief affair earlier in his marriage, he learned the error of his ways and has remained loyal to his addled wife.

During their chance encounter on the bus, Michael observes that Liz is troubled. When the two wind up at the same laundromat to wash their clothes, Michael unnerves Liz by using Auguste Dupin's technique of ratiocination to seemingly read her mind and recreate her present life circumstances. Distressed over Finnegan's accurate revelations, Liz tracks Michael down in the newsroom, fearing that the information he possesses about her could ruin the lives of her lover and his family. Michael, who now refers to Liz as Elizabeth, assuages her fears by explaining how he used his observations to form his analysis and shares some of his professional and marital history with her.

Initially wary of Michael, Elizabeth soon considers him a close confidant and regularly seeks his advice about her relationship with Paul. Paul finally leaves his wife when he discovers she, too, has been having an affair of her own and is pregnant with her lover's child. Meanwhile, Margaret is hospitalized with a poor prognosis after suffering a massive stroke during a burglary of the Finnegans' home. With Elizabeth's help, Michael organizes his house and makes plans to sell it to a neighborhood youth center after Margaret's death. After his wife has passed away, Michael, now alone, decides he needs to get away on a trip to Europe. Before Michael can take action, Elizabeth recognizes Paul's true character and ends their relationship. She immediately seeks out Michael at his home and the two soon realize the love they each need can be found in each other.

Production on the HBO movie began on June 25, but was nearly derailed by Mary Tyler Moore after the first read-through of the script. Director Joan Micklin Silver recalled Moore announced her plan to exit the production when it became clear to her that Preston's character was the main focus of the film:

> And after the first read-through, Mary Tyler Moore said to me, "Can I see you, please?" and I said "Yes," and she said, "I'm going home." And I said, "What's the problem?" and she said, "Well it's *his* movie." Well, I felt like saying, "Mary, you read the script," but, you know, it *was* [Preston's] movie, true enough. And I said, "Well, Mary, I think we can make it more your movie–why don't we work with improvisations? I'm used to that and I think we can do some wonderful stuff." And she said, "I can't improvise. I hate it, I don't want to do it, I'm not good at it." And I said, "Well, let's give it a try, and if you still hate it, we'll think of something else to do." So, after lunch, we were

going to do improvisations with Sam Waterston because he played her boyfriend and then also Mary and Pres . . . So, I said to Pres, "I'm going to start with them, so why don't you come over in about an hour, let me work with them first." So, he said, "Okay." So, I go into my room . . . and we start and there's a knock on my door and I open it and it's Pres and he says, "I don't have any place else to go." So, I said, "All right, come in and sit there and be quiet and listen." Well, it was such a lucky thing, because he laughed. And everything they did that he enjoyed–he was just one of these terrific guys, you know, and he enjoyed himself. They felt they had an audience and they came up to it. And of course, I'm madly taping everything . . . and then I . . . scripted scenes and so on. And Mary Tyler Moore proved to be fabulous at improvising and Pres was unbelievable—unbelievably good . . . Pres was just such a dream. He was a dream to work with.[16]

Moore had exhibited similar behavior in the recent past in response to another script she believed did not adequately showcase her talents. While preparing to film the television movie *Heartsounds* (1984) in which Moore starred opposite James Garner, she likewise threatened to quit and fold the production. When director Glenn Jordan determined the *Heartsounds* script was too long and needed some cuts, scenes of Moore's character Martha Lear were eliminated from the script. An unhappy Moore called the director at 2:00 a.m. to inform him she would be immediately withdrawing from the project. A contingent of panicked television executives quickly assured Moore that most of the cuts had been restored to the script and let her know that an extra scene had been added to the movie just for her. The director admitted he was only able to make these accommodations for Moore by cutting "some of [James Garner's] stuff" from the movie.[17]

As the director of *Finnegan Begin Again*, Joan Micklin Silver was tasked with bringing a script in need of revision to life. The process involved some improvisation on behalf of the cast and, as for the director herself, "it was a matter of pointing scenes up, thinning scenes out, and letting actors who know how to make dialogue crackle, find their characters, and incorporate them into their scenes."[18] At one point in the film, Preston was able to make extraordinary use of improvisation by suddenly erupting into a jig in the middle of the street to the strains of a neighborhood teen's boombox. Micklin Silver treasured the opportunity to work with Preston and appreciated that "he was a person who had a great confidence in himself and in his abilities."[19] She marveled at Preston's selfless, magnanimous nature and confidence when she observed Moore's attempts to overshadow him in the film:

> Mary Tyler Moore would often upstage him. I don't know whether she did it instinctually or how it was, but . . . I would try to prevent that from happening. So, I took him aside and I said, "Look, Pres, she's upstaging you." And he said, "Yeah, so?" And I said, "Well, if you'll cooperate with me, I can stop that from happening, I can organize it so it won't happen." And he said, "Do you like the character I'm creating?" and I said, "Well, I love

it." And he said, "Do you think my work is good?" and I said, "I think your work is fabulous," and he says, "So, forget it." I've never seen anybody so sure of himself, he just knew what he was doing. So, we went along and he emerges fantastically from the film.[20]

In addition to the opportunity to play a romantic lead in a film, Preston shared he was equally attracted to the role of Michael Finnegan because the character was "a guy I'd never played before, and I'm always looking for something entirely different from my last role."[21] The character also allowed the actor to portray a wide range of emotions. One particular scene in the movie requires his character to burst into tears at the dinner table. After the scene was filmed, Micklin Silver marveled at Preston's ability to cry on cue:

> Joan said to me, "I'm surprised you can cry so easily." I said, "I can't, but Finnegan, this sad, broken-down Irishman can." I suppose a method actor at that point would have been thinking, "My mother is dead, God how I miss her, and my father is gone." But in life, you adjust to those things. And–thank you mama, thank you papa—I don't happen to have a raft of emotional problems, at least that I'm aware of. Acting for me is a question of [the] author's intent.[22]

Acting was serious business for Preston. The star, who generally refused to comment on his acting style or his approach to his craft, would only offer this glimpse into his modus operandi:

You know, people talk about the method, but I will never talk about how I work. There are certain things I do that I can talk about that I'm doing mechanically for a reason, but I will never talk about *how* I work because if I put it into words, then it is on a conscious level and it won't work for me anymore."[23]

Preston, who had only met Mary Tyler Moore for the first time at the 1983 Tony Awards, communicated it had been "such a pleasure to work on this film with her,"[24] adding that "Mary has the thing that I look for in a leading lady which is that she's hearty. She even laughs like a man, with a loud ha-ha-ha, not one of these dainty giggles."[25] Moore likewise lauded her co-star by revealing Preston "contributed masterfully to the production as well as to our amusement in between setups. If ever the term 'pro' was appropriate for a performer, it was he. Steady, smooth, sure, patient and generous are all words he 'owned' as far as I'm concerned."[26] The actress recalled one specific lull in filming when Preston amazed the assembled crew:

One afternoon as we sat in our chairs on the sidelines waiting (as always, waiting), [Preston] began talking about *The Music Man*. I innocently asked if he still remembered the impossibly difficult lyrics to "Trouble," with which he stood up, adjusted an imaginary tie, shot his cuffs, and for an audience of about six people (most of whom were too young to have seen it) he did the entire song with choreography.[27]

Actor Bob Gunton, who portrayed newspaper reporter Christian Jamison in the film, initially met Preston in 1979 during the opening night party for the Broadway production of *Evita*, in which Gunton played the role of Juan Peron. Gunton's first encounter with Preston left an indelible impression:

> For me, the highlight of that raucous gathering was my meeting, speaking with, and accepting some very precisely observed comments and compliments for my Peron from none other than Robert Preston–the original Professor Harold Hill. His personal magnetism, conveyed with a generosity of spirit and personal warmth, was irresistible.[28]

While working together on *Finnegan Begin Again*, Gunton had the opportunity to chat with Preston during lunch on the set about the actor's Broadway career and his depiction as a screen heavy during his early years in the movie industry. Preston shared amusing and dramatic stories of his experiences on Broadway and Gunton was struck by Preston's gracious nature, captivating banter, and photographic memory:

> It was astonishing to me the extent to which he recalled the particulars of my Peron portrayal. He both chatted with me and listened to my stories as if reminiscing with an old pal. This collegiality seemed grounded in his open-hearted embrace of all who toil in the theater as members of a special and fortunate family. Most remarkable to me was the focus and intensity with which Preston listened. I think this was, in large part, the source of

his magnetism and "star-quality." I had seen only his filmed version of *The Music Man*. But after my interactions and conversations with Pres, I suspected the movie version offered only a glimpse of what he surely must have achieved live on stage—the complete and utter surrender of a theater audience to his indelible charm.[29]

Filming for *Finnegan Begin Again* wrapped in early September. The movie premiered on HBO on February 24, 1985 and was also broadcast on British television.[30] Reviews of the cable television movie were glowing. Tom Shales of *The Washington Post* dubbed *Finnegan Begin Again* "the best and most serious romantic comedy ever made for cable television." Shales described Preston's performance in the film as "rousing, endearing, masterfully rascally" and made note that "at this point in his career, it would be risky to say of Preston that he has never been better, because there've been too many memorable Preston performances." Heaping additional praise on the actor, Shales commented, "if Robert Preston had any more charm than he has, he would have to be two people."[31] Kevin Thomas of the *Los Angeles Times* deemed the film "sweet and funny," and declared "this bittersweet romantic comedy has just about everything going for it," adding that Preston "who must hold the patent on charm, is a joy to behold." Thomas additionally complimented the production for brilliantly striking "a blow at ageism" in a youth-obsessed culture.[32] Kenneth R. Clark of the *Chicago Tribune* likewise lauded the film, exclaiming, "Preston simply explodes when he hits the screen. Add Mary Tyler Moore to the equation and you have dynamite."[33]

Preston and Moore were respectively nominated for cable Ace Awards in 1985 for Best Actor and Best Actress in a Movie or Miniseries, however, it was David Sanborn and Michael Colina who received recognition for *Finnegan Begin Again* by taking home an Ace Award for Best Musical Score.

By mid-1984, an uncomfortable tension began to surface between Preston and director Blake Edwards. In July, Preston disclosed that Julie Andrews and Blake Edwards were "upset" and "very disappointed" about his decision not to re-team with Andrews in a Broadway musical version of *Victor/Victoria*. Preston indicated he never agreed to reprise the role of Toddy on Broadway, but when he was asked by Andrews and Edwards to do so and declined, "they got indignant."[34] Since the role of Toddy had already been immortalized on film, the pragmatic Preston had no intention of competing against his screen performance in a Broadway musical; he realized it would be a zero-sum game for him to do so and further suggested that such a stage show was a mistake:

> I think they're so ill-advised. Blake and Julie assumed, because we were such a family when we made that film, that I'd do the Broadway show. They were astounded and almost heartbroken when I said I didn't want to. We're almost enemies now . . . I told Blake when he first approached me, that I wanted to see a book [of the proposed musical]. He said, "We can't have a book ready before you sign." I said to him, "All you have to do is tell me you're going to do a movie and I'll do it. But I know the Broadway theater and I want to see a book. We can't end the musical the way we ended the movie." Hell,

the movie didn't end, I did this phony drag scene and they just rolled the credits over me. But Blake wouldn't tell me what would replace it.[35]

For his part, Blake Edwards realized as he was filming *Victor/Victoria* that it "was a good stage vehicle" and he "kept obsessing on that all the time."[36] He was "baffled" by Preston's assertion that he never agreed to join the Broadway production of *Victor/Victoria*, alleging there was "a table full of people, including my wife, who witnessed his agreement [to do the show]. He said it clearly, 'I'll do it if Julie does it.' On the strength of that we put the whole thing together."[37] For a variety of reasons, the Broadway version of *Victor/Victoria* did not come together until the fall of 1995, several years after Preston's death and thirteen years after the film version had been released to the public.

In early November, Preston was slated to receive the "Mr. Wonderful" award from The Thalians organization. The Thalians—a philanthropic organization established in 1955 by members of the entertainment industry and aptly named after Thalia, the Greek muse of comedy—was created to provide charitable support for mental health programs. The organization, directed by actresses Debbie Reynolds and Ruta Lee for over sixty years, raised more than $35 million for mental health-related causes, with the mental health and well-being of America's wounded heroes as their most recent focus of benefaction. A large portion of The Thalians's fundraising has been derived through their annual gala which honors a show business celebrity, a "Ms. or Mr. Wonderful," with an entertainment tribute as well as a trophy designed by Walt Disney. Disney created the trophy for The Thalians in 1966 which features the character Goofy and incorporates the theatrical masks of comedy and tragedy. The trophy is presented annually to a member of the entertainment community for their body of work and their behind-the-scenes personal philanthropy. In addition to Preston, Thalians honorees have included Peter Ustinov, Harold Lloyd, Jimmy Durante, Frank Sinatra, Ed Sullivan, Busby Berkeley, Gene Kelly, Sammy Davis, Jr., Lucille Ball, Debbie Reynolds, Dorothy Lamour, Bob Hope, Bing Crosby, James Stewart, Rita Hayworth, Count Basie, Jack Lemmon, Lena Horne, Kenny and Marianne Rogers, Jane Wyman, Mary Martin, Lana Turner, Shirley MacLaine, June Haver, Fred MacMurray, Ann-Margret, Carol Burnett, Van Johnson, Ann Miller, Whoopi Goldberg, Angela Lansbury, Liza Minnelli, Donald O'Connor, Carol Channing, Sally Field, Mary Tyler Moore, Ruta Lee, Phyllis Diller, Burt Bacharach, Red Buttons, Marc Cherry, Sir Roger Moore, Clint Eastwood, Mickey Rooney, Hugh Hefner, and Smokey Robinson.

Preston was honored with a "Mr. Wonderful" award at the twenty-ninth annual Thalians Ball, titled The Magic of Music, on November 3. The event, held at the Century Plaza Hotel, featured a black-tie dinner and show. The gala's program book explained the basis on which Preston was chosen as the 1984 "Mr. Wonderful" honoree:

Robert Preston has shared an ongoing lifetime of creativity with us. He is *our* Music Man, he is Beauregard Burnside in *Mame*, he is the hilarious Toddy, he is that dashing devil of the golden film classic era. He is all this and more. For more than forty-four years he has reached into his vast vault of talent and entertained us. And selfishly we look to him to give us just a little more, and more, and more. For Robert Preston has only just begun.[38]

Members of the Hollywood elite in attendance to honor Preston included Lloyd Bridges and wife Dorothy Dean Bridges, Dorothy Lamour, Jeff Bridges and wife Susan, Phyllis Diller, Charlton Heston, George Peppard, Ginger Rogers, Robert Stack, Dick Van Patten, Bernie Kopell and wife Yolanda Velo, Cornel Wilde, Macdonald Carey, Hal Linden, and Barbi Benton.

Ruta Lee described the tribute to Robert Preston as "a spectacular Thalians event."[39] In her memoir *Consider Your Ass Kissed*, Lee acknowledged that although all of The Thalians's galas were amazing, the one tribute "that stands out was for Robert Preston. We had Mary Martin performing "Flaming Agnes" from *I Do, I Do*, Barry Bostwick and Barbara Eden doing *Mack & Mabel*, darling Shirley Jones doing *Music Man* and the inimitable Lucy doing *Mame*."[40]

The evening's tribute to Preston, emceed by Ruta Lee and produced by Jerry Franks, consisted of several song-and-dance productions honoring the actor's lifetime body of work on stage and screen. The opening number featured dancers dressed in River City garb singing "Iowa Stubborn" and Dick Gautier performing "Ya Got Trouble" from *The Music Man*. Sammy Davis, Jr., originally scheduled to sing "Ya Got Trouble," became ill and was unable to attend the gala. Gautier was asked to fill in for Davis at the last minute, with only two days to learn the song-and-dance routine. The next segment of the show featured Barry Bostwick and Barbara Eden who performed songs from Preston's musical *Mack & Mabel*. Bostwick sang "I Won't Send Roses," and Eden performed a dance number to "Look What Happened to Mabel." Shirley Jones presented a posthumous award to the late Meredith Wilson before paying tribute to Preston with a soaring, soprano rendition of "Till There Was You" from *The Music Man*. Lucille Ball appeared on the stage dressed in her riding togs from the movie *Mame* and re-enacted the musical number "Mame" with a retinue of male dancers dressed in riding boots and hunting costumes, with Stuart Damon in the role of Beauregard Burnside. For the final performance, the 1983 Thalians award recipient Mary Martin appeared on stage dressed as Agnes, her character in the Broadway show, *I Do, I Do!* and sang "Flaming Agnes" from the musical's score.

Martin then introduced Preston to receive his "Mr. Wonderful" award, and the actor walked onto the stage and extended a two-handed kiss to the audience. After presenting her friend with the trophy, Martin remained next to a discomfited Preston at his behest; he draped his right arm around Martin's waist to anchor her at his side on stage. In accepting the award, Preston referenced his wife, Catherine, and their forty-four-year marriage:

> I have tried for well over fifty years in this business to avoid being an anti-climax and tonight, it is not going to be easy . . . I'll tell you something, this is all things to all people, and I know what it is to me. But I also know what it is to Catherine. It will be a great addition to her clown collection. She started that collection, by the way, exactly forty-four years ago this coming Thursday [their wedding anniversary], so, I think she's entitled to enjoy this even more than I am, and for many, many, many reasons. Well, Thalians, you have just put the icing on a life that's been a great big piece of cake.[41]

For the show's finale, the Pasadena College Marching Band streamed onstage while serenading Preston and the audience with a rousing rendition of the actor's signature song, "Seventy-Six Trombones." In reflecting upon the 1984 Thalians gala, Ruta Lee acknowledged, "the night for Bob Preston was one of the best [The Thalians] ever did . . . never a better lineup of stars saluting the incomparable Robert Preston . . . I'm very proud of all of our events, but this one was truly tops!"[42]

A month later, Preston was honored as a living legend with distinguished achievement in film at the second annual American Cinema Awards along with Dorothy Maguire, Robert Mitchum, and Jane Wyman. The American Cinema Award Foundation was established by producer David Gest and singer Michael Jackson in 1983 "to bring national recognition and renewed interest in those artists and individuals of the 1920s, 30s, 40s, and 50s who have made an outstanding contribution to the American cinema"[43] and to recognize "those individuals who have been responsible for creating a body of work that has left an indelible impression in the minds of the public."[44] Proceeds from the annual awards banquets benefitted the Motion Picture and Television Country House and Hospital in Woodland Hills, CA, and provided scholarships for theater arts, dance, and music at colleges nationwide.

Tristan Rogers hosted the awards banquet on December 18 in the Grand Ballroom of the Beverly Wilshire Hotel before a star-studded audience. The evening's presenters included Janet Leigh, Ray Milland, Rock Hudson, Esther Williams, Robert Young, Lew Ayres, Martha Scott, Troy Donohue, Teresa Wright, and Roddy McDowell.[45]

Preston was back in New York in February 1985 to participate in *Night of 100 Stars II*. The ABC television special, produced by Alexander Cohen on behalf of the Actors Fund of America, was taped at Radio City Music Hall on February 17. The two-hour extravaganza featuring the Radio City Rockettes as well as 286 celebrities from stage, screen, and television, was broadcast on March 10. Preston was featured on the show in the "Special Movie Stars" segment. The movie legends showcased in this portion of the telecast–Dustin Hoffman, Lana Turner, Robert Preston, Sidney Poitier, Olivia de Havilland, Robert DeNiro, Danny Kaye, and Lawrence Olivier–were introduced by Bernadette Peters after some of their famous film clips were shared with the audience. Before Preston's introduction, the audience was shown a clip of the actor in drag performing "The Shady Dame of Seville" from *Victor/Victoria* along with a short clip of him dressed as Harold Hill singing "Seventy-Six Trombones" from *The Music Man.*

Preston, dressed in a tuxedo, bounded down the staircase onto the stage to an orchestra flourish of his theme song "Seventy-Six Trombones," did a slight Harold Hill jig, and blew a two-handed kiss to the audience before exiting the stage. The segment's finale saw seven of the showcased stars flanking Olivier on stage for a final bow and a standing ovation from the audience.

Less than a month later, Preston received the honor of being inducted into the American Theater Hall of Fame. The organization was founded in New York in 1971 by Earl Blackwell, James M. Nederlander, Gerard Oestreicher, and L. Arnold Weissberger to preserve theater history and to honor those who have made outstanding contributions to the American Theater. To be eligible for induction, nominees must have at least twenty-five years of distinguished service in the American theater, in addition to a minimum of five major production credits on Broadway. Members are elected annually by the nation's drama critics, editors, and established members of the Theater Hall of Fame.

The 1985 induction ceremony was held at noon on March 4 in the rotunda of the Gershwin Theatre in New York City. Tradition called for each new inductee to be presented for membership by another theater veteran. Joe Papp, who served as the emcee of the event, signaled the start of the ceremony by taking his place center stage in the mezzanine lobby. The presenters for the ceremony, Ruth Gordon, Rosemary Harris, Jerome Lawrence, Lloyd Richards, Peter Stone, Robin Wagner, Bernadette Peters, Richard Barr, Milton Goldman, Maureen Stapleton, Anna Crouse, and Hume Cronyn, then filed into the mezzanine down a long staircase to introduce the new inductees.[46] Inducted alongside Preston that day were Edward Albee, Richard Burton (posthumously), Melvin Douglas, James Earl Jones, Garson Kanin, Tharon Muser, Alan Schneider, Lee Simonson, Kim Stanley, Dorothy Stickney, Robert Whitehead, and Alexander Wolcott.[47]

Preston, introduced by Bernadette Peters, expressed his gratitude for the honor and disclosed his favorite Broadway role was that of Pancho Villa in the ill-fated musical *We Take the Town.*[48] Ron Fassler, who crashed the event in order to see his favorite actor up close and personal, recalled Preston "made a wonderful speech, asking to be remembered for his flops as well as hits."[49]

In addition to the various film and theatrical honors, Preston also received horticultural recognition by being anthropomorphized as an iris by hybridizer David Spence in 1985. Spence, an old movie buff, had been long-enamored with *The Music Man.* It was obvious to Spence, who viewed the movie several dozen times, that Preston was a "wonderful actor and great showman" who "possessed the talent and personality to portray the perfect Harold Hill."[50] Spence hybridized two different irises with the intention of naming one of the flowers after the actor. In order to name an iris after a living person, registration guidelines require that permission be obtained from the individual for whom the iris will be named. Spence sent a letter to Preston's Montecito home detailing his plan to name an iris in honor of the actor and requested his permission for the registration. Spence included photos of the two hybrids with his correspondence and asked Preston to select the hybrid flower that would ultimately carry his moniker. Preston responded to Spence's inquiry with a gracious letter; he was flattered to have an iris named in his honor and selected the hybrid he preferred to be registered as his namesake. In addition, Preston wrote a personal letter to the American Iris Society, dated August 9, 1985, in which he gave permission for the iris hybrid S82-205-1 to be named for him.[51] Spence discerned from Preston's correspondence that the actor and his wife were "genuinely nice, down-to-earth" people. The showy, fragrant plant registered as the Robert Preston Iris (Iridaceae *Iris* 'Robert Preston'), is described as a tall bearded iris that features a plicata flower pattern and a pronounced musky fragrance. Propagation of the dazzling iris must be accomplished via rhizome and tuber division rather than from seed. The bloom itself is white with a heavily veined and dotted red border, white falls that are veined and dotted darker violet on the edge, and a medium blue beard.[52]

Preston's final performance was in a two-hour made-for-tv movie, produced by Irwin Allen and directed by Walter Grauman, that began production in the fall of 1985. The film, *Outrage*, featured Preston, Beau Bridges, Linda Purl, Mel Ferrer, Stan Haze,

Burgess Meredith, William Allen Young, and Anthony Newley in a story based on Henry Denker's novel of the same name.

The film grapples with the question of whether citizens should be permitted to take the law into their own hands when the legal system fails to dispense justice to perpetrators of crime. Acting as a vigilante, Dennis Riordan (Preston) guns down criminal Charlie Johnson (Haze) who brutally raped and murdered his daughter, Agnes, but escaped prosecution due to a legal technicality. Riordan, despondent in the aftermath of his daughter's brutal rape/murder and the recent death of his wife, Nedda, who lacked the will to live, vowed to hunt down his daughter's killer. Riordan is defended at trial by attorney Brad Gordon (Bridges) in the courtroom of Judge Aaron Klein (Meredith). When Riordan refuses an insanity defense, Gordon sees no other option than to place the legal system on trial and issues a subpoena to Judge Lengel (Ferrer), the jurist who freed Agnes's rapist and murderer on a technicality, to testify in Riordan's trial. Thrown into the mix is Gordon's girlfriend Arlene (Purl) and a smarmy agent (Newley) who unsuccessfully attempts to gain the exclusive rights to Riordan's story. The jury ultimately is sympathetic to the miscarriage of justice surrounding Agnes's murder and finds Riordan not guilty.

Outrage, shot in October 1985 at Warner Brothers Burbank Studios, marked the second time Preston acted in a film with Beau Bridges. Portraying a character depressed over the rape and murder of his daughter and the death of his wife, Preston appeared physically gaunt and fragile in several scenes of the movie.

The issue of vigilantism was one Preston understood but could not condone, as evidenced by his analysis of Dennis Riordan:

I can see the extenuating circumstances. That's what makes the character interesting to play. I've never played anyone like him. To his mind, his life is over. He has nothing left to live for. He puts up no defense and hasn't a thought of being freed. What caused him to go over the edge was the sight of the killer of his daughter walking out of the courtroom a free man–and laughing. He had to wipe the smile off that man's face.[53]

Despite his sympathy for Riordan, Preston was unable to excuse his character's actions:

All the same, I can't agree that murdering even such a despicable man is justified . . . I agree with the idea that it's better to let a criminal profit than to punish an innocent man. I'm not ready to repeal the Fourth and Fifth Amendments.[54]

The film brought Preston's past experience as a crime victim to the fore. He recalled being beaten by a gang of men in New York in January 1952, yet ultimately chose not to press charges against his main assailant, Joseph Scarlato:

I was jumped by seven hoodlums in New York City some years ago. It was the early 1950s. I was appearing on an early TV show called *Lux Video Theatre*, and these bums must have thought, "Hey, let's beat up an actor" . . . the police caught the ringleader of the gang . . . his name was Joey . . . I decided not to press charges against him . . . The boy's father came to me. He apologized and I accepted. You see, as a boxer, his fists were "deadly weapons" in the eyes of the law. He could have had a bad rap. In his case, it would have been felony assault.[55]

Outrage aired on CBS on March 2, 1986 to mixed reviews. Some television critics, such as those from The Washington Post and The Los Angeles Times, offered a harsh critique of the film. In his review in The Washington Post, Tom Shales characterized Outrage as "shamelessly preposterous on nearly every conceivable level," adding the film, "stomps on shaky ground" and "may be the looniest vigilante movie of the year."[56] Howard Rosenberg from The Los Angeles Times took CBS to task for "billing Outrage as one of those really significant movies that gives you lots to chew on. Instead, it gives new meaning to the word dumb." Rosenberg noted that "any legitimate points that Outrage tries to make about flaws in the legal system are obscured by a general witlessness in this Irwin Allen production that includes such trite characters as a grouchy-but-fair judge, played by Burgess Meredith, and a grubby literary agent, played by Anthony Newley."[57] Other news outlets, notably Newsday and The New York Times, gave the film more favorable reviews. Newsday's Leo Seligsohn acknowledged, "truth to tell, it's not bad. The acting is good–if you can get past the tortured logic" of the plotline.[58] John J. O'Connor of The New York Times indicated the film raised "troubling questions about the country's overall judicial system," adding "if it ends up being somewhat less convincing than intended, the two-hour film, largely a courtroom drama, succeeds in being unusually provocative as it outlines and explores certain gray areas of the law."[59] O'Connor went on to praise Preston's work in the film, declaring "the role of Riordan is filled to overflowing by Robert Preston, an actor with a talent for being effortlessly engaging . . . as Riordan, Mr. Preston protests with such calm rage, such savvy sincerity against the injustices of the world he lives in that to find him less than admirable would border on misanthropy."[60]

By the time *Outrage* was broadcast on television in March 1986, Preston was aware he was battling cancer. The actor, a life-long cigarette smoker, first learned of his oral cancer during a visit to the dentist in the waning days of 1985. Preston was at the dentist's office for a routine cleaning when cancer was discovered below the gum line.[61] A biopsy of the tissue confirmed malignant cells as well as a diagnosis of carcinoma of the tongue and floor of the mouth.[62] Since squamous cell carcinoma can spread quickly and aggressively, it was suspected that the disease had already metastasized to other parts of the body. The actor's first visit to Dr. Albert Medwid, a Santa Barbara surgical oncologist, took place on January 8, 1986. The initial oncology appointment was quickly followed by surgery on January 14, in which a mandibulectomy was performed to resection the left floor of the mouth, followed by reconstructive repair.

To maintain a strict level of privacy about his illness, Preston and Catherine elected not to share the news of his condition nor burden extended family members and friends with the details of his treatment. A private man, Preston hoped to avoid public scrutiny as he battled cancer and sought to prevent the press from trailing him to and from doctor and hospital visits. His diagnosis and treatment were handled privately with dignity and resolve; it was not his wish for his cancer or his treatment to become fodder for the tabloids or define his legacy.

As Preston's illness progressed, the oral cancer metastasized to his lungs and liver,[63] and was then beyond the point of successful treatment. Every effort was made to boost his stamina, including the use of dietary supplements to bolster his weight. Despite living with the heartache of the impending loss of her beloved husband, Catherine managed Preston's illness every step of the way.[64] In the last months of his life, Preston was cared for at home by Catherine, with the assistance of professional caregivers, and was able to enjoy the familiar surroundings of his home and share closeness with Catherine in the remaining time they had together.

The last four weeks of Preston's life were further impaired by renal failure. His condition eventually deteriorated to the point that he was transported to Santa Barbara Cottage Hospital on Thursday, March 19, 1987 for what amounted to hospice care. It was two days later that Preston, age sixty-eight, took his last breath at 5:15 p.m. on Saturday, March 21. In addition to seventy-two-year-old Catherine, Preston was survived by his eighty-seven-year-old father Doc, who managed to outlive his wife and both of his sons.

The actor's death, reported in every major media outlet in the United States, erroneously stated Preston died as a result of lung cancer; his underlying cause of death was primary carcinoma of the tongue and floor of the mouth which eventually led to metastatic carcinoma of the lung and liver.[65] Catherine cremated her husband's body, with the cremation performed on March 24. Preston's death came as a shock to extended family members, friends, colleagues on Broadway and in Hollywood, and fans who had no idea the star had been battling cancer.

President Reagan and his wife Nancy issued a statement in which they acknowledged the news of the actor's death came as "a great shock," adding they had known Preston "a great many years" and "he was a friend who will be missed."[66] Lucille Ball, who starred opposite Preston in the movie *Mame*, praised Preston as "a wonderful performer, a professional from the word go, and a great gentleman."[67] Actress Shirley Jones, who played Marian Paroo to Preston's Harold Hill in the movie version of *The Music Man*, described the actor as a private, unassuming man. Jones revealed that "as a human being he was, I thought, so un-Hollywood . . . he was not hungry for publicity. He liked his privacy. He was never involved in the Hollywood party scene. He just wanted to come and do his work and go home."[68] Blake Edwards, who directed Preston in *S.O.B.* and *Victor/Victoria*, recognized the actor as "one of the last of a vanished breed that I hate to see leave the scene. He was a brave and remarkable man who did not let his closest friends know he was dreadfully ill,"[69] adding Preston "was a very unique, lovely man. I really don't have the words for it; none of them do him justice."[70] Despite the outpouring of sympathy at the news of Preston's death, Catherine arranged for her husband's interment to be held in private. In the absence of fanfare, a formal funeral service, or throngs of mourners, Catherine scattered Preston's cremains in the Pacific Ocean near the coastline adjacent to their Montecito home.

The forty-first annual Tony Awards was broadcast on June 7, 1987, the day before what would have been Preston's sixty-ninth birthday. Several notable stars–Ray Bolger, James Coco, Danny Kaye, and Cary Grant, among others–had passed away between the previous and current Tony Awards ceremony, but it was Preston's death that was marked by a spectacular tribute during the broadcast. At the midpoint of the show, host Angela Lansbury introduced a special eleven-minute tribute to Preston:

For a performer, that sense of home that we spoke of can be found in many places—on the stage of a theater, the set of a film—wherever one finds that magic which makes us all come to life. Sometimes you find it in a song or in the words you're saying, or in another actor's eyes. This year, the theater lost a friend. His energy, his enthusiasm, and the joy of his great talent just came at you in a way that almost dazed you. It almost dared you not to be lifted up by its spell. His name was Robert Preston.[71]

Film clips rolled which depicted Preston as Harold Hill in *The Music Man* and, to the tune of "Goodnight My Someone," photo stills of the actor were flashed across the screen that celebrated his performances in *I Do! I Do!*, *Sly Fox*, with Barbara Cook in *The Music Man* on Broadway, *Mack & Mabel*, and as Toddy in the film *Victor/Victoria*. Lansbury, who starred with Preston in the 1960 film *Dark at the Top of the Stairs*, continued, "For all of us, whoever knew and worked with Bob, two of his leading ladies have come here tonight to remember that man and his magic."[72]

Bernadette Peters then sang "Time Heals Everything" from *Mack & Mabel* and Barbara Cook followed with "Till There Was You" from *The Music Man*. As Cook completed her vocals, the Tony stage erupted with dancers, dressed in *Music Man* band costumes, who performed a spirited routine to "Seventy-Six Trombones." A marching band, dressed in red uniforms, filed in through the audience as they played "Seventy-Six Trombones" and encircled the performing dancers on stage.

Mary Martin, Preston's co-star in *I Do, I Do!*, took the stage to share memories of working with Preston in Hollywood and on Broadway. She proceeded to sing "This House," the last song from *I Do, I Do!*, for both Catherine (Craig) Preston and "to Robert from his Agnes." As Martin prepared to honor her friend's memory by presenting a posthumous Lawrence Langner Award for Distinguished Achievement in the Theatre to Preston, she welcomed Catherine (Craig) Preston to the stage. Catherine ascended to the microphone in a floor-length, black V-neck dress and a black and gold floral jacket; her outfit was embellished with a thick, gold, waist-length rope chain. Catherine, visibly touched by the tribute, gazed intently at the award and its inscription, before exclaiming, "This is a beautiful honor. Robert loved the theater and [extending the award] this means the theater loved him back. Thank you."[73]

As Catherine exited the stage, a late 1950s still photograph of Preston and Catherine was flashed on the screen to conclude this segment of the awards show. Later in September, this Tony Awards broadcast received the 1987 Primetime Emmy Award for Outstanding Variety, Music, or Comedy Series.

Following Preston's death, Catherine settled into a quiet life dedicated to gardening and punctuated with visits from family and friends. In December 1987, thirty years after *The Music Man* premiered on Broadway, Catherine and her eighty-eight-year-old father-in-law, Doc Meservey, attended a holiday dinner at Chasens in West Hollywood hosted by Meredith Willson's widow, Rosemary. Mrs. Willson arranged the reunion dinner for members of the cast as an opportunity to reminisce and share memories of *The Music Man* and to pay tribute to Preston's dazzling performance as Harold Hill.

In early 1988 as she was still grieving Preston's death, Catherine had an emotional hand-grenade lobbed into the fabric of her existence that had been fifty-two years in the making. On February 9, 1988, a civil complaint was filed in Santa Barbara County Superior Court for a determination of paternity and heirship. The action was directed against Catherine Meservey as the executrix of Robert Preston's will by Rita Eleanora Meservey a.k.a. Laurie Tavis, who alleged she was Preston's only biological child and sought a share of her birthright.[74]

The complaint alleged Laurie had been born out of wedlock on November 26, 1952 in Los Angeles, California, conceived on or about March 7, 1952, as a result of a sexual encounter between Preston and Rita O'Leary Tavis. Laurie Tavis's complaint alleged Preston "did agree in writing to pay and did in fact pay the medical expenses for the birth" and "contributed to the support of [Tavis] during her minority" to include monthly child support and contributions to her college tuition. In filing the complaint, Tavis asked the court to legally decree that Preston was her "natural father."[75]

Definitive paternity testing was unavailable in 1952. It is unknown whether Preston knew he was the biological father of Rita Tavis's child and, as alleged, provided financial support for her. If the allegations were true and Preston did, in fact, provide child support, he may have been inclined to offer such assistance because he believed the child to be his, he could not dispute the possibility of a paternity claim, or he hoped to avoid subjecting his wife to the pain of discovering that an indiscretion resulted in the birth of a child. It is also possible that he simply wished to eschew a paternity melodrama akin to the spectacle of the 1940s-era Charlie Chaplin/Joan Berry imbroglio. If Tavis produced evidence or documentation to substantiate her allegation that Preston agreed in writing to support her as a child, such evidence would corroborate that the actor acted in good faith by providing financial support to promote the well-being and best interests of the child.

Tavis's mother, Rita Catherine O'Leary, was born in Teller, Alaska on March 6, 1920. Rita graduated from Nome High School in 1937 and the outstanding student was awarded a two-year scholarship to the Agricultural College and School of Mines in Fairbanks. With two years of college to her credit, Rita went to work in the offices of Alaska Airlines and Pan American Airlines after marriage to Seattle native, Wilbur Tavis, in 1940 and the subsequent birth of their son.[76] Following a divorce in 1947, Rita relocated to Hawaii to work as a Pan Am passenger service agent at the Honolulu Airport,[77] then moved to Los Angeles, California in 1951 to work for El Al Israel Airlines.[78] It was while living and working in Los Angeles that Rita allegedly rendezvoused with Preston in March 1952. Laurie Tavis's birth certificate, in which her name was listed as "Rita Eleanora Tavis," lists the name of the father as thirty-five-year-old "Robert Preston Meservey," with his occupation reported as being an "actor" in "motion pictures."[79] Rita and her children returned to Anchorage, Alaska in 1957 where she completed her Bachelor's degree in Education as well as a Master's degree and enjoyed a twenty-three-year tenure with the Anchorage School District.[80]

Catherine initially responded on March 21 through her attorneys to deny "each and every allegation" proffered by Laurie Tavis in the February 9 complaint.[81] Although Catherine as executrix was required to file an inventory and appraisement of Preston's estate in the probate proceeding, she had not done so as of August 26, 1988.[82] Catherine additionally prevailed upon the court to bar Tavis's complaint, arguing that it had been more than four years since Tavis reached the age of majority, she delayed filing the complaint until after Preston's death to prejudice the proceedings, failed to file a claim against the estate of Robert Preston Meservey within four months of the first issuance of Letters Testamentary,[83] and additionally filed a motion for judgment on the pleadings included in her attorney's memorandum of points and authorities.[84] In response, Tavis's attorney argued no statute of limitation existed with regard to paternity actions in the State of California.[85] On December 14, the parties received some measure of clarity when Judge Ronald C. Stevens concluded that Catherine's motion for judgment on the pleadings should be denied.[86]

As the plaintiff, Laurie Tavis requested a jury trial. The trial calendar for Santa Barbara County Superior Court, issued on December 23, 1988, indicated the jury trial had been set for February 10, 1989 and projected a five-day court proceeding. The calendar also indicated a case Readiness and Settlement conference had been scheduled for February 3, 1989.[87] On the same day the court calendar was issued, Catherine's attorneys filed a status report indicating that pre-trial discovery was incomplete and signaled the potential need for additional discovery to include a deposition of Laurie Tavis's mother and blood type testing of the plaintiff. The status report additionally acknowledged that the attorneys for both parties were awaiting the receipt of Preston's medical records from Santa Barbara Cottage Hospital.[88]

The use of DNA for paternity testing first became available in 1988.[89] Although Preston's DNA was no longer available for direct analysis, it was possible for such testing to be performed on the surviving putative paternal grandparent, Doc Meservey, who would possess genes in common with his son. Prior to the use of or without the availability of DNA testing, blood types were the most common factor considered in paternity testing, although ABO blood group information could only be used to exclude potential fathers, rather than confirm a parental relationship.[90] While it is unknown if blood type information was recorded in the medical records from Preston's brief stay at Santa Monica Cottage Hospital in March 1987, such information may have proven useful to either bolster or invalidate Tavis's paternity claim.

A definitive answer to the question of Tavis's paternity would not be resolved in court. Eight days before the commencement of the jury trial, Laurie Tavis submitted a request for dismissal of the paternity complaint with prejudice.[91] The motivation for Tavis's termination of the case is left to conjecture; it remains unclear whether Catherine Preston and Laurie Tavis reached an out-of-court settlement to end the complaint and forgo the spectacle of a public trial, or if Tavis had a change of heart and made the decision not to proceed with her paternity case.

Whatever the reason and circumstances behind the abrupt dismissal of the paternity complaint, Tavis, a self-employed artist,[92] married Jeffrey Zweiback in New York City in 1990. The Zweibacks eventually divorced in Florida in December 2000. Laurie Zweiback resided in Florida with her mother, Rita, until Rita's death on February 10, 2010 at age eighty-nine. Three years later, sixty-year-old Laurie Zweiback died at her home in Mims, Florida at 2:45 a.m. on February 18, 2013 and was later cremated. Adding to the intrigue over the dismissal of the 1988 paternity case, information on Laurie (Tavis) Zweiback's death certificate, supplied by her brother, listed her father's name as Robert Preston.[93]

Catherine continued to reside in the beautiful Montecito home that featured a large garden, and she dedicated many hours of her time to gardening, maintaining correspondence with old friends, and becoming involved in cat rescue.[94]

Catherine became frail toward the end of her life and required 24-hour nursing care at home.[95] She passed away at home at 8:22 p.m. on January 14, 2004, at age eighty-eight, as a result of long-term complications from dysphagia.[96] Like her beloved husband, Catherine was cremated and her cremains were committed to the Pacific Ocean on the coastline adjacent to her Montecito home, near the site where Preston's cremains had been scattered seventeen years earlier. Although Catherine decided to forgo any type of funeral or memorial service for Preston, her extended family arranged for a small group of her friends from the neighborhood, fellow cat rescue devotees, old friends, and the nursing staff who had provided her care to assemble for a final goodbye.[97]

A year after Catherine's death, a one-man biographical musical about Preston's life titled *Ya Got Trouble* was featured at the Village Theatre in Issaquah, Washington from May 26 to June 12, 2005. The idea for the musical emanated from actor Mark Sparks, who was assisted with the story by Bob DeDea; the end result of the collaboration was a musical book by DeDea which provided a first-person narrative of Preston's career. Sparks and DeDea conducted extensive research into Preston's life, interviewing several of Preston's fellow actors to re-create Preston's life and legacy in the musical storyline. The musical evolved into a solo performance by Sparks as Preston, punctuated by the music of Tom Jones and Harvey Schmidt, Meredith Willson, and other composers.[98] Reviews of the one-man musical were mixed. Rosemary Ponnekanti from *The News Tribune* in Tacoma described the show as "a labor of love that sometimes touches Preston's charismatic dazzle, but often falls into empty sameness." Ponnekanti observed the musical attempted to create "a narrative of Preston's life told from beyond the grave" via a monologue by Preston, as portrayed by Sparks.[99] Critics from *The Seattle Times* described the musical as showcasing Preston "holed up in an apropos afterlife room of old theater props and movie posters" and taking the audience "on his life's journey . . . and into history." They concluded Sparks and DeDea were "unhappy to settle for a musical schmooze session" and thus made the decision to add some romance to the story by depicting "Preston oozing poetic declarations to longtime wife Catherine Craig." In an otherwise tepid review of the musical, the creative team was complimented for their collaboration, taking note that "Sparks' musicality and DeDea's arrangement complement each other."[100]

EPILOGUE

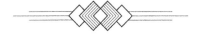

I n the end, what can be concluded about such a private man who chose to lead a very quiet existence? Despite some fits and starts in both his professional and private life, what emerges from the fabric of Preston's life is the undeniable truth of his versatility as a performer, one who possessed the innate ability to perform superbly in a variety of genres–drama, comedy, westerns, and musicals. As a testament to his skill as an actor, Preston continued to deliver remarkable performances on stage and screen and strived to reach new apogees, even when cast in flawed projects, up until his untimely death in 1987.

It was his mother, Ruth, who first recognized Preston's talent and guided him toward the path to stardom. High school provided Preston with the opportunity to shine on stage. He became the protégé of drama teacher, E.J. Wenig, and it was Wenig who arranged for additional theatrical exposure for Preston with Patia Power's Shakespearean acting troupe. It was a persistent Paramount attorney who became the conduit for Preston's studio screen test; a column by Louella Parsons became the magic bullet that allowed the actor to shed his dead-end Paramount contract; a chance encounter with José Ferrer in New York led to a Broadway career; an appearance on the 1971 Tony Awards telecast led to a role in *Junior Bonner* and a revitalization of his film career, and the list goes on and on. Preston was grateful to all those who helped him reach his potential and marveled at the way the fates continued to heap favor upon him. He was also well aware that luck played a large role in the forward trajectory of his career: each time he turned down a part or a planned project fell through, a better opportunity always seemed to materialize right around the corner.

During his fifty-year career on stage and in films, Preston appeared in forty-two Pasadena Playhouse productions, forty-five motion pictures, sixteen Broadway plays and musicals–not including *We Take the Town* or *The Prince of Grand Street*–as well as in countless 1950s television theatrical productions and made-for-television movies in the 1970s and 1980s. He began his professional career as an underrated Hollywood actor before his eventual metamorphosis into a beloved prince of Broadway. As highlighted by screenwriter William Goldman, Preston was one of the rare actors who could do it all: drama, comedy–both light and dark–and musicals.[1] Neither a trained singer nor a dancer, Preston was able to accomplish both with great aplomb and, per Richard Burton, articulate his lines with a voice of golden thunder. He possessed amazing cadence and control of his speech, and it was these skills that allowed him to sing and enunciate fast-tempo and complex song lyrics with perspicuous clarity.

Preston's perfectionism fueled the execution of precision performances in which he exuded confidence in each word and every step. He learned to act using the entirety of his body; his ability to emote through a combination of his unique voice, eyes, expressions, and gestures became the magic that captivated Broadway and film audiences everywhere.

Acting was Preston's life's work and although he appreciated awards and professional recognition, he was most proud of his ability to have successfully made the transition from film to stage. In 1957, Broadway critics and Hollywood naysayers were equally astounded by Preston's ability to dance, sing, and transmogrify into the character of Harold Hill. Preston's performance in *The Music Man* became the spark that ignited an awakening within the acting community, and was the catalyst that catapulted him into the rarified A-list of stage and screen performers.

Confident in his range as an actor, Preston did not simply portray a character: he *became* the character and inserted his essence into each and every role. Preston used his ethos and expressive gestures–a wince, a raised eyebrow, a scowl, a wave of the hand–to his advantage in film or on stage. It was the ability to completely inhabit each character, regardless of the character's likeability or lack of pathos, that allowed him to portray a convincing con man or a gay singer in 1930s Paris. It was this rare quality that allowed Preston to impart his unique brand of energy into each role and create a lasting and sympathetic impression on the audience. His performance in *The Music Man* lifted the typecasting yoke established in his films from the 1930s and 1940s and provided opportunities for him to portray an unemployed husband and father in *Dark at the Top of The Stairs*, an other-world alien in *The Last Star Fighter*, and a zany doctor in *S.O.B.* Yet, despite his extensive body of work, there is no star on the Hollywood Walk of Fame nor an imprint at Grauman's Chinese Theatre to immortalize his talent or pay tribute to his cinematic and stage accomplishments.

Because Preston consistently portrayed characters who were his own age or slightly older, stage and screen audiences saw him evolve in real time over the course of his career. His roles in midlife were some of his best, including Michael in *I Do, I Do!*, Ace in *Junior Bonner*, Centauri in *The Last Starfighter*, Foxwell J. Sly in *Sly Fox*, and Carroll Todd in *Victor/Victoria*.

Preston was impressed by Barbara Stanwyck's supportive, down-to-earth nature and emulated her professional largesse. It was not in his nature to be difficult, throw his weight around, or make excessive, unreasonable demands of directors or producers as so many others he worked with were wont to do. Preston was a decent man who achieved success in a competitive profession by virtue of his diverse talent. He managed to survive the studio system, the fickleness of the film industry, and various professional minefields in Hollywood and Broadway with aplomb while maintaining his integrity and calling his own shots. Charismatic, sophisticated, modest, and always a gentleman, Preston's easy-going, flexible professionalism made him a favorite of Hollywood producers and directors. He could be counted on to deliver a solid performance, often in a single take, without any needless theatrics or drama. Preston was also admired by his fellow actors for his talent as well as for his generosity, support, kindness, and his magnanimous nature. Members of the cast and crew on his productions were awed by his entertaining, approachable, and attentive nature, and no one had a bad word to say about him.

A master at shielding his private life, Preston remained an enigma to many of his closest co-stars and contemporaries. As a husband, Preston was imperfect. Despite several bumps in the road during the forty-six years of marriage to Catherine, he unquestionably adored and admired his wife. He could be himself with Catherine and allow his emotions to flow freely, something he was unable to do with anyone else. Catherine was the one woman who truly understood him, could meet him toe-to-toe, and knew what made him tick. Despite his legendary charisma and the public face of bold confidence, Preston was a shy child who grew into a self-effacing adult.

Catherine understood this dichotomy; it was Catherine to whom Preston allowed himself to be vulnerable–he appreciated her steady, calm nature, relied on her for advice and emotional sustenance, and loved her from the depths of his soul. Through it all, Catherine loved her husband unconditionally and cherished him until the last day of his life.

As was true of most performers' careers, Preston's path was punctuated with successes and a few flops. Although some of the movies or Broadway productions in which he appeared were savaged by critics, in the vast majority of these reviews, Preston's performances were praised as superb.

Despite his extensive body of work in Hollywood and on Broadway, the public at large tends to singularly focus on Preston's iconic performance as Harold Hill in *The Music Man*, ignoring his broader career. Preston, however, was not fixated on *The Music Man*, choosing to maintain an onward-and-upward attitude about the direction of his career. The actor had been approached on several occasions to revive *The Music Man* on Broadway, but steadfastly declined. He had no interest in resurrecting Harold Hill, believing that such a revival was pointless, especially since his performance had already "been locked on screen for all the world to see."[2]

Preston was acutely aware he was, in fact, the personification of Harold Hill and did not wish to compete against himself. In his article addressing the reluctance of actors to reprise the role of

Hill on Broadway, Michael Riedel explained most actors do not wish the inevitable comparison with Preston since he was "one of Broadway's greatest leading men" and had "enormous energy, confidence, and charm and he made singing and dancing look easy."[3] Much has been made about the difficulty of other actors in *The Music Man* revivals to displace the memories of Preston as Harold Hill. Several actors including Steve Martin, Jim Carrey, Kevin Kline, Patrick Swayze, and George Clooney were approached to reprise the role on The Great White Way, but passed on the opportunity.[4] Other actors, however, chose to forge ahead and tackle the role on Broadway or on film, often with mixed results. Critical reviews of these performances concluded that none of them managed to re-create Preston's unrivaled portrayal of Hill or matched his effortlessness, nimbly executed speech, and complete embodiment of the character that kept audiences spellbound. Each of the revival productions, thoroughly entertaining in its own right, has incorporated the requisite fanfare and razzmatazz that audiences expect from a fresh take of *The Music Man.* However, each incarnation of Harold Hill has failed to attain the archetypal prosopopoeia Preston exhibited in the original Broadway production that captivated audiences in 1957 or in the iconic performance he immortalized in the 1962 film. David Hinkley from the New York *Daily News* aptly addressed the Harold Hill conundrum in *Music Man* revivals and clarified why Preston and Hill will remain synonymous: "to most people, Robert Preston *was* the Music Man . . . for Robert Preston to ever fade out would require we also forget Harold Hill, which we will not do."[5] Although Harold Hill was admittedly not Preston's favorite character, it was this singular, spectacular role that catapulted him to stage and screen stardom and ensured he would forever remain *the* Music Man.

END NOTES

WAITING IN THE WINGS

1. Susan Meservey (Suzy), "Post about the height of Preston's parents," Facebook, July 12, 2020. https://www.facebook.com/groups/robertpreston/. [Online account/comment deleted; author has a screenshot of the original post on file].

2. Susan Meservey (Suzy), "Post about Ruth Rea Meservey," Facebook, August 1, 2020, https://www.facebook.com/groups/robertpreston/. [Online account/comment deleted; author has a screenshot of the original post on file].

3. Susan Meservey (Suzy), "Post about Preston's birth," Facebook, June 8, 2020, https://www.facebook.com/groups/robertpreston/. [Online account/comment deleted; author has a screenshot of the original post on file].

4. George S. Hage, "Happiest Actor on Broadway," *Saturday Evening Post,* December 6, 1958, 114.

5. Susan Meservey (Suzy), "Post about Ruth Rea Meservey," Facebook, June 8, 2020, https://www.facebook.com/groups/robertpreston/. [Online

account/comment deleted; author has a screenshot of the original post on file].

6. Lillian Ross and Helen Ross, *The Player: A Profile of an Art*, 2nd ed. (New York: Simon and Schuster, 1962) 404.

7. Ross and Ross, *The Player*, 404.

8. Ross and Ross, *The Player*, 404.

9. Ross and Ross, *The Player*, 404.

10. Ross and Ross, *The Player*, 405.

11. Tracy Palmgren Monroe, interview by the author, February 15, 2021.

12. Tracy Palmgren Monroe, interview by the author, February 15, 2021.

13. Ross and Ross, *The Player*, 405.

14. Susan Meservey (Suzy), "Post about Robert Preston," Facebook, June 14, 2020. https://www.facebook.com/groups/robertpreston/. [Online account/comment deleted; author has a screenshot of the original post on file].

15. Tom Prideaux, "That Music Man Is Back on Broadway, Still Making Films and Aiming at Shakespeare," *People*, October 31, 1977, 80.

16. Charles Leinenweber, interview by the author, July 2, 2021

17. Charles Leinenweber, interview by the author, July 2, 2021.

18. Charles Leinenweber, interview by the author, July 2, 2021.

19. Ross and Ross, *The Player*, 405.

20. Ross and Ross, *The Player*, 405.

21. Hage, "Happiest Actor on Broadway," 114.

22. Ross and Ross, *The Player*, 405.

23. "How the Music Man (Robert Preston) Met Houdini's Ghost (Patrick Culliton)," Houdinisghost.com, accessed February 1, 2022, http://www.houdinisghost.com/robertpreston.html.

24. David Sterritt, "Robert Preston Back on Broadway as 'Sly Fox'," *Lowell Sun*, (Lowell, MA), August 28, 1977, 57.

25. Al Cohn, "Twenty Years Later, He's Still the Con Man," *Herald News*, September 25, 1977, 70.

26. Ross and Ross, *The Player*, 408.

27. Cohn, "Twenty Years Later, He's Still the Con Man," 70.

28. Keith D. Mano, "Robert Preston," *People*, June 28, 1982, 77.

29. Charles Leinenweber, interview by the author, July 2, 2021.

30. Death Certificate of Naomi Rea, 9695 (1931), State of California Department of Public Health. [Copy in possession of author].

31. Obituary of Naomi Rea. *Los Angeles Times*, August 30, 1931, 16.

32. Ross and Ross, *The Player*, 406.

33. "Lincoln High School," Wayback Machine, December 31, 2006, accessed September 5, 2021, http://www.stampstudio.com:80/earlyL.html.

34. Abraham Lincoln High School, The 1935 Lincolnian (Los Angeles, CA) 24.

35. James Reid, "Move Over Mr. Gable-Here's Robert Preston," *Motion Picture*, September 1939, 67.

36. Ross and Ross, *The Player*, 407.

37. Abraham Lincoln High School, The 1935 Lincolnian (Los Angeles, CA) 75.

38. Gilbert Millstein, "That Brassy Man Returns to Broadway as Poor Richard," *Saturday Evening Post*, October 17, 1964, 88.

39. Mano, "Robert Preston," 77.

40. Prideaux, "That Music Man Is Back on Broadway," 80.

41. Ross and Ross, *The Player*, 407.

42. Ross and Ross, *The Player*, 408.

43. Ross and Ross, *The Player*, 408.

44. Dick Mook, "Typhoon Has Something to Blow About." *Silver Screen*, May 1940, 42.

45. Diane Alexander, *Playhouse* (Los Angeles: Dorleac-MacLeish, 1984), 31.

46. Alexander, *Playhouse*, 49.

47. Alexander, *Playhouse*, 49.

48. Alexander, *Playhouse*, 53.

49. Vernon Young, "Masks and Faces," *Arcadia Tribune* (Arcadia, CA), July 9, 1936, 5.

50. Vernon Young, "Masks and Faces," *Arcadia Tribune* (Arcadia, CA), July 13, 1936, 3.

51. Alexander, *Playhouse*, 60.

52. Sidney Fields, "The Music Man is Back," *Daily News* (New York, NY), October 15, 1974, 36.

53. Hage, "Happiest Actor on Broadway," 114.

54. Charles Leinenweber, interview by the author, July 28, 2021.

55. Charles Leinenweber, interview by the author, July 2, 2021.

56. Lotys Benning, "The Happy Mrs. Preston," *Indianapolis Star*, February 16, 1958, 10.

57. Charles Leinenweber, interview by the author, July 2, 2021.

58. Charles Leinenweber, interview by the author, July 2, 2021.

59. Hage, "Happiest Actor on Broadway," 114.

60. Hage, "Happiest Actor on Broadway," 114.

61. "Roundabout Previews Lead to Film Contract." *Los Angeles Times*, August 28, 1938, S3-5.

62. Reid, "Move Over Mr. Gable," 69.

63. Alexander, *Playhouse*, 49.

64. Alexander, *Playhouse*, 49.

65. Robert Viagas, *I'm The Greatest Star: Broadway's Top Musical Legends From 1900 to Today* (New York: Applause Theatre and Cinema Books, 2009), 224.

66. Reid, "Move Over Mr. Gable," 69.

67. Ed Jonesboy, "Presenting Preston," *Hollywood*, October 1939, 38.

68. Reid, "Move Over Mr. Gable," 69.

69. James Robert Parish and Lennard DeCarl, *Hollywood Players: The Forties* (New Rochelle, NY: Arlington House, 1976), 584.

70. Parish and DeCarl, *Hollywood Players*, 584.

RIDING THE B TRAIN THROUGH TINSELTOWN

1. James Reid, "Move Over Mr. Gable–Here's Robert Preston," *Motion Picture*, September 1939, 71.
2. James Robert Parish and Lennard DeCarl, *Hollywood Players: The Forties* (New Rochelle, NY: Arlington House, 1976), 586.
3. William Peper, "Robert Preston," *Films in Review*, March 1968, 132.
4. Frank S. Nugent, "King of Alcatraz' Rules the Screen of the Criterion–The Palace Takes 'Time Out for Murder' At the Palace," *New York Times*, October 7, 1938, 21.
5. Robbin Coons, "Hollywood Sights and Sounds," *Gallup Independent* (Gallup, NM), January 20, 1939, 5.
6. Boyd Martin, "Robert Preston May Be a Star," *Courier Journal* (Louisville, KY), December 28, 1938, 12.
7. Barbara Cook and Tom Santopietro, *Then and Now: A Memoir* (New York: Harper, 2016), 103.
8. Ron Fassler, "My Favorite Actor," *Ron Fassler* (blog), June 8, 2018, https://medium.com/@ronfassler/my-favorite-actor-c2a97dcbd584.
9. Fassler, "My Favorite Actor," 2018.
10. Kirtley Baskette, "Heavenly Hard Guy," *Modern Screen*, January 1940, 26.
11. Ed Jonesboy, "Presenting Preston," *Hollywood*, October 1939, 39.
12. Anton Karl Kozlovic, "Cecil B. DeMille," Senses of Cinema, accessed March 4, 2021, http://sensesofcinema.com/2013/great-directors/cecil-b-demille/.
13. Charles Champlin, "Straight from the 'Music Man'," *Los Angeles Times*, February 27, 1983, 256.
14. Jonesboy, "Presenting Preston," 39.
15. Paul Harrison, "Robert Preston Finds Camera Better Audience than Some in Stock," *Muncie Evening Press*, November 26, 1938, 6.
16. Parish and DeCarl, *Hollywood Players*, 584.
17. Jonesboy, "Presenting Preston," 39.

18. Doug R. Tomlinson, *Actors on Acting for the Screen: Roles and Collaborations* (New York: Garland Publications, 1994), 689.

19. Jonesboy, "Presenting Preston," 39.

20. Peper, "Robert Preston," 135.

21. Scott Eyman, *Empire of Dreams: The Epic Life of Cecil B. DeMille* (New York: Simon & Schuster, 2013), 10.

22. Margaret McManus, "Preston–An Actor's Actor," *Baltimore Sun,* February 24, 1963, 49.

23. Eyman, *Empire of Dreams,* 336.

24. Eyman, *Empire of Dreams,* 334.

25. Joseph Hurley, "Robert Preston," *Films in Review,* August-September 1982, 398.

26. Hurley, "Robert Preston," 398.

27. Parish and DeCarl, *Hollywood Players,* 584.

28. "Troupe of Screen Stars Visits City on DeMille Union Pacific Special," *Indianapolis Star,* May 13, 1939, 11.

29. "Troupe of Screen Stars Visits City," 11.

30. May Mann, "The Real Truth about Robert Preston's Surprise Marriage," *Screenland,* February 1941, 20.

31. Mann, "The Real Truth," 20.

32. Mann, "The Real Truth," 21.

33. Harrison, "Robert Preston Finds Camera Better Audience," 6.

34. Harrison, "Robert Preston Finds Camera Better Audience," 6.

35. Reid, "Move Over Mr. Gable," 71.

36. William Wellman, *Wild Bill Wellman: Hollywood Rebel* (New York: Pantheon Books, 2015), 14.

37. Wellman, *Wild Bill Wellman,* 17.

38. Wellman, *Wild Bill Wellman,* 81.

39. John A. Gallagher, "Robert Preston talks Wild Bill Wellman," interview by John A. Gallagher, *Biograph Days, Biograph Nights,* YouTube, Uploaded by tvdays, 1981. https://youtu.be/fxSDn5fnzf4.

40. Reid, "Move Over Mr. Gable," 71.

41. Reid, "Move Over Mr. Gable," 71.

42. Lillian Ross and Helen Ross, *The Player: A Profile of an Art*, 2nd ed. (New York: Simon and Schuster, 1962), 411.

43. Wellman, *Wild Bill Wellman*, 348.

44. Wellman, *Wild Bill Wellman*, 348.

45. Gallagher, interview.

46. John C. Tibbetts and James M. Welsh, *American Classic Screen Interviews* (Lanham, MD: Scarecrow Press, Inc., 2010), 75.

47. Wellman, *Wild Bill Wellman*, 349.

48. Ida Zeitlin, "Lamour's in Love," *Modern Screen*, May 1940, 41.

49. Zeitlin, "Lamour's in Love," 41.

50. Zeitlin, "Lamour's in Love," 41.

51. James B. Gladstone, *The Man Who Seduced Hollywood: The Life and Loves of Greg Bautzer, Tinseltown's Most Powerful Lawyer* (Chicago: Chicago Review Press, 2013), 48.

52. Dorothy Lamour and Dick McInnes, *My Side of the Road* (Englewood Cliffs, NJ: Prentice-Hall, 1980), 34.

53. Lamour and Innes, *My Side of the Road*, 82.

54. Lamour and Innes, *My Side of the Road*, 83.

55. Lamour and Innes, *My Side of the Road*, 83.

56. Zeitlin, "Lamour's in Love," 41.

57. Zeitlin, "Lamour's in Love," 71.

58. Ross and Ross, *The Player*, 411.

59. Parish and DeCarl, *Hollywood Players*, 585.

60. Keith D. Mano, "Robert Preston," *People*, June 28, 1982, 77.

61. Ross and Ross, *The Player*, 411.

62. Sheilah Graham, "He Got Gate He Asked For," *Boston Globe*, January 4, 1948, 75.

63. Zeitlin, "Lamour's in Love," 72.

64. Zeitlin, "Lamour's in Love," 73.

65. "Difficulties Best Love," *South Bend Tribune*, February 16, 1940, 6.

66. "Hollywood Radio Whispers," *Radio and Television Mirror*, January 1940, 64.

67. Mann, "The Real Truth," 84.

68. Dorothy Lubou, "Stars Over Broadway," *Motion Picture*, April 1940, 16.

69. "Undergoes Knife," *Chicago Tribune*, March 10, 1940, 5.

70. Lamour and Innes, *My Side of the Road*, 102.

71. Jack Holland, "What's Ahead for Dorothy Lamour," *Motion Picture*, October 1940, 98.

72. "Dorothy Lamour Says Engagement Is Off," *Honolulu Star-Bulletin*, May 9, 1940, 1.

73. Graham, Sheilah, "Noes May Be A Yes," *Kansas City Star*, November 19, 1940, 8.

74. Rita Wilson, "Why Dorothy Lamour Lost Robert Preston," *Movie Mirror*, August 1940, 74.

75. Wilson, "Why Dorothy Lamour Lost Robert Preston," 74.

76. Louella O. Parsons, "Story Angers Dorothy Lamour," *Philadelphia Inquirer,* July 1, 1940, 20.

77. "Ann Sothern Says 'Don't Let Looks Throw You'," *Oakland Tribune* (Oakland, CA), July 11, 1940, 78.

78. "Ann Sothern Says," 78.

79. Mann, "The Real Truth," 85.

80. Mann, "The Real Truth," 85.

81. Lamour and Innes, *My Side of the Road*, 83.

82. Lamour and Innes, *My Side of the Road*, 84.

83. Suzanne Adelson, "It's Toujours Lamour–Dorothy Lamour Is Back On The Road Again at Age 67," *People*, February 22, 1982, 102.

84. Mann, "The Real Truth," 84.

85. Mann, "The Real Truth," 84.

86. Bosley Crowther, "Four New Films Open Here: 'Third Finger, Left Hand,' With Myrna Loy–A Dispatch From Reuters, 'Moon Over Burma' and 'Gallant Sons'," *New York Times,* December 12, 1940, 37.

87. "The Pied Piper of Broadway," *Time*, July 21, 1958, 44.

88. Hurley, "Robert Preston," 398.

89. Irving Wallace, "Heaven-Nevada," *Modern Screen*, March 1942, 100.

90. Wallace, "Heaven-Nevada," 100.

91. "Hollywood Couple Wed in Las Vegas," *Oakland Tribune* (Oakland, CA), November 9, 1940, 20.

92. Louella O. Parsons, "Bob Preston Elopes," *Miami Herald*, November 9, 1940, 5.

93. "The Pied Piper of Broadway," 44.

94. Edward J. Funk, *Behind the Door: The Real Story of Loretta Young* (Self-published, Edward Funk International, 2015), 9.

95. Peper, "Robert Preston," 133.

96. Ronald Bergan, "Loretta Young," *The Guardian* (London, England), August 14, 2000, 18.

97. "Paramount Sues Ameche in Movie-Role Agreement," *Detroit Free Press*, April 10, 1940, 1.

98. Rex Reed, "Ayn Rand: A Woman Under Siege," *Independent Press-Telegram* (Long Beach, CA), April 1, 1973, Southland Sunday 9.

99. "Inside Stuff," *Photoplay*, September 1941, 14.

100. Susan Meservey (Suzy), "Post about Catherine's Ectopic Pregnancy," Facebook, June 8, 2020. https://www.facebook.com/groups/robertpreston/. [Online account/comment deleted; author has a screenshot of the original post on file].

101. Susan Meservey (Suzy), "Post about Catherine's Ectopic Pregnancy," Facebook, June 8, 2020. https://www.facebook.com/groups/robertpreston/. [Online account/comment deleted; author has a screenshot of the original post on file].

102. Sheilah Graham, "Hollywood Today," *Times-Tribune* (Scranton, PA), December 16, 1947, 21.

103. Graham, "He Got Gate He Asked For," 75.

104. Crosby Day, "A Star Duo Is Born," *Orlando Sentinel*, April 27, 2003, 9.

105. Beverly Linet, *Ladd: The Life, the Legend, the Legacy of Alan Ladd* (New York: Berkley, 1980), 49.

106. Douglas W. Churchill. "Signing on the Lawn: Mr. Selznick Joins United Artists at Pickfair Meet–More Hollywoodiana," *New York Times*, October 14, 1941, 5.

107. Linet, *Ladd: The Life, the Legend, the Legacy of Alan Ladd*, 60.

108. Linet, *Ladd: The Life, the Legend, the Legacy of Alan Ladd*, 61.

109. Linet, *Ladd: The Life, the Legend, the Legacy of Alan Ladd*, 62.

110. Day, "A Star Duo Is Born," 9.

111. "Robert Preston Aids Yank Air Operations," *Evening Review* (East Liverpool, OH), April 14, 1944, 1.

112. "Robert Preston in Service as Private," *San Bernardino County Sun*, October 30, 1942, 1.

113. Tibbetts and Welsh, *American Classic Screen Interviews*, 75.

114. Tom Prideaux, "That Music Man Is Back on Broadway, Still Making Films and Aiming at Shakespeare," *People*, October 31, 1977, 80.

115. Weston East, "Gossip," *Screenland*, October 1943, 57.

116. "Robert Preston Coaches Flyers," *St. Joseph News Press* (St. Joseph, MO), April 14, 1944, 7.

117. "Back to Work," *The Record* (Hackensack, NJ), August 10, 1945, 5.

118. Tibbetts and Welsh, *American Classic Screen Interviews*, 73.

119. Parish and DeCarl, *Hollywood Players*, 587.

120. "Capt. Robert Preston Reports from France," *Pittsburgh Press*, July 22, 1945, 27.

121. "Capt. Robert Preston Reports from France," 27.

122. "Robert Preston Plays Lead as 418 Disembark," *Daily News* (New York, NY), August 10, 1945, 121.

123. "Robert Preston Resumes Career," *Pittsburgh Press*, Nov 9, 1945, 31.

124. Mano, "Robert Preston," 78.

125. Louella O. Parsons, "Preston Sues for New Studio Deal," *Pittsburgh Sun-Telegraph*, December 27, 1945, 10.

126. Parsons, "Preston Sues for New Studio Deal," 10.

127. Mano, "Robert Preston," 78.

128. John L. Scott, "Film Pair Balk Hex of Hollywood," *Los Angeles Times,* January 27, 1946, 25.

129. Scott, "Film Pair Balk Hex of Hollywood," 25.

130. Scott, "Film Pair Balk Hex of Hollywood," 27.

131. Scott, "Film Pair Balk Hex of Hollywood," 27.

132. Scott, "Film Pair Balk Hex of Hollywood," 27.

133. Hurley, "Robert Preston," 398.

134. Robert E. Morsberger, "That Hemingway Kind of Love: Macomber in the Movies,'" *Literature/Film Quarterly* 4, no. 1 (1976): 57, https://www.jstor.org/stable/43796004.

135. Bosley Crowther, "'The Macomber Affair' a Film with Joan Bennett, Gregory Peck and Robert Preston, Has Premiere at Globe Theatre," *New York Times*, April 21, 1947, 21.

136. Morsberger, "That Hemingway Kind of Love: Macomber in the Movies," 55.

137. Morsberger, "That Hemingway Kind of Love: Macomber in the Movies," 55.

138. Tibbetts and Welsh, *American Classic Screen Interviews,* 75.

139. Hurley, "Robert Preston," 398.

140. Hedda Hopper, "The Music Man Sounds Off," *Chicago Tribune,* February 4, 1962, 154.

141. Peper, "Robert Preston," 131.

142. "The Pied Piper of Broadway," 44.

143. Hurley, "Robert Preston," 398.

144. Parish and DeCarl, *Hollywood Players*, 587.

145. Peper, "Robert Preston," 135.

146. "Playhouse Holds Over 'Girl of the Golden West'," *Metropolitan Pasadena Star-News*, August 16, 1947, 8.

147. "The Pied Piper of Broadway," 44.

148. Hurley, "Robert Preston," 401.

149. Peper, "Robert Preston," 135.

150. Peper, "Robert Preston," 135.

151. "Requirements for Acting Told by Robert Preston," *Los Angeles Times*, December 21, 1955, 65.

152. "Requirements for Acting Told by Robert Preston," 65.

153. "Requirements for Acting Told by Robert Preston," 65.

154. Gilbert Millstein, "That Brassy Man Returns to Broadway as Poor Richard," *Saturday Evening Post*, October 17, 1964, 90.

155. Lamour and Innes, *My Side of the Road*, 105.

156. "Meservey Signed," *Daily News* (New York, NY), February 1, 1947, 166.

157. Linet, *Ladd: The Life, the Legend, the Legacy of Alan Ladd*, 118.

158. Lamour and Innes, *My Side of the Road*, 137.

159. "Robert Preston's False Tooth in Way During Scene," *Valley Times* (North Hollywood, CA), December 23, 1947, 12.

160. Peper, "Robert Preston," 134.

161. Tibbetts and Welsh, *American Classic Screen Interviews*, 74.

162. Peper, "Robert Preston," 134.

163. Anthony Slide and Charles Brackett, *It's the Pictures That Got Small: Charles Brackett on Billy Wilder and Hollywood's Golden Age*, ed. Anthony Slide (New York: Columbia University Press, 2014), 318.

164. Peper, "Robert Preston," 134.

165. Hurley, "Robert Preston," 399.

166. Hugh Dixon, "The Hollywood Wash," *Pittsburgh Post-Gazette*, December 15, 1947, 17.

167. "Preston Heads East," *Democrat and Chronicle* (Rochester, NY), December 7, 1947, 63.

168. Graham, "He Got Gate He Asked For," 75.

169. Peper, "Robert Preston," 134.

170. Robert LaGuardia and Gene Arceri, "How a Star Saw Herself," *Chicago Tribune*, June 23, 1985, Tempo-5.

171. Sumiko Higashi, "Susan Hayward," in *Stars, Fans, and Consumption in the 1950s: Reading Photoplay* (New York: Palgrave Macmillan, 2014), 157.

172. Higashi, "Susan Hayward," 60.

173. Higashi, "Susan Hayward," 62.

174. LaGuardia and Arceri, "How A Star Saw Herself," 5.

175. Prideaux, "That Music Man Is Back on Broadway," 79.

176. Ted Thackrey, "'Music Man' Robert Preston Dies of Cancer," *Los Angeles Times*, March 22, 1987, 28.

177. Thackrey, "'Music Man' Robert Preston Dies of Cancer," 28.

178. Arnold Markoe, Kenneth T. Jackson, and Karen Markoe. *The Scribner Encyclopedia of American Lives*. Vol. Two. (New York: C. Scribner's Sons, 2002), 332.

BROADWAY FEVER

1. "4 Actors Named to Guild Board," *Valley Times* (North Hollywood, CA), August 10, 1950, 17.

2. Margaret McManus, "Preston-An Actor's Actor," *Baltimore Sun*, February 24, 1963, 49.

3. Edwin Schallert, "Preston Incorporated for Baseball Feature; Mary Wickes Returns," *Los Angeles Times*, January 29, 1949, 9.

4. Schallert, "Preston Incorporated for Baseball Feature," 9.

5. Walter Ames, "Good TV Reception Required in Home Sale," *Los Angeles Times*, September 1, 1950, 18.

6. Keith D. Mano, "Robert Preston," *People*, June 28, 1982, 78.

7. Louella Parsons, "Robert Preston-The Music Man," *San Francisco Examiner*, August 20, 1961, 18.

8. Mano, "Robert Preston," 79.

9. Tom Prideaux, "That Music Man Is Back on Broadway, Still Making Films and Aiming at Shakespeare," *People*, October 31, 1977, 79.

10. James Robert Parish and Lennard DeCarl, *Hollywood Players: The Forties* (New Rochelle, NY: Arlington House, 1976), 589.
11. Sheilah Graham, "Robert Preston Plans 2 Films," *The Spokesman-Review* (Spokane, WA), December 25, 1950, 15.
12. Graham, "Robert Preston Plans 2 Films," 15.
13. William Peper, "Robert Preston," *Films in Review*, March 1968, 136.
14. Joseph Hurley, "Robert Preston," *Films in Review*, August-September 1982, 401.
15. Lillian Ross and Helen Ross, *The Player: A Profile of an Art*, 2nd ed. (New York: Simon and Schuster, 1962), 413.
16. John Chapman, "Mainly About Theater: Run of the Mill Actors Needed," *Daily News*, (New York, NY), June 9, 1951, 197.
17. Hurley, "Robert Preston," 401.
18. Hurley, "Robert Preston," 401.
19. Parsons, "Robert Preston - The Music Man," 18.
20. Parsons, "Robert Preston - The Music Man," 18.
21. Louella O. Parsons, "Dore Schary Prepares to Screen 'Mr. Congressman'," *San Francisco Examiner*, May 2, 1951, 23.
22. Roderick Mann, "Old Man River City, He Just Keeps Rollin' Along," *Los Angeles Times*, March 16, 1982, 73.
23. Ross and Ross, "Robert Preston," 414.
24. Louis Sheaffer, "'20th Century' Still Gets There, but with Lighter Cargo of Laughs," *Brooklyn Daily Eagle*, June 6, 1951, 12.
25. Prideaux, "That Music Man Is Back on Broadway," 80.
26. Parish and DeCarl, *Hollywood Players*, 589.
27. Louis Sheaffer, "Curtain Time," *Brooklyn Daily Eagle*, June 28, 1951, 4.
28. Parish and DeCarl, *Hollywood Players*, 589.
29. Martha McHatton, "Film First Subs for Ford Theater," *Indianapolis News*, July 6, 1951, 25.
30. Paul Jones, "Martha Scott Starts in TeeVee Premiere," *Atlanta Constitution*, July 13, 1951, 31.

31. Peggy Lee, *Miss Peggy Lee: An Autobiography* (New York: Donald I. Fine, Inc., 1989), 140.

32. Lee, *Miss Peggy Lee: An Autobiography*, 140.

33. James Gavin, *Is That All There Is?: The Strange Life of Peggy Lee* (New York: Atria Paperback, 2014), 18.

34. George Jacobs and William Stadiem, *Mr. S: My Life with Frank Sinatra* (New York: Harper Entertainment, 2004) , 75.

35. Gavin, *Is That All There Is?: The Strange Life of Peggy Lee*, 450.

36. Jacobs and Stadiem, *Mr. S: My Life with Frank Sinatra*, 68.

37. Gavin, *Is That All There Is?: The Strange Life of Peggy Lee*, 127.

38. Gavin, *Is That All There Is?: The Strange Life of Peggy Lee*, 106.

39. Lee, *Miss Peggy Lee: An Autobiography*, 145.

40. "Sings the Blues and Wins Divorce," *Daily News* (New York, NY), May 16, 1951, A-7.

41. Dorothy Kilgallen, "Voice of Broadway," *The Record-Angus* (Greenville, PA), May 28, 1951, 7.

42. Lee, *Miss Peggy Lee: An Autobiography*, 145.

43. Lee, *Miss Peggy Lee: An Autobiography*, 146.

44. Louella O. Parsons, "Hollywood," *Philadelphia Inquirer*, May 28, 1951, 23.

45. Gavin, *Is That All There Is?: The Strange Life of Peggy Lee*,123.

46. Gavin, *Is That All There Is?: The Strange Life of Peggy Lee*,124.

47. Lee, *Miss Peggy Lee: An Autobiography*, 145.

48. Earl Wilson, "Joyce Only Wanted a Career," *The Times Recorder* (Zanesville, OH), July 20, 1951, 4.

49. Lee, *Miss Peggy Lee: An Autobiography*, 146.

50. Louella O. Parsons, "Big Musical Lineup Planned at RKO," *San Francisco Examiner*, July 31, 1951, 13.

51. "Robert Preston Talks Divorce," *Valley Times* (North Hollywood, CA), August 11, 1951, 3.

52. Dorothy Kilgallen, "Broadway," *Star-Gazette* (Elmira, NY), August 16, 1951, 34.

53. Dorothy Kilgallen, "Broadway," *Star-Gazette* (Elmira, NY), August 22, 1951, 16.

54. Lee, *Miss Peggy Lee: An Autobiography*, 146.

55. Gavin, *Is That All There Is?: The Strange Life of Peggy Lee,*124.

56. "Roy Feltus, 77, Longtime Circus Figure, is Dead," *Indianapolis News,* February 23, 1954, 6.

57. "Robert Preston Arriving for Roosevelt Play," *Miami News,* August 26, 1951, 27.

58. Harrison Carroll, "Behind the Scenes in Hollywood," *Lancaster Eagle-Gazette* (Lancaster, OH), September 11, 1951, 6.

59. "Letter From Betty," *Miami News,* September 3, 1951, 4.

60. Janice Pape, "Preston 'Swooney Guy' Janice Finds in Talk," *Miami News,* September 7, 1951, 25.

61. Pape, "Preston 'Swooney Guy,'" 25.

62. Carroll, "Behind the Scenes in Hollywood," 6.

63. Herb Rau, "Detective Story Well Done," *Miami News,* September 5, 1951, 9.

64. Lee, *Miss Peggy Lee: An Autobiography*, 146.

65. Lee, *Miss Peggy Lee: An Autobiography*, 146.

66. Dorothy Kilgallen, "On Broadway," *Pittsburgh Post-Gazette,* September 7, 1951, 29.

67. Al Salerno, "Brooklyn and Broadway Night Life," *Brooklyn Daily Eagle,* October 14, 1951, 31.

68. Hedda Hopper, "Hollywood," *Daily News,* October 31, 1951, 44.

69. Louella O. Parsons, "Hollywood," *Bangor Daily News,* November 8, 1951, 25.

70. Ed Sullivan, "Toast of the Town," *The Evening Sun* (Baltimore, MD), December 5, 1951, 41.

71. Ed Sullivan, "Toast of the Town," *The Evening Sun* (Baltimore, MD), December 27, 1951, 19.

72. "Screen Actor Robert Preston Charges Fighter in Beating," *Knoxville News-Sentinel,* February 1, 1952, 11.

73. "Screen Actor Robert Preston Charges Fighter in Beating," 11.

74. "Robert Preston Charges Beating to NY Fighter," *Fresno Bee* (Fresno, CA), January 31, 1952, 1.

75. "Robert Preston Tells Court of Beating," *Los Angeles Times*, February 1, 1952, 55.

76. "Robert Preston Tells Court of Beating," 55.

77. "Film Luminary Tells Judge All About New York Beating," *Santa Maria Times* (Santa Maria, CA), February 1, 1952, 5.

78. "Nugent Back in 'Male Animal,' ANTA Schedules 'Four Saints'," *Daily News* (New York, NY), February 29, 1952, 95.

79. Louis Sheaffer, "'Male Animal' Delightful Start for City Center Comedy Series," *Brooklyn Daily Eagle*, May 1, 1952, 10.

80. Hurley, "Robert Preston," 401.

81. Hurley, "Robert Preston," 401.

82. Earl Wilson, "Earl Wilson's Column," *San Francisco Examiner*, May 8, 1952, 22.

83. Gavin, *Is That All There Is?: The Strange Life of Peggy Lee*, 138.

84. Gavin, *Is That All There Is?: The Strange Life of Peggy Lee*, 138.

85. Jack Holland, "The Girl with the Sexy Voice," *Screenland*, February 1953, 41.

86. Holland, "The Girl with the Sexy Voice," 41.

87. Gavin, *Is That All There Is?: The Strange Life of Peggy Lee*, 139.

88. "Films Had No Role to Lure 'Male Animal's' Bob Preston," *Brooklyn Daily Eagle*, July 27, 1952, 25.

89. "Films Had No Role to Lure 'Male Animal's' Bob Preston," 25.

90. "Films Had No Role to Lure 'Male Animal's' Bob Preston," 25.

91. "Films Had No Role to Lure 'Male Animal's' Bob Preston," 25.

92. "Ebsen Pinch Hits in 'Male Animal'," *Daily News* (New York, NY), December 13, 1952, 255.

93. Dorothy Kilgallen, "Top Television Comic is Drinking Far Too Much," *Muncie Evening Press*, June 10, 1952, 9.

94. Ed Sullivan, "Little Old New York," *Pittsburgh Press,* July 18, 1952, 11.

95. "Films Had No Role to Lure 'Male Animal's' Bob Preston," 25.

96. John Gardiner, "Robert Preston Prefers Footlights to Studio Kliegs," *Windsor Star* (Ontario, Canada), December 24, 1953, 5.

97. Dorothy Kilgallen, "Broadway," *Star-Gazette* (Elmira, NY), August 12, 1952, 28.

98. Kilgallen, "Broadway," 28.

99. Gavin, *Is That All There Is?: The Strange Life of Peggy Lee,*124.

100. Bosley Crowther, "At the 52nd Street Trans-Lux," *New York Times,* January 14, 1953, 27.

101. Dorothy Masters, "Preston's Not the Type to be Movie-Typed," *Daily News* (New York, NY), March 1, 1953, 159.

102. Masters, "Preston's Not the Type to be Movie-Typed," 159.

103. Norris Randolph, "Jelke? Jelke? Wasn't He the Guy Who?," *Esquire Magazine,* April 1967, 137.

104. Richard Maney, "Kicking it Around Led Them to Men of Distinction," *Brooklyn Daily Eagle,* April 26, 1953, 29.

105. "'Misalliance' to Reopen Tonight; Lead for Preston," *Daily News* (New York, NY), March 6, 1953, 191.

106. Louis Shaeffer, "Men of Distinction Takes Comic View of Vice Racket," *Brooklyn Daily Eagle,* May 1, 1953, 8.

107. John Chapman, "Men of Distinction a Witless and Seedy Comedy About a Vice Case," *Daily News* (New York, NY), May 1, 1953, 459.

108. Louis Calta, "Condon's 1st Play to Close Tonight," *New York Times,* May 2, 1953, 12.

109. Morrie Gelman, "Interview with Angela Lansbury," *Television Academy Foundation,* September 15, 1998, https://interviews.televisionacademy.com/interviews/angela-lansbury.

110. Gelman, "Interview with Angela Lansbury," September 15, 1998.

111. Gelman, "Interview with Angela Lansbury," September 15, 1998.

112. "Robert Preston, Catherine Craig to Perform at Myrtle Beach," *Charlotte Observer,* May 11, 1953, 34.

113. Gardiner, "Robert Preston Prefers Footlights to Studio Kliegs," 5.

114. Gardiner, "Robert Preston Prefers Footlights to Studio Kliegs," 5.

115. Gardiner, "Robert Preston Prefers Footlights to Studio Kliegs," 5.

116. Brooks Atkinson, "*His and Hers* written by the Kanins, Stars Celeste Holm and Robert Preston," *New York Times*, January 8, 1954, 18.

117. Atkinson, "*His and Hers* written by the Kanins," 18.

118. Atkinson, "*His and Hers* written by the Kanins," 18.

119. "New Plays in Manhattan," *Time*, April 19, 1954, 86.

120. Brooks Atkinson, "Magic and Loss in Debut at the Booth," *New York Times*, April 10, 1954, Theater-10.

121. "Storm Routs Tent Audience," *Philadelphia Inquirer*, July 15, 1954, 13.

122. Brooks Atkinson, "Shulman-Smith Comedy Opens at Longacre," *New York Times*. October 14, 1954, 37.

123. Atkinson, "Shulman-Smith Comedy Opens at Longacre," 37.

124. Atkinson, "Shulman-Smith Comedy Opens at Longacre," 37.

125. "The Tender Trap," *Time*, October 25, 1954, 41.

126. Bob Thomas, "Robert Preston is Back in Hollywood," *News-Pilot* (San Pedro, CA), January 29, 1960, 2.

127. Thomas, "Robert Preston is Back in Hollywood," 2.

128. Jack Shaffer, "The Time Your Favorite Star Almost Blew His Top," *Modern Screen*, March 1957, 28.

129. Bosley Crowther, "'Last Frontier' Vague on Who's Good or Bad," *New York Times*, December 8, 1955, 45.

130. Thomas, "Robert Preston is Back in Hollywood," 2.

131. William Glover, "'Music Man' Carries 2 Show Veterans to Broadway," *Democrat and Chronicle* (Rochester, NY), December 15, 1957, 103.

132. Meredith Willson, *But He Doesn't Know the Territory: The Making of Meredith Willson's The Music Man* (Minneapolis: University of Minnesota Press, 2009), 111.

133. Sam Zolotow, "'Janus' Role Goes to Miss Sullavan," *New York Times*, May 20, 1955, 29.

134. Michael D. Rinella, *Margaret Sullavan: The Life and Career of a Reluctant Star* (Jefferson, NC: McFarland & Company, Inc., 2019), 62.

135. Harold J. Kennedy, *No Pickle, No Performance: An Irreverent Theatrical Excursion from Tallulah to Travolta* (Garden City, NJ: Doubleday & Company, Inc., 1978), 63.

136. Philip F. Crosland, "Janus," *The News-Journal* (Wilmington, DE), October 20, 1955, 55.

137. Crosland, "Janus," 55.

138. Henry T. Murdock, "'Janus' Tickling Comedy, Opens at Forrest," *Philadelphia Inquirer*, October 25, 1955, 23.

139. "Comedy Gets Mixed N.Y. Notices," *Los Angeles Evening Citizen News*, November 29, 1955, 16.

140. Brooks Atkinson, "The Theatre: 'Janus'," *New York Times*, November 25, 1955, 37.

141. Rinella, *Margaret Sullavan: The Life and Career of a Reluctant Star,* 209.

142. Kennedy, *No Pickle, No Performance,* 230.

143. William Goldman, *The Season: A Candid Look at Broadway* (New York: Limelight Editions, 2000), 146.

144. Mano, "Robert Preston," 78.

145. Mano, "Robert Preston," 78.

146. Rinella, *Margaret Sullavan: The Life and Career of a Reluctant Star,* 209.

147. Joan Hanauer, "Impulse Returns Claudette Colbert to Broadway," *Democrat and Chronicle* (Rochester, NY), April 15, 1956, 1.

148. Leonard Lyons, "Lyons Den," *Post-Standard* (Syracuse, NY), April 5, 1956, 33.

149. Hanauer, "Impulse Returns Claudette Colbert to Broadway," 1.

150. Lyons, "Lyons Den," 33.

151. Kennedy, *No Pickle, No Performance,* 61.

152. "Margaret Sullavan Dead; Overdose of Pills is Hinted," *New York Times*, January 2, 1960, 1.

153. David Richards, "The Music Man Has Far More Than One Tune in Him," *Democrat and Chronicle* (Rochester, NY), September 2, 1984, 1-D.

154. John Chapman, "Claudette Colbert Returns," *Daily News* (New York, NY), April 11, 1956, 56.

155. Hedda Hopper, "Hollywood," *Daily News* (New York, NY), April 21, 1956, 18.

156. Goldman, *The Season: A Candid Look at Broadway*, 17.

157. Goldman, *The Season: A Candid Look at Broadway*, 17.

158. Rev. Dr. E. E. Jackson, Jr., "Hero Tales," *Pittsburgh Sun-Telegraph*, March 17, 1956, 18.

159. Douglas Watt, "Let's Look at the Records," *Daily News* (New York, NY), July 17 1955, 12.

160. "Robert Preston in 'Bon Voyage'," *Daily News*, September 7, 1956, 48.

161. Henry Murdock, "'Hidden River' at Walnut," *Philadelphia Inquirer*, January 8, 1957, 10.

162. Arnold Zeitlin, "West Philadelphia's Gabel," *Philadelphia Inquirer*, March 31, 1957, 24.

163. Zeitlin, "West Philadelphia's Gabel," 24.

164. John Gassner, "Broadway in Review," *Educational Theatre Journal* 9, no. 2 (May 1957): 116.

165. John Mosedale, "Legitimate Theater's New Problem is 'Hit or Miss' Philosophy," *St. Louis Globe-Democrat*, March 24, 1957, 74.

166. Harry Harris, "Patti Page Flops as Actress," *Philadelphia Inquirer*, June 20, 1957, 20.

THE HAPPIEST ACTOR ON BROADWAY

1. Charles Leinenweber, interview by the author, July 28, 2021.

2. Albin Krebs, "Kermit Bloomgarden, Producer of Many Outstanding Plays, Dead," *New York Times*, September 21, 1976, 40.

3. Meredith Willson, *But He Doesn't Know the Territory: The Making of Meredith Willson's The Music Man* (Minneapolis: University of Minnesota Press, 2009), 110.

4. "Pied Piper of Broadway," *Time*, July 21, 1958, 45.

5. David Richards, "The Music Man Has Far More Than One Tune in Him," *Democrat and Chronicle* (Rochester, NY), September 2, 1984, 19-D.

6. Willson, *But He Doesn't Know the Territory*, 110.

7. "Pied Piper of Broadway," 45.

8. Willson, *But He Doesn't Know the Territory*, 111.

9. Willson, *But He Doesn't Know the Territory*, 118.

10. Willson, *But He Doesn't Know the Territory*, 118.

11. Lillian Ross and Helen Ross, *The Player: A Profile of an Art*, 2nd ed. (New York: Simon and Schuster, 1962) 414.

12. Willson, *But He Doesn't Know the Territory*, 118.

13. Willson, *But He Doesn't Know the Territory*, 119.

14. Willson, *But He Doesn't Know the Territory*, 119.

15. "Grist Mill has Inherit the Wind," *The Item of Millburn and Short Hills*, July 11, 1957, 8.

16. "Willson to Stage His Own Musical," *Los Angeles Times*, August 16, 1957, 2.

17. Leonard Lyons, "It Was Safer to Wear Gems," *Morning Call* (Allentown, PA), September 23, 1957, 23.

18. Barbara Cook and Tom Santopietro, *Then and Now: A Memoir* (New York: Harper, 2016), 113.

19. "'Music Man' Says Secret to Success: His Shoes," *Valley Times* (North Hollywood, CA), March 27,1962, 18.

20. "How the Music Man (Robert Preston) Met Houdini's Ghost (Patrick Culliton)," Houdinisghost.com, accessed February 1, 2022, http://www.houdinisghost.com/robertpreston.html.

21. Willson, *But He Doesn't Know the Territory*, 151.

22. Willson, *But He Doesn't Know the Territory*, 153.

23. Henry Murdock, "Happy Premier at Shubert," *Philadelphia Inquirer*, November 19, 1957, 25.

24. Murdock, "Happy Premier at Shubert," 25.

25. George S. Hage, "Happiest Actor on Broadway," *Saturday Evening Post*, December 6, 1958, 113.

26. Hage, "Happiest Actor on Broadway," 113.

27. Hage, "Happiest Actor on Broadway," 113.

28. William Goldman, *The Season: A Candid Look at Broadway* (New York: Limelight Editions, 2000), 17.

29. Goldman, *The Season: A Candid Look at Broadway*, 18.

30. Willson, *But He Doesn't Know the Territory*, 176.

31. Willson, *But He Doesn't Know the Territory*, 176.

32. Willson, *But He Doesn't Know the Territory*, 178.

33. Willson, *But He Doesn't Know the Territory*, 179.

34. Brooks Atkinson, "Music Man," *New York Times*, December 20, 1957, 31.

35. "Pied Piper of Broadway," 43.

36. Hage, "Happiest Actor on Broadway," 112.

37. "Pied Piper of Broadway," 43.

38. Ron Miller, "Robert Preston," in *You Ain't Heard Nothin' Yet: Interviews with Stars from Hollywood's Golden Era* (Lexington, KY: University Press of Kentucky, 2017), 57-61.

39. Richards, "The Music Man Has Far More Than One Tune in Him," 67.

40. Jim Bishop, "Happiest Actor on Broadway," *St. Louis Post-Dispatch*, October 11, 1959, 97.

41. Willson, *But He Doesn't Know the Territory*, 119.

42. Willson, *But He Doesn't Know the Territory*. 119.

43. Hage, "Happiest Actor on Broadway," 113.

44. Joseph Hurley "Robert Preston," *Films in Review*, August-September 1982, 403.

45. Emery Wister, "Robert Preston Talks About 'The Music Man," *Charlotte News*, November 23, 1961, 29.

46. Hage, "Happiest Actor on Broadway," 113.

47. Hage, "Happiest Actor on Broadway," 113.

48. Dennis McGovern and Deborah Grace Winer, *Sing out, Louise! - 150 Broadway Musical Stars Remember 50 Years* (New York: Schirmer Books, 1996), 180.
49. Michael Riedel and Susan Haskins, "Interview with Barbara Cook," *Theater Talk*, YouTube, uploaded by Theater Talk Archive, April 21, 2000. https://www.youtube.com/watch?v=DPF5R5iTwQ0.
50. Cook and Santopietro, *Then and Now: A Memoir*, 103.
51. Cook and Santopietro, *Then and Now: A Memoir*, 103.
52. Cook and Santopietro, *Then and Now: A Memoir*, 111.
53. Hage, "Happiest Actor on Broadway," 113.
54. Hage, "Happiest Actor on Broadway," 113.
55. Robert W. Schneider and Kevin David Thomas, "Interview with Patti Mariano, Golden Age Actress," *Behind the Curtain: Broadway's Living Legends*, Broadway Podcast Network, October 1, 2018, podcast audio, https://broadwaypodcastnetwork.com/behind-the-curtain/140-patti-mariano-golden-age-child-actress/.
56. Cook and Santopietro, *Then and Now: A Memoir*, 105.
57. Cook and Santopietro, *Then and Now: A Memoir*, 111.
58. Cook and Santopietro, *Then and Now: A Memoir*, 108.
59. Cook and Santopietro, *Then and Now: A Memoir*, 112.
60. Lotys Benning Stewart, "The Happy Mrs. Preston," *Indianapolis Star*, February 16, 1958, 14.
61. Hage, "Happiest Actor on Broadway," 114.
62. Cook and Santopietro, *Then and Now: A Memoir*, 112.
63. Cindy Adams, "Cindy says . . . ," *Brooklyn Daily*, October 2, 1959, 8.
64. Stewart, "The Happy Mrs. Preston," 14.
65. Stewart, "The Happy Mrs. Preston," 10.
66. Keith D. Mano, "Robert Preston," *People*, June 28, 1982, 78.
67. Mano, "Robert Preston," 78.
68. Stewart, "The Happy Mrs. Preston," 14
69. Stewart, "The Happy Mrs. Preston," 10.

70. Stewart, "The Happy Mrs. Preston," 14.

71. Stewart, "The Happy Mrs. Preston," 14.

72. Stewart, "The Happy Mrs. Preston," 10.

73. Stewart, "The Happy Mrs. Preston," 14.

74. "Pied Piper of Broadway," 42.

75. "Pied Piper of Broadway," 42.

76. Frankie Groaner, "See Selves as 'Music Man'," *Daily News* (New York, NY), March 27, 1958, 7.

77. John De Lorenzi, "TV Plus Record Albums Give Broadway Performer Nation-Wide Popularity," *Daily News* (Murfreesboro, TN), September 9, 1958, 2.

78. De Lorenzi, "TV Plus Record Albums Give Broadway Performer Nation-Wide Popularity," 2.

79. Ward Morehouse, "Bob Preston's a Rare Actor – He's Happy," *Long Island Star-Journal*, June 30, 1959, 5.

80. McGovern and Winer, *Sing out, Louise!*, 180.

81. Morehouse, "Bob Preston's a Rare Actor – He's Happy," 5.

82. Morehouse, "Bob Preston's a Rare Actor – He's Happy," 5.

83. Margaret McManus, "Preston – An Actor's Actor," *Baltimore Sun*, February 24, 1963, 49.

84. Vivian Brown, "Robert Preston at Home," *The Progress*, July 25, 1964, 18.

85. Margaret McManus, "Robert Preston Slated to Star in TV's 'Bells of St. Mary's'," *Asbury Park Press* (Asbury Park, NJ), October 24, 1959, 11.

86. Morehouse, "Bob Preston's a Rare Actor - He's Happy," 5.

87. Bishop, "Happiest Actor on Broadway," 97.

88. Brown, "Robert Preston at Home," 18.

89. McManus, "Preston – An Actor's Actor," 49.

90. Charles Leinenweber, interview by the author, July 2, 2021.

91. Charles Leinenweber, interview by the author, July 2, 2021.

92. McManus, "Robert Preston Slated to Star in TV's 'Bells of St. Mary's'," 11.

93. Bishop, "Happiest Actor on Broadway," 97.

94. "Preston Set to Star in 'Stairs' Film," *Valley Times* (North Hollywood, CA), December 4, 1959, 17.

95. Bob Thomas, "Robert Preston Is Back in Hollywood," *News-Pilot* (San Pedro, CA), January 29, 1960, 2.

96. Dick Williams, "Films' New Realism Astounds Preston," *Mirror News* (Los Angeles, CA), February 16, 1960, 21.

97. "New Music Man," *Independent* (Long Beach, CA), December 18, 1959, 1.

98. Leanne Wood, "'Persuasive Americanism'?: The Reactionary Promotion and Reception of Warner Bros. The Music Man (1962)," *American Music* 31, no 4: (Winter 2013): 480.

99. Thomas, "Robert Preston Is Back in Hollywood," 2.

100. David C. Tucker, *Eve Arden: A Chronicle of All Film, Television, Radio and Stage Performances* (Jefferson, NC: McFarland & Company, Inc., 2012), 128.

101. Kate Cameron, "'Music Man' Back to Films," *Daily News* (New York, NY), September 11, 1960, 28.

102. "Studios Rush to Beat Actor Strike Deadline," *Motion Picture Daily*, March 1, 1960, 7.

103. "Studios Rush to Beat Actor Strike Deadline," 7.

104. "Studios Rush to Beat Actor Strike Deadline," 7.

105. Richard F. Shepard, "Preston Stars in 'Years Ago'," *New York Times*, April 22, 1960, 61.

106. Val Adams, "Ruth Gordon Play to Be On TV Again," *New York Times*, March 28, 1960, 55.

107. "Plays Reopen on Broadway as Strike Ends," *Pasadena Independent*, June 14, 1960, 4.

108. "Plays Reopen on Broadway as Strike Ends," 4.

109. "The Dark at the Top of The Stairs," *Film Bulletin*, September 19, 1960, 18.

110. "The Dark at the Top of The Stairs," *Variety*, December 31, 1959, https://variety.com/1959/film/reviews/the-dark-at-the-top-of-the-stairs-1200419571/.

111. "Dark At the Top of the Stairs," *Motion Picture Daily*, September 14, 1960, 3.

112. "Bluer Movies, Not-So-Blue Noses," *Life*, December 5, 1960, 46.

113. Bosley Crowther, "Screen: Vulgarized Inge," *New York Times*, September 23, 1960, 33.

114. Hedda Hopper, "Bob Preston Sought for 'Music Man' Here," *Los Angeles Times*, January 26, 1960, 16.

115. Vernon Scott, "It's Show Biz," *Daily Record*, May 12, 1961, 11.

116. Erskine Johnson, "'Little Things' Still 'Music Man' Secret," *Progress-Bulletin* (Pomona, CA), May 15, 1961, 9.

117. Shirley Jones and Wendy Leigh, *Shirley Jones: A Memoir* (New York: Gallery Books, 2013), 128.

118. Nancy Nelson and Cary Grant, *Evenings with Cary Grant: Recollections in His Own Words and by Those Who Knew Him Best* (New York: William Morrow, 1991), 270.

119. James Robert Parish and Lennard DeCarl, *Hollywood Players: The Forties* (New Rochelle, NY: Arlington House, 1976), 591.

120. Erskine Johnson, "'Little Things' Still 'Music Man' Secret," 9.

121. Peter S. Haigh, "Hey Preston!," *Film Review*, September 1962, 6.

122. Haigh, "Hey Preston!," 6.

123. Wood, "Persuasive Americanism'?," 480.

124. Production Budget, February 28, 1961, Folder 1410, Warner Brothers archive. University of Southern California, Los Angeles, CA.

125. Dick Williams, "Returns to Life for 'Music Man'," *Los Angeles Mirror*, June 19, 1961, 13.

126. Bob Thomas, "Preston Wins Music Man Role," *Fresno Bee* (Fresno, CA), May 5, 1961, 15.

127. Steven Smith, "The Lost Art of Evocative Film Titles," *Los Angeles Times*, March 30, 1997, Calendar 44.

128. Jones and Leigh, *Shirley Jones: A Memoir*, 129.

129. Jones and Leigh, *Shirley Jones: A Memoir*, 130.

130. Jones and Leigh, *Shirley Jones: A Memoir*, 131.

131. Jones and Leigh, *Shirley Jones: A Memoir*, 131.

132. Jones and Leigh, *Shirley Jones: A Memoir*, 132.

133. Sidney Skolsky, "Preston Leaves 'Music Man'," *Los Angeles Evening Citizen News*, August 10, 1961, 12.

134. Haigh, "Hey Preston!," 6.

135. Robert Preston, vocalist, "Chicken Fat" by Meredith Willson, recorded 1962, Capitol Records, vinyl LP.

136. Robert Elisberg, "Go, You Chicken Fat, Go!," *Elisberg Industries* (blog), April 15, 2013. http://www.elisbergindustries.com/blog/ go-you-chicken-fat-go.

137. Elisberg, "Go, You Chicken Fat, Go!," 2013.

138. Skolsky, "Preston Leaves Music Man," 12.

ROLLER COASTER

1. Hedda Hopper, "Robert Preston Has a Gambler's Attitude on Life," *Kansas City Star*, February 25, 1962, 89.

2. "MGM Making 2 Cinerama Films," *Evening Vanguard* (Venice, CA), August 7, 1961, 7.

3. Earl Wilson, "'Rifleman' Shooting at Minow; Connors Asks How He Stands," *Los Angeles Mirror*, October 10, 1961, 15.

4. Erskine Johnson, "MGM Turns Cinerama Camera on Old West," *Progress-Bulletin* (Pomona, CA), October 26, 1961, S3-7.

5. Johnson, "MGM Turns Cinerama Camera on Old West," S3-7.

6. Jim Murray, "Bob Plays Through," *Los Angeles Times*, January 10, 1963, Section 3-2.

7. Bob Thomas, "Episodic 'West' In Can at Last; It's an Epic," *Valley Times* (North Hollywood, CA), June 5, 1962, 8.

8. Thomas, "Episodic 'West' In Can at Last," 8.

9. Bosley Crowther, "'How the West was Won,' Familiar Saga," *New York Times*, April 1, 1963, 53.

10. Bob Thomas, "'How West Was Won' Termed Hit Here After London, Paris," *San Bernardino County Sun*, Feb 28, 1963, C-9.

11. Jerry Gaghan, "'Pancho Villa' Takes Town," *Philadelphia Daily News*, January 18, 1962, 41.

12. Stuart Ostrow, *Present at the Creation, Leaping in the Dark, and Going against the Grain: 1776, Pippin, M. Butterfly, La bête, & Other Broadway Adventures* (New York: Applause Theatre & Cinema Books, 2006), 18.

13. Ostrow, *Present at the Creation*, 18.

14. Aaron Netsky, "When Robert Preston Played Pancho Villa," *Onstage Blog* (blog), January 2016, www.onstageblog.com/columns/2016/1/7/when-robert-preston-played-pancho-villa.

15. Gaghan, "Pancho Villa Takes Town," 41.

16. "Robert Preston in New Musical," *Record-Journal* (Meriden, CT), January 20, 1962, 8.

17. Ostrow, *Present at the Creation*, 18.

18. Fred Russell, "Gossip of the Rialto," *Bridgeport Post* (Bridgeport, CT), February 11, 1962, 51.

19. Russell, "Gossip of the Rialto," 51.

20. Gaghan, "Pancho Villa Takes Town," 41.

21. Gilbert Millstein, "That Brassy Music Man Returns to Broadway as Poor Richard," *Saturday Evening Post*, October 17, 1964, 88.

22. Millstein, "That Brassy Music Man," 88.

23. John Cullum and Emily Frankel, "Who Inspired John Cullum?," *Artists in Residence Broadcasting*, New York, October 12, 2013, Vidcast, *YouTube*, Uploaded by AI.R Broadcasting, https://www.youtube.com/watch?v=dHN63sUlZ9E&list=PLA67BD971925A2859&index=142.

24. John Cullum and Emily Frankel, "Why John Cullum Admires Robert Preston," *Artists in Residence Broadcasting*, New York, January 6, 2014,

Vidcast, *YouTube*, Uploaded by AI.R Broadcasting, https://www.you-tube.com/watch?v=CEXUtR5vC5k&feature=youtu.be

25. Barbara Comstock White, "Have You Seen We Take the Town at the Shubert," *Record-Journal* (Meriden, CT), February 21, 1962, 14.

26. Theodore H. Parker, "Musical Comes to Shubert," *Hartford Courant* (Hartford, CT), February 21, 1962, 17.

27. Parker, "Musical Comes to Shubert," 17.

28. Millstein, "That Brassy Music Man," 87.

29. William Peper, "Robert Preston," *Films in Review*, March 1968, 138.

30. Barbara Wilson, "Birdie's Boss Gets Wrinkles from Musical," *Philadelphia Inquirer*, March 11, 1962, 75.

31. Henry Murdoch, "'We Take Town' is Musical Tale of Pancho Villa," *Philadelphia Inquirer*, March 1, 1962, 34.

32. Jerry Gaghan, "'We Take the Town' at Schubert," *Philadelphia Daily News*, March 1, 1962, 42.

33. Ostrow, *Present at the Creation*, 18.

34. Millstein, "That Brassy Music Man," 87.

35. Ostrow, *Present at the Creation*, 19.

36. Ostrow, *Present at the Creation*, 19.

37. "Preston Musical Ends Run Early," *Philadelphia Inquirer*, March 18, 1962, 59.

38. Ken Mandelbaum, *Not Since Carrie: 40 Years of Broadway Musical Flops* (New York: St. Martin's Press, 1991), 61.

39. Cullum and Frankel, *Why John Cullum Admires Robert Preston*, 2014.

40. Tracy Palmgren Monroe, interview by the author, February 15, 2021.

41. Tracy Palmgren Monroe, interview by the author, February 15, 2021.

42. Kristin Buehner, "Hotel Hanford Hosted Elegant Party after 'Music Man' premiere," *Globe Gazette* (Mason City, IA), May 25, 2012, 1.

43. Buehner, "Hotel Hanford Hosted Elegant Party," 1.

44. Buehner, "Hotel Hanford Hosted Elegant Party," 1.

45. James Robert Parish and Lennard DeCarl, *Hollywood Players: The Forties* (New Rochelle, NY: Arlington House, 1976), 591.

46. Brenda Davies, "The Music Man," *Sight and Sound* 31, no 3 (Summer 1962), 147.

47. Hedda Hopper, "Huckster Don Kent Future Film Star," *Los Angeles Times*, March 26, 1963, 60.

48. Leanne Wood, "Persuasive Americanism'?: The Reactionary Promotion and Reception of Warner Bros.' The Music Man (1962)," *American Music* 31, no 4 (Winter 2013): 480.

49. Wood, "Persuasive Americanism'?," 480.

50. Louella Parsons, "Best of Hollywood," *Philadelphia Inquirer*, March 28, 1962, 32.

51. Hedda Hopper, "Hollywood," *Daily News*, March 21, 1962, C-14.

52. Howard Thompson, "Preston To Star in Comedy Movie," *New York Times*, March 31, 1962, 16.

53. Thompson, "Preston to Star in Comedy Movie," 16.

54. Vernon Scott, "Filmland Wants Robert Preston," *Indianapolis News*, September 5, 1962, 16.

55. "Island of Love," AFI Catalog. https://aficatalog.afi.com/.

56. Hedda Hopper, "McQueen Will Star Himself In 'Kimona'," *Los Angeles Times*, September 12, 1962, 63.

57. Harrison Carroll, "Behind the Scenes in Hollywood," *Morristown Gazette Mail* (Morristown, TN), September 5, 1962, 9.

58. Harold Heffernan, "Robert Preston's Wife 'Refuses' to Interfere," *Indianapolis Star*, November 7, 1962, 24.

59. Heffernan, "Robert Preston's Wife Refuses to Interfere," 24.

60. Heffernan, "Robert Preston's Wife Refuses to Interfere," 24.

61. Hopper, "McQueen Will Star Himself In 'Kimona'," 63.

62. "Preston and Randall Return Home," *Brooklyn Daily*, August 30, 1962, 7.

63. Heffernan, Robert Preston's Wife Refuses to Interfere, 24.

64. Dorothy Masters, "Preston and Randall Top Albee Dualler," *Daily News* (New York, NY), May 23, 1963, 82.

65. "Greek Travesty," *Time*, July 5, 1963, 86.

66. Marlene Matouk, "Professor Harold Hill Finds 'Island of Love'," *Tampa Bay Times*, June 19, 1963, 41.

67. "Chastity Lightly Held," *Variety*, March 13, 1963, 17.

68. "Island of Love," AFI Catalog. https://aficatalog.afi.com/.

69. Hedda Hopper, "Hollywood," *Daily News* (New York, NY), July 3, 1964, 38.

70. "All the Way Home stars Preston, Simmons," *Philadelphia Inquirer*, September 2, 1962, 13.

71. Howard Thompson, "Tennessee Testament," *New York Times*, October 21, 1962, 135.

72. Eugene Archer, "'No Strings' Sold to Film Company," *New York Times*, August 29, 1962, 20.

73. "Robert Preston Figures His Career in Upsurge," *Lexington Herald-Leader* (Lexington, KY), November 10, 1963, 27.

74. "Robert Preston Figures His Career in Upsurge," 27.

75. "'All Way Home' Sets Rehearsals," *Daily News* (New York, NY), September 27, 1962, 76.

76. Pat Fields, "Film Cast Arrives to Begin Work," *Knoxville Journal*, October 8, 1962, 1.

77. Wanda Hale, "'Music Man,' He Just Keeps Rolling Along," *Daily News* (New York, NY), November 10, 1963, 8.

78. "Robert Preston and Pat Hingle Get Clipped for Film," *Brooklyn Daily*, October 31, 1962, 9.

79. "Rooters Out Susskind Troupe at Knoxville," *Los Angeles Times*, October 15, 1962, 70.

80. "Pair of Horses (Iron) Pull 'All the Way Home'," *Knoxville News-Sentinel*, October 30, 1962, 7.

81. Vic Weals, "Old Cars–ET Model T Owners Recall the Filming of 'All the Way Home'," *Knoxville Journal*, June 11, 1986, C-1.

82. Weals, "Old Cars," C-2

83. Dorothy Kilgallen, "Voice of Broadway," *Tribune* (Coshocton, OH), October 24, 1963, 4.

84. Pat Fields, "'Simpatico' Key Word to Preston's Success," *Knoxville Journal*, October 25, 1962, 22.

85. Sheilah Graham, "Hope Lange Plans Play in New York," *Des Moines Tribune*, March 13, 1963, 24.

86. Paul F. Brown, *Rufus: James Agee in Tennessee* (Knoxville: The University of Tennessee Press, 2018), 309.

87. "Preston Hurt on Movie Set," *Knoxville News-Sentinel*, October 27, 1962, 1.

88. "Michael Kearney, The Child Actor of 'All the Way Home,' Revisits Knoxville," *Knoxville History Project*, September 2, 2015, https://knox-villehistoryproject.org/2015/09/02/michael-kearney-the-child-actor-of-all-the-way-home-revisits-knoxville/.

89. Brown, *Rufus: James Agee in Tennessee*, 325.

90. Brown, *Rufus: James Agee in Tennessee*, 325.

91. "Michael Kearney, The Child Actor of 'All the Way Home,' Revisits Knoxville," September 2, 2015.

92. "$1 Butterflies in Abundance," *Valley Times* (North Hollywood, CA), November 1, 1962, 44.

93. Brown, *Rufus: James Agee in Tennessee*, 318.

94. "First Boar," *Knoxville Journal*, October 16, 1962, 1.

95. "Preston Bags Boar, But Loses Shirttail," *Knoxville News-Sentinel*, October 16, 1962, 6.

96. Georgiana Fry, "Waterman Gets Divorce, Wife Given Custody," *Knoxville News-Sentinel*, June 28, 1968, 1.

97. "Filming of Agee Movie Ends Today," *Knoxville News-Sentinel*, November 11, 1962, 7.

98. Judy Collins, *Sweet Judy Blue Eyes: My Life in Music* (New York: Three Rivers Press, 2011), 116

99. Collins, *Sweet Judy Blue Eyes,* 116.

100. Collins, *Sweet Judy Blue Eyes,* 118.

101. Collins, *Sweet Judy Blue Eyes,* 118.

102. Dwight Newton, "Command Program," *San Francisco Examiner,* February 4, 1963, 19.

103. Cecil Smith, "Carol Plays It for Laughs," *Los Angeles Times,* February 24, 1963, 447.

104. Harry Harris, "Modest Carol Burnett Likes Comedy With 'Heart'," *Philadelphia Inquirer,* February 24, 1963, 2.

105. Harris, "Modest Carol Burnett," 2.

106. Frank Langley, "Carol Burnett Tremendous Talent, Warm Character," *Arizona Republic* (Phoenix, AZ), February 24, 1963, 45.

107. Langley, "Carol Burnett Tremendous Talent," 45.

108. Langley, "Carol Burnett Tremendous Talent," 45.

109. Langley, "Carol Burnett Tremendous Talent," 45.

110. Dwight Newton, "A Triumph for Carol," *San Francisco Examiner,* February 26, 1963, 51.

111. Ken Welch, "I Died a Thousand Deaths," Performed by Robert Preston on *An Evening with Carol Burnett, CBS,* New York, February 24, 1963.

112. Alan Gill, "Preston Recalls His 1000 Deaths," *Philadelphia Inquirer,* February 21, 1963, 18.

113. Rick DuBrow, "Carol Burnett Talented, TV Show Entertaining," *Cumberland Evening Times* (Cumberland, MD), February 25, 1963, 6.

114. Langley, "Carol Burnett Tremendous Talent," 45.

115. Carol Burnett, *In Such Good Company* (New York: Three Rivers Press, 2016), 58.

116. Burnett, *In Such Good Company,* 58.

117. DuBrow, "Carol Burnett Talented, TV Show Entertaining," 6.

118. Newton, "A Triumph for Carol," 51.

119. Cynthia Lowry, "Carol Burnett Show Sure 'Nuff Special," *Fort Worth Star Telegraph,* February 25, 1963, 14.

120. Jack Gould, "TV Series Begun by Carol Burnett," *New York Times,* February 26, 1963, 9.

121. Gould, "TV Series Begun by Carol Burnett," 9.

122. Ward Morehouse, "Buff Cobb Gets Galaxy of Stars to Play Shaw," *The Star Press* (Muncie, IN), May 26, 1963, C-9.

123. Hedda Hopper, "Hollywood," *Daily News* (New York, NY), September 2, 1963, 41.

124. Hopper, "Hollywood," September 2, 1963, 41.

125. "Robert Preston Plays Lead," *The Gazette*, March 5, 1963, 10.

126. "Robert Preston Plays Lead," 10.

127. Gay Pauley, "She's Still Got It," *Tucson Citizen*, May 4, 1963, 29.

128. Christopher Plummer, *In Spite of Myself: A Memoir* (New York: Alfred A. Knopf, 2008), 602.

129. Plummer, *In Spite of Myself: A Memoir*, 472.

130. James Bacon, "The Pixy Forgot Her Car," *Tampa Tribune*, March 24, 1963, 59.

131. Hopper, "Hollywood," September 2, 1963, 41.

132. Howard Taubman, "'Too Good To Be True' in a Pert Revival," *New York Times*, March 14, 1963, 8.

133. "Too Bad To Be True," *Time*, March 22, 1963, 74.

134. William Glover, "'Too True'-Good Try, No Show," *Morning Call* (Allentown, PA), March 13, 1963, 10.

135. Glover, "'Too True'-Good Try, No Show," 10.

136. "Robert Preston, Wife Separate," *Bridgeport Post* (Bridgeport, CT), May 16, 1963, 61.

137. Charles McHarry, "On the Town," *Daily News* (New York, NY), May 13, 1963, 362.

138. Earl Wilson, "Actor Robert Preston and Wife Separate," *Los Angeles Times,* May 17, 1963, 26.

139. Wilson, "Actor Robert Preston and Wife Separate," 26.

140. "Glynis Signed," *Tyler Morning Telegraph* (Tyler, TX), May 23, 1963, 17.

141. Hedda Hopper, "Zanuck Picks Sandra Dee, Jimmy Stewart, Fabian," *Tampa Tribune*, March 13, 1963, 19.

142. James Davis, "Too Poor Biz to Close 'Too True to be Good'," *Daily News* (New York, NY), May 24, 1963, 233.

143. Walter Winchell, "Panama Lures U.S. Tourists," *Indianapolis Star*, June 1, 1963, 25.

144. Walter Winchell, "In New York," *Greenville News*, June 8, 1963, 4.

145. Harrison Carroll, "Behind The Scenes in Hollywood," *Wilkes-Barre Times Leader* (Wilkes-Barre, PA), June 20, 1963, 16.

146. Carroll, "Behind the Scenes in Hollywood," 16.

147. Carroll, "Behind the Scenes in Hollywood," 16.

148. Dorothy Kilgallen, "Divorce Ruled Out for Robert Preston," *Philadelphia Daily News,* June 17, 1963, 31.

149. Sheilah Graham, "Sheilah Graham Column," *Des Moines Tribune*, June 11, 1963, 17.

150. Susan Meservey (Suzy), email to author, August 11, 2020.

151. Susan Meservey (Suzy), email to author, August 11, 2020.

152. Harrison Carroll, "Behind the Scenes in Hollywood," *Morristown Gazette Mail* (Morristown, TN), June 19, 1963, 11.

153. "Discovering With Decie," *Los Angeles Times*, June 30, 1963, 2.

154. Susan Meservey (Suzy), email to author, August 11, 2020.

155. Ward Morehouse, "Electric Bob Preston Blazes Bright Career," *Edmonton Journal* (Edmonton, Canada), June 17, 1963, 13.

156. "Robert Preston Chest Chairman," *Independent* (Long Beach, CA), July 4, 1963, 16.

157. Hedda Hopper, "Preston Wants Broadway Show," *Los Angeles Times*, July 2, 1963, 49.

158. Hedda Hopper, "Stars on the Patio," *Daily News* (New York, NY), July 3, 1963, 204.

159. Jerry Gaghan, "Preston's Split Puts Wife Back on Stage," *Philadelphia Daily News*, July 19, 1963, 35.

160. Dorothy Kilgallen, "Nixon Is Favorite Candidate for Top Job in Hollywood," *Daily Journal* (Vineland, NJ), July 23, 1963, 6.

161. Harold Cohen, "At Random," *Pittsburgh Post-Gazette*, July 22, 1963, 18.

162. Harold Heffernan, "Rush Call Went into Two Years of Work," *The Evening Sun* (Baltimore, MD), July 29, 1962, 21.

163. Lorraine Gauguin, "Hollywood Callboard," *Argus Leader* (Sioux Falls, SD), August 11, 1963, 25.

164. Louella Parsons, "Big Seal for Stanwyck," *San Francisco Examiner*, August 13, 1963, 17.

165. "School Official Admits Bank Robberies," *Independent* (Long Beach, CA), August 24, 1963, 2.

166. Sheilah Graham, "Sheilah Graham Reports," *Calgary Herald* (Calgary, Canada), September 21, 1963, 7.

167. Sheilah Graham, "Sheilah Graham Column," *Des Moines Tribune*, September 24, 1963, 6.

168. Hank Grant, "TV News Beat," *Press and Sun-Bulletin* (Binghamton, NY), September 22, 1963, 36.

169. George Maksian, "TV Off Beat," *Daily News* (New York, NY), August 4, 1963, 15.

170. "Glynis Johns is Engaged," *New York Times*, June 25, 1964, 25.

171. James Gavin, *Is That All There Is?: The Strange Life of Peggy Lee* (New York: Atria Paperback, 2014), 245.

172. Peggy Lee, *Miss Peggy Lee: An Autobiography* (New York: Donald I. Fine, Inc., 1989), 146.

173. Lee, *Miss Peggy Lee: An Autobiography*, 146.

174. Lee, *Miss Peggy Lee: An Autobiography*, 147.

175. Gavin, *Is That All There Is?: The Strange Life of Peggy Lee*, 245.

176. Louella Parsons, "Hollywood," *Philadelphia Inquirer*, September 18, 1963, 37.

177. "Preston To Do Comedy Now, Musical in 1964," *Journal-Herald* (Dayton, OH), September 13, 1963, 47.

178. Louella Parsons, "Hollywood," *Philadelphia Inquirer*, September 18, 1963, 37.

179. "Preston Signs for Pair of Stage Roles," *The Pantagraph* (Bloomington, IL), September 29, 1963, 33.

180. Kate Cameron, "Plane Delay Inspires Film," *Daily News* (New York, NY), September 1, 1963, S2-1.

181. Sheilah Graham, "Shirley Films Effervescent Exit," *Indianapolis Star*, October 1, 1963, 20.

182. Charles Leinenweber, interview by the author, July 2, 2021.

183. Leonard Lyons, "Kept His Crossword Puzzles for 3 ½ Months," *Journal News* (White Plains, NY), October 21, 1963, 14.

184. Earl Wilson, "Prestons Patch Up 23-Year Marriage," *Philadelphia Daily News*, September 27, 1963, 48.

185. Earl Wilson, "It Happened Last Night," *Reno Gazette-Journal* (Reno, NV), September 30, 1963, 16.

186. "TV Key Preview," *The Fresno Bee* (Fresno, CA), October 8, 1963, 6-D.

187. Kay Gardella, "'Telephone Hour' returns; Burnett on with Benny," *Daily News* (New York, NY), October 9, 1963, 82.

188. Brown, *Rufus: James Agee in Tennessee*, 326.

189. Raymond Flowers, "City Basks in Glow of Film Premiere," *Knoxville Journal*, October 18, 1963, 1.

190. Brown, *Rufus: James Agee in Tennessee*, 326.

191. Rod Gibson, "Knoxville Had Its Stars For 'All the Way Home'," *Kingsport Times-News* (Kingsport, TN), October 20, 1963, 8-B.

192. "Arrive in Style," *Knoxville Journal*, October 16, 1963, 1.

193. Flowers, "City Basks in Glow of Film Premiere," 1.

194. Mike McGrady, "'All The Way Home' Rates As 2-Handkerchief Film," *Newsday*, October 30, 1963, 3C.

195. Kate Cameron, "'All The Way Home' Touches the Heart," *Daily News* (New York, NY), October 30, 1963, 16.

196. Cameron, "'All the Way Home' Touches the Heart," 16.

197. Bosley Crowther, "'All The Way Home' is Here," *New York Times*, October 30, 1963, 46.

198. Brown, *Rufus: James Agee in Tennessee*, 329.

199. James Bawden, "Jean Simmons," interview in *You Ain't Heard Nothin' Yet: Interviews with Stars from Hollywood's Golden Era* (Lexington, KY: University of Kentucky Press, 2017), 189–200.

200. The National Board of Review of Motion Pictures, December 22, 1963, www.nbrmp.org.

201. "Preston to get Union's Award," *Daily News* (New York, NY), October 17, 1963, 79.

202. Dorothy Kilgallen, "Preston Play Satirizes Lucy, Others in Video," *Times-Tribune* (Scranton, PA), November 25, 1963, 11.

203. Marie Wallace, *On Stage & In Shadows: A Career Memoir* (New York: iUniverse, Inc., 2005), 50.

204. Leslye Hunter, interview by the author, August 4, 2021.

205. Leslye Hunter, interview by the author, August 4, 2021.

206. Wallace, *On Stage & In Shadows: A Career Memoir*, 51.

207. "Have You Seen . . . Nobody Loves an Albatross at New Haven's Shubert?," *Record-Journal* (Meriden, CT), November 29, 1963, 12.

208. "Have You Seen . . . Nobody Loves an Albatross," 12.

209. Wallace, *On Stage & In Shadows: A Career Memoir*, 52.

210. Kevin Kelly, "Sharp Comedy Misses Its Intended Target," *Boston Globe*, December 8, 1963, 80-A.

211. Kelly, "Sharp Comedy Misses Its Intended Target," 80-A.

212. Richard Andrews, "Nobody Loves an Albatross," *Harvard Crimson* (Cambridge, MA), December 5, 1963.

213. Richard F. Shepard, "TV Refugee: Author of 'Nobody Loves an Albatross' Discusses His Coast Adventures," *New York Times*, March 15, 1964, X-3.

214. Wallace, *On Stage & In Shadows: A Career Memoir*, 54.

215. Howard Taubman, "Preston Stars in Satire of Coast's TV World, " *New York Times*, December 20, 1963, 20.

216. John Chapman, "It's The Same Old Hollywood with TV," *Daily News* (New York, NY), December 29, 1963, 25-C.

217. "Move Over, Sammy Glick," *Time*, December 27, 1963, 39.

218. Leslye Hunter, interview by the author, August 4, 2021.

219. Leonard Lyons, "Best of Broadway," *Philadelphia Inquirer*, December 30, 1963, 10.

220. Robert Viagas, *I'm The Greatest Star: Broadway's Top Musical Legends from 1900 to Today* (New York: *Applause Theatre and Cinema Books*, 2009), 228.

221. William Glover, "Goofs Made Playwrights Out of Performers," *Asbury Park Press* (Asbury Park, NJ), September 27, 1964, 36.

222. "'48 Presidential Opponents in Accord at Broadway Play," *New York Times*, April 22, 1964, 54.

223. "Fancy Meeting You Here," *News Leader* (Staunton, VA), May 6, 1964, 9.

224. "N.A.A.C.P. to Stage Telecast on May 14 to Raise $1Million," *New York Times*, April 11, 1964, 9.

225. "NAACP Will Reap $Million from May 14 TV Spectacle," *Pittsburgh Courier*, May 9, 1964, 13.

226. "Multi-talent NAACP Show Set Thursday," *Express and News* (San Antonio, TX), May 10, 1964, 6.

227. "List Still Growing for Coming NAACP 'Freedom Spectacular'," *Black Dispatch* (Oklahoma City, OK), May 8, 1964, 6.

228. Mike Connolly, "Mike Connolly On TV," *Sunday News* (Lancaster, PA), May 10, 1964, 4.

229. "Preston Wins Barter Award," *New York Times*, May 16, 1964, 13.

230. David Henderson, "Robert Preston: The Music Man Becomes Mr. Broadway," *The Players Showcase* (Summer 1965), 26.

231. Leslye Hunter, interview by the author, August 4, 2021.

232. Peter Filichia, *The Great Parade* (New York: St. Martin's Press, 2015), 147.

233. Filichia, *The Great Parade*, 147.

234. Douglas Watt, "Shirley Verrett to Sing Carmen for City Opera," *Daily News* (New York, NY), May 14, 1964, 19C.

235. Millstein, "That Brassy Music Man Returns to Broadway as Poor Richard," 87.

236. Hal Boyle, "Robert Preston Portraying Ben Franklin on Broadway," *Greenwood Commonwealth* (Greenwood, MS), December 17, 1964, 4.

237. Robert Viagas, *I'm The Greatest Star: Broadway's Top Musical Legends*, 228.

238. Ken Mandelbaum, *Not Since Carrie* (New York: St. Martin's Press, 1991), 61.

239. Robert Wahls, "A Swinging Swede," *Daily News* (New York, NY), November 15, 1964, S2-2.

240. William Glover, "The Sweetish Baroness Played a Hunch," *Press and Sun Bulletin* (Binghamton, NY), September 5, 1964, 9.

241. Lee Silver, "Ben Franklin Preston Counsels Wife to Fly Kite & Dates Ulla," *Daily News* (New York, NY), November 17, 1964, 25.

242. "Summer Brings Unusual Broadway Changes," *Desert Sun* (Palm Springs, CA), May 30, 1964, 3.

243. Watson Crews, Jr., "Preston Meets Co-star, and Presto!," *Daily News* (New York, NY), December 6, 1964, 26.

244. Earl Wilson, "Preston to Wed His Leading Lady," *Philadelphia Daily News*, April 7, 1965, 34.

245. Vivian Brown, "Robert Preston Loves Home Life," *Rocky Mount Telegram* (Rocky Mount, NC), August 11, 1964, 3.

246. Henderson, "Robert Preston: The Music Man Becomes Mr. Broadway," 29.

247. Henderson, "Robert Preston: The Music Man Becomes Mr. Broadway," 28.

248. Millstein, "That Brassy Music Man Returns to Broadway as Poor Richard," 87.

249. Millstein, "That Brassy Music Man Returns to Broadway as Poor Richard," 87.

250. "The Start of Something Big?," *Daily News* (New York, NY), August 11, 1964, 41.

251. Henry T. Murdoch, "Preston Stars in 'Franklin'," *Philadelphia Inquirer*, August 25, 1964, 16.

252. Jerry Gaghan, "'Ben Franklin in Paris' Opens at Shubert," *Philadelphia Daily News*, August 25, 1964, 41.

253. Henderson, "Robert Preston: The Music Man Becomes Mr. Broadway," 56.

254. Kevin Kelly, "A History Book Musical That Won't Make History," *Boston Globe*, September 27, 1964, A55.

255. James Davis, "'Lovely War' Will Open; 'Ben Franklin' Delayed," *Daily News* (New York, NY), September 30, 1964, 69.

256. Millstein, "That Brassy Music Man Returns to Broadway as Poor Richard," 88.

257. William Goldman, *The Season: A Candid Look at Broadway* (New York: Limelight Editions, 2000), 17.

258. Tom Prideaux, "That Music Man Is Back on Broadway, Still Making Films and Aiming At Shakespeare," *People,* October 31, 1977, 80.

259. Howard Taubman, "Ben Franklin in Paris," *New York Times*, October 28, 1964, 52.

260. "Showman in Knee Britches," *Time*, November 6, 1964, Vol 84, no 19, 52.

261. "Showman in Knee Britches," 52.

262. John Chapman, "Robert Preston Perfect Choice to Portray Ben Franklin in Paris," *Daily News* (New York, NY), October 28, 1964, 78.

263. Silver, "Ben Franklin Preston Counsels Wife to Fly Kite & Dates Ulla," 25.

264. "'Franklin' Has Actress on String," *Philadelphia Daily News*, November 17, 1964, 3.

265. Silver, "Ben Franklin Preston Counsels Wife to Fly Kite & Dates Ulla," 25.

266. "'Franklin' Has Actress on String," 3.

267. "Preston's Costar Will Ask Divorce," *Los Angeles Times*, November 19, 1964, 30.

268. Eugene Spagnoli, "Now Ulla's Shedding Mate, Insists It's Her Own Show," *Daily News* (New York, NY), November 19, 1964, 4.

269. "'Franklin' Has Actress on String," 3.

270. *American Musical Theatre,* (Broadcast), New York, NY: CBS, November 28, 1964.

271. *American Musical Theatre,* November 28, 1964.

272. Thomas Allen Greenfield, "Ben Franklin in Paris," in *American Musicals in Context: From the American Revolution to the 21st Century,* 47–58. (Santa Barbara, CA: Greenwood, 2021), 49.

273. Greenfield, "Ben Franklin in Paris," 49.

274. Ben Gross, "Who Killed Anne Frank? A Meaningful TV Study," *Daily News* (New York, NY), December 14, 1964, 65.

275. Ward Morehouse, "Two Foreign 'Intrigues'," *Detroit Free Press,* December 1, 1964, 4-D.

276. Morehouse, "Two Foreign 'Intrigues'," 4-D.

277. Walter Winchell, "In New York," *The Greenville News* (Greenville, SC), December 23, 1964, 4.

278. Crews, "Preston Meets Co-Star, and Presto," 25-26.

279. Crews, "Preston Meets Co-Star, and Presto," 25-26.

280. Crews, "Preston Meets Co-Star, and Presto," 25-26.

281. "Deaths Over Weekend," *Los Angeles Evening Citizen News* (Hollywood, CA), February 15, 1965, 2.

282. Hedda Hopper, "Fast Work," *Daily News* (New York, NY), May 14, 1965, 19C.

283. Earl Wilson, "Preston to Wed His Leading Lady," *Philadelphia Daily News,* April 7, 1965, 34.

284. Wilson, "Preston to Wed His Leading Lady," 34.

285. Earl Wilson, "It Happened Last Night," *Tyler Morning Telegraph* (Tyler, TX), March 26, 1965, S2-8.

286. Dorothy Kilgallen, "Prestons Reunite, And Ulla Is Riled," *Philadelphia Daily News,* March 5, 1965, 38.

287. Wilson, "Preston to Wed His Leading Lady," 34.

288. Wilson, "Preston to Wed His Leading Lady," 34.

289. William Federici, "Preston and Co-Star Exchange 'I Wills'," *Daily News* (New York, NY), April 25, 1965, 4.

290. Wilson, "Preston to Wed His Leading Lady," 34.

291. Ken Mandelbaum, *Not Since Carrie* (New York: St. Martin's Press, 1991), 61.

292. Charles Leinenweber, interview by the author, July 28, 2021.

293. Hopper, "Fast Work," 19C.

ROARING BACK

1. Don Royal, "Preston Opens 'Proud Land' Vistas," *El Paso Herald-Post*, November 6, 1965, 32.

2. Kay Gardella, "Preston Hosts Specs," *Daily News* (New York, NY), April 23, 1965, 27-C.

3. Don Royal, "Bob Preston Opens 'This Proud Land'," *Kenosha News* (Kenosha, WI), November 6, 1965, 31.

4. Aleene MacMinn, "Preston Sees U.S.A. in 7-League Boots," *Los Angeles Times*, August 25, 1965, 16.

5. David H. Rhinelander, "Harwinton Farmer Postpones Chores to Watch TV Actors Work on Farm," *Hartford Courant*, June 5, 1965, 13.

6. MacMinn, "Preston Sees U.S.A. in 7-League Boots," 16.

7. Marion Purcelli, "Robert Preston Talks of His 'Rediscovery'," *Chicago Tribune*, November 7, 1965, TV-10.

8. Purcelli, "Robert Preston Talks of His 'Rediscovery'," TV-10.

9. Joan Crosby, "Robert Preston Learns Television Is Magic," *Independent* (Long Beach, CA), December 12, 1965, 23.

10. Crosby, "Robert Preston Learns Television Is Magic," 23.

11. MacMinn, "Preston Sees U.S.A. in 7-League Boots," 16.

12. Howard Pearson, "Bob Preston, Man of U.S.," *Deseret News* (Salt Lake City, UT), July 30, 1965, 18.

13. Matt Messina, "TVer on '64 Election Set," *Daily News* (New York, NY), June 1, 1965, 30.
14. Rhinelander, "Harwinton Farmer Postpones Chores," 13.
15. Margaret McManus, "'Music Man' Preston Passes River City on Western Tour," *Post Standard* (Syracuse, NY), December 11, 1965, 13.
16. Matt Messina, "Drop Tracy TV Debut," *Daily News*, June 8, 1965, 31-C.
17. Allen Rich, "TV Week," *Los Angeles Evening Citizen News*, November 12, 1965, B-16.
18. Rich, "TV Week," B-16.
19. "Blackout Follies," *The Indianapolis News*, November 18, 1965, 10.
20. Kay Gardella, "Radio Comes to Rescue During the Big Blackout," *Daily News* (New York, NY), November 11, 1965, 110.
21. Crosby, "Robert Preston Learns Television Is Magic," 23.
22. Crosby, "Robert Preston Learns Television Is Magic," 23.
23. "Sights and Sounds of the Big Sky Country." *Chicago Tribune*, December 11, 1965, TV Week-5.
24. "Sights and Sounds of the Big Sky Country," TV Week-5.
25. "Sights and Sounds of the Big Sky Country," TV Week-5.
26. McManus, "'Music Man' Preston Passes River City on Western Tour," 13.
27. Barbara Delatiner, "Cause for Shame in 'Proud Land'," *Newsday*, December 20, 1965, 101.
28. "'Proud Land' Features the Sun Country," *Sandusky Register* (Sandusky, OH), January 26, 1966, 30.
29. "'Proud Land' Visits Sun Country," *Hartford Courant* (Hartford, CT), January 23, 1966, 8.
30. Terry Shain, "Series' Third Try a Successful Trip," *Boston Globe*, January 27, 1966, 47.
31. Sam Zolotow, "Robert Preston to Play Henry II," *New York Times*, August 14, 1965, 10.
32. "Way Out West Fourth Show on Proud Land," *Daily Herald* (Provo, UT), February 14, 1966, 21.

33. "Way Out West Fourth Show on Proud Land," 21.

34. "Way Out West Fourth Show on Proud Land," 21.

35. Cynthia Lowry, "Critics Corner," *Press-Telegram* (Long Beach, CA), February 27, 1966, 21.

36. Harold Stern, "Bob Preston Narrator for 'This Proud Land'," *Herald and Review* (Decatur, IL), November 9, 1965, 9.

37. Stern, "Bob Preston Narrator for 'This Proud Land'," 9.

38. "Proud Land Series Looks at Middle West," *Times Herald* (Port Huron, MI), April 23, 1966, 17.

39. "Proud Land Series Looks at Middle West," 17.

40. Pearson, "Bob Preston, Man of U.S.," 18.

41. "Proud Land Series Looks at Middle West," 17.

42. Richard K. Shull, "They Say in Sheboygan: 'This Was the Wurst Yet'," *Indianapolis News*, April 26, 1966, 13.

43. James Davis, "'Kill One-Eyed Man' Ought to Be Arrested," *Daily News* (New York, NY), October 22, 1965, 76.

44. "Rosemary Harris Signed for 'Lion'," *Daily News*, December 2, 1965, 17-C.

45. McManus, "'Music Man' Preston Passes River City on Western Tour," 13.

46. "Preston Grows Beard for His Role as Henry II," *Morning Call* (Patterson, NJ), March 8, 1966, 14.

47. Rosemary Harris, interview by the author, May 12, 2021.

48. Rosemary Harris, interview by the author, May 12, 2021.

49. Rosemary Harris, interview by the author, May 12, 2021.

50. Rosemary Harris, interview by the author, May 12, 2021.

51. "Ballet Bows at Center," *Daily News* (New York, NY), January 4, 1966, 35.

52. Leonard Lyons, "'Lion in Winter' Rehearsing in Theater on the Actual Site," *Journal News* (White Plains, NY), January 24, 1966, 21.

53. Christopher Walken, interview by the author, May 29, 2021.

54. Christopher Walken, interview by the author, May 29, 2021.

55. Christopher Walken, interview by the author, May 29, 2021.

56. Christopher Walken, interview by the author, May 29, 2021.

57. Kevin Kelly, "'Lion in Winter' Literate, but People Remote," *Boston Globe*, February 8, 1966, 19.

58. Kevin Kelly, "'Lion in Winter' Caged in Rhetoric," *Boston Globe*, February 13, 1966, A-21.

59. Kelly, "'Lion in Winter' Caged in Rhetoric," A-21.

60. Kelly, "'Lion in Winter' Literate, but People Remote," 19.

61. Timothy S. Mayer, "The Lion in Winter at the Colonial," *Harvard Crimson* (Boston, MA), February 19, 1966.

62. Stanley Kauffmann, "'Lion in Winter Opens," *New York Times*, March 4, 1966, 23.

63. Rosemary Harris, interview by the author, May 12, 2021.

64. Rosemary Harris, interview by the author, May 12, 2021.

65. Rosemary Harris, interview by the author, May 12, 2021.

66. Rosemary Harris, interview by the author, May 12, 2021.

67. Rosemary Harris, interview by the author, May 12, 2021.

68. Frank Wesley Meservey, Jr., death certificate, February 19, 1972, file no. 7097-008014, State of California, County of Los Angeles. [Copy in possession of author].

69. John Anthony Gilvey, *Before the Parade Passes By: Gower Champion and the Glorious American Musical* (New York: St. Martin's Press, 2005), 156.

70. Gilvey, *Before the Parade Passes By*, 160.

71. Mary Martin, *My Heart Belongs* (New York: William Morrow and Company, Inc., 1977), 284.

72. David Kaufman, *Some Enchanted Evenings: The Glittering Life and Times of Mary Martin* (New York: St. Martin's Press, 2016), 253.

73. Hobe Morrison, "Merrick Gets Preston to Say 'I Do' For Musical on 'Fourposter'," *Morning Call* (Patterson, NJ), June 23, 1966, 26.

74. Morrison, "Merrick Gets Preston to Say 'I Do'," 26.

75. Martin, *My Heart Belongs*, 284.

76. Gilvey, *Before the Parade Passes By*, 161.

77. Martin, *My Heart Belongs*, 284.

78. Gilvey, *Before the Parade Passes By*, 161.

79. "Robert Preston Says 'I Do, I Do'," *Daily News* (New York, NY), June 20, 1966, 48.

80. Kaufman, *Some Enchanted Evenings*, 257.

81. Abe Laufe, *Broadway's Greatest Musicals* (New York: Funk & Wagnalls, 1977), 352.

82. Martin, *My Heart Belongs*, 286.

83. Martin, *My Heart Belongs*, 283.

84. Kaufman, *Some Enchanted Evenings*, 262.

85. Martin, *My Heart Belongs*, 283

86. Shirley Eder, "Jackie Gleason's Pet Peeve," *Detroit Free Press*, September 19, 1966, 6B.

87. Gilvey, *Before the Parade Passes By*, 167.

88. Kaufman, *Some Enchanted Evenings*, 262.

89. Samuel Hirsch, "Musical 'I Do!' New Wrinkle in Matrimony," *Boston Herald*, September 27, 1966, 14.

90. Hirsch, "Musical 'I Do!' New Wrinkle in Matrimony," 14.

91. Kevin Kelly, "Enchanted Team in Sentimental Romp," *Boston Globe*, September 27, 1966, 55.

92. Rex Reed, "Champion–Almost Always," *New York Times*, February 19, 1967, Section 2-3.

93. Kaufman, *Some Enchanted Evenings*, 259.

94. Earl Wilson, "Show People Get Threats; New York Is Fun City," *Cincinnati Enquirer*, November 22, 1966, 15.

95. Louis R. Cedrone, Jr., "Yes, Yes, Yes For 'I Do! I Do!'," *Evening Sun* (Baltimore, MD), October 24, 1966, A-10.

96. R.H. Gardner, "Pre-Broadway Show at National," *Baltimore Sun*, October 26, 1966, 28.

97. Cecil Smith, "Musical Taking Long Way to N.Y.," *Los Angeles Times*, October 27, 1966, 13.

98. Gilvey, *Before the Parade Passes By*, 178.

99. Kaufman, *Some Enchanted Evenings*, 260.

100. E.B. Radcliffe, "Martin, Preston in 'I Do! I Do!'," Scheduled Here," *Cincinnati Enquirer*, October 25, 1966, 1.

101. William A. Raidy, "Robert Preston's Hard Day's Night," *Argus* (Fremont, CA), July 20, 1967, 6.

102. Raidy, "Robert Preston's Hard Day's Night," 6.

103. Raidy, "Robert Preston's Hard Day's Night," 6.

104. Kaufman, *Some Enchanted Evenings*, 260.

105. Kaufman, *Some Enchanted Evenings*, 260.

106. Reed, "Champion–Almost Always," Section 2-3.

107. E.B. Radcliffe, "'I Do, I Do' Fine Show," *Cincinnati Enquirer*, November 10, 1966, 57.

108. "'I Do, I Do' Due in Cincy," *Xenia Daily Gazette* (Xenia, OH), November 8, 1966, 3.

109. Gilvey, *Before the Parade Passes By*, 178.

110. Kaufman, *Some Enchanted Evenings*, 261.

111. Kaufman, *Some Enchanted Evenings*, 261.

112. "Bold New Pitch in Song-and-Dance," *Life*, January 13, 1967, 83.

113. "Bold New Pitch in Song-and-Dance," 85.

114. John Chapman, "'I Do! I Do!' a Charming Musical with Mary Martin, Bob Preston," *Daily News* (New York, NY), December 6, 1966, 68.

115. "Anniversary Schmalz," *Time*, December 16, 1966, 87.

116. Walter Kerr, "'I Do! I Do!' Arrives," *New York Times*, December 6, 1966, 58.

117. Cecil Smith, "Mary Martin, Robert Preston Do Everything in 'I Do! I Do!,'" *Los Angeles Times*, December 7, 1966, IV-2.

118. Martin, *My Heart Belongs*, 290.

119.Tom Prideaux, "That Music Man Is Back on Broadway, Still Making Films and Aiming at Shakespeare," *People*, October 31, 1977, 80.

120.Prideaux "That Music Man Is Back on Broadway," 80.

121.Martin, *My Heart Belongs*, 287.

122.Kaufman, *Some Enchanted Evenings*, 262.

123."Remembering the Tony-Winning Musical Performers– Part 2," *Playbill*, May 13, 1996. https://www.playbill.com/article/ remembering-the-tony-winning-musical-performers-part-2-com-67848.

124.Sam Zolotow, "'I Do!' is Closed While Star is Ill," *New York Times*, May 11, 1967, 50.

125.Richard F. Shepard, "'I Do! I Do!' Will Tour with Original Stars," *New York Times*, November 21, 1967, 53.

126.Earl Wilson, "'I Do! I Do!' Star Says 'I Won't, I Won't'," *Independent* (Long Beach, CA), August 1, 1967, 8.

127.Wilson, "'I Do! I Do!' Star Says 'I Won't, I Won't," 8.

128.Martin, *My Heart Belongs*, 290.

129.Kaufman, *Some Enchanted Evenings*, 264.

130.Lawrence Devine, "Meet Mr. Robert Preston–Man of Many Roles," *Detroit Free Press*, February 23, 1969, 40.

131.Martin, *My Heart Belongs*, 290.

132.Martin, *My Heart Belongs*, 290.

133.Kaufman, *Some Enchanted Evenings*, 266.

134."Mary Martin Seriously Ill, Show Closes," *Bangor Daily News*, February 28, 1969, 22.

135.Devine, "Meet Mr. Robert Preston–Man of Many Roles," 40.

136."Musical Lauded as Sure-Fire Hit," *Monroe News Star* (Monroe, LA), September 3, 1974, 6-A.

137."Star's Illness Perils 'I Do, I Do' Here," *Philadelphia Daily News*, March 1, 1969, 17.

138.Shirley Eder, "Barbra's Marriage: Shades of Fanny?," *Detroit Free Press*, March 7, 1969, 11.

139. Martin, *My Heart Belongs*, 290.

TRIUMPH AND TRAGEDY

1. Bob Thomas, "Talent—and Luck for Robert Preston," *Kansas City Times*, July 13, 1971, 29.
2. Thomas, "Talent—and Luck for Robert Preston," 29.
3. Marshall Terrill, *Steve McQueen: Portrait of an American Rebel* (New York: Donald I. Fine, Inc., 1993), 214.
4. Keith B. Woods, "An Afternoon with Jeb Rosebrook," December 3, 2016, video, https://vimeo.com/194298437.
5. John Bustin, "Show World," *Austin American-Statesman*, August 18, 1972, 49.
6. Robert Taylor, "I Want You to Feel Very Old," *Oakland Tribune* (Oakland, CA), July 2, 1972, 2-EN.
7. Bustin, "Show World," 49.
8. Dale McIntyre, "Robert Preston Returns to Films," *News-Pilot* (San Pedro, CA), June 30, 1972, A-7.
9. Phil Strassberg, "'Junior Bonner' Features Prescott and Stars Suave Steve McQueen," *Arizona Republic* (Phoenix, AZ), July 2, 1972, N-5.
10. Shirley Eder, "Want A New View? Turn House Around," *Detroit Free Press*, June 25, 1971, 9.
11. Jeb Rosebrook and Stuart Rosebrook, *Junior Bonner: The Making of a Classic with Steve McQueen and Sam Peckinpah in the Summer of 1971* (Albany, GA: Bear Manor Media, 2018), loc. 433 of 2718, Kindle.
12. Penina Spiegel, *McQueen: The Untold Story of a Bad Boy in Hollywood* (Garden City, NY: Doubleday & Company, Inc, 1986), 12.
13. Spiegel, *McQueen: The Untold Story of a Bad Boy in Hollywood*, 11.
14. Spiegel, *McQueen: The Untold Story of a Bad Boy in Hollywood*, 12.
15. William F. Nolan, *McQueen* (New York: Congdon & Weed, Inc., 1984), 9.
16. Spiegel, *McQueen: The Untold Story of a Bad Boy in Hollywood*, 29.

17. Spiegel, *McQueen: The Untold Story of a Bad Boy in Hollywood*, 40.

18. Spiegel, *McQueen: The Untold Story of a Bad Boy in Hollywood*, 41.

19. Spiegel, *McQueen: The Untold Story of a Bad Boy in Hollywood*, 58.

20. Spiegel, *McQueen: The Untold Story of a Bad Boy in Hollywood*, 194.

21. Spiegel, *McQueen: The Untold Story of a Bad Boy in Hollywood*, 199.

22. Spiegel, *McQueen: The Untold Story of a Bad Boy in Hollywood*, 199.

23. Marc Eliot, *Steve McQueen: A Biography* (New York: Three Rivers Press, 2011), 172.

24. James Garner and Jon Winokur, *The Garner Files: A Memoir* (New York: Thorndike Press, 2011), 137.

25. Toni Fletcher, "The Day Steve McQueen Met His New Nazi Neighbor, Keith Moon," *Newsweek*, February 20, 2014, https://www.newsweek.com/day-steve-mcqueen-met-his-new-nazi-neighbor-keith-moon-229741.

26. Terrill, *Steve McQueen: Portrait of an American Rebel*, 215.

27. Barbara Leigh and Marshall Terrill, *The King, McQueen, and the Love Machine: My Secret Hollywood Life with Elvis Presley, Steve McQueen, and James Aubrey* (Bloomington, IN: Xlibris Corporation, 2001), 164.

28. Barbara Leigh, email to author, November 1, 2021.

29. Barbara Leigh and Marshall Terrill, *The King, McQueen, and the Love Machine*, 164.

30. Terrill, *Steve McQueen: Portrait of an American Rebel*, 214.

31. Eliot, *Steve McQueen: A Biography*, 244.

32. Barbara Leigh, email to author, November 1, 2021.

33. Robert Preston interview by Lewis Archibald, 1982, sound recording, *Rodgers and Hammerstein Archives of Recorded Sound at The New York Public Library*, New York.

34. Robert Preston interview by Lewis Archibald, 1982.

35. Rosebrook, *Junior Bonner: The Making of a Classic*, loc. 1422 of 2718, Kindle.

36. Rosebrook, *Junior Bonner: The Making of a Classic*, loc. 1422 of 2718, Kindle.

37. Terrill, *Steve McQueen: Portrait of an American Rebel*, 214.

38. Terrill, *Steve McQueen: Portrait of an American Rebel*, 215.

39. Robert Preston interview by Lewis Archibald, 1982.

40. Terrill, *Steve McQueen: Portrait of an American Rebel*, 215.

41. Rosebrook, *Junior Bonner: The Making of a Classic*, loc. 1655 of 2718, Kindle.

42. Rosebrook, *Junior Bonner: The Making of a Classic*, 214.

43. Keith B. Woods, "Jeb Rosebrook Talks About Opening Night of Junior Bonner," 2016, video, https://vimeo.com/288089744

44. Terrill, *Steve McQueen: Portrait of an American Rebel*, 216.

45. Vincent Canby, "'Junior Bonner' is a Rodeo Family Close-up," *New York Times*, August 3, 1972, 24.

46. Kathleen Carroll, "Old Pros Give New Western Bullwhip Bite," *Daily News* (New York, NY), August 3, 1972, 86.

47. Gene Siskel, "Junior Bonner," *Chicago Tribune*, September 18, 1972, Section 2-18.

48. George Anderson, "McQueen is Junior Bonner at the Gateway," *Pittsburgh Post-Gazette*, September 15, 1972, 25.

49. Bustin, "Show World," 49.

50. Roger Ebert, "Junior Bonner," September 20, 1972, https://www.rogerebert.com.

51. Charles Michener, "Bull Story," *Newsweek*, June 19, 1972, 64.

52. Terrill, *Steve McQueen: Portrait of an American Rebel*, 216.

53. Robert Preston interview by Lewis Archibald, 1982.

54. Christopher Sandford, *McQueen: The Biography* (New York: Taylor Trade Publishing, 2002), 294

55. "'Child's Play' Direction by Lumet," *The Evening Sun* (Baltimore, MD), September 22, 1971, 21.

56. "James Mason Gets a Star Role," *Calgary Herald* (Alberta, Canada), October 26, 1971, 74.

57. Stefan Kanfer, *Somebody: The Reckless Life and Remarkable Career of Marlon Brando* (New York: Vintage Books, 2009), 250.

58. Doris Brown, "'Child's Play' Isn't for N.J. Actors, Photographer," *Central New Jersey Home News* (New Brunswick, NJ), December 19, 1971, 79.

59. Brown, "'Child's Play' Isn't for N.J. Actors, Photographer," 79.

60. Kanfer, *Somebody: The Reckless Life and Remarkable Career of Marlon Brando*, 251.

61. David Downing, *Marlon Brando* (Briarcliff Manor, NY: Stein and Day, 1984), 160.

62. Kanfer, *Somebody: The Reckless Life and Remarkable Career of Marlon Brando*, 251.

63. Peter Manso, *Brando: The Biography* (New York: Hyperion, 1994), 734.

64. "Brando Fails to Please Merrick; Robert Preston In," *Variety*, November 3, 1971, 2.

65. Brown, "'Child's Play' Isn't for N.J. Actors, Photographer," 79.

66. Sidney Lumet, *Making Movies* (New York: Vintage Books, 1996), 143.

67. Lumet, *Making Movies*, 168.

68. Frank Wesley Meservey, Jr., death certificate, February 19, 1972, file no. 7097-008014, State of California, County of Los Angeles. [Copy in possession of author].

69. Tracy Palmgren Monroe, interview by the author, February 15, 2021.

70. Charles Leinenweber, interview by the author, July 28, 2021.

71. Charles Leinenweber, interview by the author, July 28, 2021.

72. Roger Ebert, "Child's Play," May 15, 1973, https://www.rogerebert.com.

73. Barry Westgate, "Movies: Striking Melodrama," *Edmonton Journal* (Edmonton, Canada), March 6, 1973, 60.

74. Paul D. Zimmerman, "Boys Will Be Boys," *Newsweek*, December 18, 1972, 93.

75. "'Child's Play' Wins Three Cork Awards," *Los Angeles Times*, July 5, 1973, 75.

76. Vincent Canby, "Weird Pupils of Child's Play," *New York Times*, December 13, 1972, 58.

77. Pauline Kael, *Reeling* (Boston: Little, Brown and Company, 1976), 73.

78. Richard Tyler Jordan, *But Darling, I'm Your Auntie Mame! The Amazing History of the World's Favorite Aunt* (Santa Barbara, CA: Capra Press, 1998), 190.

79. Norma Lee Browning, "Lovable Lucy is the Updated Mame," *Chicago Tribune*, January 4, 1973, 21.

80. Shirley Eder, "Did 'Bonanza' Axe Jolt Jim Arness?," *Charlotte News*, November 18, 1972, 17C.

81. William V. Madison, *Madeleine Kahn: Being the Music–A Life* (Jackson: University Press of Mississippi, 2015), 91.

82. Stephen Citron, *Jerry Herman: Poet of the Showtune* (New Haven: Yale University Press, 2004), 158.

83. Bob Rose, "Maude and Lucy Ready for Mame," *Morning Call* (Allentown, PA), January 14, 1973, F-2.

84. Marilyn Back, "Robert Preston Didn't Appreciate Lucy's Gift," *San Francisco Examiner*, January 8, 1973, 22.

85. Citron, *Jerry Herman: Poet of the Showtune*, 158.

86. Back, "Robert Preston Didn't Appreciate Lucy's Gift," 22.

87. Radie Harris, "Bea Arthur Quits 'Mame' Film After Role Disagreement," *Hollywood Reporter*, December 22, 1972.

88. Rose, "Maude and Lucy Ready for Mame," F-2.

89. Nancy Anderson, "Robert Preston Has Had Four Careers," *Dispatch* (Moline, IL), June 2, 1973, A-12.

90. Robert Kerwin, "Lucy Going Like 61," *Chicago Tribune*, April 22, 1973, 18.

91. Kerwin, "Lucy Going Like 61," 19.

92. Jordan, *But Darling, I'm Your Auntie Mame!*, 195.

93. Jordan, *But Darling, I'm Your Auntie Mame!*, 197.

94. Jordan, *But Darling, I'm Your Auntie Mame!*, 198.

95. Jordan, *But Darling, I'm Your Auntie Mame!*, 204.

96. Citron, *Jerry Herman: Poet of the Showtune*, 158.

97. Stefan Kanfer, *Ball of Fire: The Tumultuous Life and Comic Art of Lucille Ball* (New York: Alfred A. Knopf, 2003), 279.

98. Paul D. Zimmerman, "On the Ball," *Newsweek*, March 18, 1974, 112-A.

99. Kael, *Reeling*, 298

100. Vincent Canby, "Mame Puts on New but Familiar Face–Lucille Ball," *New York Times*, March 8, 1974, 18.

101. James Cook, "Maimed," *Time*, March 25, 1974, 68.

102. Milton Krims, "Mame," *Saturday Evening Post*, March 1974, 36.

103. 28th Annual Tony Awards, directed by Clark Jones, April 21, 1974 on ABC, uploaded to YouTube by MissPoochSmooch on May 26, 2013, https://www.youtube.com/watch?v=qWfRrQtL9Bc.

104. Steven Suskin and Ellen Stern, "Mack & Mabel: Goodbye, Mabel!," in *Second Act Trouble: Behind the Scenes at Broadway's Big Musical Bombs* (Guilford, CT: Applause Books, 2006), 127.

105. Shirley Eder, "Bob Will Make Music Again," *Philadelphia Inquirer*, February 21, 1974, 19-D.

106. Earl Wilson, "Backstage Plotting," *Press-Telegram* (Long Beach, CA), May 31, 1974, A-33.

107. Ken Mandelbaum, *Not Since Carrie* (New York: St. Martin's Press, 1991), 315.

108. John Anthony Gilvey, *Before the Parade Passes By: Gower Champion and the Glorious American Musical* (New York: St. Martin's Press, 200), 244.

109. Jerry Herman and Marilyn Stasio, *Showtime: A Memoir* (New York: Donald I. Fine Books, 1996), 193.

110. Marilyn Lerner, Letter to the Editor, *Los Angeles Times*, August 11, 1974, 20.

111. Herman and Stasio, *Showtime: A Memoir*, 193.

112. Herman and Stasio, *Showtime: A Memoir*, 194.

113. Herman and Stasio, *Showtime: A Memoir*, 193.

114. Herman and Stasio, *Showtime: A Memoir*, 194.

115. Herman and Stasio, *Showtime: A Memoir*, 192.

116. Citron, *Jerry Herman: Poet of the Showtune*, 200.

117. Citron, *Jerry Herman: Poet of the Showtune*, 200.

118. Joe Pollack, "'Mack and Mabel' Opens Run for Week at Municipal Opera," *St. Louis Post-Dispatch*, August 20, 1974, 4-B.

119. Pollack, "'Mack and Mabel' Opens Run for Week at Municipal Opera," 4-B.

120. Mimi Avins, "Robert Preston: Brag and Bluster," *St. Louis Post-Dispatch*, August 15, 1974, 1-D.

121. Avins, "Robert Preston: Brag and Bluster," 1-D.

122. Ellen Stock, "Mack & Mabel: Getting the Show Off the Road," *New York Magazine*, October 7, 1974, 49.

123. "Ford At Performance Of 'Mack and Mabel'," *St. Louis Post-Dispatch*, September 5, 1973, 8-A.

124. Herman and Stasio, *Showtime: A Memoir*, 195.

125. Steven Suskin, *More Opening Nights on Broadway: A Critical Quotebook of the Musical Theatre, 1965 through 1981* (New York: Schirmer Books, 1997), 565.

126. Herman and Stasio, *Showtime: A Memoir*, 195.

127. Herman and Stasio, *Showtime: A Memoir*, 196.

128. Jim Lowe, "Interview with Robert Preston," *Jim Lowe's New York*, WNEW Metromedia Radio 1130 in New York, October 7, 1974.

129. Lowe, "Interview with Robert Preston."

130. Lowe, "Interview with Robert Preston."

131. Clive Barnes, "'Mack & Mabel' and Silent Film Era," *New York Times*, October 7, 1974, 54.

132. Rex Reed, "A Musical You Just Can't Put Down," *Daily News* (New York, NY), October 13, 1974, 5.

133. Douglas Watt, "'Mack & Mabel' Giddy Look at Silent -Film Era," *Daily News* (New York, NY), October 7, 1974, 46.

134. Walter Kerr, "'Mack & Mabel' Makes Gloomy Stage Music," *New York Times*, October 13, 1974, S2-1.

135. T. E. Kalen, "Reel Sad," *Time*, October 21, 1974, 93.

136. "Musical Lauded as Sure-Fire Hit," *Monroe News Star* (Monroe, LA), September 3, 1974, 6-A.

137. Herman and Stasio, *Showtime: A Memoir*, 197.

138. Suskin, *More Opening Nights on Broadway: A Critical Quotebook of the Musical Theatre*, 565.

139. Citron, *Jerry Herman: Poet of the Showtune*, 201.

140. Charles Leinenweber, interview by the author, July 28, 2021.

141. Ruth Rea Meservey, death certificate, December 29, 1973, file no. 7097-053737, State of California, County of Los Angeles. [Copy in possession of author].

142. Charles Leinenweber, interview by the author, July 28, 2021.

BOOMERANG

1. "Bell Telephone Salute Friday," *Daily Independent Journal* (San Rafael, CA), March 22, 1976, 31.

2. Edgar Penton, "Bell Telephone Slates 'Jubilee'," *Post-Star* (Glen Falls, NY), March 20, 1976, 26.

3. "Award-Winning Cast Featured in Four Original Miniplays," *Times Colonist* (Victoria, British Columbia), April 4, 1975, 53.

4. "Tonight's 'Happy Ending' is Given Praise," *The Bee* (Danville, VA), April 10, 1975, 6-D.

5. "Award-Winning Cast Featured in Four Original Miniplays," 53.

6. Harry Harris, "'Happy Endings' Off to a Promising Start," *Philadelphia Inquirer*, April 10, 1975, 5-C.

7. Tom McMahon, "No King of the Heap Here," *Windsor Star* (Windsor, Canada), April 11, 1975, 15.

8. Jay Sharbutt, "'Happy Endings' Restores Faith," *Greeley Daily Tribune* (Greeley, CO), April 9, 1975, 34.

9. Tom Green, "'Happy Endings' Opening Weak," *Journal News* (White Plains, NY), April 10, 1975, 25.

10. Paul Henniger, "'My Father's House' Finally Makes It," *Ithaca Journal* (Ithaca, NY), May 31, 1975, 7.

11. Henniger, "'My Father's House' Finally Makes It," 7.

12. Bob MacKenzie, "Family Memories on ABC," *Oakland Tribune* (Oakland, CA), June 6, 1975, 18.

13. Tom Prideaux, "That Music Man Is Back on Broadway, Still Making Films and Aiming at Shakespeare," *People*, October 31, 1977, 84.

14. Prideaux, "That Music Man Is Back on Broadway," 79.

15. Keith D. Mano, "Robert Preston," *People*, June 28, 1982, 79.

16. Charles Leinenweber, interview by the author, July 28, 2021.

17. Prideaux, "That Music Man Is Back on Broadway," 79.

18. Prideaux, "That Music Man Is Back on Broadway," 79.

19. Charles Leinenweber, interview by the author, July 2, 2021.

20. Robert Viagas, *I'm The Greatest Star: Broadway's Top Musical Legends from 1900 to Today* (New York: Applause Theatre and Cinema Books, 2009), 229.

21. Murray Olderman, "Ritchie Gets 'Tough'," *Shreveport Journal* (Shreveport, LA), July 12, 1976, B-7.

22. Olderman, "Ritchie Gets 'Tough'," B-7.

23. Winston Daniel, "Star Gossip," *San Antonio Express*, September 19, 1976, 9.

24. "Pearl Bailey TV Pitches Rattle UN," *Wilkes Barre Times Leader* (Wilkes-Barre, PA), November 26, 1976, 9.

25. Thom Smith, "Burt: The People Just Love You," *Palm Beach Post* (West Palm Beach, FL), December 23, 1976, C-1.

26. Smith, "Burt: The People Just Love You," C-1.

27. Liz Smith, "Liz Smith," *San Francisco Examiner*, November 18, 1976, 33.

28. Vincent Canby, "'Semi-Tough' Film Winson Field Goals," *New York Times*, November 19, 1977, 12.

29. David Ansen, "Incomplete Pass," *Newsweek,* November 28, 1977, 98.

30. Kathleen Carroll, "Semi-Tough: Flab but Fun," *Daily News* (New York, NY), November 19, 1977, 13.

31. Richard Schickel, "Good Ole Boys," *Time,* November 21, 1977, 85.

32. Earl Wilson, "Music Man Turns into A Sly Fox," *Detroit Free Press,* April 30, 1977, 17.

33. Charles Leinenweber, interview by the author, July 2, 2021.

34. Burt Reynolds, *My Life* (New York: Hyperion, 1994), 296.

35. Reynolds, *My Life,* 295.

36. Reynolds, *My Life,* 295.

37. John Corry, "Robert Preston Going Into 'Sly Fox' Will Do It with Tonality," *New York Times,* April 1, 1977, 49.

38. Patricia O'Haire, "Once A Fast Talker . . . ," *Daily News* (New York, NY), May 6, 1977, 60.

39. William Glover, "Robert Preston, Dick Cavett, Larry Kert Took Over Show Roles Created by Others This Summer," *The Danville Register* (Danville, VA), August 31, 1977, 8-B.

40. Bethe Austin, interview by the author, January 17, 2022.

41. Bethe Austin, interview by the author, January 17, 2022.

42. George Anderson, "A Master Con Artist at Work Again," *Pittsburgh Post-Gazette,* May 12, 1977, 9.

43. Walter Kerr, "The Sly, Foxy Genius of Robert Preston," *New York Times,* July 31, 1977, 3.

44. Douglas Watt, "Preston Tops as Comedy Man," *Daily News* (New York, NY), May 20, 1977, 49.

45. Emory Lewis, "Foxy Preston," *The Record* (Hackensack, NJ), May 20, 1977, B-12.

46. Emory Lewis, "A Very Foxy Sly," *The Record* (Hackensack, NJ), May 29, 1977, 53.

47. Bethe Austin, interview by the author, January 17, 2022.

48. Bethe Austin, interview by the author, January 17, 2022.

49. Prideaux, "That Music Man Is Back on Broadway," 83.

50. Prideaux, "That Music Man Is Back on Broadway," 83.

51. Jean Robson, "Top Lincoln Grad is Greatest 'Hamlet'," *Highland Park News Herald & Journal* (Palm Springs, CA), May 26, 1968, 9.

52. Margaret McManus, "'Music Man' Preston Passes River City on Western Tour," *Post Standard* (Syracuse, NY), December 11, 1965, 13.

53. David Henderson, "Robert Preston: The Music Man Becomes Mr. Broadway," *The Players Showcase* (Summer 1965), 57.

54. John Cullum and Emily Frankel, "Why John Cullum Admires Robert Preston," Artists in Residence Broadcasting, New York, January 6, 2014, Vidcast, YouTube, Uploaded by AI.R Broadcasting, https://www.youtube.com/watch?v=CEXUtR5vC5k&feature=youtu.be.

55. Pat O'Haire, "A King for a Day," *Daily News* (New York, NY), July 29, 1977, 5.

56. Glenn Currie, "Broadway Beginning New Season," *Daily Breeze*, (Torrance, CA), October 9, 1977, 43.

57. Jonathan Takiff, "'Grand Street' Is Right Up Saks' Avenue," *Philadelphia Daily News*, March 3, 1978, 41.

58. Robert Merrill, *The Prince of Grand Street*, digital recording of the First Theatre Party Preview on September 26, 1977 at the Alvin Theatre in New York City.

59. Earl Wilson, "Last Night," *Pittsburgh Post-Gazette*, January 6, 1978, 19.

60. Maggie Daly, "No Percy-Lance Love Match," *Chicago Tribune*, December 8, 1977, 20.

61. David Krane, *The Prince of Grand Street*, email to the author, October 24, 2021.

62. Jerry Adler, "Okay, Okay–So He Looks Terrific!," *Daily News* (New York, NY), February 19, 1978, 3.

63. Adler, "Okay, Okay–So He Looks Terrific!", 3.

64. David Krane, *The Prince of Grand Street*, email to the author, October 24, 2021.

65. Neva Small, interview by the author, October 23, 2021.

66. Neva Small, interview by the author, October 23, 2021.

67. Neva Small, interview by the author, October 23, 2021.

68. Ken Mandelbaum, *Not Since Carrie: 40 Years of Broadway Musical Flops* (New York: St. Martin's Press, 1991), 63.

69. William B. Collins, "'Prince' Wears a Bent Crown at the Forrest," *Philadelphia Inquirer*, March 9, 1978, 4-B.

70. Stuart Bykofsky, "Did the 'Prince of Grand Street' Really Slander Yiddish Theater?," *Philadelphia Daily News*, March 24, 1978, 37.

71. Larry Fields, "Quincy's Cutting Edge," *Philadelphia Daily News*, March 20, 1978, 27.

72. Jack Lloyd, "A Favorable Impression Pays Off," *Philadelphia Inquirer*, March 23, 1978, 4-B.

73. Neva Small, interview by the author, October 23, 2021.

74. George McKinnon, "Tryout Treatment for 'Grand Street'," *Boston Globe*, March 29, 1978, 35.

75. Dan Dietz, *The Complete Book of 1970s Broadway Musicals* (Lanham, MD: Rowman & Littlefield, 2015), 395.

76. George McKinnon, "No Room for 'Angel'," *Boston Globe*, March 15, 1978, 63.

77. Nathan Cobb, "Goodnight Sweet 'Prince'," *Boston Globe*, April 14, 1978, 29.

78. Jonathan Mandell, "'Prince' Still Seeks a Crown That Fits," *Boston Globe*, April 2, 1978, C-1.

79. Mandell, "'Prince' Still Seeks a Crown That Fits," C-1.

80. Kevin Kelly, "Merrill's 'Fiddler in the Basement'," *Boston Globe*, April 6, 1978, 26.

81. Kelly, "Merrill's 'Fiddler in the Basement'," 26.

82. Ken Mandelbaum, *Not Since Carrie: 40 Years of Broadway Musical Flops*, 63.

83. Cobb, "Goodnight Sweet 'Prince'," 29.

84. Cobb, "Goodnight Sweet 'Prince'," 29.

85. David Krane, *The Prince of Grand Street*, email to the author, October 24, 2021.

86. David Krane, *The Prince of Grand Street*, email to the author, October 24, 2021.

87. *The Prince of Grand Street* by Robert Merrill with Robert Preston, Neva Small, and cast, recorded live in April 1978 at the Shubert Theatre in Boston, Massachusetts.

88. Ron Spivak, *The Prince of Grand Street*, email to the author, October 27, 2021.

89. John Corry, "Funny Thing Happens to 'Tribute' On Its Way to New York," *New York Times*, April 14, 1978, 49.

90. Cobb, "Goodnight Sweet 'Prince'," 30.

91. Neva Small, interview by the author, October 23, 2021.

92. Dennis McGovern and Deborah Grace Winer, *Sing out, Louise!–150 Broadway Musical Stars Remember 50 Years* (New York: Schirmer Books, 1996), 180.

93. Mandelbaum, *Not Since Carrie: 40 Years of Broadway Musical Flops*, 63.

94. Matthew Murray, "Off Broadway Reviews: The Prince of Grand Street," *Talkinbroadway.com*, May 29, 2003, https://www.talkinbroadway.com/page/ob/05_29_03.html.

95. Nancy Anderson, "Robert Preston Reflects Life," *Newark Advocate* (Newark, OH), April 19, 1978, 9.

96. Paul Henniger, "Wagon Ho!," *The Spokesman-Review* (Spokane, WA), March 23, 1979, 7.

97. Jerry Buck, "'Chisholms' Taps a Neglected Period," *Green Bay Press-Gazette* (Green Bay, WI), March 25, 1979, 10.

98. Ada Lynn Shrewsbury, interview by the author, January 14, 2022.

99. "New Salem, Clayville setting for 'Chisholms'," *Decatur Daily Review* (Decatur, IL), October 11, 1978, 29.

100. "About People," *Daily Review* (Morgan City, LA), October 20, 1978, 12.

101. Rosemary Harris, interview by the author, May 12, 2021.

102. Lee Winfrey, "'The Chisholms' Hits Trail with Fine Cast, Script, Music," *Philadelphia Inquirer*, March 29, 1979, 19-D.

103. David Bianculli, "CBS Hits the Trail and Heads West, Returns with Six-hour 'Chisholms'," *Fort Lauderdale News*, March 23, 1979, 245.

104. David Mott, "Three Towns Go Back a Century When Film Crew Arrives," *Rutland Daily Herald* (Rutland, VT), August 20, 1979, 20.

105. Mott, "Three Towns Go Back a Century When Film Crew Arrives," 20.

106. Brandon Maggart, interview by the author, November 26, 2021.

107. "American Short Story," *The Pantagraph* (Bloomington, IL), March 15, 1980, 7.

108. Robert Preston interview by Lewis Archibald, 1982, sound recording, *Rodgers and Hammerstein Archives of Recorded Sound at The New York Public Library*, New York.

109. Rosemary Harris, interview by the author, May 12, 2021.

110. "The Chisholms." *Star-News TV Week* (Pasadena CA), February 3, 1980, 7.

111. "The Chisholms," *Star-News TV Week*, 7

112. "The Chisholms," *Star-News TV Week*, 7.

113. "The Chisholms," *Star-News TV Week*, 7.

114. Johna Blinn, "Outdoorsman Robert Preston Also Possesses Cooking Skills," *Times-Mall* (Bedford, IN), January 20, 1979, 29.

115. Robert Preston interview by Lewis Archibald, 1982.

RETURN TO THE SILVER SCREEN

1. Bernard Drew, "Robert Preston: Acting is His Life," *The Daily Times* (Mamaroneck, NY), July 19, 1981, F-1.

2. Sam Wasson, *A Splurch in The Kisser: The Movies of Blake Edwards* (Middletown, CT: Wesleyan University Press, 2009), 224.

3. Wasson, *A Splurch in The Kisser: The Movies of Blake Edwards*, 225.

4. Loretta Swit, interview by the author, January 10, 2022.

5. Loretta Swit, interview by the author, January 10, 2022.

6. Chris Chase, "Is Hollywood Really 'S.O.B.' Decadent?," *New York Times*, July 9, 1981, C-17.

7. Drew, "Robert Preston: Acting is His Life," F-1.

8. Pat Taggart, "New Film Career is Music to Robert Preston," *Star Tribune* (Minneapolis, MN), May 28, 1982, 18-B.

9. Bruce R. Miller, "Preston's Back in Hollywood in a Big Way," *Sioux City Journal*, April 9, 1982, 2.

10. Vincent Canby, "Blake Edwards' S.O.B. A Farce," *New York Times*, July 1, 1981, 68.

11. Vincent Canby, "Why *S.O.B.* deserves to be S.R.O.," *New York Times*, July 12, 1981, D-15.

12. Dean Johnson, "Edwards' Vendetta," *Orlando Sentinel*, July 10, 1981, 4.

13. Desmond Ryan, "Blake Edwards' S.O.B. is Hilarious Bronx Cheer," *Dispatch* (Moline, IL), July 12, 1981, B-4.

14. Kirk Honeycutt, "'S.O.B.' Intelligent, Malicious Film," *Times Advocate* (Escondido, CA), July 2, 1981, 17.

15. Lawrence O'Toole, "A Venomous Valentine to Hollywood," *Macleans* 94, no. 27, July 6, 1981, 52.

16. Kathleen Carroll, "*S.O.B.* is Blake's Hollywood Hatchet Job," *Daily News* (New York, NY), July 1, 1981, 41. 17.

17. "S.O.B.," *People*, July 20, 1981, 15.

18. Rick Brough, "'S.O.B.'s Not Lively Bull, but Blandness," *The Newspaper* (Park City, UT), July 23, 1981, B-5.

19. Robert Alan Ross, "'S.O.B.' Movie About a Film Flop is Also a Scenario of Failure," *Tampa Bay Times* (St. Petersburg, FL), July 3, 1981, 3-D.

20. Wasson, *A Splurch in The Kisser: The Movies of Blake Edwards*, 239.

21. Shirley Eder, "Jackson and McCartney Do a Crossover of Their Own," *Detroit Free Press*, June 28, 1981, 9-C.

22. Wasson, *A Splurch in The Kisser: The Movies of Blake Edwards*, 239.

23. Aljean Harmetz, "Blake Edwards in Tiff Over *S.O.B*," *New York Times*, June 25, 1981, C-17.

24. Eder, "Jackson and McCartney Do a Crossover of Their Own," 9-C.

25. Wasson, *A Splurch in The Kisser: The Movies of Blake Edwards*, 239.

26. George Anderson, "'S.O.B. Stars Take Show on Road to Save Their Movie," *Pittsburgh Post-Gazette*, July 13, 1981, 21.

27. Loretta Swit, interview by the author, January 10, 2022.

28. Anderson, "S.O.B.' Stars Take Show on Road to Save Their Movie," 24.

29. Anderson, "S.O.B.' Stars Take Show on Road to Save Their Movie," 24.

30. Tim Sacco, "And The Winner Is: 'The Avant-garde Mastodon'," *Des Moines Register*, February 21, 1982, 3-H.

31. Robert Windeler, *Julie Andrews: A Life on Stage and Screen* (Secaucus, NJ: Carol Publishing Group, 1997), 187.

32. Taggart, "New Film Career is Music to Robert Preston," 18-B.

33. Pat Taggart, "Robert Preston is Delighted with his New Movie Image," *Morning Call* (Allentown, PA), May 20, 1982, D-13.

34. Larry King, "Interviews with Blake Edwards and Jack Valenti; Experts Debate on Nuclear Policy," *CNN Larry King Weekend* (Los Angeles, CA), CNN, July 27, 2002.

35. David Craig, *On Performing: A Handbook for Actors, Dancers, Singers on the Musical Stage* (New York: McGraw-Hill, 1987), 122.

36. Bob Thomas, "Leading Man Robert Preston Portrays Gay Entertainer," *The Item* (Sumter, SC), April 1, 1982, 8-C.

37. Taggart, "Robert Preston is Delighted with his New Movie Image," D-13.

38. Wasson, *A Splurch in The Kisser: The Movies of Blake Edwards*, 241.

39. Wasson, *A Splurch in The Kisser: The Movies of Blake Edwards*, 241.

40. Robert Preston interview by Lewis Archibald, 1982, sound recording, *Rodgers and Hammerstein Archives of Recorded Sound at The New York Public Library*, New York.

41. Robert Preston interview by Lewis Archibald, 1982.

42. "Robert Preston–From 'The Music Man' to Dr. Finegarten in 'S.O.B.',"
    Bennington Banner (Bennington, VT), July 16, 1981, 10.

43. Robert Preston interview by Lewis Archibald, 1982.

44. Robert Preston interview by Lewis Archibald, 1982.

45. Richard Stirling, *Julie Andrews: An Intimate Biography* (New York: St.
    Martin's Press, 2007), 274.

46. Craig, *On Performing: A Handbook for Actors, Dancers, Singers on the
    Musical Stage*, 123.

47. Robert Preston interview by Lewis Archibald, 1982.

48. Robert Preston interview by Lewis Archibald, 1982.

49. Robert Preston interview by Lewis Archibald, 1982.

50. *Julie Andrews Online*, Facebook post, "The Shady Dame from Seville,"
    September 14, 2016, https://www.facebook.com/JulieAndrewsOnline/photos/
    the-shady-dame-from-seville-film-fact-the-costume-worn-by-julie-andrews-
    in-the-n/10154548692844628/.

51. Robert Preston interview by Lewis Archibald, 1982.

52. Tom Fitzgerald and Lorenzo Marquez, "Very Harlow," *Metrosource LA*
    (Los Angeles, CA), 2012.

53. Lesley Ann Warren, interview by the author, July 6, 2021.

54. Lesley Ann Warren, interview by the author, July 6, 2021.

55. Lesley Ann Warren, interview by the author, July 6, 2021.

56. Lesley Ann Warren, interview by the author, July 6, 2021.

57. Stirling, *Julie Andrews: An Intimate Biography*, 275.

58. Vincent Canby, "*Victor/Victoria*, a Blake Edwards Farce," *New York
    Times*, March 19, 1982, C-8.

59. Sheila Benson, "Blake Edwards' VICTOR/IA: A Fresh Look at
    Sexuality," *Los Angeles Times*, March 14, 1982, 29.

60. Roger Ebert, "Victor/Victoria." *Chicago Sun-Times*, January 1, 1982.

61. "Film Review: Victor/Victoria," *Variety*, December 31, 1981, https://va-
    riety.com/1981/film/reviews/victor-victoria-1200425063/.

62. Bruce Miller, "Preston's Back in Hollywood in a Big Way," *Sioux City Journal*, April 9, 1982, 22.

63. Lee Grant, "Gays Give Media Credit – Where Credit Is Due," *Los Angeles Times*, October 6, 1982, 89.

64. Charles Champlin, "7 Career Accidents Proved to be Lucky for Robert Preston," *Asbury Park Press* (Asbury Park, NJ), March 6, 1983, G-3.

65. Bettylou Peterson, "Retirement is Not in Preston's Script," *Detroit Free Press*, May 25, 1982, 8.

66. Stacy Smith, "Finding Joy in Limelight–Even TV," *Courier-Post* (Camden, NJ), March 18, 1982, 10-C.

67. Vernon Scott, "Robert Preston Enters Career No. 5," *Sentinel* (Carlisle, PA), April 3, 1982, D-19.

68. "I Was Truly Looking for Something to Do in Television," *Daily Spectrum* (St. George, UT), May 26, 1982, 11.

69. Bill Carter, "'Rehearsal': Whodunit Dun Right," *Baltimore Sun*, May 26, 1982, C-18.

70. Dianne Holloway, "Rehearsal for Murder Makes Viewers Think," *Austin American-Statesman* (Austin, TX), May 26, 1982, D-20.

71. Marvin Kitman, "Lack of Suspense No Mystery," *Newsday*, May 26, 1982, 80.

72. 72 "Ebullient Robert Preston Stars in the Role of Crafty Playwright," *The State* (Columbia, SC), May 23, 1982. 13.

73. David Richards, "Robert Preston With a Capital P," *Washington Post*, July 22, 1984, G-5.

74. Dick DuBrow, "Showbiz: All Around Leading Man," *Scrantonian Tribune* (Scranton, PA), November 6, 1983, E-8.

75. Dubrow, "Showbiz: All Around Leading Man," E-8.

76. Charles Champlin, "Straight from the Music Man," *Los Angeles Times*, February 27, 1983, 27.

77. Bob Hope's *Pink Panther Thanksgiving Gala*, directed by Tony Charmoli, aired on November 21, 1982, NBC.

78. Bob Hope's *Pink Panther Thanksgiving Gala*, November 21, 1982, NBC.

79. Bob Hope's *Pink Panther Thanksgiving Gala*, November 21, 1982, NBC.

80. Richards, "Robert Preston with a Capital P," G-5.

81. Town Clerk of Greenwich, "Bargain and Sale Deed," Book 1334, Page 151, Greenwich, CT, recorded August 29, 1983. [Author has copy of documents].

82. "Preston Fleeing Connecticut," *Daily News* (New York, NY), December 30, 1982, 9.

83. Paul Henniger, "Gunsmoke in the September Sun," *San Francisco Examiner*, October 2, 1983, 54.

84. "Grizzled Veteran Stars in Rare TV Horse Opera," *Columbia Record* (Columbia, SC), October 10, 1983, 11-D.

85. John O'Connor, "September Gun, a Comedy Drama," *New York Times*, October 7, 1983, 31.

86. Juliane Hastings, "'September Gun' Holds No Surprises, Lots of Fun," *Daily Press* (Newport News, VA), October 7, 1983, 25.

87. Harriett Van Horne, "Rivaling the Big Ball Game," *Newsday*, October 7, 1983, III-52.

88. Richards, "Robert Preston with a Capital P," G-5.

89. Charles Leinenweber, interview by the author, July 28, 2021.

90. Pat Berman, "Don't Typecast Me," *The State* (Columbia, SC), April 9, 1982, 8-D.

91. David Richards, "There's Quite a Range Preston Can Play: Villainous, Charming, Or Gay," *Journal Herald* (Dayton, OH), August 3, 1984, 25.

92. The VES Society, "The Last Starfighter Q&A," *YouTube* Video, 40:12, April 23, 2015, https://www.youtube.com/watch?v=DT6d08G7hb8.

93. The VES Society, "The Last Starfighter Q&A."

94. David J. Hogan, "Digital Drama in Outer Space," *Marquee* 9, no. 4, May 1984, 21.

95. Hogan, "Digital Drama in Outer Space," 21.

96. FilmIsNow Movie Bloopers & Extras, "Behind the Scenes of Starfighter Cult Movie #1", *YouTube* video, 12:25, January 1, 2021, https://www.youtube.com/watch?v=WHwjWZKDx18.

97. The VES Society, "The Last Starfighter Q&A,"

98. Bart Mills, "Preston Resurrects Con-man Character," *Asbury Park Press* (Asbury Park, NJ), July 8, 1984, G-1.

99. Bryan Garner, "The Last Starfighter–Lance guest joins us to chat about his career including Halloween 2 and Jaws," *YouTube* video, 59:20, May 2, 2021, Uploaded by Be More Super, https://www.youtube.com/watch?v=h62WYn-awqA.

100. Garner, "The Last Starfighter–Lance guest joins us to chat about his career."

101. Garner, "The Last Starfighter–Lance guest joins us to chat about his career."

102. Ryan Plummer, "Everything You Never Knew About the Making of Last Starfighter," *Gizmodo*, July 10, 2014, https://gizmodo.com/everything-you-never-knew-about-the-making-of-last-star-1602703884.

103. "Summer Fare," *Evening Sentinel* (Carlisle, PA), December 14, 1983, A-2.

104. Mike Joy, "Interview: Catherine Mary Stewart (The Last Starfighter, Night of the Comet)," *Horror News*, January 17, 2011, https://horrornews.net/28305/interview-catherine-mary-stewart-the-last-starfighter-night-of-the-comet/.

105. The VES Society, "The Last Starfighter Q&A.".

106. Lawrence Van Gelder, "More Wars In 'Last Starfighter'," *New York Times*, July 13, 1984, C-5.

107. Roger Ebert, "The Last Starfighter," *Chicago Sun-Times*, January 1, 1984.

108. Richard Schickel, "Styles For a Summer Night," *Time*, July 23, 1984, 102.

FINAL CURTAIN

1. Michael London, "Depiction of Gays Honored by Group," *Los Angeles Times*, September 21, 1983, 86.

2. "Robert Preston to Host Gay Artists Awards," *Philadelphia Daily News*, August 23, 1983, 36.

3. Michael London, "Gay Artists Alliance Lauds 'Lianna'," *Miami Herald*, September 26, 1983, 28.

4. Ted Thackrey Jr., "'Music Man' Robert Preston Dies of Cancer," *Los Angeles Times*, March 22, 1986, 28.

5. Morton DaCosta, "A Tribute to Robert Preston," Program for the 41st Annual Tony Awards at the Mark Hellinger Theatre, New York, NY, *Playbill*, 1987, 18.

6. Sylvie Drake, "South Coast Rep Steals Scene," *Los Angeles Times*, April 4, 1984, V1-7.

7. Drake, "South Coast Rep Steals Scene," V1-7.

8. "The 38th Annual Tony Awards (June 3, 1984)," *YouTube* video, 1:55:56, posted by "MissPoochSmooch", September 6, 2013, https://www.youtube.com/watch?v=XtmrHztScb8.

9. Clarke Taylor, "HBO Film Excites Mary Tyler Moore," *Los Angeles Times*, September 7, 1984, 13.

10. Joe Kaliff, "Magic Carpet Over Broadway," *Canarsie Courier* (Brooklyn, NY), May 24, 1984, 38.

11. "Ask Them Yourself," *Lansing State Journal* (Lansing, Michigan), June 3, 1984, 3.

12. David Richards, "Robert Preston," *Journal Herald* (Dayton, OH), August 3, 1984, 25.

13. "Never Too Late for Romance, Preston Finds," *Daily World* (Opelousas, LA), December 28, 1984, 15-C.

14. "Never Too Late for Romance, Preston Finds," 15-C.

15. Stephen Farber, "Robert Preston Adopts a Coast Focus: Films," *The New York Times*, February 20, 1985, C-22.

16. Michael Pressman, Visual History with Joan Micklin Silver, *Directors Guild of America*, September 19, 2005, https://www.dga.org/Craft/VisualHistory/Interviews/Joan-Micklin-Silver.aspx.

17. Mary Tyler Moore, *After All* (New York: Dell Publishing, 1995), 334.

18. Taylor, "HBO Film Excites Mary Tyler Moore," 13.

19. Pressman, "Visual History with Joan Micklin Silver," interview.

20. Pressman, "Visual History with Joan Micklin Silver," interview.

21. Farber, "Robert Preston Adopts a Coast Focus: Films," C-22.

22. Richards, "Robert Preston," 25.

23. David Craig, *On Performing: A Handbook for Actors, Dancers, Singers on the Musical Stage* (New York: McGraw-Hill, 1987), 109.

24. "Never Too Late for Romance, Preston Finds," 15-C.

25. Farber, "Robert Preston Adopts a Coast Focus: Films," C-22.

26. Moore, *After All*, 336.

27. Moore, *After All*, 337.

28. Bob Gunton, email to the author, March 22, 2022.

29. Bob Gunton, email to the author, March 22, 2022.

30. Bill Kaufman, "Cable-TV Film Role for Moore," *Newsday*, July 26, 1984, 11.

31. Tom Shales, "Love With a Lilt: Preston and Moore in HBO's 'Finnegan'," *Washington Post*, February 23, 1985, G-7

32. Kevin Thomas, "'Finnegan' Strikes Down Ageism," *Los Angeles Times*, February 22, 1985, 22.

33. Kenneth R. Clark, "Robert Preston Explodes in 'Finnegan'," *Chicago Tribune*, February 22, 1986, 15.

34. Marilyn Beck, "Hollywood," *Daily News* (New York, NY), July 16, 1984, 41.

35. David Richards, "Robert Preston With a Capital P," *Washington Post*, July 22, 1984, G-5.

36. Charlie Rose, Interview with Blake Edwards, *The Charlie Rose Show,* PBS, November 20, 1996, https://charlierose.com/videos/2327.

37. Roderick Mann, "Edwards' Year of Living Dangerously," *The Los Angeles Times*, November 25, 1984, 21.

38. The Thalians, 1984 Program Book, *The Thalians 29th Annual Gala Ball honoring Robert Preston*, Beverly Hills, CA, 20.

39. Ruta Lee, email to the author, February 1, 2022.

40. Ruta Lee, *Consider Your Ass Kissed* (Batavia, OH: Briton Publishing, LLC, 2021), 78.

41. Robert Preston, "Thalians Award Acceptance Speech," 29th Annual Thalians Gala, Century Plaza Hotel, Century City, CA, November 3, 1984, Academy of Motion Picture Arts and Sciences Archive.

42. Ruta Lee, email to the author, January 11, 2022.

43. American Cinema Awards 1984, *The Second Annual American Cinema Awards Program Book*, Beverly Hills, CA.

44. "Four To Receive Cinema Awards," *Los Angeles Times*, December 13, 1984, VI-3.

45. Frederick Heider, "The Gadabout," *The Desert Sun* (Palm Springs, CA), December 21, 1984, C-5.

46. Kathy Larkin, "Theater Greats to Hall of Fame," *Daily News* (New York, NY), March 5, 1985, M-11.

47. Terry Hodge Taylor, email to author, March 3, 2022.

48. Larkin, "Theater Greats to Hall of Fame," M-11.

49. Ron Fassler, "A View from The Audience," *Playbill*, April 1987, 43.

50. David Spence, interview by the author, March 26, 2022.

51. Robert Preston, *Letter to the American Iris Society,* August 9, 1985, courtesy David Spence.

52. "Robert Preston Iris," Iris Encyclopedia, *The American Iris Society,* March 7, 2011 (revised November 6, 2019), https://wiki.irises.org/TbPthruT/TbRobertPreston.

53. Bart Mills, "Actor Raps Vigilantism Promoted by His Character," *The Indianapolis News*, March 1, 1986, 5.

54. Mills, "Actor Raps Vigilantism Promoted by His Character," 5.

55. Mills, "Actor Raps Vigilantism Promoted by His Character," 5.

56. Tom Shales, "TV Previews: Diluted Disaster," *Washington Post*, March 1, 1986, C-7.

57. Howard Rosenberg, "Outrage-Offense Against Viewers," *Los Angeles Times*, March 1, 1986, V-11.

58. Leo Seligsohn, "Putting the Supreme Court on Trial," *Newsday*, March 1, 1986, 20.

59. John J. O'Connor, "TV View: 'Outrage' Gives a New Twist to Vigilantism," *New York Times*, March 2, 1986, S2-3.

60. O'Connor, "TV View: 'Outrage' Gives a New Twist to Vigilantism," S2-3.

61. Charles Leinenweber, interview by the author, July 2, 2021.

62. Robert Preston, death certificate, issued March 23, 1987, file no. 87-046169, State of California Department of Public Health. [Copy in possession of author].

63. Death Certificate of Robert Preston, March 23, 1987.

64. Charles Leinenweber, interview by the author, July 2, 2021.

65. Death Certificate of Robert Preston, March 23, 1987.

66. Thackrey Jr, "'Music Man' Robert Preston Dies of Cancer," 1.

67. Thackrey Jr, "'Music Man' Robert Preston Dies of Cancer," 1.

68. "'Music Man' Robert Preston Remembered as Shunning Glamour," *Desert Sun* (Palm Springs, CA), March 23, 1987, A-4.

69. "Actor Robert Preston Dies of Lung Cancer," *The Kilgore News* (Kilgore, TX), March 23, 1987, 7.

70. "Friends Remember Preston as 'Quiet Man'," *Tulare Advance-Register* (Tulare, CA), March 23, 1987, 2.

71. "The 41st Annual Tony Awards (June 7, 1987)," *YouTube* video, 2:03:44, posted by "MissPoochSmooch", August 14, 2014, https://www.youtube.com/watch?v=VYBo5eulYgA&t=230s.

72. Lansbury, "41st Annual Tony Awards."

73. Catherine Preston, "41st Annual Tony Awards.

74. Complaint For Determination of Paternity and Heirship, In the Superior Court for the State of California, Santa Barbara County, Case Number 170100, February 9, 1988. [Copy in possession of author].

75. Complaint For Determination of Paternity and Heirship, In the Superior Court for the State of California, Santa Barbara County, Case Number 170100, February 9, 1988. [Copy in possession of author].

76. Obituary of Rita Tavis, *Anchorage Daily News*, February 21, 2010.

77. "Alaska Girl Here with AAA Staff," *Honolulu Star Bulletin*, August 26, 1947, 17.

78. Obituary of Rita Tavis, February 21, 2010.

79. Rita Eleanora Tavis, birth certificate, issued November 26, 1952, file no. 3761, State of California, County of Los Angeles. [Copy in possession of author].

80. Obituary of Rita Tavis, February 21, 2010.

81. Answer To Complaint for Determination of Paternity and Heirship, In the Superior Court of the State of California for the County of Santa Barbara, Case Number 170100, March 21, 1988. [Copy in possession of author].

82. John H. Park to Barry Langberg and Mary Muir, memorandum, Los Angeles, CA, August 26, 1988. [Copy in possession of author].

83. Barry Langberg to John H. Parke, memorandum, "Memorandum of Points and Authorities," Los Angeles, CA, November 22, 1988. [Copy in possession of author].

84. Notice of Motion and Motion for Judgment on The Pleadings: Memorandum of Points and Authorities. In the Superior Court of the State of California for the County of Santa Barbara, Case Number 170100, November 23, 1988. [Copy in possession of author].

85. Points and Authorities in Opposition to Motion for Judgment on the Pleadings, Superior Court of the State of California for the County of

Santa Barbara, Case Number 170100, December 7, 1988, 7. [Copy in possession of author].

86. Judge Ronald Stevens, memorandum, "Memorandum of Intended Decision," Case Number 170100, In the Santa Barbara Superior Court, December 14, 1988. [Copy in possession of author].

87. Trial Setting/Status Conference Calendar, Santa Barbara Superior Court, December 23, 1988, 1. [Copy in possession of author].

88. Status Report, Superior Court of the State of California for the County of Santa Barbara, Case Number 170100, December 23, 1988. [Copy in possession of author].

89. Jill Abrams, "Paternity Testing: Blood Types and DNA," *Nature Education* 1 (1): 146.

90. Abrams, "Paternity Testing: Blood Types and DNA," 146.

91. Request for Dismissal, Superior Court of the State of California for the County of Santa Barbara, Case Number 170100, February 3, 1989. [Copy in possession of author].

92. Laurie Eleanora Zweiback, death certificate, February 18, 2013, file no. 2013023333, State of Florida Bureau of Vital Statistics. [Copy in possession of author].

93. Death Certificate of Laurie Eleanora Zweiback, February 18, 2013.

94. Charles Leinenweber, interview by the author, July 2, 2021.

95. Charles Leinenweber, interview by the author, July 2, 2021.

96. Catherine Preston, death certificate, January 15, 2004, file no. 3052004029046, State of California Department of Public Health. [Copy in possession of author].

97. Charles Leinenweber, interview by the author, July 28, 2021.

98. Kenneth Jones, "Preston's Life Explored in New Musical, *Ya Got Trouble!* in Pacific Northwest," May 26-June 12," *Playbill*, May 26, 2005

99. Rosemary Ponnekanti, "TAG Stirs Memories of a Music Man," *The News Tribune* (Tacoma, WA), November 6, 2006, D-1.

100. Leah B. Green and Mischa Berson, "Renewed TAG Borrows a Little 'Trouble'," *The Seattle Times*, November 10, 2006.

EPILOGUE

1. William Goldman, *The Season: A Candid Look at Broadway* (New York: Limelight Editions, 2000), 17.
2. Emory Lewis, "A Very Foxy Sly," *The Record* (Hackensack, NJ), May 29, 1977, 53.
3. Michael Riedel, "Is There A "Music Man' In the House? - Harold Hill Is One Of Broadway's Best Roles. So Why Doesn't Anyone Want It?," *New York Post*, June 21, 1999, https://nypost.com/1999/06/21/is-there-amusic-manin-the-house-harold-hill-is-one-of-broadways-best-roles-so-why-doesnt-anyone-want-it/.
4. Riedel, "Is There A "Music Man' In the House?"
5. David Hinkley, "The Role and The Man Were in Tune," *Daily News* (New York, NY), March 23, 1987, 4.

FILMOGRAPHY, THEATER, TELEVISION, RADIO

FILM

King of Alcatraz (1938)

Director: Robert Florey

Studio: Paramount

<u>Cast</u>: Gail Patrick (as Dale Borden), Lloyd Nolan (as Raymond Grayson), Harry Carey (as Captain Glennan), J. Carrol Naish (as Steve Murkil), **Robert Preston** (as Robert MacArthur), Anthony Quinn (as Lou Gedney), Dennis Morgan (as First Mate Rogers [as Richard Stanley]), Richard Denning (as Harry Vay), Konstantin Shayne (as Murok), Eddie Marr (as Dave Carter), Emory Parnell (as Olaf), Paul Fix (as 'Nails' Miller), Virginia Vale (as Dixie [as Dorothy Howe]), Monte Blue (as Officer), John Hart (as 1st Radio Operator).

Illegal Traffic (1938)

Director: Louis King

Studio: Paramount

Cast: J. Carrol Naish (as Lewis Zomar), Mary Carlisle (as Carol Butler), **Robert Preston** (as Charles Bent Martin), Judith Barrett (as Marie Arden), Pierre Watkin (as Jigger), Buster Crabbe (as Steve), George McKay (as Frank 'Old Man' Butler), Richard Denning (as Silk Patterson), Phil Warren (as Dittmar), Sheila Darcy (as Mathilde), Dolores Casey (as Mamie), Dennis Morgan (as Cagey Miller), John Hart (as Davis), Regis Toomey (as Windy), William B. Davidson (as Dalton), Joseph Crehan (as Chief Daley), Monte Blue (as Captain Moran), Archie Twitchell (as Duke), Morgan Conway (as State's Attorney Ryan), Emory Parnell (as Lieutenant).

Disbarred (1939)
Director: Robert Florey
Studio: Paramount
Cast: Gail Patrick (as Joan Carroll), **Robert Preston** (as Bradley Kent), Otto Kruger (as Tyler Craden), Sidney Toler (as G.L. 'Mardy' Mardeen), Helen MacKellar (as Abbey Tennant), Virginia Dabney (as Miss Gita LaRue), Clay Clement (as Attorney Roberts), Frank M. Thomas (as D.A. Blanchard), John Hart (as Reporter), Virginia Vale (as Stewardess [as "Dorothy Howe"]), Paul Fix (as Stone).

Union Pacific (1939)
Director: Cecil B. DeMille
Studio: Paramount
Cast: Barbara Stanwyck (as Mollie Monahan), Joel McCrea (as Captain Jeff Butler), Akim Tamiroff (as Fiesta), **Robert Preston** (as Dick Allen), Lynne Overman (as Leach Overmile), Brian Donlevy (as Sid Campeau), Robert Barrat (as Duke Ring), Anthony Quinn (as Jack Cordray), Stanley Ridges (as General Casement), Henry Kolker (as Asa M. Barrows), Francis McDonald (as General Grenville M. Dodge), Willard Robertson (as Oakes Ames), Harold Goodwin (as E.E. Calvin), Evelyn Keyes (as Mrs. Calvin), Richard Lane (as Sam Reed), Emory Parnell (as Foreman),

John Marston (as Durant), Guy Usher (as Leland Stanford), Adrian Morris (as Railwayman).

Beau Geste (1939)
Director: William A. Wellman
Studio: Paramount
Cast: Gary Cooper (as Michael "Beau" Geste), Ray Milland (as John Geste), **Robert Preston** (as Digby Geste), Brian Donlevy (as Sergeant Markoff), Susan Hayward (as Isobel Rivers), J. Carrol Naish (as Rasinoff), Albert Dekker (as Schwartz), Broderick Crawford (as Hank Miller), Charles Barton (as Buddy McMonigal), James Stephenson (as Major Henri de Beaujolais), Heather Thatcher (as Lady Patricia Brandon), James Burke (as Lieutenant Dufour), G.P. Huntley Jr. (as Augustus Brandon), Harold Huber (as Voisin), Donald O'Connor (as Beau s a child), Billy Cook (as John as a child), Martin Spellman (as Digby as a child), Ann Gillis (as Isobel as a child), David Holt (as Augustus as a child), Harvey Stephens (as Lieutenant Martin), Stanley Andrews (as Maris), Harry Woods (as Renoir), Arthur Aylesworth (as Renault), Henry Brandon (as Renouf), Barry Macollum (as Krenke), Ronald R. Rondell (as Bugler).

Typhoon (1940)
Director: Louis King
Studio: Paramount
Cast: Dorothy Lamour (as Dea), **Robert Preston** (as Johnny Potter), Lynne Overman (as Skipper Joe), J. Carrol Naish (as Mekaike), Chief Thundercloud (as Kehi), Frank Reicher (as Doctor), John Rogers (as Barkeep), Paul Harvey (as Dea's father), Norma Gene Nelson (as Dea as a child), Angelo Cruz (as Kehi's bodyguard), Jack Carson (as Mate), Al Kikume (as Cook).

North West Mounted Police (1940)

Director: Cecil B. DeMille

Studio: Paramount

Cast: Gary Cooper (as Texas Ranger Dusty Rivers), Madeleine Carroll (as April Logan), Paulette Goddard (as Louvette Corbeau), Preston Foster (as Sergeant Jim Brett), **Robert Preston** (as Ronnie Logan), George Bancroft (as Jacques Corbeau), Lynne Overman (as Tod McDuff), Akim Tamiroff (as Dan Duroc), Walter Hampden (as Big Bear), Lon Chaney Jr. (as Shorty), Montagu Love (as Inspector Cabot), Francis McDonald (as Louis Riel), George E. Stone (as Johnny Pelang), Willard Robertson (as Supt. Harrington), Regis Toomey (as Constable Jerry Moore), Richard Denning (as Constable Thornton), Douglas Kennedy (as Constable Carter), Robert Ryan (as Constable Dumont), Ralph Byrd (as Constable Ackroyd), Rod Cameron (as Constable Underhill), Chief Thundercloud (as Wandering Spirit), David Dunbar (as Vitale), Cecil B. DeMille (as Narrator), Noble Johnson (as Indian), Paul Newlan (as Indian), Emory Parnell (as George Higgins).

Moon Over Burma (1940)

Director: Louis King

Studio: Paramount

Cast: Dorothy Lamour (as Arla Dean), **Robert Preston** (as Chuck Lane), Preston Foster (as Bill Gordon), Doris Nolan (as Cynthia Harmon), Albert Bassermann (as Basil Renner), Frederick Worlock (as Stephen Harmon), Addison Richards (as Art Bryan), Harry Allen (as Sunshine), Frank Lackteen (as Khran), Stanley Price (as Khuda).

The Lady from Cheyenne (1941)

Director: Frank Lloyd

Studio: Universal Pictures/Frank Lloyd Productions

Cast: Loretta Young (as Annie Morgan), **Robert Preston** (as Steve Lewis), Edward Arnold (as James 'Jim' Cork), Frank Craven (as Hank Foreman),

Gladys George (as Elsie), Jessie Ralph (as Mrs. McGuinness), Stanley Fields (as Jerry Stover), Willie Best (as George), Samuel S. Hinds (as Governor Howard), Spencer Charters (as Dr. McGuinness), Clare Verdera (as Mrs. Matthews), Al Bridge (as Mr. Matthews), Charles Williams (as Clerk), Erville Alderson (as Ike Fairchild), Emmett Vogan (as Stanton), Roger Imhof (as Uncle Bill), William B. Davidson (as Nye Dunbar), James Kirkwood (as Politician), Wade Boteler (as Turk), Emory Parnell (as Crowley).

Parachute Battalion (1941)
Director: Leslie Goodwins
Studio: RKO Radio Pictures, Inc.
Cast: **Robert Preston** (as Donald Morse), Nancy Kelly (as Kit Richards), Edmond O'Brien (as Bill Burke), Harry Carey (as Bill Richards), Buddy Ebsen (as Jeff Hollis), Paul Kelly (as Tex), Richard Cromwell (as Spence), Robert Barrat (as Col. Burke), Edward Fielding (as Chief of Infantry), Erville Alderson (as Pa Hollis), Selmer Jackson (as Thomas Morse), Grant Withers (as Captain).

New York Town (1941)
Director: Charles Vidor
Studio: Paramount
Cast: Fred MacMurray (as Victor Ballard), Mary Martin (as Alexandra Curtis), Akim Tamiroff (as Stefan Janowski), **Robert Preston** (as Paul Bryson, Jr.), Lynne Overman (as Sam), Eric Blore (as Vivian), Fuzzy Knight (as Gus Nelson), Cecil Kellaway (as Shipboard Host), Edward McNamara (as Brody), Oliver Blake (as Bender, the lawyer), Ken Carpenter (as Master of Ceremonies), Sam McDaniel (as Henry), Iris Adrian (as Toots O'Day).

The Night of January 16ᵗʰ (1941)
Director: William Clemens
Studio: Paramount

Cast: **Robert Preston** (as Steve Van Ruyle), Ellen Drew (as Kit Lane), Nils Asther (as Bjorn Faulkner), Clarence Kolb (as Tilton), Willard Robertson (as Inspector Donegan), Cecil Kellaway (as Oscar, the Drunk), Donald Douglas (as Attorney Polk), Paul Stanton (as the District Attorney), Margaret Hayes (as Nancy Wakefield).

Pacific Blackout (1941)
Director: Ralph Murphy
Studio: Paramount
Cast: **Robert Preston** (as Robert Draper), Martha O'Driscoll (as Mary Jones), Philip Merivale (as John Runnell), Eva Gabor (as Marie Duval), Louis Jean Heydt (as Harold Kermin), Thurston Hall (as Williams), Mary Treen (as Irene), J. Edward Bromberg (as Pickpocket), Spencer Charters (as Cornelius), Cy Kendall (as Hotel Clerk), Russell Hicks (as Commanding Officer), Paul Stanton (as Judge), Clem Bevans (as Night-watchman), Robert Emmett Keane (as Defense Attorney), Edwin Maxwell (as District attorney), Rod Cameron (as Pilot).

Reap the Wild Wind (1942)
Director: Cecil B. DeMille
Studio: Paramount
Cast: Ray Milland (as Steven Tolliver), John Wayne (as Jack Stuart), Paulette Goddard (as Loxi Claiborne), Raymond Massey (as King Cutler), **Robert Preston** (as Dan Cutler), Lynne Overman (as Captain Philpott), Susan Hayward (as Drusilla Alston), Milburn Stone (as Lieutenant Farragut), Charles Bickford (as Bully Brown), Walter Hampden (as Commodore Devereaux), Louise Beavers (as Maum Maria, the Claiborne Maid), Martha O'Driscoll (as Ivy Devereaux), Elisabeth Risdon (as Mrs. Claiborne), Hedda Hopper (as Aunt Henrietta Beresford), Victor Kilian (as Mathias Widgeon), Oscar Polk (as Salt Meat), Raymond Hatton (as Master Shipwright), Lane Chandler (as Sam), William 'Wee Willie' Davis (as The Lamb), Ben Carter

(as Chinkapin), Janet Beecher (as Mrs. Mottram), Dave Wengren (as 'Claiborne' Lookout), Davison Clark (as Judge Marvin), Louis Merrill (as Captain of the 'Pelican'), Frank M. Thomas (as Dr. Jepson), Victor Varconi (as Lubbock), Sue Thomas (as Belle at Ball), Cecil B. DeMille (as Narrator).

This Gun for Hire (1942)
Director: Frank Tuttle
Studio: Paramount
Cast: Veronica Lake (as Ellen Graham), **Robert Preston** (as Michael Crane), Laird Cregar (as Willard Gates), Alan Ladd (as Philip Raven), Tully Marshall (as Alvin Brewster), Marc Lawrence (as Tommy), Olin Howland (as Blair Fletcher), Roger Imhof (as Senator Burnett), Pamela Blake (as Annie), Frank Ferguson (as Albert Baker), Victor Kilian (as Drew), Patricia Farr (as Ruby), Harry Shannon (as Steve Finnerty), Charles C. Wilson (as the Police Captain), Mikhail Rasumny (as Slukey), Bernadene Hayes (as Albert Baker's Secretary), Mary Davenport (as Salesgirl), Chester Clute (as Rooming House Manager), Charles Arnt (as Male Dressmaker), Earle S. Dewey (as Mr. Collins), Clem Bevans (as Scissor Grinder), Lynda Grey (as Gates' Secretary), Virita Campbell (as Little Girl).

Wake Island (1942)
Director: John Farrow
Studio: Paramount
Cast: Brian Donlevy (as Major Geoffrey Caton), Macdonald Carey (as Lieutenant Bruce Cameron), **Robert Preston** as (Private Joe Doyle), William Bendix (as Private Aloysius K. Randall), Albert Dekker (as Shad McClosky), Walter Abel (as Commander Roberts), Mikhail Rasumny (as Ivan Probenzky), Rod Cameron (as Captain Pete Lewis), Bill Goodwin (as Sergeant Higbee), Damian O'Flynn (as Captain Bill Patrick), Frank Albertson (as Johnny Rudd), Philip Van Zandt (as Cpl. Gus Goebbels).

Star Spangled Rhythm (1942)

Director: George Marshall

Studio: Paramount

Cast: Victor Moore (as William "Pop" Webster), Betty Hutton (as Polly Judson), Eddie Bracken (as Johnny Webster), Walter Abel (as B.G. DeSoto), Cass Daley (as Mimi), Cecil B. DeMille (as himself), Preston Sturges (as himself), Edward Fielding (as Y. Frank Freemont), Boyd Davis (as Captain Kingsley), Anne Revere (as Sarah), Paul Newlan (as Stage Door Guard), **Robert Preston** (Uncredited).

Night Plane from Chungking (1943)

Director: Ralph Murphy

Studio: Paramount

Cast: **Robert Preston** (as Captain Nick Stanton), Ellen Drew (as Ann Richards), Stephen Geray (as Doctor Ven Der Lieden), Otto Kruger (as Albert Pasavy), Victor Sen Yung (as Captain Po), Tamara Geva (as Countess Olga Karagin), Soo Yong (as Madame Wu), Ernest Dorian (as Major Raoul Brissac), Angel Cruz (as Japanese soldier), Allen Jung (as Lieutenant Tang), Leonard Strong (as Lieutenant Karuma), Lee Tung Foo (as Bus driver).

The Macomber Affair (1947)

Director: Zoltan Korda

Studio: United Artists

Cast: Gregory Peck (as Robert Wilson), Joan Bennett (as Margaret "Margot" Macomber), **Robert Preston** (as Francis Macomber), Reginald Denny (as Police Inspector), Jean Gillie (as Aimee), Carl Harbord (as Coroner), Vernon Downing (as Reporter Logan), Frederick Worlock (as Clerk).

Variety Girl (1947)

Director: Robert Florey

Studio: Paramount

Cast: Mary Hatcher (as Catherine Brown), Olga San Juan (as Amber La Vonne), DeForest Kelley (as Bob Kirby), Frank Ferguson (as R.J. O'Connell), Glenn Tryon (as Bill Farris), Nella Walker (as Mrs. Webster), Torben Meyer (as Andre), Jack Norton (as Busboy at Brown Derby), William Demarest (as Barker), Frank Faylen (as Stage manager), **Robert Preston** (as himself, celebrity cameo).

Wild Harvest (1947)
Director: Tay Garnett
Studio: Paramount
Cast: Alan Ladd (as Joe Madigan), Dorothy Lamour (as Fay Rankin), **Robert Preston** (as Jim Davis), Lloyd Nolan (as Kink), Richard Erdman (as Mark Lewis), Allen Jenkins (as Higgins), Will Wright (as Mike Alperson), Griff Barnett (as Rankin), Anthony Caruso (as Pete), Walter Sande (as Long), Frank Sully (as Nick), Caren Marsh (as Natalie).

Big City (1948)
Director: Norman Taurog
Studio: Metro-Goldwyn-Mayer Corp.
Cast: Margaret O'Brien (as Midge), **Robert Preston** (as Rev. Andrews), Danny Thomas (as Cantor Feldman), George Murphy (as Pat O'Donnell), Karin Booth (as Florence Bartlett), Edward Arnold (as Judge Abercrombie), Butch Jenkins (as Lewis Keller), Betty Garrett (as "Shoo Shoo" Grady), Lotte Lehmann (as Mama Feldman).

Blood on the Moon (1948)
Director: Robert Wise
Studio: RKO Radio Pictures, Inc.
Cast: Robert Mitchum (as Jim Garry), Barbara Bel Geddes (as Amy Lufton), **Robert Preston** (as Tate Riling), Walter Brennan (as Kris Barden), Phyllis Thaxter (as Carol Lufton), Frank Faylen (as Jake Pindalest), Tom Tully

(as John Lufton), Charles McGraw (as Milo Sweet), Clifton Young (as Joe Shotten), Tom Tyler (as Frank Reardon), George Cooper (as Fred Barden), Tom Keene (as Ted Elser), Bud Osborne (as Cap Willis), Zon Murray (as Nels Titterton), Robert Bray (as Bart Daniels).

Whispering Smith (1948)
Director: Leslie Fenton
Studio: Paramount
Cast: Alan Ladd (as Luke "Whispering" Smith), **Robert Preston** (as Murray Sinclair), Brenda Marshall (as Marian Sinclair), Donald Crisp (as Barney Rebstock), Fay Holden (as Emmy Dansing), William Demarest (as Bill Dansing), Murvyn Vye (as Blake Barton), Frank Faylen (as Whitey Du Sang), John Eldredge (as George McCloud), Ward Wood (as Leroy Barton), J. Farrell MacDonald (as Bill Baggs), Will Wright (as Sheriff McSwiggin).

Tulsa (1949)
Director: Stuart Heisler
Studio: Eagle-Lion Films, Inc.; Walter Wanger Pictures, Inc.
Cast: Susan Hayward (as Cherokee Lansing), **Robert Preston** (as Brad Brady), Pedro Armendáriz (as Jim Redbird), Lloyd Gough (as Bruce Tanner), Chill Wills (as Pinky Jimpson), Ed Begley (as John J. "Johnny" Brady), Jimmy Conlin (as Homer Triplette), Roland Jack (as Steve), Bill Hickman (as Bill, the Caterpillar tractor driver).

The Lady Gambles (1949)
Director: Michael Gordon
Studio: Universal Pictures Company, Inc.
Cast: Barbara Stanwyck (as Joan Phillips Boothe), **Robert Preston** (as David Boothe), Stephen McNally (as Horace Corrigan), Edith Barrett (as Ruth Phillips), John Hoyt (as Dr. Rojac), Elliott Sullivan (as Barky), John Harmon (as Frenchy), Philip Van Zandt (as Chuck Benson), Leif Erickson (as

Tony), Curt Conway (as Bank Clerk), Houseley Stevenson (as Pawnbroker), Don Beddoe (as Mr. Dennis Sutherland), Nana Bryant (as Mrs. Dennis Sutherland), Tony Curtis (as Bellboy), Peter Leeds (as Jack Harrison, Hotel Clerk), Frank Moran (as Murphy), John Indrisano (as Bert).

The Sundowners (1950)
Director: George Templeton
Studio: Eagle-Lion Films, Inc.
Cast: **Robert Preston** (as James Cloud/'Kid Wichita'), Robert Sterling (as Tom Cloud), Chill Wills (as Sam Beers), Cathy Downs (as Kathleen Boyce), John Litel (as John Gall), Jack Elam (as Earl Boyce), Don Haggerty (as Sheriff Elmer Gall), Stanley Price (as Steve Fletcher), Clem Fuller (as Turkey), Frank Cordell (as Jim Strake), Dave Kashner (as Gill Bassen), John Drew Barrymore (as Jeff Cloud).

When I Grow Up (1951)
Director: Michael Kanin
Studio: Eagle-Lion Classics, Inc.; Horizon Productions, Inc.
Cast: Bobby Driscoll (as Josh / Danny Reed), **Robert Preston** (as Father Reed), Martha Scott (as Mother Reed), Sherry Jackson (as Ruthie Reed), Johnny McGovern (as Duckface Kelly), Frances Chaney (as Mrs. Kelly), Poodles Hanneford (as Bobo), Ralph Dumke (as Carp), Paul Guilfoyle (as Doc), Paul Levitt (as Carp's Assistant), Griff Barnett (as Dr. Bailey), Margaret Lloyd (as Volunteer Nurse), Charley Grapewin (as Grandpa Reed), Harry Morgan (as Father Reed), Elisabeth Fraser (as Mother Reed), Robert Hyatt (as Binks), Hamilton Camp (as Bully), Ruth Lee (as Bully's Mother), Donald Gordon (as Harmonica Boy).

Cloudburst (1951)
Director: Francis Searle
Studio: Hammer Film Productions

Cast: **Robert Preston** (as John Graham), Elizabeth Sellars (as Carol Graham), Colin Tapley (as Inspector Davis), Sheila Burrell (as Lorna Dawson), Harold Lang (as Mickie Fraser / Kid Python), Mary Germaine (as Peggy Reece), George Woodbridge (as Sergeant Ritchie), Lyn Evans (as Chuck Peters), Thomas Heathcote (as Jackie), Edith Sharpe (as Mrs. Reece), Daphne Anderson (as Kate), Edward Lexy (as Cardew), James Mills (as Thompson), Noel Howlett (as Johnson), Martin Boddey (as Desk Sergeant).

Best of the Badmen (1951)
Director: William D. Russell
Studio: RKO Radio Pictures, Inc.
Cast: Robert Ryan (as Jeff Clanton), Claire Trevor (as Lily), Jack Buetel (as Bob Younger), **Robert Preston** (as Matthew Fowler), Walter Brennan (as 'Doc' Butcher), Bruce Cabot (as Cole Younger), John Archer (as Curley Ringo), Lawrence Tierney (as Jesse James), Barton MacLane (as Joad), Tom Tyler (as Frank James), Robert J. Wilke (as Jim Younger), John Cliff (as John Younger), Lee MacGregor (as Lieutenant Blaine), Emmett Lynn (as Oscar), Carleton Young (as Wilson).

My Outlaw Brother (1951)
Director: Elliot Nugent
Studio: Benedict Bogeaus Production, Inc.; Eagle-Lion Classics, Inc.
Cast: Mickey Rooney (as J. Dennis "Denny" O'Moore), Wanda Hendrix (as Señorita Carmelita Alvarado), **Robert Preston** (as Joe Warder), Robert Stack (as Patrick O'Moore), José Torvay (as Enrique Ortiz), Carlos Múzquiz (as Col. Sanchez), Fernando Wagner (as Burger), Hilda Moreno (as Señora Alvarado).

Face to Face (1952)
Director: John Brahm and Bretaigne Windust
Studio: RKO Radio Pictures, Inc.

Cast: James Mason (as The Captain), Gene Lockhart (as Capt. Archbold), Michael Pate (as Leggatt), Albert Sharpe (as First Mate Brown), Sean McClory (as Second Mate Robinson), Alec Harford (as Smithers), **Robert Preston** (as Sheriff Jack Potter), Marjorie Steele (as the Bride), Minor Watson (as Scratchy' Wilson), Dan Seymour (as Drummer), Olive Carey (as Laura Lee), James Agee (as Frank).

The Last Frontier (1955)
Director: Anthony Mann
Studio: Columbia Pictures Corp.
Cast: Victor Mature (as Jed Cooper), Guy Madison (as Captain Glenn Riordan), **Robert Preston** (as Colonel Frank Marston), James Whitmore (as Gus), Anne Bancroft (as Corinna Marston), Russell Collins (as Captain Phil Clarke), Peter Whitney (as Sergeant Major Decker), Pat Hogan (as Mungo).

The Dark at the Top of the Stairs (1960)
Director: Delbert Mann
Studio: Warner Bros. Pictures, Inc.
Cast: **Robert Preston** (as Rubin Flood), Dorothy McGuire (as Cora Flood), Eve Arden (as Lottie Lacey), Angela Lansbury (as Mavis Pruitt), Shirley Knight (as Reenie Flood), Lee Kinsolving (as Sammy Golden), Frank Overton (as Morris Lacey), Robert Eyer (as Sonny Flood), Penney Parker (as Flirt Conroy), Ken Lynch (as Harry Ralston).

The Music Man (1962)
Director: Morton DaCosta
Studio: Warner Bros. Pictures
Cast: **Robert Preston** (as Harold Hill), Shirley Jones (as Marian Paroo), Buddy Hackett (as Marcellus Washburn), Hermione Gingold (as Eulalie Mackechnie Shinn), Paul Ford (as Mayor George Shinn), Pert Kelton (as Mrs. Paroo), The Buffalo Bills ([Vern Reed, Al Shea, Wayne "Scotty" Ward,

Bill Spangenberg] as The School Board), Timmy Everett (as Tommy Djilas), Susan Luckey (as Zaneeta Shinn), Ronny Howard (as Winthrop Paroo), Harry Hickox (as Charlie Cowell), Charles Lane (as Constable Locke), Mary Wickes (as Mrs. Squires), Peggy Mondo (as Ethel Toffelmier), Sara Seegar (as Mrs. Maud Dunlop), Adnia Rice (as Alma Hix), Jesslyn Fax (as Avis Grubb), Monique Vermont (as Amaryllis).

How the West Was Won (1962)
Director: John Ford, Henry Hathaway, George Marshall, Richard Thorpe
Studio: Cinerama, Inc.; Metro-Goldwyn-Mayer, Inc.
Cast: Spencer Tracy (as Narrator), James Stewart (as Linus Rawlings), Carroll Baker (as Eve Prescott Rawlings), Debbie Reynolds as (Lillith Prescott van Valen), Karl Malden (as Zebulon Prescott), Agnes Moorehead (as Rebecca Prescott), Walter Brennan (as Col. Jeb Hawkins), Brigid Bazlen (as Dora Hawkins), Gregory Peck (as Cleve Van Valen), **Robert Preston** (as Roger Morgan), Thelma Ritter (as Agatha Clegg), George Peppard (as Zeb Rawlings), Andy Devine (as Corporal Peterson), Harry Morgan (as Gen. Ulysses S. Grant), John Wayne (as Gen. William Tecumseh Sherman), Russ Tamblyn (as Confederate deserter), Raymond Massey (as President Abraham Lincoln), Henry Fonda (as Jethro Stuart), Richard Widmark (as Mike King), Lee J. Cobb (as Marshal Lou Ramsey), Eli Wallach (as Charlie Gant), Carolyn Jones (as Julie), Mickey Shaughnessy (as Deputy Stover).

Island of Love (1963)
Director: Morton DaCosta
Studio: Warner Bros. Pictures
Cast: **Robert Preston** (as Steve Blair), Tony Randall (as Paul Ferris), Giorgia Moll (as Elena Harakas), Walter Matthau (as Tony Dallas), Betty Bruce (as Cha Cha Miller), Vassili Lambrinos (as Professor Georg Pappas), Michael Constantine (as Andy), Oliver Johnson (as Professor Krumwitz), Titos Vandis (as Father Anaxagoras), Miranta Myrat (as

Mama Harakas), Lewis Charles (as Louie), Peter Mamakos (as Nick), Lilian Miniati (as Eunice Miranda).

All the Way Home (1963)

Director: Alex Segal

Studio: Paramount

<u>Cast</u>: Jean Simmons (as Mary Follet), **Robert Preston** (as Jay Follet), Pat Hingle (as Ralph Follet), Aline MacMahon (as Aunt Hannah), Thomas Chalmers (as Joel), John Cullum (as Andrew), Helen Carew (as Mary's mother), Ronnie Claire Edwards (as Sally), John Henry Faulk (as Walter Starr), Mary Perry (as Great-aunt Sadie), Lylah Tiffany (as Great-great-grandmaw), Edwin Wolfe (as John Henry), Michael Kearney (as Rufus Follet).

Junior Bonner (1972)

Director: Sam Peckinpah

Studio: ABC Pictures, Joe Wizan-Booth Gardner Productions, Solar Productions

<u>Cast</u>: Steve McQueen (as Junior 'J.R.' Bonner), **Robert Preston** (as Ace Bonner), Ida Lupino (as Elvira Bonner), Ben Johnson (as Buck Roan), Joe Don Baker (as Curly Bonner), Barbara Leigh (as Charmagne), Mary Murphy (as Ruth Bonner), Bill McKinney (as Red Terwiliger), Dub Taylor (as Del), Sandra Deel (as Nurse Arlis), Don "Red" Barry (as Homer Rutledge), Charles H. Gray (as Burt).

Child's Play (1972)

Director: Sidney Lumet

Studio: Paramount

<u>Cast</u>: James Mason (as Jerome Malley), **Robert Preston** (as Joseph Dobbs), Beau Bridges (as Paul Reis), Ron Weyand (as Father Frank Mozian), Charles White (as Father William Griffin), David Rounds (as Father George Penny), Kate Harrington (as Mrs Carter), Brian Chapin (as O'Donnell), Bryant

Fraser (as Jennings), Mark Hall Haefeli (as Wilson), Tom Leopold (as Shea), Julius Lo Iacono (as McArdle), Christopher Man (as Travis), Paul O'Keefe (as Freddie Banks), Robert D. Randall (as Medley).

Mame (1974)
Director: Gene Saks
Studio: Warner Bros.
Cast: Lucille Ball (as "Auntie Mame" Dennis Burnside), Beatrice Arthur (as Vera Charles), **Robert Preston** (as Beauregard Jackson Pickett Burnside), Bruce Davison (as Patrick Dennis), Kirby Furlong (as young Patrick Dennis), Jane Connell (as Agnes Gooch), Joyce Van Patten (as Sally Cato), Lucille Benson (as Mother Burnside), George Chiang (as Ito), Doria Cook-Nelson (as Gloria Upson), Don Porter (as Mr. Upson), Audrey Christie (as Mrs. Upson), John McGiver (as Mr. Babcock), Bobbi Jordan (as Pegeen), Patrick Labyorteaux (as Peter), Ruth McDevitt (as Cousin Fan), Burt Mustin (as Uncle Jeff), Roger Price (as Ralph Divine), John Wheeler (as Judge Bregoff), Ned Wertimer (as Fred Kates), Michele Nichols (as Midge), Eric Gordon (as Boyd), Barbara Bosson (as Emily).

Semi-Tough (1977)
Director: Michael Ritchie
Studio: United Artists
Cast: Burt Reynolds (as Billy Clyde Puckett), Kris Kristofferson (as Marvin "Shake" Tiller), Jill Clayburgh (as Barbara Jane Bookman), **Robert Preston** (as Big Ed Bookman), Bert Convy (as Friedrich Bismark), Roger E. Mosley (as Puddin Patterson Sr.), Lotte Lenya (as Clara Pelf), Richard Masur (as Phillip Hooper), Carl Weathers (as Dreamer Tatum), Brian Dennehy (as T.J. Lambert), Mary Jo Catlett (as Earlene Emery), Joe Kapp (as Hose Manning), Ron Silver (as Vlada Kostov), Jim McKrell (as Bud McNair), Peter Bromilow (as Kostov's Interpreter), Norman Alden (as Coach Alvin Parks).

_S.O.B._ (1981)
Director: Blake Edwards
Studio: Paramount
Cast: Julie Andrews (as Sally Miles), William Holden (as Tim Culley), Richard Mulligan (as Felix Farmer), **Robert Preston** (as Dr. Irving Finegarten), Robert Webber (as Ben Coogan), Robert Vaughn (as David Blackman), Marisa Berenson (as Mavis), Larry Hagman (as Dick Benson), Stuart Margolin (as Gary Murdock), Loretta Swit (as Polly Reed), Craig Stevens (as Willard Pratt), Shelley Winters (as Eva Brown), Robert Loggia (as Herb Maskowitz), Jennifer Edwards (as Lila), Rosanna Arquette (as Babs), John Lawlor (as the Capitol Studios Manager), John Pleshette (as the Capitol Studios Vice-President), Ken Swofford (as Harold P. Harrigan), Hamilton Camp (as Lipschitz), Paul Stewart (as Harry Sandler), Larry Storch (as Swami), Mimi Davis (as Joyce Benson), David Young (as Sam Marshall), Herb Tanney (as Burgess Webster), Joe Penny (as Officer Buchwald), Erica Yohn (as Agnes), Colleen Brennan (as Tammy Taylor), Gene Nelson (as Clive Lytell).

Victor/Victoria (1982)
Director: Blake Edwards
Studio: Metro-Goldwyn-Mayer
Cast: Julie Andrews (as Victoria Grant / Count Victor Grazinski), James Garner (as King Marchand), **Robert Preston** (as Carroll "Toddy" Todd), Lesley Ann Warren (as Norma Cassidy), Alex Karras (as "Squash" Bernstein), John Rhys-Davies (as Andre Cassell), Peter Arne (as Labisse), Malcolm Jamieson (as Richard Di Nardo), Herb Tanny (as Charles Bovin), Ina Skriver (as Simone Kallisto), Maria Charles (as Madame President), Glen Murphy (as Boxer), Geoffrey Beevers (as Police Inspector), Jay Benedict (as Guy Longois).

The Last Starfighter (1984)
Director: Nick Castle
Studio: Universal Pictures

Cast: Lance Guest (as Alex Rogan / Beta Alex), **Robert Preston** (as Centauri), Dan O'Herlihy (as Grig), Catherine Mary Stewart (as Maggie Gordon), Norman Snow (as Xur), Kay E. Kuter (as Enduran), Barbara Bosson (as Jane Rogan), Chris Hebert (as Louis Rogan), Dan Mason (as Lord Kril), Vernon Washington (as Otis), Peter Nelson (as Jack Blake), Peggy Pope (as Elvira), Meg Wyllie (as Granny Gordon), Ellen Blake (as Clara Potter), Britt Leach (as Mr. Potter), Bunny Summers (as Mrs. Boone), Owen Bush (as Mr. Boone), Marc Alaimo (as Hitchhiker), Wil Wheaton (as Louis' friend), Cameron Dye (as Andy), Geoffrey Blake (as Gary).

THEATER

Twentieth Century (1950-1951)
Venue: Broadway Theatre: Fulton Theatre
Playwrights: Ben Hecht and Charles MacArthur
Role Dates: June 4, 1951 – June 30, 1951
Role: Oscar Jaffe (Replacement for José Ferrer)

The Male Animal (1952-1953)
Venue: Broadway
Theatre: Music Box Theatre
Playwrights: James Thurber and Elliott Nugent
Role Dates: April 30, 1952 – December 14, 1952
Role: Joe Ferguson

Men of Distinction (1953)
Venue: Broadway
Theatre: 48th Street Theatre
Playwright: Richard Condon
Role Dates: April 30, 1953 – May 02, 1953
Role: Peter Hogarth

His and Hers (1954)

Venue: Broadway

Theatre: 48th Street Theatre

Playwrights: Fay Kanin and Michael Kanin

Role Dates: January 7, 1954 – March 13, 1954

Role: Clem Scott

The Magic and the Loss (1954)

Venue: Broadway

Theatre: Booth Theatre

Playwright: Julian Funt

Role Dates: April 9, 1954 – May 1, 1954

Role: George Wilson

The Tender Trap (1954-1955)

Venue: Broadway

Theatre: Longacre Theatre

Playwrights: Max Shulman and Robert Paul Smith

Role Dates: October 13, 1954 – January 8, 1955

Role: Joe McCall

Janus (1955-1956)

Venue: Broadway

Theatre: Plymouth Theatre

Playwright: Carolyn Green

Role Dates: November 24, 1955 – June 30, 1956

Role: Gil

The Hidden River (1957)

Venue: Broadway

Theatre: Playhouse Theatre

Playwrights: Augustus Goetz and Ruth Goetz
Role Dates: January 23, 1957 – March 16, 1957
Role: Jean Monnerie

The Music Man (1957-1961)
Venue: Broadway
Theatre: Majestic Theatre
Playwright: Meredith Willson
Role Dates: December 19, 1957 – January 9, 1959 | Replacement for Bert
Parks: June 13, 1960 – June 25, 1960
Role: Harold Hill

We Take the Town (1962) [*Closed on The Road in Philadelphia*]
Venue: New Haven, CT and Philadelphia, PA
Theatre: Forrest Theatre (New Haven), Shubert Theatre (Philadelphia)
Playwrights: Matt Dubey, Felice Bauer, and Harold Karr
Role Dates: February 17, 1962 – March 17, 1962
Role: Pancho Villa

Too True to be Good (1963)
Venue: Broadway
Theatre: 54th Street Theatre
Playwright: George Bernard Shaw
Role Dates: March 12, 1963 – June 1, 1963
Role: The Burglar

Nobody Loves an Albatross (1963-1964)
Venue: Broadway
Theatre: Lyceum Theatre
Playwright: Ronald Alexander
Role Dates: December 19, 1963 – May 30, 1964

Role: Nat Bentley

Ben Franklin in Paris (1964-1965)
Venue: Broadway
Theatre: Lunt-Fontanne Theatre
Playwrights: Sidney Michaels
Role Dates: October 27, 1964 – May 1, 1965
Role: Benjamin Franklin

The Lion in Winter (1966)
Venue: Broadway
Theatre: Ambassador Theatre
Playwrights: James Goldman
Role Dates: March 3, 1966 – May 21, 1966
Role: Henry II

_I Do, I Do!_ (1966-1968)
Venue: Broadway
Theatre: 46th Street Theatre
Playwright: Tom Jones
Role Dates: December 5, 1966 – December 6, 1967
Role: Michael

_I Do, I Do!_ - **National Tour** (1968-1969)
Venue: National Tour
Tour Dates: April 4, 1968 – February 21, 1969
Cities: Rochester, New York; Indianapolis, Indiana; Minneapolis, Minnesota; Los Angeles, California; Portland, Oregon; Vancouver, British Columbia; Seattle, Washington; San Diego, California; Denver, Colorado; Phoenix, Arizona; Kansas City and St. Louis, Missouri; Omaha, Nebraska; St. Paul, Minnesota; Milwaukee, Wisconsin; Memphis, Tennessee; Dallas,

Texas; Houston, Texas; Oklahoma City, Oklahoma; Hershey, Pennsylvania; Baltimore, Maryland; and Detroit, Michigan.
Role: Michael

__Mack & Mabel__ (1974)
Venue: Broadway
Theatre: Majestic Theatre
Playwright: Michael Stewart
Role Dates: October 6, 1974 – November 30, 1974
Role: Mack Sennett

__Sly Fox__ (1976-1978)
Venue: Broadway
Theatre: Broadhurst Theatre
Playwright: Larry Gelbart
Role Dates: May 10, 1977 – December 31, 1977 (Replacement for George C. Scott)
Role: Foxwell J. Sly and The Judge

__The Prince of Grand Street__ (1978) [*Closed on The Road in Boston*]
Venue: Philadelphia, PA and Boston, MA
Theatre: Forrest Theatre (Philadelphia), Shubert Theatre (Boston)
Playwrights: Robert Merrill
Role Dates: March 7, 1978 – April 15, 1978
Role: Nathan Rashumsky

TELEVISION: ACTING ROLES

Studio One in Hollywood (CBS)
Episode: *The Survivors* (aired March 20, 1950)
Cast: Donald Curtis, Leslie Nielsen, Stanley Ridges, Robert Cromwell, Svea Grunfeld, **Robert Preston**. Dudley Sadler.

Lux Video Theatre (CBS)

Episode: *The Old Lady Shows Her Medals* (aired April 2, 1951)

Cast: Rosalind Ivan (as Mrs. Mickleham), Jay Jackson (as Self/Announcer), Stuart MacIntosh (as Mr. Willings), Phoebe Mackay (as Mrs. Haggerty), **Robert Preston** (as Dowey), Maida Reade (as Mrs. Twymley), Evelyn Wall (as Woman in Street), Margaret Wycherly (as Mrs. Dowey).

Host: James Mason, Otto Kruger, Gordon MacRae, Ken Carpenter.

Man Against Crime (CBS)

Episode: Recurring role as Pat Barnett (aired June 29 – August 3, 1951)

Lux Video Theatre (CBS)

Episode: *Cafe Ami* (aired October 15, 1951)

Cast: **Robert Preston** (as Jed Kennedy), Maria Riva (as Hilda), Rod Steiger (as Victor Honegger), Walter Matthau (as Craig), Susan Wayne (as Girl Singer), Andrew Duggan (as Thug), Lawrence Breitman (as Waiter).

Host: James Mason, Otto Kruger, Gordon MacRae, Ken Carpenter.

Schlitz Playhouse of Stars (CBS)

Episode: *The Nymph and the Lamp* (aired December 7, 1951)

Cast: **Robert Preston**, Margaret Sullavan

Host: Irene Dunne

Lux Video Theatre (CBS)

Episode: *Kelly* (aired February 2, 1952)

Cast: Geraldine Brooks (as Odette), Marcel Hillaire (as Frenchman), Jay Jackson (as Self/Announcer), Horace McMahon (as Capt. Hodges), **Robert Preston** (as Kelly), Jack Warden (as Sgt. Stivers).

Host: James Mason, Otto Kruger, Gordon MacRae, Ken Carpenter.

Pulitzer Prize Playhouse (ABC)
Episode: *The Jungle* (aired April 9, 1952)
Cast: Elmer Davis, Nina Foch, Hanna Landy, **Robert Preston**, Kent Smith.
Host: Elmer Davis

Curtain Call (NBC)
Episode: *The Promise* (aired June 20, 1952)
Cast: Carol Bruce, **Robert Preston**

Lux Video Theatre (CBS)
Episode: *Happily, But Not Forever* (aired September 22, 1952)
Cast: Bramwell Fletcher (as President Maynard), Jay Jackson (as Self/
Announcer), Malcolm Keen (as Dean Truitt), June Lockhart (as Sally Eaton),
Robert Preston (as Isaac Eaton).
Host: James Mason, Otto Kruger, Gordon MacRae, Ken Carpenter.

Robert Montgomery Presents (NBC)
Episode: *Maggie, Pack Your Bags* (aired January 19, 1953)
Cast: **Robert Preston** (as Jeff Frazer), Margaret Hayes (as Maggie Frazer)
Host: Robert Montgomery

Lux Video Theatre (CBS)
Episode: *The Betrayer* (aired May 14, 1953)
Cast: Richard Carlyle (as Detective), Bruce Gordon (as Labrutte), Jay
Jackson (as Self/Announcer), Grace Kelly (as Meg), Louis Lytton (as
Mac), **Robert Preston** (as Tom), Doris Rich (as Mrs. Curtis).
Host: James Mason, Otto Kruger, Gordon MacRae, Ken Carpenter.

The Plymouth Playhouse (ABC)
Episode: *Baby and Me* (aired June 14, 1953)
Cast: Janis Paige, Stanley Prager, **Robert Preston**

Host: David Cook

Medallion Theatre (CBS)
Episode: *The Quiet Village* (aired August 22, 1953)
Cast: **Robert Preston**, Rod Steiger

Danger (CBS)
Episode: *The Boys on the Corner* (aired September 8, 1953)
Cast: **Robert Preston**, Madeleine Sherwood
Host: Dick Stark

The United States Steel Hour (ABC)
Episode: *Hope for a Harvest* (aired November 10, 1953)
Cast: **Robert Preston** (as Elliott Martin), Faye Emerson (as Mathilda
Martin), Sophie Treadwell (as Carlotta Thatcher), Dino Di Luca (as Victor
de Lucchi).
Host: Lawrence Langner, Roger Pryor

Campbell Summer Soundstage (NBC)
Episode: *Al Toolum and His Buddy Leo* (aired April 30, 1954)
Cast: Leo Durocher, Van Dyke Parks, **Robert Preston**.

The United States Steel Hour (ABC)
Episode: *The End of Paul Dane* (aired May 11, 1954)
Actors: **Robert Preston** (as Dr. Abbott), Warren Stevens (as Paul Dane),
Teresa Wright (as Margaret Swift).
Host: Lawrence Langner, Roger Pryor

The United States Steel Hour (ABC)
Episode: *The Bogey Man* (aired January 18, 1955)

Actors: Humphrey Davis (as Mr. King), Celeste Holm (as Madge Collins), **Robert Preston** (as Jack Roberts), Darryl Richard (as Tony), Ann Thomas (as Miss Orchard), James Westerfield (as Sam Moreno).
Host: Lawrence Langner, Roger Pryor.

Climax! (CBS)
Episode: *The Box of Chocolates* (aired February 24, 1955)
Cast: Vanessa Brown (as Vera), Victor Jory (as Robert), Pat O'Brien (as Police Lieutenant Moore), **Robert Preston** (as William Struthers).
Host: William Lundigan, Mary Costa

The Elgin Hour (ABC)
Episode: *Crime in the Streets* (aired March 8, 1955)
Cast: **Robert Preston** (as Ben Wagner), Glenda Farrell (as Mrs. Dane), John Cassavetes (as Frankie Dane), Mark Rydell (as Lou Macklin), Van Dyke Parks (as Richie Dane), Will Kuluva (as Mr. Gioia), Ivan Cury (as 'Baby' Gioia), David Winters (as Glasses), Jerry Wynne (as Blockbuster), Robert Brivic (as Fighter), Tony Mitchell (as Benny).

Lux Video Theatre (CBS)
Episode: *It Grows on Trees* (aired March 17, 1955)
Cast: Robert Bruce (as Policeman), Alexander Campbell (as Carrollman), Ken Carpenter (as Self/Announcer), Lauren Chapin (as Midge Baxter), Richard H. Cutting (as Leatherbee), Dabbs Greer (as MacGuire), Henry Hunter (as Murchison), Ruth Hussey (as Polly Baxter), David Janssen (as Ralph), Charlotte Knight (as Mrs. Pryor), Forrest Lewis (as Dr. Burrows), Tom Nolan (as Flip Baxter), **Robert Preston** (as Phil Baxter), Ralph Sanford (as Police Sgt.), Leigh Snowden (as Diane Baxter), Pierre Watkin (as Sleamish).
Host: James Mason, Otto Kruger, Gordon MacRae, Ken Carpenter.

General Electric Theater (CBS)

Episode: *It Gives Me Great Pleasure* (aired April 3, 1955)

Cast: Myrna Loy (as Kate Kennedy), Zachary Scott (as David Wadsworth), **Robert Preston** (as Jim Tweedy), Harold J. Kennedy (as Trumbull), Loïs Bolton (as Mrs. Tweedy), Jeff Elliott (as Johnny Kennedy).

Host: Ronald Reagan

Kraft Theatre (NBC)

Episode: *Drop on the Devil* (aired June 22, 1955)

Cast: Everett Chambers, **Robert Preston**, Ford Rainey, Dick York.

Host: Charles Stark

Robert Montgomery Presents (NBC)

Episode: *Woman in the Window* (aired September 12, 1955)

Cast: **Robert Preston** (as Professor Richard Wanley), Maria Riva (as Alice Reed)

Host: Robert Montgomery

The Alcoa Hour (NBC)

Episode: *Undertow* (aired December 11, 1955)

Cast: John Kerr (as Jamie Hallock), Hanna Landy (as Gail Parr), Thomas Mitchell (as Cap'n Jarvis), Cathleen Nesbitt (as Mother Hallock), **Robert Preston** (as Doug Hallock), Teresa Wright (as Sylvia Hallock).

The Alcoa Hour (NBC)

Episode: *Long After Summer* (aired February 5, 1956)

Cast: Ben Astar (as Manuel), Raymond Bramley (as Minister), Donald Harron (as Jack), Susan Kohner (as Joanna), Augusta Merighi (as Josie), Simon Oakland (as Bert), **Robert Preston** (as Tom Waycroff), Cameron Prud'Homme (as Alben).

The 20th Century-Fox Hour (CBS)

Episode: *Child of the Regiment* (October 3, 1956)

Cast: Teresa Wright (as Janice Walner), Louise Arthur (as Mrs. Carsten), Paul Birch (as Provost Marshal), John Close (as First MP), Gary Hunley (as Tommy Carsten), Candace Lee (as Mari), Grace Lem (as Mrs. Yamoto), **Robert Preston** (as Capt. Bob Walner), Grandon Rhodes (as Col. Jamison), Everett Sloane (as Maj. Carsten), Katherine Warren (as Mrs. Jamison), Reba Waters (as Alicia Carsten).

Goodyear Playhouse (NBC)

Episode: *Missouri Legend* (aired October 7, 1956)

Cast: Barbara Baxley (as Mrs. Weeks), Thomas A. Carlin (as Bob Ford), James Gavin (as Billy Gashade), Louise Platt (as Mrs. Howard), **Robert Preston** (as Thomas Howard / Jesse James).

Climax! (CBS)

Episode: *The Midas Touch* (aired October 18, 1956)

Cast: Walter Abel (as Stewart), George Dolenz (as Cortino), Margaret Hayes (as Sylvia), Anna Navarro (as Teresa), **Robert Preston** (as Cleve Gordon). Host: William Lundigan, Mary Costa

Playhouse 90 (CBS)

Episode: *Made in Heaven* (aired December 6, 1956)

Cast: **Robert Preston** (as Zachary Meredith), Phyllis Kirk (as Nancy Tennant), Jacques Bergerac (as Laszlo Vertes), Imogene Coca (as Elsa Meredith), Mark Roberts (as Mr. Tennant), Benny Baker (as Bartender), Benay Venuta (as Marian Hunt), Sheila Bond (as June), Eddie Mayehoff (as Philip Dunlap). Host: Richard Joy

The Alcoa Hour (NBC)

Episode: *The Animal Kingdom* (aired February 17, 1957)

Cast: Alan Hale Jr. (as Red Regan), Joanne Linville (as Daisy Sage), Paul McGrath (as Rufus Collier), Meg Mundy (as Cecelia Henry), **Robert Preston** (as Tom Collier), Mary Welch (as Franc).

Omnibus (ABC)
Episode: *The Fall River Legend – The Trial of Lizzie Borden* (aired March 24. 1957)
Cast: Katharine Bard (as Lizzie Borden), Loïs Bolton, Margaret Hamilton (as Mrs. Gifford), Richard Kiley (as The Prosecuting Attorney), Christopher Plummer, **Robert Preston** (as The Defense Attorney), Diana Adams, Lucia Chase, Nora Kaye, John Kriza, Dimitri Romanoff, Katharine Ross.
Host: Alistair Cooke

Kraft Theatre (NBC)
Episode: *Nothing Personal* (aired June 19, 1957)
Cast: Nina Foch, **Robert Preston**
Host: Charles Stark

Climax! (CBS)
Episode: *Trail of Terror* (aired August 8, 1957)
Cast: Diana Lynn (as Julie Morton), **Robert Preston** (as Lt. Hogue), Kurt Kasznar (as Jean Duclerc), Arthur Hanson (as Sgt. Russell), Katherine Warren (as Miss Nolan), Walter Reed (as Dr. Frank Morton), James McCallion (as Kielty), Claire Du Brey (as The Landlady), Ben Wright (as Dr. Billings), Kay E. Kuter (as The Pharmacist), Maurice Solomon (as The Coroner), Paul Siemion (as Bonaventure), Perry Ivins (as The Bartender), Barbara Bell Wright (as Nurse), Patrick Sexton (as The Intern).
Host: William Lundigan, Mary Costa

The Bells of St. Mary's (CBS)
TV Movie: (aired October 27, 1959)

Cast: Claudette Colbert (as Sister Benedict), Marc Connelly, Glenda Farrell, Nancy Marchand (as Sister Michael), Barbara Myers, **Robert Preston** (as Father Chuck O'Malley), Charles Ruggles (as Horace Bogardus).

The DuPont Show of the Month (CBS)
Episode: *Years Ago* (aired April 21, 1960)
Cast: **Robert Preston** (as Clinton Jones), Peggy Conklin (as Annie Jones), Sandra Church (as Ruth Gordon Jones), Janice Mars (as Miss Glavin), Arthur Malet (as Mr. Bagley), Roy Fant (as Mr. Sparrow), Jo Anna March (as Katherine Follett), Abigail Kellogg (as Anna Witham), Carl Reindel (as Fred Whitmarsh).

Happy Endings (ABC)
TV Movie (aired April 10, 1975)
Cast: Lauren Bacall, Lisa Rochelle, Nancy Andrews, Jimmy Fields, Art Carney, Elizabeth Wilson, John Cunningham, Alan King, **Robert Preston**, James Earl Jones.

My Father's House (ABC)
TV Movie (aired June 1, 1975)
Cast: Cliff Robertson (as Tom Lindholm Jr.), **Robert Preston** (as Tom Lindholm Sr.), Eileen Brennan (as Mrs. Lindholm Sr.), Rosemary Forsyth (as Judith Lindholm), Ruth McDevitt (as Anna), Michael-James Wixted (as Tom Jr., as a boy), Lark Geib (as Susan), Michael Cornelison (as Steven), Brad Savage (as Brad), Carlene Olson (as Ellen), Gail Strickland (as Paula), Laurie Main (as Food Editor), Clarke Gordon (as Flaherty).

The Chisholms (CBS)
Episodes: Miniseries and Primetime TV Series
Cast: **Robert Preston** (as Hadley Chisolm), Rosemary Harris (as Minerva Chisolm, Ben Murphy (as Will Chisolm), James Van Patten (as Bo Chisolm),

Stacy Nelkin / Delta Burke (as Bonnie Sue Chisolm), Brian Kerwin / Brett Cullen (as Gideon Chisolm), Charles Frank / Reid Smith (as Lester Hackett), Victoria Racimo (as Keewidinok), Mitchell Ryan (as Cooper Hawkins), Devon Ericson (as Betsy O'Neal), and Susan Swift (as Annabel Chisolm and Mercy Hopwell).

Season 1 – 4 Episode Miniseries (aired March 29, 1979 - April 19, 1979)

Season 2 – 9 Episode Primetime Series (aired January 19, 1980 – March 15, 1980)

(Preston's character was killed in Season 2, Episode 5, which aired on February 16, 1980)

The Man That Corrupted Hadleyburg (PBS)

TV Short (aired March 17, 1980)

Cast: **Robert Preston** (as The Stranger), Tom Aldredge (as Edward Richards), Fred Gwynne (as Rev. Burgess), Frances Sternhagen (as Mary Richards).

Rehearsal for Murder (CBS)

TV Movie (aired May 26, 1982)

Cast: **Robert Preston** (as Alex Dennison), Lynn Redgrave (as Monica Welles), Patrick Macnee (as David Mathews), Lawrence Pressman (as Lloyd Andrews), William Russ (as Frank Heller), Madolyn Smith Osborne (as Karen Daniels), Jeff Goldblum (as Leo Gibbs), William Daniels (as Walter Lamb), John Finnegan (as Damon), Wallace Rooney (as Ernie), Buck Young (as Lieutenant McElroy).

September Gun (CBS)

TV Movie (aired October 8, 1983)

Cast: **Robert Preston** (as Ben Sunday), Patty Duke Astin (as Sister Dulcina), Geoffrey Lewis (as Sheriff Johnson), Sally Kellerman (as Mama Queen), David Knell (as Jason, Ben's Nephew), Jacques Aubuchon (as Father

Jerome), Christopher Lloyd (as Jack Brian), Jon Gries (as Brian Brian), Clayton Landey (as Boomer Brian), Pat Anderson (as Billie Sue), Gene Blakely (as Merchant), Henry Kendrick (as Lawyer), Grizzly Green (as Luke), Roy Gunsberg (as Jasper), Austin Judson (as Henry).

Finnegan Begin Again (HBO)
Cable TV Movie (aired February 24, 1985)
Cast: Mary Tyler Moore (Liz DeHaan), **Robert Preston** (as Mike Finnegan), Sam Waterston (as Paul Broadbent), Sylvia Sidney (as Margaret Finnegan), David Huddleston (as Jack Archer), Bob Gunton (as Christian Jamison), Giancarlo Esposito (as Intruder), Russell Horton (as Mort), Peter Friedman (as John Jewell), Jon DeVries (as Dr. Binder), Frederick Strother (as Elias Williams), Rick Warner (as Charlie DeWitt), Jan Guarino (as Ticket Seller).

Outrage! (CBS)
TV Movie (aired March 2, 1986)
Cast: **Robert Preston** (as Dennis Riordan), Beau Bridges (as Brad Gordon), Burgess Meredith (as Judge Aaron Klein), Linda Purl (as Arlene Robbins), Mel Ferrer (as Judge Michael Lengel), Anthony Newley (as Victor Coles), William Allen Young (as Lester Crewe), Bill Dearth (as Spence), Steven Marlo (as William Simmons), Stan Haze (as Charlie Johnson), Brent Jennings (as Wilbert Ward), Ric Mancini (as Sgt. Kalbfus), Robert Miano (as Santini), Vince Howard (as Prouty), Lou Valenzi (as District Attorney).

TELEVISION AND DOCUMENTARY SHORTS: AS HIMSELF

Wings Up (1943) [Documentary Short]
Cast: Clark Gable, **Robert Preston**, General Henry H. "Hap" Arnold, Gilbert Roland, William Holden, Brenda Marshall.

Screen Snapshots: Hawaii in Hollywood (1948) [Documentary Short]
Cast: Jud Allen, Don the Beachcomber, Lee Bowman, Georgia Carroll, Alice Faye, Phil Harris, John Huston, Danny Kaye, Evelyn Keyes, Frank Morgan, **Robert Preston.**

Footlights and Kleiglights [NBC TV Series]
Episode: Episode 1.67 (aired July 24, 1951)
Cast: Ben Grauer, **Robert Preston**
Host: Ben Grauer

Your Show of Shows [NBC TV Series]
Episode: Episode #3.12 (aired November 24, 1951)
Cast: Sid Caesar, Imogene Coca, Carl Reiner, Howard Morris
Guest Performer: **Robert Preston**
Host: Sid Caesar and Imogene Coca

Your Show of Shows [NBC TV Series]
Episode: Guest Host – **Robert Preston** (aired January 24, 1953)
Cast: Carl Reiner, Howard Morris, Bill Hayes, Bambi Linn, Rod Alexander, Judy Johnson, Jack Russell
Host: **Robert Preston**

Anywhere, U.S.A. [ABC TV Series]
Episode: Aired November 23, 1952 - January 25, 1953
Host: Eddie Dowling, **Robert Preston**

The Martha Raye Show [NBC TV Series]
Episode: May 15, 1954
Guests: Jake LaMotta, **Robert Preston**, Margaret Truman
Host: Martha Raye

Omnibus (CBS)
Episode: *The Adams Family* (1955)
Cast: Alan Hewitt, **Robert Preston**, Thomas B. McCabe, Eliot Noyes, Richard Purdy, Robert Duke, Ray Johnson.
Host: Alistair Cooke

Sentinels in the Air [Documentary Short]
February 10, 1956
Cast: **Robert Preston** (Narrator), Sam Campbell, Edward White, Joe Reilly, John Train, Tim Selden, Doug Wood.

New Family in Town [Documentary Short]
1956
Narrator: **Robert Preston**. Twelve-minute black-and-white civil defense documentary focusing on the importance of air raid shelters for personal protection.

Playhouse 90 [CBS TV Series]
Episode: *Eloise* (aired November 22, 1956)
Role: Self - Announcing Next Week's Show

Playhouse 90 [CBS TV Series]
Episode: *Confession* (aired November 29, 1956)
Guest Host: **Robert Preston**

What's My Line? [CBS TV Series]
Episode: "Dr. Norman Vincent Peale & Judy Holliday" (aired March 17, 1957)
Panelists: Arlene Francis, **Robert Preston**, Dorothy Kilgallen, Bennett Cerf
Host: John Charles Daly

What's My Line? [CBS TV Series]
Episode: "Cyril Ritchard" (aired December 22, 1957)
Panelists: Dorothy Kilgallen, **Robert Preston**, Arlene Francis, Bennett Cerf
Host: John Charles Daly

The 12th Annual Tony Awards [aired April 13, 1958]
Venue: Waldorf-Astoria Hotel, New York, NY
Role: Self – Winner of the Tony Award for Distinguished Featured Musical
Actor

Perry Como's Kraft Music Hall [CBS TV Series]
Episode: "Maureen O'Hara, Robert Preston and Jimmy Van Heusen" (aired
September 13, 1958)
Guests: Maureen O'Hara, **Robert Preston**, Jimmy Van Heusen.
Host: Perry Como

You Asked for It [ABC TV Series]
Episode: "Backstage Broadway" (aired March 1, 1959)
Cast: Vivian Blaine, Eddie Cantor, Gypsy Rose Lee, **Robert Preston**,
Joseph Schildkraut.
Host: Jack Smith

The 13th Annual Tony Awards [aired April 12, 1959]
Venue: Waldorf-Astoria Hotel, New York, NY
Broadcast on local television station WCBS-TV (Channel 2) in New York
City Role: Self – Presenter

The Bell Telephone Hour [NBC TV Series]
Episode: "One Nation Indivisible" (aired October 28, 1960)
Guests: Dorothy Collins, Mahalia Jackson, Jo Stafford
Host: **Robert Preston**

The Bell Telephone Hour [NBC TV Series]

Episode: "Encore!" (aired April 28, 1961)

Guests: Rosemary Clooney, Mahalia Jackson, **Robert Preston**.

The 16th Annual Tony Awards [aired April 29, 1962]

Venue: Waldorf-Astoria Hotel, New York, NY

Broadcast on local television station WCBS-TV (Channel 2) in New York City

Host: **Robert Preston** – along with Ray Bolger

The Dinah Shore Show [NBC TV Series]

Episode: "Salute to the Month of June with Togetherness" (aired June 1, 1962)

Guests: **Robert Preston**, Rita Moreno, Vic Damone, The Frank DeVol Orchestra.

Damone sings "Flamingo;" **Preston** sings "Ya Got Trouble;" Damone and Shore sing "June" medley, Moreno sings "Teamwork", "Jim," "I Walk Alone," "Mad About Him Blues;" Moreno and Shore sing "The Lady Wants to Twist;" and Damore, **Preston**, Moreno, and Shore sing "Ain't Down Yet."

Host: Dinah Shore

Dinner with the President [CBS TV Special]

Air Date: January 31, 1963

Venue: Sheraton-Park Hotel, Washington DC

Guests: President John F. Kennedy, Will Holt, Judy Collins, Lynn Gold, the Clancy Brothers and Tommy Makem, Josh White, and Odetta.

Host: **Robert Preston**

An Evening with Carol Burnett [CBS TV Special]

Episode (Air Date): February 24, 1963 Guest: **Robert Preston**

Host: Carol Burnett

What's My Line? [CBS TV Series]
Episode: "Robert Preston" (aired March 3, 1963)
Panelists: Dorothy Kilgallen, Allen Ludden, Arlene Francis, Bennett Cerf
Mystery Guest: **Robert Preston**
Host: John Charles Daly

The Bell Telephone Hour [NBC TV Series]
Episode: "Episode #6.1" (October 8, 1963)
Guests: Svetlana Beriosova, Anna Moffo, Rudolf Nureyev, Richard Tucker
Host: **Robert Preston**

The Tonight Show Starring Johnny Carson [NBC TV Series]
Episode: January 2, 1964
Guests: Henny Youngman, **Robert Preston**, Selma Diamond.
Host: Johnny Carson

Password [CBS TV Game Show]
Episode: Carol Burnett vs. Robert Preston (aired January 9, 1964)
Panelists: Carol Burnett, **Robert Preston**
Host: Allen Ludden

What's My Line? [CBS TV Series]
Episode: "Marion Ladewig, W.J. Kelly, Noël Coward" (aired January 12, 1964)
Panelists: Dorothy Kilgallen, **Robert Preston**, Arlene Francis, Bennett Cerf
Host: John Charles Daly

The 18th Annual Tony Awards [aired May 24, 1964]
Venue: New York Hilton, New York, NY
Broadcast on local television station WWOR-TV (Channel 9) in New York City

Master of Ceremonies: **Robert Preston** - along with Steve Lawrence

NAACP Freedom Spectacular [CBS TV Special]
Air Date: May 14, 1964
Role: Self – Performer

The Les Crane Show [ABC TV Premiere Pilot]
Air Date: August 3, 1964
Panelists: Harry Belafonte, **Robert Preston**, Riccardo Montalban, Celeste Holm, Mel Brooks. Kay Mulvey, Irving Shulman, Adela Rogers St. Johns, Dr. Harold Smith
Host: Les Crane

American Musical Theater [CBS TV Series]
Air Date: November 28, 1964
Panelists: **Robert Preston**, Ulla Sallert, Donald Pippin.
Host: Earl Wrightson

The Ed Sullivan Show [CBS TV Series]
Episode: Episode #18.12 (aired December 13, 1964)
Guests: Daniele Barioni, Anita Bryant, Con Conwally, Julie Harris, Alan King, Anne Meara, **Robert Preston**, Jerry Stiller, Arthur Worsley
Host: Ed Sullivan

What's My Line? [CBS TV Series]
Episode: "Ruth Ansom, Joe Dogan, **Robert Preston**" (aired March 13, 1966)
Panelists: Tony Randall, Jeanne Parr, Arlene Francis, Bennett Cerf
Mystery Guest: **Robert Preston**
Host: John Charles Daly

The Bell Telephone Hour [NBC TV Series]

Episode: "Great Moments" (aired April 27, 1965)
Guests: Harry Belafonte, Maurice Chevalier, **Robert Preston**, Rudolf
Nureyev, Joan Sutherland

The Merv Griffin Show [Westinghouse Broadcasting TV Series]
Episode: "Robert Preston, David Burns, Bruce Scott, Jackie Mason" (aired
July 9, 1965)
Guests: **Robert Preston**, David Burns, Bruce Scott, Jackie Mason
Host: Merv Griffin

The Young Set [ABC TV Series]
Episode: "Robert Preston" (aired November 9, 1965)
Guests: **Robert Preston**
Host: Phyllis Kirk

The Merv Griffin Show [Westinghouse Broadcasting TV Series]
Episode: "Robert Preston, Pat Harrington, Hermione Gingold, London Lee,
Allen & Rossi" (aired April 4, 1966)
Guests: **Robert Preston**, Pat Harrington, Hermione Gingold, London Lee,
Steve Rossi, Marty Allen
Host: Merv Griffin

The Tonight Show Starring Johnny Carson [NBC TV Series]
Episode: April 19, 1966
Guests: **Robert Preston**, Godfrey Cambridge, Selma Lee, Rosetta Shaw
Host: Johnny Carson

This Proud Land [ABC TV Mini-Series / Documentary]
6 Episodes: "The Wild, Wild East" (aired November 9, 1965), "Big Sky
Country" (aired December 18, 1965), "The Sun Country" (aired January 26,

1966), "The Way Out West" (aired February 25, 1966), "The South" (aired March 31, 1966), "The Surprising Midwest" (aired April 25, 1966).
Host / Guide: **Robert Preston**

The 21st Annual Tony Awards [aired May 26, 1967]
Venue: Shubert Theatre, New York, NY Broadcast on ABC television
Host: **Robert Preston** - along with Mary Martin
Winner - Best Performance by a Leading Actor in a Musical: **Robert Preston**

The 9th Annual Grammy Awards [aired March 2, 1967]
Role: Self - Presenter
Venue: Beverly Hilton Hotel, Los Angeles, CA

The 23rd Annual Tony Awards [aired April 20, 1969]
Role: Self – Presenter
Venue: Mark Hellinger Theatre, New York, NY Broadcast on NBC television
Host: **Robert Preston**

The 25th Annual Tony Awards [aired March 28, 1971]
Role: Self – Presenter and Performer: Sang "Ya Got Trouble" for the Salute to 25 Years of Tony Award Winning Musicals
Venue: Palace Theatre, New York, NY Broadcast on ABC television

The 28th Annual Tony Awards [aired April 21, 1974]
Venue: Shubert Theatre, New York, NY Broadcast on ABC television
Host: **Robert Preston** – along with Peter Falk, Florence Henderson, and Cicely Tyson

The 29th Annual Tony Awards [aired April 20, 1975]
Venue: Winter Garden Theatre in New York, NY Broadcast on ABC television

Role: Self – Nominee for Best Performance by a Leading Actor in a Musical (Mack & Mabel)

Dinah! [TV Series distributed by 20th Century Fox Television]
Episode: Episode #2.46 (aired November 17, 1975)
Guests: Abraham Beame, Yul Brynner, Dick Cavett, Ethel Merman, **Robert Preston**.
Host: Dinah Shore

The 31st Annual Tony Awards [aired June 5, 1977]
Venue: Shubert Theatre in New York, NY Broadcast on ABC television
Role: Self – Presenter and Performer

The Mike Douglas Show [Westinghouse Broadcasting TV Series]
Episode: Episode #17.133 (aired April 3, 1978)
Guests: Daryl Dragon, **Robert Preston**, Jay Redack, Joan Rivers, Toni Tennille.
Host: Mike Douglas

Looks Familiar [Thames Television]
Episode Date: April 28, 1981
Guests: Diana Dors, **Robert Preston**, Dick Vosburgh
Host: Dennis Norden

The 39th Annual Golden Globe Awards [aired January 30, 1982]
Venue: The Beverly Hilton Hotel in Los Angeles, CA. Broadcast on CBS Television
Host: **Robert Preston** – along with Linda Gray

Night of 100 Stars [ABC TV Special]
Air Date: March 8, 1982
Venue: Radio City Music Hall in New York, NY.
Robert Preston – Star performer

The 36th Annual Tony Awards [aired June 6, 1982]
Role: Self - Presenter and Performer (**Robert Preston**)
Venue: Imperial Theatre, New York, NY

Bob Hope's Pink Panther Thanksgiving Gala [NBC TV Special]
Air Date: November 21, 1982
Guests: Julie Andrews, Dean Martin, Dudley Moore, Willie Nelson,
Bernadette Peters, **Robert Preston**, Robert Wagner
Host: Bob Hope

The 40th Annual Golden Globe Awards [Syndicated TV Special]
Venue: Beverly Hilton Hotel, Beverly Hills, CA Air Date: January 29, 1983
Role: Nominee for Best Performance of an Actor in a Motion Picture –
Comedy or Musical for *Victor/Victoria* (1982)

The 9th Annual People's Choice Awards [aired March 17, 1983]
Venue: Santa Monica Civic Auditorium, Santa Monica, CA. Broadcast on
CBS Television
Role: Self – Presenter

The 55th Annual Academy Awards [April 11, 1983]
Venue: Dorothy Chandler Pavilion, Los Angeles, CA Broadcast on ABC
Television
Role: Nominee for Best Supporting Actor for *Victor/Victoria* (1982)

Eighth Annual Circus Of The Stars [CBS TV Special]
Air Date: December 18, 1983
Venue: Caesar's Palace in Las Vegas, NV.
Host: **Robert Preston** (as Ringmaster) – with Louis Gossett, Jr., Beverly
D'Angelo, and Dottie West.

The Laurence Olivier Awards [CBS TV Special]
Hosted by the Society of London Theatre, London, England
Presenters: Michael York, Angela Lansbury, Ellen Burstyn, **Robert Preston**, Tony Randall Broadcast on January 19, 1984

The 38th Annual Tony Awards [CBS TV Special]
Venue: The Gershwin Theatre in New York, NY Air Date: June 3, 1984
Role: Self - Host & Presenter & Performer
Host: **Robert Preston** – along with Julie Andrews

Going Hollywood: The 30s [Movie Channel TV Documentary]
Air Date: April 1, 1984
Role: Self - Host

Night of 100 Stars II [ABC TV Special]
Air Date: March 10, 1985
Role: Performer
Robert Preston featured in the "Special Movie Stars" segment.

RADIO PERFORMANCES

1940
Alice Faye, Ray Milland, **Robert Preston**, "Alexander's Ragtime Band", *Lux Radio Theater*, CBS Radio, Los Angeles, CA: CBS, June 3, 1940.

1941
Loretta Young, **Robert Preston**, "The Lady from Cheyenne", *Lux Radio Theater*, CBS Radio, Los Angeles, CA: CBS, June 16, 1941.

1942

Alice Faye, **Robert Preston**, "City for Conquest", *Lux Radio Theater*, CBS Radio, Los Angeles, CA: CBS, February 9, 1942.

Pat O'Brien, **Robert Preston**, Ralph Bellamy, "The Fighting 69th", *Lux Radio Theater*, CBS Radio, Los Angeles, CA: CBS, April 6, 1942

Rita Hayworth, Robert Taylor, **Robert Preston**, "Test Pilot", *Lux Radio Theater*, CBS Radio, Los Angeles, CA: CBS, May 25, 1942.

Brian Donlevy, Broderick Crawford, **Robert Preston**, "Wake Island", *Lux Radio Theater*, CBS Radio, Los Angeles, CA: CBS, October 10, 1942.

AWARDS, NOMINATIONS, PROFESSIONAL RECOGNITION

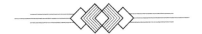

September 23, 1952 [Recognition]
Robert Preston is the guest of honor at a tea given by the Twelfth Night Club theatrical group in New York, NY.

April 13, 1958 [Winner]
The Tony Award for Distinguished Featured Musical Actor was awarded to Robert Preston for his role as Harold Hill in *The Music Man*.

April 21, 1959 [Winner]
The Aegis Theater Club presents an award to Robert Preston at the Plaza Hotel in New York, NY for his role in *The Music Man*.

March 5, 1963 [Nominee]

Robert Preston is a nominee for a Golden Globe for Best Actor - Comedy or Musical for *The Music Man* (1962).

September 1963 [Winner]

The annual Laurel Award for Top Male Musical Performance was presented to Robert Preston for his role in *The Music Man* (1962).

October 18, 1963 [Winner]

The International Alliance of Theatrical Stage Employees (IATSE) recognized Robert Preston's contributions to the stage, film, and television by presenting the actor with the union's 50th Anniversary Award at a dinner held at the Americana Hotel in New York, NY.

May 15, 1964 [Winner]

Robert Preston receives the 25th Annual Barter Prize from the Barter Theater in Abingdon, VA for his outstanding contribution to the theater.

May 26, 1967 [Winner]

The Tony Award for Best Performance by a Leading Actor in a Musical is awarded to Robert Preston for his role as Michael in *I Do!, I Do!*

April 20, 1975 [Nominee]

Robert Preston is nominated for a Tony Award for Best Performance by a Leading Actor in a Musical for his role as Mack Sennett in *Mack & Mabel*.

May 1975 [Nominee]

Robert Preston is nominated for a Drama Desk Award for Outstanding Actor in a Musical for his role as Mack Sennett in *Mack & Mabel*.

January 5, 1982 [Winner]

Robert Preston receives the award for Best Supporting Actor from the National Society of Film Critics for his role as Dr. Irving Finegarten in *S.O.B.* (1981).

February 14, 1982 [Winner]

Robert Preston received the Best Supporting Actor Award from the National Board of Review for his role as Toddy in *Victor/Victoria* (1982).

October 4, 1982 [Winner]

Robert Preston receives an award for his portrayal of Toddy in *Victor/Victoria* (1982) at the second annual Alliance for Gay Artists Awards at the L.A. Stage Company Theater in Hollywood.

January 13, 1983 [Winner]

Robert Preston is honored with a Career Achievement Award from the Los Angeles Film Critics Association.

January 29, 1983 [Nominee]

Robert Preston is a Golden Globe nominee for Best Actor in a Motion Picture - Comedy or Musical for *Victor/Victoria* (1982).

January 30, 1983 [Nominee]

Robert Preston is a nominee for Best Supporting Actor for his role as Toddy in *Victor/Victoria* (1982) from the New York Film Critics Circle.

April 11, 1983 [Nominee]

Robert Preston is nominated for an Academy Award for Best Actor in a Supporting Role for his role as Toddy in *Victor/Victoria* (1982).

April 2, 1984 [Recognition]
Robert Preston is the honored guest at the 50th annual Los Angeles Drama Critics Circle Awards.

April 1984 [Winner]
The Western Heritage Awards present Robert Preston, Patty Duke Astin, Bill Brademan, and Edwin Self with the Bronze Wrangler Award for *September Gun* (1983).

November 3, 1984 [Winner]
Robert Preston receives the "Mr. Wonderful" award from The Thalians at the gala held in his honor at the Century Plaza Hotel in Los Angeles, CA.

December 18, 1984 [Winner]
Robert Preston is honored as a living legend along with Dorothy Maguire, Robert Mitchum, and Jane Wyman at the 2nd Annual American Cinema Awards at the Beverly Wilshire Hotel in Los Angeles, CA.

March 4, 1985 [Recognition]
Robert Preston is inducted into the American Theater Hall of Fame in the rotunda of the Gershwin Theatre in New York City.

June 9, 1985 [Nominee]
Robert Preston is nominated for a Saturn Award for Best Supporting Actor for his role as Centauri in *The Last Starfighter* (1984).

August 1985 [Recognition]
Robert Preston has a hybrid iris, the Tall Bearded Robert Preston Iris, named in his honor.

December 3, 1985 [Nominee]

Robert Preston is a nominee for the Cable Ace Award for Actor in A Movie or Miniseries for his role as Michael Finnegan in *Finnegan Begin Again* (1985).

June 7, 1987 [Recognition]

Robert Preston is posthumously awarded the Lawrence Langner Award for Distinguished Achievement in the Theatre at the 41st Annual Tony Awards; Catherine Preston accepts the award on behalf on her late husband.

RECIPES SHARED
BY ROBERT PRESTON

Although his wife Catherine was an excellent cook, Preston was no stranger to the kitchen and grill. He shared two of his favorite recipes, Ham Steaks Hawaiian Style and Shrimp Scampi in newspapers:

ROBERT PRESTON'S HAM STEAKS HAWAIIAN STYLE
(Serves 2)

- 2 one-inch-thick center cut ham steaks
- 4-6 Pineapple slices (reserve juice from can)
- 1/3 cup brown sugar or molasses
- Maraschino cherries for garnish (optional)
- 2 Tablespoons butter, more if needed

For best results, select a hearty smoked ham weighing about 8 to 10 pounds. Have butcher cut steaks from center side, 1-inch thick. Place ham steaks in a Large, greased roasting pan. Coat each steak with a thin layer of brown sugar or molasses, dot generously with butter.

Place in a preheated 350°F oven and lower heat immediately to 275°F. Baste frequently, adding more butter if needed. When ham is thoroughly heated, place pineapple slices in center of each steak, pour pineapple juice over ham, decorate with maraschino cherries. Run under broiler at low heat for 5 minutes to brown. Serve piping hot with your favorite vegetables and salad.

For a nice flavor, add 1 Tablespoon prepared mustard to brown sugar or molasses. For a sweet-sour effect, dilute pineapple juice with a few teaspoons of vinegar.

Ham Steaks Hawaiian Style reprinted from the *Philadelphia Daily News*
Blin, Johna, "Celebrity Cookbook," *Philadelphia Daily News*, January 30, 1980, F-7.

SHRIMP SCAMPI
(2 Portions)

This was one of Preston's favorite dishes at Danny's Hideaway in New York. The Prestons asked the chef for the recipe so they could enjoy it at home.

- ½ cup butter
- 1-pound raw shrimp, shelled and deveined
- clove garlic, crushed
- ¼ cup minced parsley
- teaspoons Worcestershire Sauce
- 2 cups hot cooked rice
- Juice of ½ lemon

- Parmesan cheese [grated]
- ¼ cup Sherry wine
- 1 Tablespoon sugar
- 2 Tablespoons chopped fresh dill

In shallow pan melt butter over low heat. Add next 6 ingredients; mix well. Arrange shrimp in a single layer in the sauce. Spoon sauce over shrimp. Broil at low heat 8 minutes. Remove from broiler. Let stand for 15 minutes. Sprinkle on parsley. Broil at high heat for 3 minutes. Arrange shrimp over rice, spoon sauce over shrimp and rice. Sprinkle with parmesan cheese. A green salad and white wine can accompany the dish.

Shrimp Scampi recipe reprinted from the *Los Angeles Times*
Paddleford, Clementine, "Actor's Scampi," *Los Angeles Times*,
June 28, 1964, This Week-10.

INDEX

Q

Printed in Great Britain
by Amazon